CW00392556

Tibet and China in the Twenty-first Century

Contents

Acknowledgments

There are many experts on Tibet and China upon whose writings I have drawn and acknowledge in the endnotes to this book. I have also spoken with a great many people and thank especially His Holiness the Dalai Lama, the Seventeenth Karmapa, the Kalon Tripa Professor Samdhong Rinpoche, Mitchell Albert and André Gaspard of Saqi Books with my thanks for their patience and help, Jimmy Cooper, Ian Cumming of Tibet Images, Professor Robert McCorquodale, Thierry Dodin of Tibet Information Network, Kasur Lodi Gyari, Eddie Hughes, Karma Lhundup, Malcolm Moorhouse, Professor Dawa Norbu, Kalon Lobsang Nyandek, Paul Orm⋯⋯⋯ for his fine map, Jetsun Pema, Michael van Walt van Praag, Mrs K. Y. Takhla, Mrs Namgyal Lhamo Taklha, T. C. Tethong, Tempa Tsering and Kasur Tashi Wangdi. However, my greatest debt of gratitude is to my wife, Chris Michell, for her idea that I should embark on this venture in the first place, for her sympathetic and perceptive thoughts, comments and corrections on drafts and for the sacrifices she has made to ensure that I had the time and space to do the job. Our three cats have been endlessly interested in what I have been doing and are still trying to puzzle it out. For any errors and omissions I, of course, remain responsible.

A Note on Translation

For convenience I follow current usage for readers primarily interested in Tibet, giving also the Chinese or Tibetan name where it seems most relevant. Thus, 'Kumbum' monastery (in Amdo near the border of Qinghai and Gansu) rather than its Chinese name 'Ta'er Si'. Also, I mostly follow the *pinyin* (Pi) romanisation of Chinese characters which was introduced in China in the 1950s and became official in 1979. *Pinyin* was invented by the Chinese government to help foreigners pronounce Chinese words, but it is based on Latin pronunciation, not English. It has not, however, completely replaced the earlier Wade-Giles system. In this book I use the earlier place name 'Peking' for the period up to the formation of the People's Republic of China in 1949 and 'Beijing' (Pi) for after that time. Similarly, 'Chiang Kai-shek' is used instead of 'Jiang Jieshi' (Pi). Jonathan D. Spence, in *The Search for Modern China* (W. W. Norton and Co.), second edition, 1999, p. xxxi, gives conversions for 392 letters and common groups of letters from *pinyin* to Wade-Giles.

Foreword

by His Holiness
The Dalai Lama

However we look at the Tibetan situation, as a nation we are passing through a very difficult time. Some of us are living in exile as refugees, without protection. Tibetans in Tibet live under the control of a totalitarian system, with no freedom over their own destinies.

The problem seems set to get worse. An overwhelming number of Chinese are arriving in Tibet, and the whole Tibetan way of life is changing as a result. Although new generations of Tibetans may feel patriotic about Tibet, the fact that they have been born and brought up in a Chinese culture means their sense of their Tibetan identity will have altered.

I understand that these days, in and around Lhasa, the Tibetans' way of life – from the food they eat to the way they speak – has become sinocised. To take one small example, greater numbers of Tibetans eat rice and vegetables for breakfast, which is a Chinese habit. (The traditional Tibetan morning custom is to eat *tsampa* [roasted barley flour, a Tibetan staple food].) I find such changes quite alarming, because from this deceptively minor change we can see that the whole attitude of the younger generation is changing. If things go on like this, imagine what will happen in another thirty years.

This is the reality from the worst point of view. More optimistically, I think it will be difficult for large numbers of Chinese to settle in Tibet. The altitude is high, for one thing, and it will not be easy for them to transfer everything from China that they need to feel comfortable.

On the other hand, the Tibetan and Chinese peoples have lived side by side for centuries. I have always attached great importance to our relationship, which for the most part has been friendly and peaceful. In future, too, we will have no alternative but to live as neighbours. Therefore, in our struggle for freedom and justice I have always tried to pursue a path of nonviolence in order to ensure that a relationship based on mutual respect, friendship and genuine good neighbourliness can be sustained between our two peoples.

Moreover, I believe that it is more important to look forward to the future than to dwell in the past. It is not impossible that the 6 million Tibetans could benefit from joining the 1 billion Chinese of their own free will, if a relationship based on equality, mutual benefit and mutual respect can be established. But if China wants Tibet to stand by her, it is up to China to create the necessary conditions. However, it has now become clear that Tibetan efforts alone will not be sufficient to achieve our goal; we need international support.

Tibet's historical relationship with China is very complex. Unfortunately, even before the Communist revolution, the history of Tibet and its relations with China was distorted. The fact is that mutual relations go back many centuries. Public and formal acknowledgment of this can be found as early as the seventh century, when King Song-tsen Gampo took a Chinese princess as his wife. Even then, respect for Tibet extended far beyond its relationship with its neighbour to the east, for at the same time Song-tsen Gampo married a Nepalese princess and developed strong religious and cultural ties with India that have continued to the present day.

The international community and even the Chinese still do not fully comprehend the extent of the destruction, suffering and injustice experienced by the Tibetans under Chinese rule. Today the Chinese people, especially the intellectuals, closely follow what happens outside China. Chinese authorities are no longer able to isolate the population from outside sources of information. It is therefore immensely important that in democratic countries there is open and honest discussion of all aspects of the Tibetan issue, from the historical relations between Tibet and China to the current violations of human rights.

In this book John Heath has attempted to present a balanced account of relations between Tibet and China, giving due weight not only to the Tibetan point of view but also to events and changes that have taken place in China. I feel this is a very healthy approach. I firmly believe that the Tibetan problem can eventually be solved through open dialogue.

February 2004

Introduction

At the end of September 1987 I was comfortably installed in the Malla Hotel in Kathmandu, soon to meet the other eighteen members of an expected seven-week geological expedition to the high Himalaya. They were nearly all scientists, mostly American. I was there because I was not a scientist. The American leader, Dr Maynard Miller ('Mal'), was a close friend of mine from postgraduate days at Cambridge University in England, and I had twice been on expeditions to the icefield in Alaska with him. He knew I was experienced on glaciers and could well support their scientific work. Also, I was a management consultant with international experience and could talk about things other than geomorphology and glaciers, which he thought was a good idea. Our aim was to survey 'the highest icefield in the world' situated at about 20,000 feet. The reasons for this have become apparent as the effects of global warming are better understood. Many of Asia's great rivers have their origins in this great icefield and its melting would be catastrophic. The state of its health needed monitoring.

So there we were, extravagantly kitted out, with a pile of scientific equipment, waiting for Mal to collect the trekking permits which had been approved six months before, following a full year of negotiation. The icefield was in a restricted area, so permits were essential. 'They have withdrawn their permission,' Mal gasped as he entered the room. 'We cannot go.'

When we recovered from the devastating news we tried to discover what was wrong, and if possible put it right. It was unthinkable to return home. We did, however, learn what had happened. On 21 September, just before our arrival in Kathmandu, the Dalai Lama had addressed a group from the US Congress and had put forward his 'Five-Point Peace Plan'. It was his first attempt to appeal directly to the American legislature and thus to the world community about the plight of Tibet since the Chinese invasion of that country in 1950 and its subsequent occupation.

The Chinese reacted to this peace plan with fury. Tibet was seen by them as an internal matter, and in their view the international community had no right to interfere. Tibet was and always had been part of China, they said. The US government in particular was blamed for permitting the address to take place. We were an American expedition planning to go – at exactly the wrong time – to an area which we were now told was the subject of current controversy between the Chinese and Nepalese governments. A Chinese delegation had only just left Kathmandu.

We hastily replanned the entire expedition. Half the party, including myself, was to try to find out what was going on in the only ruby mine in Nepal in an extremely remote part of the country at about 16,000 feet, discovered and developed by an American geologist friend of Mal's who was not now permitted to visit there. That sounded much more interesting to me. I walked with Lhakpa, our Sirdar, the leader of our accompanying Sherpas, a Buddhist responsible for the porters and cooks and for finding the way. He told me about the Dalai Lama and about Tibet, about his distant relatives who still lived there and their terrible suffering under the Chinese. He would slip into Tibet from time to time, he said, to take money to them, to tell them not to lose hope for eventual freedom and to bring back news.

At high altitudes we passed many small Buddhist villages (at lower levels most villages were Hindu). There were many people there with Tibetan features, and often I spoke with the village headmen about their lives, their politics and how they related to the central government in Kathmandu. So the expedition proved to be an unexpected learning experience, which I decided to develop further.

In April 1988, during the Dalai Lama's ten-day visit to the UK a few months after my return, I went to hear him speak at a packed Central Hall in Westminster, London. Although I knew a little about Buddhism from attending both the London Buddhist Centre and Rigpa (one of the main centres of Tibetan Buddhism in the UK), much of his talk went over my head. But I saw him in action, most dramatically when – in the middle of expounding an idea – a man jumped from his seat and headed for him, shouting something as he ran. At once the Dalai Lama's discreetly positioned bodyguards leaped forward to protect him, but he waved them away. He beckoned to the man to sit in front of him, then leaned down to listen intently to what he had to say.

The rest of us in this vast hall waited in tense silence while the Dalai Lama spoke quietly with the intruder, who then rose and walked back to his seat. 'Now, where was I?' asked the Dalai Lama with his characteristic laugh, before resuming his talk as though nothing had happened. His presence dominated the hall and its huge audience.

At the entrance there were piles of books about Tibet. I bought a handful. On the way downstairs I ran into John Rowley, a friend who was one of the Dalai Lama's protectors onstage. Seeing my books he said, 'Why don't you come and join us and write something yourself?' So, once I had read those books and spoken with friends, I did.

In December 1988 I sent my first report to the Dalai Lama, called 'The Economic Viability of Tibet'. I had just retired after sixteen years at the London Business School, and economic development was a special interest of mine. Some weeks later I met with Michael van Walt van Praag, a tall, distinguished-looking Dutchman with a pleasant lilt in his voice and a powerful mind. He turned out to be the Dalai Lama's legal advisor, a brilliant international lawyer who was on his way back to the Netherlands from Dharamsala, the north Indian hill station where the Dalai Lama now lives in exile. He had been asked to talk with me about my report. I could tell that he thought it in some ways a pretty naive effort, but he encouraged me to continue writing. I argued that a free Tibet could become economically viable without China by releasing the natural talents and enthusiasm of its people. Many Tibetans in exile had received good training and experience in business, and would return to help a free Tibet, while many of Tibet's Western supporters were businessmen and women who could contribute in different ways. There were also international institutions that would help, especially the United Nations Development Programme (UNDP).[1] The main political point I made was that somehow China's economic and other interests in Tibet must be met through negotiation if they were to be persuaded to grant Tibet any degree of autonomy, a joint venture with the Chinese perhaps in a genuine partnership which would recognise the needs of both peoples. (Later in this book I shall return to this theme and develop it further.) Thus it was that I found myself more and more deeply involved in the problems facing Tibet, talking with Tibetans, writing reports and in other ways trying to find solutions.

Tibet[1] Today under Chinese Occupation

'Today people of all ethnic groups [in Tibet]
are fully enjoying political, economic,
cultural and other rights, and have
complete control of their destiny.'
*From a speech by Hu Jintao,
then Vice-President of China,
19 July 2001, Lhasa*

Tibet was invaded in October 1950 by the recently formed People's Republic of China (PRC), and has been continuously occupied since 1951. Its ancient semi-feudal order was torn apart. The institution of the Dalai Lama became powerless; government by aristocracy was overturned; and almost all Tibet's Buddhist monasteries were destroyed. Ordinary working people were freed from their obligations to private landlords and from the monastic system. But in their place came the Marxist principles and practices of Mao Zedong, now the master of all China, and a Chinese administration which exercised a harsh authority and alienated the people. U-Tsang, the central part of Tibet, became the Tibet Autonomous Region (TAR), with a Communist-led administration headed by the Party Secretary. Lhasa remained the capital.

To the east of the former U-Tsang lay the Tibetan territories of Kham and Amdo, where most Tibetans live, areas now incorporated into the Chinese provinces of Sichuan, Qinghai, Gansu and Yunnan.[2] Most Tibetans in these provinces have their own designated prefectures and counties, with lower levels of Chinese administration. Kham and Amdo had long been infiltrated by the Chinese, but from at least the eighteenth century and until the early 1950s had been relatively peaceful.

After more than fifty years Tibetans remain dissatisfied with the Chinese occupation. Every aspect of society has its problems: religion, education, health, housing, economy, politics and human rights. In general, the last ten years or so are sufficient to gain a sense of the situation today. During this time some things have improved and others have worsened. It is not possible to conduct any kind of impartial nationwide survey of Tibetans – although the Chinese Academy of Social Sciences did conduct an enquiry in Tibet during July and August 2003 (published in May 2004) – as the Chinese are convinced of the benefits they have brought to the Tibetan people, and evidence to the contrary is suppressed. Therefore, we must piece together fragments from many sources to form an impression of what life there must truly be like.

Buddhism, at the heart of the Tibetan people's belief system, culture and everyday life, is under attack. Its spiritual head, the Fourteenth Dalai Lama, is revered with passionate devotion by Tibetan monks, nuns and most lay people. Living in exile in India, he is not under the control of the Chinese government and is thus seen by it as an alternative power base, a focus for loyalty and a potential political threat. He constantly travels the world to give teachings and rally support for Tibetan autonomy, and is greeted with enthusiastic support wherever he goes. But he is seen by the Chinese government as the leading 'splittist', together with the so-called 'Dalai clique' – meaning the Tibetan government-in-exile – aiming to achieve independence for his people and thus to split China apart.

Moreover, Communist politics is the main problem, the authorities believe that religion prevents or distracts the people from becoming rich – 'to be rich is glorious', as Deng Xiaoping said. (Tibetans prefer to spend their money on such projects as rebuilding and supporting monasteries, and not so much on consumer goods.) Communist Party members must swear an oath of commitment to atheism. So, for many reasons, Buddhism in Tibet is perceived to be an enemy and must be contained; the methods of doing so vary.

Early in June 2001[3] Chinese officials, based locally and from Beijing, burst into a crowded lecture room at a Buddhist institute near the town of Serthar, in a Tibetan Autonomous Prefecture of Sichuan province.[4] In all, there were about 6,000–7,000 monks and nuns living at the institute (and sometimes as many as 9,000[5]), Tibetans and Han Chinese students from many provinces all over the country and from Taiwan, Hong Kong, Inner Mongolia and elsewhere. About half were nuns. The officials allegedly shouted, 'It is time for you to go home! You must leave NOW!' Four-fifths of the residents were told to go immediately – first the thousand or so Han Chinese students, then most of the nuns. This unexpected and dramatic intervention marked the beginning of a new and more sinister phase of the Chinese containment of Tibetan Buddhism.

The Serthar institute, called Larung Gar, was founded in 1980 by the Tibetan monk Khenpo Jigme Phuntsok, an important teacher of the Thirteenth Dalai Lama. Khenpo Jigme had seen the teaching and practice of Buddhism undermined and slowly destroyed by Chinese restrictions and arrests,[6] and by the flight abroad of so many of its most cherished and experienced *lamas*. He felt driven to create a place where anyone could come for the highest levels of instruction in the *Dharma*, the sacred texts, teachings and practices of Tibetan Buddhism. It was an opportune moment, because restrictions at that time were being loosened by Hu Yaobang, the compassionate General Secretary of the Communist Party in Beijing, known in Tibet as 'China's Buddha', and one of two protégés of Deng Xiaoping for the highest office in the Communist Party.

The students lived in small one-room huts which had spread across previously uninhabited 13,000-foot hillsides like an enchanted forest. Labourers soon arrived with sledgehammers, and were paid the equivalent of US$16 for every hut they destroyed and allowed to keep any belongings they found. They started by tearing down the nuns' huts. A year later, by mid-2002, they had knocked down over 2,400 huts in total, and had removed the structural timber. The roofs of some huts were ripped apart with their inhabitants still inside. Old and sick people were expelled as well as the young and fit. By December 2002 some nuns had rebuilt their huts, which local officials attempted to prevent. Then some monks started sneaking back, hoping to go unnoticed, because Larung Gar – unlike a monastery – was very loosely organised.

Those dismissed from Larung Gar could not go to another monastery or nunnery because entry is controlled by the Chinese, and since most had taken vows not to enter into lay life they were left in limbo. There have been two suicides, and many have had mental breakdowns. Khenpo Jigme was held in custody in Chengdu, the capital city of the Chinese province of Sichuan, for one and a half years, but in November 2002 he returned to the institute, which was now much smaller in size. Teaching was resumed, though under heavy security and constant surveillance. However, in January 2004, one week after he was due to have a heart operation at a military hospital in Chengdu, Khenpo Jigme died, aged seventy.

Not only is Buddhist higher education suffering from China's policies, but, since 1954, about 90 percent of Tibet's monasteries have been physically destroyed. From 1980 to 1987, some rebuilding took place, although the institutions were now much smaller. Controls over Tibetan Buddhist education in the remaining monasteries became tighter following the June 1994 Third Work Forum on Tibet. In that year, Chinese-dominated Democratic Management Committees (DMCs) were set up to replace the traditional authority of abbots and *lamas*. Committee members are now appointed by the local branches of the Beijing-based Religious Affairs Bureau. Since 1996 the Chinese have held frequent 'patriotic re-education' campaigns for monks and nuns in support of socialism, to promote a Marxist outlook on culture and religion and to implement China's anti-Dalai Lama policies. They occupy much time and interrupt teaching, and have resulted in beatings, expulsions and deaths for those who refuse to accept what the Chinese say.

The DMCs, which quickly became an arm of state control,[7] reduced the number of monks and nuns at each institution. Entrants are restricted by quotas and a minimum age of eighteen (it was common previously for a boy to enter at age seven, traditionally 'when he could chase a raven'). In addition to studying Buddhist texts and undertaking Buddhist practices, he would learn reading and writing. In rural communities where there were no schools, most children went to the monasteries for their general education. Now this possibility is denied to them. The teaching of religion in both private and public schools in China remains prohibited, contrary to China's international obligations, although in many rural areas where Tibetans live there are still no secular schools.[8] Moreover, leading *lamas* are forced to retire at age sixty, when they are at their most experienced and influential in transmitting the *Dharma*, thus preventing the direct teaching of their wisdom to the young.

The destruction of the monasteries from 1954 and the theft of their wealth and precious artifacts did much more than dislocate the teaching and practice of Buddhism. Monasteries were also important financial centres, owners of land, trading organisations and the basis of Tibet's welfare system.[9] Since there were no banks in old Tibet, it was the monasteries that provided loans and support for the development of farms and small businesses and gave food aid to families stricken by bad harvests, illness or death.

Their destruction is a cause of the present poverty in rural Tibet, where most Tibetans live. The Chinese have not replaced the role of the monasteries in the welfare and development needs of rural Tibetans, and as a result families in these areas are now poorer than in any other part of rural China.

The Chinese have even interfered with appointing the spiritual leadership of Buddhists in Tibet, to secure their own candidates. There is the tragic and farcical story of the Chinese substitution of their own successor to the Panchen Lama following his death in January 1989, instead of the child selected by the traditional Tibetan method. The young boy they chose was the same age as the one authorised by the Dalai Lama and came from the same village – but his parents were both members of the Communist Party.

Thus do the atheist Chinese authorities attempt to undermine and ridicule Tibet's religious inheritance and to do away with the Dalai Lama as Tibet's spiritual leader. Both the Dalai Lama and Chadrel Rinpoche, who led the search for the Panchen Lama's rebirth, were called 'the scum of Buddhism'. At the same time the authorities identified being religious with patriotism. According to Chen Kuiyan, then the Communist Party Secretary in the TAR:

A qualified religious leader should, first of all, be a patriot. Any legitimate religion invariably makes patriotism the prime requirement for believers. A person who is unpatriotic ... cannot be tolerated by religion.[10]

In July 1997 Chen announced that Tibetan Buddhism had no essential connection to Tibetan culture, and in November he declared that criticism of China's cultural policy in Tibet was 'the Dalai's rubbish in disguised form'.

These deliberate and sustained attacks on Buddhism and the person of the Dalai Lama constitute cultural imperialism, racial and religious discrimination, and would appear to be genocidal. In the United Nations Convention on the Prevention and Punishment of the Crime of Genocide, to which the government of China is committed by virtue of its ratification of this convention in April 1983 (when Hu Yaobang was the Communist Party General Secretary), genocide is defined as 'any act committed with the intent to destroy, in whole or in part, a national, ethnic, racial or religious group ...'. The International Commission of Jurists, in their 365-page report 'Tibet: Human Rights and the Rule of Law' (December 1997), did not at that time use the term 'genocide' for Chinese actions against Buddhism, but the situation has worsened significantly since then.

Lay Tibetans participate in numerous religious celebrations as part of their traditional culture, at home and collectively. Practically all Tibetan families have a Buddhist shrine in their dwellings, sometimes in a small part of a room or, in richer households, occupying a whole room. Even these expressions of faith are now harassed. Since the end of 1997, 'patriotic re-education' programmes, at first confined to the monasteries, have been extended to lay people. In the TAR, pictures of the Dalai Lama have been forbidden in ordinary homes and persons caught watching a video of the Dalai Lama have been condemned to six years' imprisonment. During searches of homes by the police in Lhasa, religious artifacts such as altars, *thangkas* (religious paintings on silk or other fabrics), butter lamps and statues have been taken and dumped in the river. Large incense burners, for smouldering branches of juniper, have been destroyed. At certain festivals the circumambulation of religious sites has been forbidden. It is a political offence for *thangkas* to depict snow lions or mountains, symbols used on the Tibetan flag, and Tibetans who make such paintings have been arrested and fined.

Paradoxically, in areas to the east of the TAR where most Tibetans live – formerly Kham and Amdo – the local authorities were, until late 2001, much less strict about such matters as openly supporting the Dalai Lama and control over the monasteries. Now, in Sichuan, the Chinese have found excuses for persecuting Tibetans who support the Dalai Lama. One has been executed on inadequate evidence, and a well-respected *lama*, Tenzin Deleg Rinpoche, has been sentenced to death with a two-year suspension by the Intermediate People's Court in Karze, Sichuan province, for allegedly 'causing explosions and inciting separatism'. Torture has become more prevalent. Also, 'long life' prayers and ceremonies for the Dalai Lama, which had been permitted in these areas, were forcibly ended in November 2002 by Chinese troops.

The underlying problem for the Chinese is that Buddhism unifies all Tibetans and in adversity it helps to encourage in them a sense of nationhood. It is the living symbol of Tibet as a whole and its culture. Tibetans in Kham and Amdo had always acknowledged the Dalai Lama as their spiritual leader, but had never been administratively controlled by the government in Lhasa. Now they identify themselves as being just as Tibetan as those who live in the TAR.

The policies and beliefs of the Communist Party in relation to Buddhism were described by President Jiang Zemin in his 13,500-word policy statement of 1 July 2001 in Beijing:

> The socialist culture has become dominant in China. Because of past and present reasons, however, there still exist some backward cultures in society that have features of superstition, ignorance, decadence and vulgarity, and there even exist some decadent cultures that corrode people's mental world and jeopardise the socialist cause. We should remould the backward cultures, prevent and resolutely resist the corrosion of people by decadent cultures and various erroneous ideological concepts, and gradually reduce and root out the soil on which they rely to breed ...[11]

This confirms that he saw further action necessary to contain or eradicate

Buddhism. A few days beforehand he had just made important decisions concerning the future of Tibet at the Fourth Tibet Work Forum, held in Beijing on 25–7 June 2001. It was attended by Jiang, Premier Zhu Rongji, Li Peng (Chairman of the National People's Congress, China's legislature) and all other members of the Politburo Standing Committee – effectively the cabinet of the Communist Party and its principal policy-making body – together with the Party leadership. One of their decisions was to extend the restrictions in the TAR to Buddhism in the Tibetan areas of the four Chinese provinces.

A couple of weeks after Jiang's speech, on 19 July 2001, then Vice President Hu Jintao (since November 2002 the General Secretary of the Communist Party and China's new leader) spoke in Lhasa at the fiftieth anniversary of the signing of the 1951 'Seventeen-Point Agreement', the peace treaty following the Chinese invasion in 1950 (see Appendix for the text of the full speech):

> The fine traditional culture in Tibet has not only been protected, inherited and carried forward, but also substantiated to reflect people's new lives and meet the new requirements of social development called for by the times … People's freedom of religious belief has been fully respected and protected … It is essential to correctly and comprehensively implement the Party's policy of freedom of religious belief so that people of all ethnic groups will unite and cooperate with each other politically, respect each other's beliefs and throw all their weight behind faster development and continued stability in Tibet.

The paradox is that while Buddhism is being slowly strangled in Tibet, in China itself it is rapidly growing in popularity – its best period since the terrible destruction wrought by Mao Zedong during the Cultural Revolution – although it is strictly controlled. In 1949 there were some 200,000 Buddhist monasteries and temples throughout China, but by 1976 barely 100 were left. In the last twenty years more than 10,000 have been rebuilt with private money. There is, however, a shortage of monks and nuns, and the Han Chinese studying at the Serthar Institute were part of this revival.

Education is at the heart of continuity of culture and the development of skills. Yet Tibetan education, controlled by Han Chinese, has languished. The leader of a special United Nations (UN) *Report on Education in China* in December 2003 was 'dismayed at the illiteracy rate in the TAR of 39.5 percent'.[12] (In rural areas that figure is 49 percent, with only 15 percent of the TAR population over six years old having some form of secondary education against 40 percent in neighbouring Qinghai.) The report continued:

An education that would affirm minority rights necessitates full recognition by the majority of the worth of minority languages and religions in all facets of life. Otherwise education is seen as assimilationist and, hence, not compatible with China's human rights obligations.

In Tibet, education has been more concerned with political indoctrination than with preparation for personal adulthood and future work in a Tibetan society. As Chen Kuiyan put it in October 1994:

> Schools should be captured by socialism ... The success of our education does not lie in the number of diplomas issued to graduates from universities, colleges, polytechnic schools and secondary schools. It lies, in the final analysis, in whether our graduating students are opposed to, or turn their hearts to, the Dalai clique, and in whether they are loyal to, or do not care about, our great motherland and the great socialist cause. This is the most salient and the most important criterion for assessing right and wrong, and the contributions and mistakes of our educational work in Tibet. To successfully solve the problem we must improve political and ideological work in schools.[13]

So, in Tibetan schools, the time spent on ideological education was increased. A Tibetan teacher said that 'the curriculum for both higher and basic education must depend on whether it can guarantee the unity and territorial integrity of the country ... and the students had to read from a collection of Mao's quotations every day, as well as to spend time studying the policies of other great Chinese leaders.'

From 1997, teaching from Grade 1 in urban primary schools in the TAR has had to be in Chinese.[14] By November 2001 it had become apparent that Chinese was also to be the language of education in all primary schools in Tibet. The only course to be taught in Tibetan was to be 'Tibetan language'. Where English is taught, it is through the medium of Chinese, not Tibetan. This emphasis on learning Chinese has reversed the 1987 regulations, a legacy of Hu Yaobang, which stated that by 1993 all junior middle-school students should be taught in Tibetan and that by 1997 most lessons in senior middle schools and technical secondary schools should be in Tibetan.

There are, however, signs of change, at least in the TAR. In 'the first government regulation ever passed in China on preserving an ethnic language', in March 2002, new TAR regulations were passed on the 'Use and Development of the Tibetan Language'.[15] It pronounced the 'principle of equality of all nationalities' languages'. Tibetan and 'the common national language' (*putonghua*, with standard Han characters) will now 'have equal effect':

> 'Commonly issued documents from all levels of state organs must use both Tibetan and the common language' (Article 4 of the new regulation);

> 'The TAR is actively to develop Tibetan-language undertakings including education, news, publishing, broadcasting and films ... and is to give importance to publishing Tibetan-language children's books, books for popular consumption and popular science books ...' (Article 9);

> 'Packaging, user manuals ... of goods produced and sold within the TAR region must simultaneously use Tibetan and the common national language ...' (Article 12).

Detailed implementing regulations are to follow. There is, understandably, some scepticism whether these regulations will make much difference. However, some Chinese cadres (officials in government, industry and the Party) are now being taught Tibetan at the University of Tibet in Lhasa, which suggests that the authorities may be serious about the new law.

There has been an important question about the continuing usefulness of the Tibetan language in Tibet, which the new law may dispel. Chinese is the working language. Letters addressed in Tibetan will not be delivered. Buses and street signs are all designated in Chinese. Even discussing publicly the usefulness of the Tibetan language has led to charges of 'splittism'. Once a nation becomes dominated by a completely foreign language and culture it has lost its soul. The Chinese have said that the Tibetan language prohibits the development and use of science. That is not so. The Tibet Education and Resource Centre in Dharamsala, India, has ensured that Tibetan can be used correctly in scientific discourse.

Tibetan student enrolment was seriously below that of China as a whole. Since Tibetan children were struggling with learning Chinese, and since the curriculum was geared to urban living while overall 87 percent of Tibetans live in rural areas or are nomads, education became heavily overloaded, unreal and remote. For example, Chamdo, a town in the TAR, has been continuously occupied by the Chinese since October 1950 and is a relatively affluent Tibetan Autonomous Prefecture. One might expect superior results. Yet in 1993, with 110,000 school-age children, 64 percent had no educational opportunities and 79 percent of the Tibetan adult population was illiterate or semi-literate. The school enrolment rate for Tibetans was only 34 percent.

Racial discrimination in education is widespread in Tibet. Chinese students in mixed schools, mainly in urban areas, get new or nearly new books. Tibetans in the same school may get old books with pages missing, and they may have to pay for them while to the Chinese they are free. When a school was asked to explain the difference, teachers said that the Chinese students were 'more intelligent' and needed better-quality books. In another school, textbooks were issued to the Chinese pupils first and only if there were any left over did Tibetans receive them. 'We were always looked down on and called "uncivilised, backward fools",' said a Tibetan refugee. Others were called 'foolish *tsampa*-eaters who do not have the brain to study', while the Chinese were 'intelligent rice-eaters with a bright future'. A Tibetan with bad eyesight went to sit at the front of the class but the teacher told him he was an 'uncivilised animal' and must sit at the back.

Considering that most Tibetans live in rural areas, it is tragic that in 1998 only 2 percent of secondary schools in the TAR were in rural areas, compared with 57 percent in rural areas in China. Moreover, in a rising proportion of Tibetan secondary school pupils in the TAR, the brightest children are sent to China for their education. The 'Education of Tibetan Children in China Programme' was started in November 1984, and 14 percent of Tibetan secondary schoolchildren – some 4,000 pupils – were then taken to China.[16] By 1994 this figure had risen to 28 percent and about 13,000 children, and by November 2002 the total had increased to over 20,000 sent to more than twenty Chinese provinces and cities. Eighteen of these schools were designated 'Tibetan Secondary Schools' while the remainder had special classes for Tibetans.

Tibetan language is supposed to be part of the curriculum but is frequently not so. Children will normally spend seven years at these schools starting at aged twelve and leaving at age nineteen, during which time they are permitted to return to their homes only once. They will have become assimilated into Chinese culture, history, policies and ideas, and may have become Party members. On their return, they may form a new elite in Tibetan society and perhaps be treated with suspicion by their own people. For Tibetans to receive the best in Chinese secondary education is extremely good; to receive it in Tibet, which would be perfectly possible given the large numbers now involved, would be much better. In 1989 the programme was extended to cover technical/vocational education for Tibetans in China. In a new development in November 2002, 120 Tibetan postgraduate students are to be enrolled annually in eight leading Chinese universities. Those who lose out are the young Tibetans not selected to go to China, who could benefit from such education.

All examinations, except those relating to the Tibetan language, are in Chinese. And at the end of Twelfth Grade, in some schools, Tibetans had to achieve a minimum mark of 590 before they could proceed to higher education. Chinese students needed to achieve only a minimum of 490. Also, 'academic marks do not seem to matter for further education – it was money and connections – *guanxi* – that counted'. For many university courses in China the new entrant has to know English, especially in the sciences. But earlier, Tibetans would still be learning Chinese while the Chinese students would be learning English.

In 1985 responsibility for funding education was transferred from Beijing to local governments. There appear to have been no firm rules set from the centre about the minimum that should be spent per child according to the level of schooling or in total according to the local school-age population. There were no rules about the division between capital and current expenditures. Local authorities were expected to raise the money locally, which in Tibet was an added burden on an already poor people.

In 1986 the Chinese 'Law on Compulsory Education' stated that 'the State shall not charge tuition fees for students attending compulsory education', which covers the first nine years. This was too narrowly drawn and left the possibility of charging for other aspects of schooling. A ten-year-old girl now living in exile explained why she was unable to attend school:

> At school the teacher demanded 50 *yuan* a month to sit on a chair, 50 *yuan* to have a table, and another 25 *yuan* for the books. My father earned 50 *yuan* a month. With this money we had to buy a sack of *tsampa* to have some food.[17]

The Chinese make all executive decisions in local government under the unelected Chinese Communist Party Secretary. Naturally the secretary will make sure that the urban schools Chinese children (including their own) mostly attend will be adequately financed, while schools for rural Tibetans receive lower priority. The result has been that rural Tibetans are forced to finance and construct educational institutions at their own expense, difficult where 85 percent of the population is living below the poverty line. Practically all schools charge fees of one kind or another, and the parents of Chinese children pay at much lower rates than Tibetans, or sometimes pay nothing at all. The most blatant discrimination, very widely reported, is in schools attended by both Chinese and Tibetans. At a school in Lhasa Tibetan parents had to pay 400 *yuan* for admission (Chinese paid 200 *yuan*) in addition to a 600–700 *yuan* school fee every six months (Chinese paid no more than 450 *yuan*). When

Tibetan parents complained, they were told that the school was really just for Chinese pupils, and that the Tibetan children were lucky to be there.

By 1993 an official Chinese report in the TAR said that 'the main problems and difficulties we encounter in primary education, especially in the countryside, include funding shortages, arrears in payment of teachers' salaries, the collection of unwarranted fees and the rising dropout rate among primary and secondary school students'.[18] As a result, six kinds of educational fees were cancelled and some funding became the responsibility of the central government. The basic situation, however, did not change and, according to recently arrived refugees in India, in 2002 fees and/or payments in kind were still being levied.

Thus, throughout the whole education system in Tibet, there appears to be institutionalised racial discrimination and assumptions of Han Chinese superiority. We can only conclude that it is a deliberate policy to marginalise the Tibetans educationally and to make them feel inferior and subordinate. It is little wonder that most Tibetans leave school very early and that between one third and one half of those who escape from Tibet over the Himalaya are under the age of eighteen. They take huge risks to seek a proper education. We should acknowledge, however, that in 2003 the Chinese announced their aim of reducing illiteracy in the TAR by 100,000 per annum.[19] How they will do this is unclear.

The International Covenant on the Elimination of All forms of Racial Discrimination, which the Chinese government ratified in 1981, guarantees without discrimination 'the right to education and training'. And the UN Convention on the Rights of the Child, which China ratified in 1992, emphasises that the primary consideration in schools should be 'the development of respect for the child's parents, his or her own cultural identity, language and values'. This was put before 'the national values of the country in which the child is living'. Moreover, China's own Education Law stipulates that 'every citizen shall enjoy equal educational opportunities regardless of race, nationality, sex, occupation, financial status and religion'.

Health services are a similar problem. One eighteen-year-old man who escaped from Tibet in April 1998 reported:

> There were no Chinese people living in our area [Nye Shi village in Kandze, Tibet Autonomous Prefecture] so we had no electricity, no roads, no schools and no health services. The authorities have no interest in developing areas where they themselves have no benefit and so if anyone in our village became sick we had no one around to help us.[20]

In 1996 a scheme to improve the existing rural health system through insurance and service charges, the Cooperative Medical System (CMS), was introduced in China. In 1998 the Chinese government admitted that 'the Central Government and Tibetan governments at all levels are greatly concerned about the health of the Tibetan people' and announced that they had a 'preferential medical policy' in Tibet.[21] However, the long-standing problems remain. A report by medical specialists and others at the end of 2002 makes dismal reading:

> Health and healthcare in Tibet are among the worst in the vast territory controlled by the People's Republic of China. There is a high incidence of diseases resulting from malnutrition ... occasional outbreaks of the plague and many people suffer from Iodine Deficiency Disorders leading to retardation and goitres ... Child and infant mortality – and deaths during childbirth – are so high that in this regard Tibet can be categorised as one of the least-developed regions on earth.[22]

The tragedy is that so many of these conditions are easily preventable. There is a severe shortage of properly trained township and village health workers; money is often spent on unusable equipment and technology when such basic facilities as clean water and electricity are absent; education on hygiene, sanitation and adequate housing is neglected.

Both the allocation of investment in healthcare facilities and the charges for treatment are discriminatory. Under the CMS everything has a price. This starts with the need for a 'green pass', which may be free but more usually will cost 10–35 *yuan*. It is supposed to guarantee free medical treatment but is just a pass entitling a person to treatment for which further payments are required. Without it the sick person may be charged double for the treatment received. Tibetans report that for them the pass is difficult to obtain, although not for Chinese.

The first payment is a substantial deposit of cash at a hospital before a doctor will even see a patient. Usually this is between 1,800 and 5,000 *yuan*, but varies between hospitals and may be decided by individual doctors. Chinese will be charged less, or the fee waived altogether. Since the average per capita annual income for Tibetan farmers and herders in rural areas was only 1,158 *yuan* in 1998, clearly, as a Swiss Red Cross inspection confirmed, this deters rural people from seeking hospital treatment. Hospitals will simply refuse admission for Tibetans without the deposit, no matter how serious the condition. Some Tibetans die within days of being refused admission.

Evidently dispensing date-expired or incorrect drugs is widespread, and many Tibetans have died as a result. The authorities reckon that Tibetans, especially nomads, are uneducated and illiterate and will not understand what they are being given. There are numerous other instances of malpractice. For example, 'the hospital administration actively encourages doctors to prescribe expensive medicines to Tibetans for which they get a kickback equivalent to about one third of their monthly wage', and 'hospitals routinely refuse to dispense drugs at the state-mandated prices, claiming they have no stock. Patients are instructed to buy them from private clinics at market prices. But [these] are often operated by the hospital staff or officials and are outlets for hospital inventory at inflated prices.'

One of the most serious conditions, affecting as many as 80 percent of Tibetans in some villages, is 'big bone' disease (*kashin-beck*), on which Médecins sans Frontières (MSF) has focused. It was not a good sign that in December 2002 MSF, after fourteen years in Tibet, decided to withdraw 'for operational and human resources reasons', although some of its projects will be taken over by other charities.[23] MSF, in addition to its well-known medical assistance projects, also undertakes 'advocacy positions when dealing with specific abuses of endangered populations', which caused difficulties when the charity felt that some of Beijing's health directives were unsuited to Tibetan conditions, including the CMS, for medical payments, which MSF were required to implement, and the lack of a 'community approach' to health care.

In September 1995 in Beijing, the Fourth UN World Conference on Women put forward a wide range of goals and objectives for the improvement of the status, role and active participation of women in all spheres, public and private, through their full and equal share in economic, social, cultural and political decision-making. Women's health was a major feature. In June 2000 a Special Session of the UN General Assembly considered progress and problems during the previous five years. One might think that, China having ratified the UN Convention on the Elimination of All Forms of Discrimination against Women on 4 November 1980, and hosting the Fourth World Conference in 1995, it would have been in the lead with regard to the lawful and compassionate treatment of women in Tibet. Not so. The Tibetan Women's Association, in a special report, found that the situation for women in Tibet has become worse since 1995.[24]

This is true especially where child-bearing is concerned. In rural China, the so-called 'one child' policy is harsh and inhuman. China's two-child policy in Tibet was introduced in 1984, and until 1999 Tibetans in rural areas were permitted to have three children. Then the law was tightened to one child per family in urban areas and two in rural areas. The crude, violent and damaging means of implementation make the policy grotesquely inhuman. They are systematic and premeditated and in direct violation of international and humanitarian law. The problem is that if local officials do not meet the established government quotas for family size, they themselves face penalties and financial sanctions. Enforced abortion (which can take place very late in a pregnancy) and enforced sterilisation are the most common means of meeting the quotas. Both can be so crudely undertaken that some women suffer psychological and physical damage for the rest of their lives. They both contravene declared Chinese central government policy.

Punishments for families exceeding the birth quotas include excessive fines totally beyond their means; reduction of pay; loss of jobs; loss of housing; denial of basic rights such as having a food ration card; denial of education to the child; denial of health care; and the forfeit of any land rights due to the parents. Husbands may be beaten and arrested. One Tibetan woman who was two months pregnant was told that if she did not have an abortion her child's name would not be 'registered', she would be given only 30 percent of her salary and it would never increase. Both she and her husband could be dismissed from their jobs. So she said 'yes'. The operation was unbelievably crude and extremely damaging, involving a knife on the end of a stick, for which she had to pay – with no aftercare.

Then there is eugenics. Since China passed the 'Maternal and Infant Care Law' in 1995, the government has the right to control marriages and birth according to their perception of the health of a man and woman and their children. The aim is to prevent couples from passing on diseases and mental disabilities to their children, especially, it would appear, in 'minority nationalities'. In 1990 the Chinese authorities announced without citing evidence that there were 10,000 'inferior' Tibetans in the TAR. The absence of medical criteria and the coercive power of local officials means that sterilisation, abortion and marriage bans can be used arbitrarily and simply on their say-so. The UN Committee on the Rights of the Child (the convention was ratified by the Chinese in March 1992) stated that this law in China virtually amounts to the practice of 'selective infanticide', as deployed in Nazi Germany.

Adequate housing is a basic human right; the Chinese government agrees.[25] Yet there is gross discrimination in the availability and quality of housing in Tibet, especially in Lhasa. The problem arises because of the great influx of Chinese into the TAR. Officially approved migrants are guaranteed housing. Those who arrive unofficially know how the Chinese administrative system works and can ensure that they too are allocated housing. Housing needs for Tibetans are given low priority. In 1950, at the time of the Chinese invasion, virtually 100 percent of housing in Lhasa was for Tibetans. By the year 2000 it had fallen to 2 percent. Lhasa has become a typical Chinese city. Traditional Tibetan buildings in the centre of Lhasa, many declared by UNESCO to be protected sites, are being systematically destroyed. A survey in 2002 by Scandinavian architects show that two-thirds of Tibetan traditional buildings inside the pilgrimage circuit had already disappeared.

(While Tibetans are justifiably angry at such desecration of their cultural heritage, their feelings are probably matched by the fury of the Chinese themselves at the destruction of 91 percent of Beijing within the old city walls, in preparation for the 2008 Olympic Games.[26] The ancient tree-lined streets, the tiled one-storey courtyards where rich and poor lived side by side, and the remaining parts of its fifteenth-century Ming dynasty heritage are now being swept away without consulting any of the 2.5 million people living within the old city walls. In their place are rising, in one part of the city alone [Chaoyang], more than three hundred 140-storey skyscrapers; this process is being repeated in another part of the city. In all, some 6 million people are being rehoused in satellite towns of high-rise blocks.)

Tibetans in what is left of old Lhasa are caught in a multiple bind. The incoming Chinese take virtually all the new housing. Many Tibetan houses are demolished to make space for them. The excuse is that their houses are 'unsafe'. Tibetans, who may be given as little as two days' notice to leave, may then be told to return to the villages from which, perhaps a very long time ago, they came originally. Others may be offered accommodation in a newly built block, but at unaffordably high rents. So they also may move out – many to flee the country. Tibetans and Chinese both have to obtain the appropriate residence permits to live in Lhasa and elsewhere, but while Chinese have little difficulty with this, Tibetans from rural areas find it virtually impossible.

Some of the Tibetan housing and commercial buildings being demolished are explicitly to make Lhasa 'beautiful' for 'a modern socialist city, rich, civilised and clean'. Architecture has been used for millennia to express local or national pride, a powerful symbol of national identity. However, 'beauty' consists of putting functional uniformity above aesthetics. A few Chinese buildings have facades that pick up Tibetan designs – and distort them. Inside they are just like any other Chinese buildings.

Most housing for Tibetans is significantly inferior in space and available facilities. Chinese housing will have running water, internal toilets and electricity. Although money is allocated for improving the quality of traditional Tibetan housing, in practice most goes to improve Chinese housing. New housing is made from concrete, where traditional Tibetan housing has thick mud or brick walls. Concrete is not suitable for the extremes of climate in Tibet. In winter rooms become cold and damp and heating is a problem. Few Tibetan houses have electricity, except where Chinese live close by, and have to rely on kerosene for heating, cooking and light. Kerosene has to be purchased with special coupons, which are available only to those who attend work sessions or neighbourhood meetings (largely for political indoctrination). Coupons can be bought on the black market at high prices, and there is a risk that their validity may be cancelled without notice.

The economy in the TAR creates large inequalities in income and wealth. By 1998 rural incomes in the TAR had become the lowest of all rural incomes in China. By contrast, urban household incomes, mainly Chinese, have consistently been above the national average. The result has been one of the highest urban–rural inequalities anywhere in China. Moreover, in urban areas Chinese cadre households have much higher incomes than non-cadres, in part because they receive high incomes to induce them to live in Tibet.

From 1990 to 2000, incomes from farming and animal husbandry have stagnated, and in real terms have fallen. The livelihood of about 80 percent of Tibetans depends on the land.[27] Grasslands cover some 70 percent of the high Tibetan Plateau. Land is allocated to settled farmers near their communities at both high and low altitudes, although it is owned by the state. Fencing is now required, for which there are few or no government subsidies. In winter, farmers at high altitudes would normally move their animals to lower levels (as I observed in Nepal), but in Tibet they are increasingly frustrated in doing so by the fencing or allocations of land to local farmers. Likewise, in summer, low-altitude farmers move their animals to higher-level grasslands, and they too are finding land enclosed or at least allocated to others. Disputes break out, people are hurt, even killed, and the Chinese do not intervene. Nomads are worst affected. Their traditional livelihood and use of land are heading for extinction. In November 2001 it was announced that in the next ten years a further 1 million hectares of grassland will be fenced. The Chinese say that the nomadic way of life is an inefficient use of land, and that all nomads should be in settlements.[28] This will make control and political education by the authorities easier, and taxes simpler to collect. Many Tibetans believe also that settlements with fenced lands will free the remaining land for Chinese mineral exploitation. Farmers in the TAR have to pay high and increasing taxes, on land (in 2001 it was about three times what it was the previous year) on animals when alive, when killed and when sold. Since the end of 2001 they are also limited in the number of livestock they can own, to five per person.

Excess numbers of livestock are confiscated. However, in Chapter Three of China's White Paper on Tibet (23 May 2004), it is noted that 'farmers and herdsmen are exempt from taxes and administrative charges'.

In many areas, farmers are required to sell their produce directly to government agencies at low prices, and the authorities make a significant profit on resale. Chinese farmers can sell directly to the market and earn more. Tibetans are required to buy fertiliser from the authorities at what they consider to be unduly high prices; Chinese farmers have no such requirement. Until 1999, in some areas ordinary Tibetan nomads could buy food from any shops, but after that time they could buy only from local government-owned shops. Many private shops were closed down. Government shops were more expensive and the quality often poor.

Not only is rural life being fundamentally changed, but work for Tibetans in urban areas is also being made more difficult. Case studies show a distressing picture. The International Covenant on the Elimination of All Forms of Racial Discrimination, ratified by the Chinese government in December 1981, says that everyone, without discrimination, should enjoy 'the right to work, to free choice of employment, to just and favourable conditions of work, to protection against unemployment, to equal pay for equal work and favourable remuneration' (Art 5 [c] [i]). Moreover, the 1994 Labour Act of The People's Republic of China states that 'labourers shall not be discriminated against in employment, regardless of their ethnic community, race, sex or religious belief' (Section Twelve, Chapter Eleven). The evidence shows that both pieces of legislation are disregarded in Tibet.

Tibetans returning from their education in China may find that they are more easily accepted by Chinese employers, but the large majority of Tibetan refugees who have not been on this educational programme report that employers demand fluency in Chinese, regardless of the job itself, and no matter how well-qualified they are. Job selections are conducted in Chinese and those who do not speak it well enough may be immediately rejected. Tibetans who can speak Chinese may be transferred to remote districts where their influence is minimal and their skills under-utilised. Chinese employers appear to assume that Tibetans are backward, inefficient, ill-educated and incapable of doing anything other than menial tasks. So the Chinese get the higher-level jobs and Tibetans get the lower ones which the Chinese do not want. Even when the work is similar, Tibetans may be paid less.[29] The effects of such prejudice are to cause the richer Tibetans to pay for their children to learn Chinese language and behaviour. *Guanxi*, the network of connections between individuals, families and organisations so common in China, is as important in work as in education. Connections are cemented with gifts and favours. Tibetans with no Chinese connections may have to resort to bribes. So Tibetans without connections or ready cash may have to take the lower-level jobs.

There is discrimination also in funding business start-ups and expansion. Banks, which rarely give loans to Tibetans, will require a deposit of all their personal valuables and possessions – even to an amount exceeding the value of the loan. Chinese do not have to do this. And business permits are difficult to obtain for Tibetans, whereas the Chinese are given them automatically. In Lhasa, Chinese are permitted to construct market stalls in front of Tibetan ones, and when the latter go out of business the Chinese extend their selling area backwards. 'To get a construction contract a Tibetan needs to have a bank balance of 100,000 *yuan* … this does not apply to Chinese contractors.'[30] There are, however, a small number of Tibetan entrepreneurs who are high earners, but most people are restricted by their poor education and training and their lack of the Chinese language.

One consequence of discrimination in retailing is that the proportion of Tibetan shops in Tibetan towns and villages has reached a low level. A 1995 survey of the Tromsekhang market in Lhasa showed that of 1,061 businesses only 34 percent were Tibetan. In 1998 in Drayab County in Chamdo, a Tibetan area, only 8 percent of businesses were Tibetan. Surveys show that in no town or village in areas predominantly occupied by Tibetans are the majority of businesses owned by Tibetans.

Unemployment and poverty amongst Tibetans are high – in some areas as high as 40 percent. Their high rate of illiteracy works against them and migrants, principally from Sichuan, are much better educated – and, of course, Chinese. For most Tibetans it is an enormous struggle to survive. The dice are loaded against them. Many old people have to resort to begging. Many young people turn to thieving; many young women turn to prostitution. All this is a terrible tale of enforcement, discrimination and unfair practice. It is demeaning and frustrating, with a significant loss of Tibetans' self-esteem. Many feel that they are worthless, an attitude already instilled in the schools. However, as exiles, with all the disadvantages of separation from family and friends, there is training on offer and work opportunities. They are valued for who they are and many are very successful. In the right environment they are not at all as the Chinese portray them. The overall result is that many Tibetans escape from Tibet, braving the hazards of the Himalaya, avoiding Chinese security, risking harsh treatment by the Nepalese police, hoping for a better life.

Melvyn Goldstein's solution to the problem that non-farming employment in Tibet, especially the manual and low-paid jobs, is being taken over by non-

Tibetan migrants from China is to change the 'open-door' policy and allow in fewer migrants, or to give job preferences or 'set asides' in favour of Tibetans. However, the authors of the wide-ranging Chinese Academy of Social Sciences research study of the changing conditions in the TAR, published in May 2004, argued robustly:

> Tibet is an inseparable part of China. No matter whether they are Tibetan or belong to other ethnic groups, they are all Chinese citizens. Only on this basis can we talk about the impact of public policies on workers of different ethnic background, sex and age. Allowing the free flow of labour contributes to poverty alleviation and making the country a fairer place for all. Thus, from a national perspective labour policies should not discriminate against certain regions and ethnic people.

One can see the 'free trade' argument for the movement of labour. Giving preference to Tibetans would discriminate against the poor would-be migrants from China. If there were a 'level playing field' without discrimination in education or training against Tibetans, for example, or without prejudice by Chinese employers against Tibetans who do not speak Chinese, or the need for *guanxi* (connections), then the Chinese Academy of Sciences' argument would hold. Meanwhile, in reality the playing field is tilted in favour of the Chinese. Until racial discrimination is eliminated, educational standards match those of the Chinese or provision is made for non-Chinese speakers by employers, then there is a legitimate case for protection in favour of Tibetans.

In June 1999 President Jiang Zemin launched the much-publicised Western Development Programme, breathtaking in scope and scale – it will cover 56 percent of the whole of China. Tibet's traditional lands cover nearly one half of 'the West'.[31] Its impact will be vast (see Chapter Ten).

The Tibetan people have not been consulted about this extensive programme of development in their lands. It is being imposed upon them. They will gain benefits in terms of extra employment opportunities and income, but it is absurd to expect these massive developments to achieve lift-off in Tibetan standards of living. However, in a welcome change in policy, in September 2002 Xinhua (China's official news agency) announced that the government had undertaken 'to approve any project benefiting the Tibetan people'. But the report does not state whether it will be Chinese or Tibetans who decide which projects will benefit the Tibetan people, whether Tibetans will be given assistance to formulate such projects in a suitable manner, where the funds will come from, whether there are budget constraints or whether there are hidden strings attached. Whether the new policy will attract Tibetan cadres, international non-governmental organisations (NGOs) and some well-trained Tibetans-in-exile is doubtful.

> Economic statistics for the scale and growth of the Gross Domestic Product (GDP) in the TAR are very misleading. A detailed Special Report by the Tibet Information Network in April 2003, 'Deciphering Economic Growth in the Tibet Autonomous Region', showed that growth, where it does take place, is heavily fuelled by government spending through subsidies and is overwhelmingly concentrated in the state sector and/or urban areas. It therefore bypasses most Tibetans, who are rural and non-salaried. Productive sectors such as agriculture (which accounted for about 75 percent of Tibetan employment), mining and industry are either stagnant or growing much more slowly than the economy in general. The 'vital engine behind its current growth' is 'government agencies, party agencies and social organisations' (which do not include social services such as education and health). Indeed, the under-supply of rural education has not been addressed. Rural Tibetans have thus been more or less marginalised from the reported rapid growth in GDP and inequalities have increased sharply throughout the TAR.

The principal political problem for Tibetans is lack of control over their own affairs. The Chinese say that in the Tibet Autonomous Region and in Tibet Autonomous Prefectures outside the TAR, Tibetans already have autonomy. But the Law on Regional National Autonomy says that 'the organs of self-government of national autonomous areas shall place the interests of the state as a whole above anything else and make positive efforts to fulfil the tasks assigned by state organs at higher levels'. Thus the Chinese see autonomy as relating only to executing policies decided at higher levels. Even so, the chief administrator in the TAR is always Chinese, the Communist Party Secretary. Since the Third Work Forum on Tibet in 1994 Beijing has been taking a leading role in the determination of policy in Tibet. At lower levels, many Tibetan cadres in Tibet act only with Chinese authority, sometimes from Chinese who may be junior to them in the administrative hierarchy.

A Chinese survey in June 1988 made an attempt to find out what Tibetan people want, including whether respondents wanted 'complete independence, greater autonomy or continuing the present arrangements'.[32] But it was undertaken on the basis of a biased sample and on technical grounds was improperly conducted. It remains unpublished. Then, as mentioned above, in May 2004 the Chinese Academy of Social Sciences published the findings of a study in the TAR looking into the progress made in food production and security, the development of human resources and social welfare in rural areas and the creation of non-farming work and the growth of public services in these areas. This very political document, although admitting that some areas are 'poverty stricken', asserted that the general trend was upwards with improvements all round. Yet the study was not very convincing. More useful comparisons could have been made through cross-section studies (through 'paired comparisons', for example, stratified by similar altitudes, age structure and type of activity) between the TAR and other mountainous rural areas in China and, better still, with the mountainous rural areas in Ladakh, to the west of Tibet. There the pastures rise to 15,000–18,000 feet and much of the land is high-altitude desert, criss-crossed by giant mountain ranges, as in the TAR. The people have common origins with the Tibetans and their culture is similar. Ladakh is, however, part of Jammu and Kashmir in India and comparisons with Tibetans in the TAR as part of China would then be highly meaningful. This opportunity was not taken.

The Dalai Lama is seen by the Chinese as the epicentre of potentially damaging forces determined to destroy China, the ultimate counter-revolutionary who 'endangers state security'. In states which respect the rule of law, such a phrase would be tested in the courts and its boundaries would be determined through cases. This does not happen in China. At the Third Work Forum on Tibet in 1994 the Chinese government announced that 'total war was to be waged against the Dalai Lama', and in 1996 it launched a Strike Hard campaign in Tibet against 'splittists' and other political activists, a campaign which had to be repeated in 2001. Instead of responding positively to protestors in Tibet in support of 'freedom' and their legitimate right of self-determination to decide such matters for themselves (see Chapter Eleven), the authorities arrest and imprison them. Such political prisoners receive the worst treatment – beatings and torture so terrible that even to write about them is painful. Yet to form a clear picture, the truth must be told.

There is no lack of information. In a most moving book,[33] Palden Gyatso, released in 1992 and now in exile, has described his experiences during thirty-three years in prison for taking part in a nonviolent protest against the Chinese occupation. Just to hold his thin, bony hand, as I have done, transmits a lifetime of pain and anger. The Venerable Bhagdro, whom I have met many times, has also described his three years of torture (1988–91).[34] A great many Tibetan refugees have been interviewed, and their reports make solemn reading. In 1999, the Danish quarterly journal *Torture*[35] published a special 52-page supplement, 'Torture in Tibet 1949–1999'. Examples of torture methods used against Tibetans are given in the notes to this chapter.[36] Here, let a 28-year-old nun, Tenzin Choedon, describe her experience in the Gutsa Detention Centre and speak for the rest:

We were all hit with rifle butts … then an official set a dog upon me … We were then taken to a hall and ordered to remove our clothes, except for out waistcoat and petticoat … I was stripped and told to lie down as if prostrating. I saw them bring knotted ropes, electric batons and sticks … First I was hit with a stick all over my body … I saw my fellow nuns being abused with electric batons in their anuses. When the electric baton was used on my body, I felt as if a nerve in my heart was being pulled out and my stomach was in pain … I was told to stand up and lean against a wall … they inserted a stick in my vagina four times with full force, which resulted in pain that lasted for three days and also gave me problems when urinating. Then the stick was rammed into my mouth . . after this incident I was unable to move and they had to take me to my cell. When I recovered my senses, I saw that my skin had become green and that I had marks on my buttocks.[37]

She received no medical attention after these tortures. As the report remarks, 'her story is not unusual. In fact, it is quite common'.

Tibetan political prisoners have been treated so badly that in Dharamsala an 'Ex-Political Prisoners' Association' has been formed (*Gu-Chu-Sum*) and a Japanese charity has funded a special building for them. Their publications list the several thousand names of such persons. However, since January 2002 it appears that China's policy on long-serving political prisoners may have changed. So far seven have been released early, including the 74-year-old Takna Jigme Sangpo, who has spent most of the past forty years in prison and was not due for release until 3 September 2011, and five nuns from Drapchi Prison. Whether this foretells a more compassionate approach remains to be seen. The number of Tibetan political prisoners has fallen in the TAR owing to fewer detentions, as in Qinghai and Gansu provinces, and has risen in Sichuan – overall, since 2003, it has stabilised.

The ideological background to Chinese policy in Tibet, confirmed by Jiang's speech on 1 July 2001, remains Marxism:

Marxism is the fundamental guiding principle for the consolidation of the Party and the development of the country. It also constitutes the common theoretical foundation of the concerted efforts of the people of all ethnic groups. The fundamental tenets of Marxism must never be abandoned, otherwise we would get lost or come to failure in the pursuit of our cause due to lack of a correct theoretical basis and ideological soul.

The Chinese campaign against 'splittism' has now been associated with the

American 'war on terror'. On 27 October 2001 the Chinese State Council, with the enthusiastic support of Li Peng, responded positively to the invitation by US President George W. Bush to join his 'war'. The council then condemned 'terrorism, splittism and fanaticism', encompassing Tibetans, Uyghurs and the Falun Gong. Two weeks later Mary Robinson, UN High Commissioner for Human Rights, on a visit to China, warned that the US-led campaign against terrorism must not be used as a pretext to suppress ethnic minority groups. She was too late.

To escape is the only solution. Walking over the high Himalaya is always hazardous, and many have perished on the way. (I have some idea what it's like. On the 1987 expedition we struggled through ice and snow to reach a pass at about 17,000 feet. It was completely blocked by snow from a ferocious storm which had lasted thirty-four hours. As we came down to our previous camp at 13,000 feet to find another route, crossing on a narrow ledge above a near-vertical icefall, my foot slipped and I went tumbling down, head over heels. With my ice axe looped round my wrist I knew what to do. But that was nothing compared with escaping over such terrain, sometimes in soft trainers, no ice axes, short of food and probably with inadequate clothing.)

The sheer physical exertion required is daunting; the possibility of frostbite, the fear of being caught, and now the possibility of a hostile reception in Nepal (in spite of the best endeavours of the United Nations High Commission for Refugees [UNHCR]) would discourage all but the most determined. Children, pregnant women and the sick, especially those who have suffered torture, are most at risk. Venerable Baghdro, the aforementioned Tibetan monk, has described the agony of wanting to give up many times during his escape over the mountains through complete exhaustion, in great pain, bleeding from nose and mouth, with his kidneys failing, and being dragged, half carried, pushed and constantly encouraged by his companions, until he made it to freedom.

Since the renewed 'Strike Hard' programme in June 2001, the possibility of being caught before such people cross the border has increased. The Chinese have stepped up their surveillance and security forces to prevent escapes. In the second half of 2001, about 2,500 Tibetans were caught by Chinese security forces while trying to flee. There are many reports of local Chinese police stealing their possessions and beating and torturing them before handing them over to the Public Security Bureau. Those apprehended will be imprisoned, and many are sentenced to 're-education through labour' or perhaps to work on the Golmud–Lhasa railway construction.

The attitude of the Nepalese police towards escapees arriving without visas has also hardened. The Maoist insurgents in Nepal have targeted their police, who have become more cautious in seeking out Tibetan arrivals. Since the Chinese may pay for the return of each escapee, or present the policemen concerned with medals, the incentive is there. Even so, in 2001, 1,735 Tibetans arrived safely, more than one half of them children and young people, a much lower figure than in previous years (about 2,000–2,500). The heightened security is leading Tibetans to choose the winter months to escape because the surveillance is less keen, but the hazards are increased. In December 2003 the Chinese completed a road to Gyaplung towards the Nangpa Pass at over 19,000 feet, close to a major glacier, over which many Tibetans escape. Floodlights have been installed at another crossing point some sixteen miles from Nangpa. The Nepalese have sown thousands of anti-personnel mines near their more remote police stations to protect them from Maoist insurgents, and Tibetan escapees may be unaware of these deadly dangers. China's ambassador to Nepal, Sun Heping, told reporters on 14 November 2003 that 'we are going to make the necessary arrangements to stop such illegal [Tibetan] immigrants'.[38] But in January 2004 the Nepalese government said it will hand over all Tibetan refugees to the UNHCR, not to the Chinese, although after the announcement they were still being deported back to China.

These examples of Chinese behaviour in Tibet in recent times are indicative of widespread colonialist attitudes, of a lack of respect for Tibet's indigenous people and of assumed Chinese superiority. Whichever way one looks there is a sad story to tell. But much of the above is anecdotal, not derived from impartially conducted and independent cultural, social and economic surveys, for these do not exist. Careful observers who have travelled the terrain, such as Patrick French (*Tibet, Tibet: A Personal History of a Lost Land*), also catch glimpses of the truth, and report on the fear and suspicion beneath the surface and the constraints under which most Tibetans live.

There is a major discrepancy between Chinese reporting of the situation in Tibet and what Tibetans themselves say when free to speak, supplemented by foreign observers. While one may dismiss Chinese reporting as propaganda in support of the state's policies, unfortunately the Chinese themselves appear to believe it. There is both an information gap between reality and Chinese perception and, it would seem, a failure to correctly analyse the statistical and other reporting that reaches Beijing, so the truth is obscured. But this is not the whole story, and one must ask why the Chinese behave in the ways described and what their purpose is. The answers are complex and interwoven with history, ideology, personality, fear, greed and intolerance.[39]

PART ONE

Origins

ONE

—

Influences from Chinese History

'A way can be a guide, but not a fixed path;
names can be given, but not permanent labels.'
Lao-tzu, Tao Te Ching,[1] *Chapter One*

Mao Zedong's influence on the modern history of China can hardly be exaggerated. The earthquakes he provoked shattered Chinese society, and their distant rumblings can still be felt today. His influence on Tibet was also intense, deep and long-lasting. It was he who initiated the policies in Tibet which, with only a short respite in the 1980s, were carried forward by Deng Xiaoping and, with greater severity, by Jiang Zemin. They led directly to the current problems.

Mao was a zealous reader. His great wooden bed, half as big again as a normal double bed, was always strewn with books. Whenever possible, he carried a book in his pocket; he loved Chinese history and early romances. His abiding passions were the ancient landmark figures who achieved great change in China, especially the most ruthless and cruel, about whom he read and reread many times. Reading about the past, for Mao, was not so much a stimulating form of leisure as a source of inspiration, learning and the basis for action. The imperial bureaucrats of old were masters of accurate note-taking and reporting. Almost all of imperial history is in the ancient records. (So often, even today, when one asks an educated Chinese person why something is as it is, his or her reply will refer back to China's ancient history.)

One might think that history is immutable. Unfortunately, so-called 'facts' do change. For example, Jonathan Spence writes of the changes that occurred between the first and second editions of his book *The Search for Modern China* (Autumn 1989 and August 1997):

> Our knowledge of China's past has been prodigiously extended. Rich archaeological discoveries inside China are transforming our view of early Chinese society and early texts on the theory of government. And also in countless areas closer to our current age, studies by Chinese and foreign scholars have profoundly altered what we thought we knew ... I have been compelled to alter many old ideas, and to introduce many new ones.

Moreover, Chinese history is sometimes reinvented for political purposes, to 'prove' a point. Disinformation is a game played by many international players, and China excels in it. None of this must paralyse writers into inactivity for fear of being found wrong. It is a warning: writers on China should use either first-hand observation or the most up-to-date information available from reputable sources.

Unfortunately the disease of unreliability plagues Chinese statistics as well. 'Anyone who spends time working in China,' writes Jasper Becker, 'eventually comes to doubt even basic facts, [such as] how many people are there in China?'[2] The former premier Zhu Rongji has admitted that many Chinese statistics are unreliable. The Chinese National Bureau of Statistics, in February 2002, uncovered endemic falsification of data. In a system where rewards may be based on the achievement of national and local targets, there is an ever-present temptation to call upon puffed-up statistical reporting. A former township party secretary in Tibet, who fled to India in 2002, said that his responsibility was to make fake reports on the development of the people, places and animals: 'When we write the reports and submit them to higher levels they also exaggerate more before submitting them to their superiors.'[3] It is also the case that 'since 1998 nearly all Chinese provincial authorities have over-reported growth rates, leading to a situation in which the sum of the parts adds up to more than the whole'. Moody's Investors' Service in 1996 described China's financial statistics as 'meaningless'. A World Bank Report in 1994 exploded the whole statistical basis on which foreign companies had based estimates of the size of China's markets and had spent millions of dollars.

The language itself in China is a problem for the unwary. The written language has no tenses. Thus referring to the historical past is the same as if it were in the present. There is no distinction in the written characters between 'was' in the past and 'is' today. It is as though the past is actually here and now, a ready guide to current action, an immediacy that makes it seem especially relevant. So history and language conspire to bring ancient China alive. Also, in discussion, the Chinese eschew a straightforward 'yes' or 'no'. Sometimes one has to follow a circuitous route to determine what exactly is meant. Alarmingly for Westerners, the spoken word can reverse its meaning if spoken with a different accent.[4]

Chinese history is a remarkable record of immense talent, ancient wisdom, invention, art, war – and catastrophe. The most ancient and famous history book is the *Shiji*, written by Sima Qian, who was the Grand Historian in 107 BC. There is little doubt that Mao will have read it, for it depicts the intrigues, actions and extraordinary achievements of his hero, the First Emperor of China – the first of three 'greats' from China's past who influenced Mao and later generations mentioned here.

The First Emperor was called Qin (Ch'in), or Qin Shihuangdi.[5] Qin donned the cap and sword of adulthood in 238 BC and became King Zheng. He made himself Emperor in 221 BC and his conquests of 270 territories, some of which were little more than city-states, took place from then to his death in 210 BC. Mao is thought to have spent at least as much time studying the First Emperor as he did Marxism.

With superior technology and the natural protection of geography – the mountains of Qin and the curve of the Yellow River – the First Emperor trained his forces thoroughly. He conquered his six Warring States neighbours and their neighbours too, destroyed their weapons, pulled down their fortresses (other than those he needed for the Great Wall) and extinguished their distinctive cultures, languages and systems of governance to form the 'Middle Kingdom' – the first united China.[6] His conquered territory ranged from the Gobi desert, in what is now Inner Mongolia in the west, to the Gulf of Tonkin in the east. (It was, however, only about one half of today's China.) His capital was Xi'an, now the provincial capital of modern Shaanxi. He thus acquired many palaces in different parts of his empire, decorated in the style of each locality in which they were situated and supplied lavishly with the best local food and concubines for his visits of inspection.

His system of government was known as the Legalist system. It drew heavily on the past, was highly bureaucratic and ruled in an austere, totalitarian fashion, enforced through fear and terror. All books in his conquered territories, other than Legalist works and those on agriculture, medicine and divination, were destroyed. Confucianism was anathema to the Legalists. Scholars were conscripted or killed; legends of the period say they were buried alive. A single written script was introduced, the basis of the system today, and their former languages extinguished. Thus all traces of the existing cultures of these besieged peoples were eradicated. Laws and regulations were standardised throughout the empire, and all were written down. People in the new empire who critically compared what they no doubt saw as the halcyon past with the terrible present, were executed with all their families – even remote relatives.

There was a system of mutual responsibility for wrongdoing, family group units of five or ten, the entire population being divided along with a system of informers. People spied and reported on each other. All traces of free expression were eradicated. The Qin state also recognised 'thought crimes' which were severely punished as acts of rebellion. The people had many duties, but only the Emperor and the elite bureaucrats, who had been chosen entirely by merit, had rights. While he encouraged agriculture, controlled in the minutest detail,[7] the privileges of the feudal land-owning aristocracy were eliminated. Everything was now owned by the state. Taxes were extortionate and the people suffered. Trade was repressed.

To consolidate his conquests, from 219 BC the Emperor moved large numbers of his own Qin people into the new territories, many of them merchants, to engage in trade and to colonise the local people. Some of the enforced migrants were convicts, fugitives, bonded servants and other people in disfavour, all reckoned to be superior to the non-Qin 'barbarians'. As a result of inspection tours of his conquests, he moved, for example, 50,000 families to Yum-yang; 30,000 families to the Ordos plateau region on the way to Inner Mongolia; another 30,000 families to Shandong, bordering the ocean to the east; and 120,000 families of the leaders of territories he conquered into replica palaces built near his own, to ensure that they were kept in submission: the emperor needed their experience and skills.

The First Emperor also introduced a single metallic currency for the whole of his empire, and weights and measures were standardised. He built over 4,250 miles of imperial highways and standardised the width between the wheels of all vehicles. This enabled him to build some very long, straight and wide roads described as 'speedways' for rapid travel to and from the more distant parts of the empire, including the 'Straight Road' of 500 miles to Inner Mongolia. He also built 1,200 miles of canals and inland waterways to carry water, people and goods, and to irrigate the land. There is controversy about his building the Great Wall; probably he linked together various existing sections of fortification to form 'the longest unbroken defence installation ever made by man'.[8]

With the destruction of so many cultures, excessive control, an extensive range of fearsome punishments for misdemeanours and the widespread transference of Qin people – including some unsavoury characters – into the new colonial territories, it is not surprising that at the first opportunity the indigenous inhabitants rebelled. When the First Emperor died, still searching in vain for the elixir of eternal life, he had failed to satisfy and motivate the people and acknowledge the faults of his system; he had also refused to take any advice (although he did have some foreign technical help). The system he created had failed to display any humanity towards his subjects, their beliefs and their traditional ways of living. It was doomed.[9] He had proclaimed that it would last 'unto a thousand and ten thousand generations', but in fact the Second Emperor, his younger son Hu Hai, was the last of the line. He had gained power through deceit and fraud, and for three years used the Qin empire for his personal pleasures. Vast numbers of his subjects were executed for supposed misdemeanours, and he presided over a reign of terror. There were armed uprisings throughout the whole of China; the country disintegrated, and the Second Emperor committed suicide in 206 BC.

Amongst those who rose against the Second Emperor was a peasant called Liu Bang. He was a natural leader, wise and compassionate, caring for his followers and for all people who came under his authority. He had fought for what he knew to be right and won many battles against other warlords and against the Qin forces still loyal to the imperial throne, and triumphed. In 201 BC, by popular acclaim, he became Emperor of China and founder of the Han dynasty, which lasted for 400 years. Even today, after more than 2,200 years, the Chinese people are still called 'Han'.

The history and experiences of the period made a deep impression on Mao. During the Cultural Revolution it was considered extremely dangerous to criticise the First Emperor, and in 1973 Mao ordered a three-year campaign for the whole country to study the Emperor's policies and actions. Scholars read and praised him. In the 1980s Chinese students were still reading textbooks that explained and justified the purposes and methods of the Qin dictatorship. It is not surprising that Chinese rule in Tibet bears many resemblances to that imposed by the First Emperor on his conquered and beleaguered neighbours. In some ways Mao felt that he had outdone Qin. In 1978 Mao said, 'Qin Shihuangdi did not amount to much. He buried only 460 scholars. We buried 46,000 of them.' (He was referring to his vanquishing of intellectuals following the 'Hundred Flowers' movement.)

However, the unified bureaucratic system under the First Emperor developed into a professional scholar-gentry class with its own strict and sensible rules – and, one would say, some rather less desirable privileges – to which admission could be achieved only by success in imperial civil examinations, later based on the nine Classics of Confucianism. As an administrative system it became a model for civil service systems in other Asian and Western countries. The

Qin dynasty and its system of governance have remarkable parallels in China today.

Sun Tzu also had great influence over Mao, but in quite a different way. He lived at the end of the sixth century BC or thereabouts.[10] It was a time of major conflict, the period of the Warring States. The Zhou dynasty was collapsing, and the military was in the ascendant. Sun Tzu was a master strategist whose inspiration has reached across millennia to the present day. (Some strategists in today's British army and navy have said that they know about Sun Tzu.)

Sun Tzu's treatise, *The Art of War*, is one of the great classics of Chinese literature.[11] Its main thesis is how to win against one's enemies without fighting, to accomplish the most by doing the least, to engage in physical conflict only as a last resort and when the circumstances will ensure victory – 'weapons are instruments of ill-omen, to be used only when unavoidable'.[12] To subdue the enemy's forces without fighting is the summit of skill.[13] The best approach is to attack the other side's strategy; next best is to attack his alliances; next best is to attack his soldiers; the worst is to attack cities.

Thomas Cleary remarks in the introduction to his translation from the original that '*The Art of War* has an incalculable abstract reserve and metaphorical potential. And, like other Taoist literature, it yields its subtleties in accord with the mentality of the reader and the manner in which it is put into practice.'[14] Although its origin is in ancient China around 2,400 years ago, it has found application throughout history, even into the present day, in many spheres: military, diplomatic, business and management.

Mao's military writings *On Guerrilla Warfare*, *On the Protracted War* and *Strategic Problems of China's Revolutionary War* show the measure of his debt to Sun Tzu.[15] Mao's own immense ability and powerful intuition enabled him to use *The Art of War* in ways which contributed to his spectacular military successes. It is apparent, too, that the Chinese invasion of Tibet in 1950 and the resulting 'Seventeen-Point Agreement' in 1951 were in accordance with Sun Tzu's precepts. From the Chinese point of view the invasion achieved complete success at small cost in terms of men and materials. That, and the negotiations in 1951, involved deception by the Chinese; surprise; threat; superior military and civilian intelligence through the use of spies; superior public relations; disruption of the enemy's communications; and – in a particular triumph which would have made Sun Tzu's eyes shine with delight – capturing one of the enemy's leaders and securing him at the head of the opposing Tibetan negotiating team.[16] In recent times, the Chinese conditions attached to offers of negotiation with the Dalai Lama are part of China's negotiating tactics and strategy.[17] They have their clear origins in Sun Tzu.

The last in this trio of main influences on Mao and Chinese thinking from the ancient past, with particular reference to Tibet, is Kong Fuzi (or Kung Fu-tzu), better known as Confucius. He was thought to have been born in 551 BC and to have died in 479 BC, a truly remarkable man – but not at all as generally represented. An enthusiast for everything which touched his interest, keen on sport, a skilled horseman and adept at archery, hunting and fishing, he was also a deeply emotional man.[18] Love and ecstasy were to him superior forms of knowledge. On hearing a particular piece of music, evidently, the emotion took him by surprise and 'for three months he forgot the taste of meat'. He was also a (frustrated) politician and a renowned sage. His *Analects* are the 'oldest complete intellectual and spiritual portrait of a man. It strikes one as a modern book.'[19] As a man of action, his political ambition was to put into practice his carefully worked-out political philosophy and administrative system. He trained capable men in his ideas. These emphasised the importance of education for rulers and the application of high moral principles. He was, however, thwarted. He travelled widely but, unsurprisingly, could not find a part of China with a sufficiently enlightened ruler who would engage him and his trained administrative team to run their affairs.

Confucius lived at a time when the parts of China that the Zhou dynasty had created 500 years or so earlier – which seemed like a 'golden age' – were in danger of disintegration.[20] The world as he knew it was set to disappear in violence and barbarity. The period of the Warring States began towards the end of his life. In such circumstances Confucius emphasised that a strong authoritarian leadership was necessary under which the people would obey the ruler as they did parents in their family lives, where they would show filial piety and respect. 'The good subject is the obedient subject ... absolute obedience to the masters of society.' To later generations, therefore, Confucius was seen as advocating a strong dictatorship at the head of a state, which Mao well remembered. But this distorted his true political ideal of moral virtue and ethical administration.

Confucianism was an elegant system for living and for governing – except that it taught discrimination against women. For a woman to be uneducated was a special virtue. According to Jonathan Spence, even in 1909 – some 1,400 years later and near the end of China's imperial system – there were only 13,000 girls enrolled in schools in the whole of China, and a few hundred more abroad – in a population then of about 430 million. Confucianism encouraged education for all men, and the family as the bridge between the individual and society.[21] 'Filial piety' was life's most important virtue. Religion should exist for the purpose of education and moral cultivation. Goodness would lead to happiness; evil would invite suffering and chaos. He advised men to direct their own destiny and not to resort to fatalistic reliance on spirits. Amongst the wise sayings of the Master there are many parallels in Christianity and Buddhism (in fact, the Buddha lived at about the same time as Confucius).

In government, Confucius counselled, 'kings should reign but not rule'. The government should be administered by the most talented and capable people, chosen for their character, education and ability. Ministers should be sincere and incorruptible, and should rule by moral example. Humanity could find happiness only if the nation existed as a cooperative community of free men. Force must be made subordinate to the power of justice and used only as a last resort. Although Confucius never saw himself as a great teacher, that is how history perceived his contribution to humanity. In China, his birthday – 28 September – is celebrated annually as 'Teachers' Day'.

Mao's early education was steeped in the ideas of Confucius, as was the custom of the time. Until he discovered Marxism he was greatly influenced by the moral precepts of Confucius. Later, when he was in power and became the 'Great Helmsman', he gave most emphasis to the authoritarian influences; morality then played no part in his politics. However, Confucius is not forgotten in China. In October 1994 the Communist Party held a large symposium in Beijing to celebrate the 2,545th anniversary of his birth; and in his keynote policy speech of 1 July 2001, then President Jiang Zemin spoke of the 'rule of virtue', not the 'rule of law'.

However, the downside of this great outpouring of ideas was that for 2,000 years, from about 140 BC until 1905 AD, educational, professional and political advancement in China was based on a person's knowledge of Confucian classics and commentaries. They constituted the imperial civil examinations. To do well in one or more of the three levels of testing was usually the only way of advancement. But the studies consisted of extensive memorisation. They stifled critical thinking and intellectual curiosity. Moreover, those who failed the examinations had not been prepared to do anything else – except to become teachers or professional letter-writers. For the peasants there was no point in education, and so the overwhelming majority of the people were illiterate. Being trained in classical Chinese, many who succeeded in the examinations could not write a modern type of report. They looked down on the farmers and peasants who had no formal education at all, thus creating class divisions. Even in recent times, many of the student demonstrators in Tiananmen Square in 1989 believed that the peasants should be excluded from the democratic process.

These three Chinese ancients, the First Emperor, Sun Tzu and Confucius, were amongst the principal influences on Mao's thought. In modern times, V. I. Lenin and especially Josef Stalin were his mentors. Their common bond was Marxism and the Soviet methodology. Stalin's aim was to promote the Communist cause and thus further aid the Chinese Communist Party (CCP) after Lenin died. Later chapters will show how extensive Stalin's influence was, and how much damage it did.

TWO

The Rise of Mao Zedong: Triumph

'Let the past serve the present.'
Mao Zedong

Mao Zedong was born on 26 December 1893 in a country of mounting confusion, chaos and strife.[1] His parents were a hard-working and increasingly rich peasant family in Shaoshan, a rural village in Hunan province. There he grew up in a well-run farm, upon fertile soil. While he lacked affection from his stern but not unsympathetic father, he adored his gentle Buddhist mother, and as a child he observed Buddhist rituals with her. His early education until the age of fourteen was, however, based on Confucius, rote learning and memorising the commentaries in classical Chinese. He learned and long remembered three key ideas. First, every human being and every society must have a moral compass, if not Confucianism then something else that fulfils that role; second, the primacy of 'right thinking', which Confucius called 'virtue'; and third, the importance of self-cultivation. He was constantly quoting Confucius and later returned to his works more and more often.

While farming for his father, he began reading about China and the world outside. His country had been occupied by foreign powers, Mongolia in the thirteenth century and now, for over 250 years, Manchuria in what was called the Qing dynasty. Also, the sovereignty of small but significant parts of China had been lost to Britain, France, Germany and the US some fifty years previously. They were growing in influence, and Japan was pressing from the north. Many young Chinese were attracted by the new technologies and political ideas of Japan, and paid visits there.

While the young Mao read avidly, he was profoundly influenced also by the political facts of life. He felt depressed about China and began to realise that it was the duty of all people to help save his country. He decided to return to studying, and at the age of fourteen went to one of the new-style (post-Confucian) junior-middle boarding schools, paid for by his father. He became involved in popular protests and movements against the Manchus and briefly joined the regular army. In February 1912, when he was eighteen, the Qing dynasty disintegrated; many Manchus were murdered. The future looked bleak, and he took up reading again.

While the Manchus were struggling to survive, a republic of China was being born. In October 1910 an elected National Assembly had met for the first time. A year later it chose Yuan Shikai as China's president and the experienced and able Lu Zhengxiang, a diplomat and foreign minister, as its premier. Yuan, 'father of the warlords', was an experienced administrator under the Manchus and had been responsible for educating their new army. Although he inherited a crazy revenue system and had little or no money, with Lu as premier, much was achieved.[2] In 1913 a new revolutionary leader, Song Jiaoren, joined with the Revolutionary League and others to form the Nationalist Party. Later that year there were elections, with some 40 million qualified voters – predominately rich and educated men – at which the Nationalists won power. Song became leader of the parliament, and was promptly assassinated. It was thought that Yuan was the instigator, fearing Song's strength and popularity. In 1913 he also forced Sun Yat-sen, the short-lived leader of the Nationalist Party, into exile. Yuan believed that only a single autocratic leader could sort out China's appalling mess.

In 1914 the Japanese, who had been steadily infiltrating China, imposed 'Twenty-one Demands' on Yuan, which would have left China a subordinate state. Yuan accepted the demands and suspended the constitution and parliament. To strengthen his own position, in December 1915 he arranged to be invited to become Emperor under the name 'Hongxian'. The military could see where this was leading, and one after another the provinces declared themselves independent of the Peking government. In 1916 Yuan was overthrown by a 'revolt of the generals', and Japan's demands were nullified. He died in the same year. Sun Yat-sen returned to active politics and helped to reorganise the Nationalist party. Then, in 1917, General Zhang – a fanatical supporter of the Manchus – attempted to revive Manchu power, marched on Peking and declared Pu Yi as Emperor. He was soon defeated by generals loyal to the Chinese and Pu Yi, still only eleven years old, was deposed.

Amidst all this disarray and confusion, it was hardly surprising that leaders in the provinces took power into their own hands; the era of fighting amongst warlords had begun. There were constant battles, and scores of large and small groups under local leaders fought for territorial control. The government in Peking was too weak to impose order. From 1918, the Japanese began further penetration into China from captured bases in Manchuria, down as far as Tianjin, one of the great trading seaports 1,000 miles north of Shanghai. This complicated the political and military scene. The Nationalist Party, or Kuomintang (KMT; also called 'Guomindang'), from the late 1920s, endeavoured to assert authority over the warlords. It was to be a long process. (They were not finally overcome until after October 1949, by Mao.)

However, the warlord era was not all war. While each leader had his own fighting force of local men, some were enlightened citizens and introduced social and economic reforms. There was social change but with no common pattern, a variety of experiments in governance and economic development. They showed that a federal system was feasible, more appropriately perhaps a confederal system with a weak centre and strength residing in the almost independent federations, once peace had been established. It could unleash the inherent genius of the Chinese people, which, over the vast period of their history, had persistently reasserted itself. At first Mao's ideas in Hunan were in accordance with these federal principles, but later they began to develop along quite different lines.

In 1912 Mao first encountered the word 'socialism' in his readings. In 1913, at the age of twenty, he embarked on a five-year course to become a teacher, but his mind was on politics. He developed three long-lasting core ideas: first, the need for a strong state with wise and paternalistic centralised political power; second, the overriding importance of individual will – 'if we do not have the will to act', he wrote, 'even though the exterior and objective [conditions] are perfect, they still cannot benefit us'; and third, the complex of relationships between China and Western intellectual traditions. Grounding foreign ideas in Chinese reality to establish their relevance became a cardinal principle. 'The law,' Mao declared, 'was an instrument for procuring happiness'. (Later he was to take a different view, that it was a bourgeois device for oppressing the masses, and he abolished it.) But then Hunan itself, where Mao lived, was engulfed in warlord violence. The Hunanese were amongst the most conservative people in all China, hostile to outsiders, stubborn, independent and aloof. Neighbouring warlords from Guangxi and Guangdong entered Hunan to try to stop marauding armies entering from the north, but they were unsuccessful. A new governor of Hunan province was appointed – 'Zhang the Venomous', a cruel and sadistic dictator appointed by the northern warlords. Mao's college was taken over by Zhang's troops. The education budget was stopped, teachers went unpaid and students fled. Hunan, 'one of the fairest provinces in all China', became a scene of 'daily ruin and lamentation'. A network of special agents and informers cowed the population, as in the First Emperor's time.

Mao's thoughts when he received his teaching diploma in June 1918 seemed to reflect the *I Ching*, the ancient book of wisdom and divination – 'all phenomena in the world are simply in a state of constant change' – along with some anti-Confucianism: 'I believe that there must be a complete transformation [in China]'. He denounced the churches, capitalists, monarchy and state. However, he said, 'no new order can be achieved until the old is destroyed'. Arriving in Peking, he found ill-paid and menial work at the university library and became influenced by the anarchists. He set up the New Peoples' Study Society, which argued about such matters and their practicality.

At the 1919 Peace Conference in Versailles, Japan sought to acquire the German Treaty Concession in Shandong, a strategically important eastern peninsula which covered approaches to Peking and was well placed to dominate the Yellow River. The US, in recognition of Chinese manpower assistance to the Allies during the war, supported China, citing the principle of self-determination and advocating the return of this territory to China.[3] However, under a secret loan agreement, the Chinese government had already committed it to the Japanese. Once this was known, US President Woodrow Wilson, British Prime Minister David Lloyd George and French Premier Georges Clemenceau, under pressure to complete all decisions before signing the Treaty of Versailles, ratified Japan's takeover of all German treaty rights.[4] This evoked fury in China. Three thousand young people demonstrated outside Tiananmen's Gate of Heavenly Peace, entered and sacked the residence of the Minister of Communications in the warlord cabinet responsible for the secret loan and proclaimed that 'China's territory may be conquered but it cannot be given away ... the Chinese people may be massacred but they will not surrender'. Protests were widespread in which Mao and Zhou Enlai were active. It became known as the May Fourth Movement; there were riots in other provinces calling for 'national renewal'; Japanese goods were boycotted; there was a run on Japanese banks. It was a turning point in China's self-esteem and a catalyst for wider action. Students became better organised and democracy and new ideas were openly discussed.

Mao started a weekly newspaper, *The Xiang River Review*, and in the first issue wrote:

Today we must change our old attitudes ... question the unquestionable. Dare to do the unthinkable ... Religious oppression, literary oppression, political oppression, social oppression, educational oppression, economic oppression, intellectual oppression and international oppression no longer have the slightest place in this world. All must be overthrown under the great cry of democracy.

In later editions he spelt out more clearly the means by which these changes could take place. The chances of reform are brightest when 'the decadence of the state, the sufferings of humanity and the darkness of society have all reached an extreme'. What was needed was a 'great union' of all progressive forces in society formed from 'a multitude of small unions'. He championed women's rights and educational policy and questioned whether to retain the nation, the family and marriage, and whether property should be public or private. He also saw clearly that the harsh conditions imposed by the Allies on a defeated Germany in 1919 'made another cycle of conflict inevitable'. These leading articles won national recognition for Mao, and they were reprinted in Peking.

But when Mao attacked the governor of Hunan in *The Xiang River Review*, it was closed down. Mao took over as editor another journal, *New Hunan*, and it, too, was closed down. After eighteen months of cruelty and oppression from Zhang the Venomous, the economy had collapsed and even the troops were not being paid. The local gentry decided that Zhang must go.

In November 1919 Mao read Marxist economic theory for the first time. He realised that the system he wanted to change was essentially economic. If society were to change, the old economic relationships would have to go. If the marriage system were to change, women must obtain economic independence. Moreover, since 1913 Hunan had been ruled by 'Butcher Tang', 'Fu the Tyrant' and 'Zhang the Venomous', each more tyrannical than the one before. It became obvious that Hunan would be better off under Hunanese control, and in 1920 the watchwords were 'Hunan for the Hunanese'. The problem was not just Hunan. All provinces and areas of China had suffered. So the right approach was to start by applying the principle of self-determination in one area, Hunan, as a model for other provinces. They would be joined together to provide a general solution. In a letter to a Shanghai newspaper in June 1920, just after Zhang was ousted by southern warlords, Mao wrote that now was the time 'to build the people's rule ... Hunan had best protect its own boundaries and implement its own self-rule ... we want to narrow the scope and talk about self-rule and self-government in Hunan' (it had a population of some 30 million). He wrote that 'Hunan should become the first of twenty-seven small Chinas'.[5] The arguments raged, and in October Mao chaired a public meeting which proposed a constitutional convention, elected through universal suffrage, by all people in Hunan over the age of eighteen (Mao preferred fifteen). However, 'people's rule' greatly alarmed the better educated, who realised that about 90 percent of the population was illiterate and uneducated.

Then Tan Yanki, Commander-in-Chief of the forces from the south, which had liberated Changsha, the capital of Hunan, replaced Zhang until he himself was overthrown by Zhao Hengti, who, like Mao, also advocated federalism in China.[6] He, in turn, was overthrown in 1926 in yet another military takeover. Mao was in total despair: 'In political circles [the Hunanese] are lethargic and extremely corrupt and we can say that there is absolutely no hope for political reform.'

Mao Zedong at this time had clear views about human rights democracy: the self-determination of peoples; confederation; women's rights; children's rights; education for all; kindness to the defeated. He had a vision of a society that could be happy if the right conditions were obtained. The problem was how to get from where they were at the time to where they wanted to be. In November 1920 he wrote:

> We really must create a powerful new atmosphere ... To [do this] naturally requires a group of hard-working and resolute people, but even more than that it requires an 'ism' that everyone holds in common ... An 'ism' is like a banner; only when it is raised will the people have something to hope for and know in which direction to go.

Mao was at first reluctant to accept that Marxism, Bolshevism, socialism or communism might be the 'ism' he was seeking, although he could see from the terrible experiences at the end of the Tang dynasty that anarchism was not the right direction either. By the end of 1920 Mao and others considered setting up a Socialist Youth League branch. He came to see that 'a Russian-style revolution looked like being the only one that would work':

> The Russian method represents a road newly discovered after all the other roads have turned out to be dead ends. This method alone has more potential than other methods of transformation ...[7] Social policy is not a method at all, because all it does is patch up some leaks. Social democracy resorts to a parliament as its tool for transforming things, but in reality the laws passed by a parliament always protect the propertied class. Anarchism rejects all authority, and I fear that such a doctrine can never be realised. The moderate type of communism, such as the extreme freedom advocated by [Bertrand Russell], lets the capitalists run wild and therefore it will

not work either.[8] The radical type of communism, or the ideology of the workers and peasants, which employs the method of class dictatorship, can be expected to achieve results. Hence it is the best method to use.

At the end of 1920, therefore, Mao came to the conclusion that Marxism – the 'materialist conception of history'– should be the philosophical basis for the new political party he and his friends were planning to create. The long search for a practical 'ism' was over.

Karl Marx had taught that socialism was inevitable and that communism would then become possible. It would be a classless, collectivist society in which the social product would be distributed according to the need of individuals and their families; in which the state, law, money and the concept of economic value would have 'withered away'. Victory was promised to the working class – the active workers for social change. Economic development would promote social evolution and was the first step.

The 'labour theory of value', central to Marx's *Das Kapital* – published in 1867 – held that the value of a commodity depends upon the labour time necessary for its production. A human's labour power is sold like any other commodity. The price paid would be the minimum necessary for providing workers their subsistence and education. But workers do not stop working when they have earned their keep and the surplus – the 'surplus value' or profit – then goes to the capitalist. Thus labour is 'exploited'. However, competitors buying machines to increase productivity will force others to invest too, at great expense. Profit falls to zero and wages are then forced below subsistence level. The system collapses and the working class inherits the power.

At this time there were about 250 million peasant farmers in China and fewer than 2 million industrial workers. Some 70 percent of the land was owned by about 10 percent of the population and about 80 percent of the population lived in rural areas. The rents charged by the landowners for agriculture by the peasants were often extortionate, and sometimes as high as 70 percent of the crop – with no remission for bad harvests. Local warlords needed food and cash to sustain their armies, and this came from the peasants. Moreover, the military took the youth from the land and invading warlord forces wreaked havoc and destruction.

The manufacturing industry in China was generally small-scale, and the capitalist owners were just as cruel and exploitative as the landlords. In 1923 an American YMCA investigation of working conditions in China found barbaric practices:

At the Beijing match factory there are 1,100 workers, many of them boys between the ages of nine and fifteen years old. Work starts at 4.00 AM and stops at 6.30 PM with a few minutes' rest at midday ... seven days a week. The ventilation is inadequate and the vapour from low-grade phosphorus damages the lungs. After thirty minutes my throat was burning. The workers breathe it all day long ... on average, eighty workers fall ill each day.

A Beijing textile plant employs 15,000 young people. The workers are paid nine dollars a month for an eighteen-hour day, seven days a week. Half are apprentices who receive no training and are paid no wages but are simply given food. Their families are too poor to feed them and are glad to give them to the factory.[9]

Although this was China, such conditions seemed to bear out Marx's theory of value. Paradoxically, one year after Marx wrote *Das Kapital* while in England on the basis of his observations there, the British Trades Union Congress (TUC) was set up (in 1868) and 150 small and ineffective trades unions joined. Membership grew rapidly as the TUC began to take effective action to protect workers from the exploitation Marx had observed. Eventually, and with much opposition, this led to a large body of social legislation protecting the health and safety of workers and giving them rights. At first Mao also tried this path, but because the parliament was so weak there was no progress. So he then chose a fundamentally different route towards the elimination of worker exploitation in line with Marxism. His aim was to solve the problem by eliminating the landlords, capitalist employers and bearing down on the bourgeoisie. The proletariat, the labouring classes, would then take command.

A series of strikes for better working conditions, with Mao in the front line, caused concern amongst Hunan's leaders and wealthy class. He petitioned the Peking parliament to enact a labour law that would provide for a maximum eight-hour working day, paid holidays, maternity leave and an end to child labour. But the warlords had had enough, and clamped down on all such activities in what became known as the 1923 'February Seventh Massacre'. Work stoppages fell sharply and those held were brutally suppressed. There were many deaths. It was the end of the first attempt to mobilise the labour movement into revolutionary action. The Communist Party was forced to operate underground, in disarray and riven with internal conflict. Mao became very depressed.

By then the Chinese Communist Party (CCP), formed in 1921 in Shanghai with Lenin's support, was gaining adherents. Mao joined, and through the clarity of his thinking and arguments became one of its leaders. In principle the Nationalist and Communist parties had similar long-term aims: to unite the Chinese people, eliminate warlordism, lead the country forward to prosperity and social justice and expel all foreigners and foreign influences, thus regaining Chinese sovereignty. In particular the two largest Treaty Ports of Shanghai and Tienjin, dating from the end of the Opium Wars, had been occupied by Britain, France and the US with their own administrations, police and troops. This was deeply humiliating to the Chinese and greatly resented. Both Nationalist and Communist parties saw that dictatorial powers were necessary to rid China of these eighty or so foreign enclaves in which Chinese sovereignty had been surrendered.

The KMT dominated the first parliament and Chinese politics until 1949, first under Sun Yat-sen and, after his death in 1925, under Chiang Kai-shek. Chiang based the parliament in Canton. The KMT had been a left-wing party, reflecting the aims of Sun. Chiang was Christian and a fervent anti-Communist, which later won him massive US support. Soon, however, he began to distance himself from the left wing of the Nationalist party and moved it towards the political right. Chiang became more authoritarian, militarist, right-wing – and extremely corrupt. He was a member of the Ch'ing Pang gangster secret society, which controlled the profitable traffic in opium, gambling, prostitution and kidnapping under the protection of the International Settlement (formed by merging the British and US Concessions) and the French Concession Authorities in Shanghai.[10] This gangster society helped Chiang destroy Communist-led unions and other Communists, carrying out the 'Shanghai Massacre' in 1927, which resulted in many deaths. It marked the beginning of an all-out effort by the KMT to eliminate the Communists which continued until 1937, when they joined forces against the Japanese invaders.

In September 1931 the Japanese began their main attack on Manchuria, capturing first the strategic centre of Jinzhou, capital of one of the nine provinces. In 1932 they named Pu Yi as Emperor of what they then called 'Manchukuo' – the very same Pu Yi (a Manchu of course) who was Emperor of China as a child. Having been ousted by the Manchu princes and later held prisoner by the Japanese in the Forbidden City, he was now a puppet of the Japanese conquerors in his home country. The Japanese starved the local people and pursued an extreme policy of apartheid, especially in education. Chinese people had to bow to every Japanese person they passed in the street; but the Japanese brought much industry and modernisation.

In 1920 Lenin had declared that in a backward country the rural peasants were the key to power, that a proletarian party of workers would not be sufficient. He saw that the peasants could unite with the industrial workers against their oppressors, and he coined the terms 'revolutionary-democratic dictatorship of the proletariat and the peasantry'.

Two years later Mao began to see the possibilities of peasant rule, but took no action. Then, in May 1925, following the shooting by Japanese guards of Chinese workers during a strike and the shooting of rioting Chinese by British police fearing they would be overrun, a general strike was called. Anti-British and anti-Japanese demonstrations broke out all over China, with boycotts against British and Japanese goods. Mao seized the opportunity and sprang into action. He formed several peasant associations in Hunan against the landlords who were hoarding rice during a drought to force up the price. The governor of Hunan sent an urgent telegram to the Xiangtan County Defence Bureau: 'Arrest Mao Zedong immediately. Execute him on the spot.'[11] Word was quickly sent to Mao who, dressed as a doctor, escaped by travelling in a closed sedan chair. He was now, at the age of thirty-one, convinced that mobilising the vast mass of peasants against their landlord oppressors was the only way forward in China. It was, however, a daunting task.

The Russians had been intervening in Chinese affairs since 1920. After Lenin's death in 1924, Stalin became closely involved. The Soviets sent a series of so-called 'advisors' to China, who exercised much authority both in the political and economic spheres. Their interest was in spreading communism in China and in helping both the KMT and the CCP to gain effective power in a land still ravaged by warlords. The Communists were a tiny group – even in 1925, there were still fewer than 1,000 members, against the KMT's more than 100,000 – but the left wing of the KMT had much in common with the Communists, and there were several important joint appointments. The twenty-eight-year-old Zhou Enlai was Deputy Commissioner in the First Corps of Chiang Kai-shek's army and Director of the Political Department in the KMT's military academy; at the same time he was responsible for military affairs in the Canton Chinese Communist Party. Mao became the KMT's specialist in peasant affairs and a member of its Peasant Movement Committee, together with his Communist affiliates. However, much support for the KMT came from landowning families and, although many favoured reform, the idea of violent overthrow of the existing order was not on their agenda.

While 75,000 troops of the Revolutionary Army of the KMT set out in 1926 to crush the warlords and reunify China, Mao continued his work with the peasants and to develop his ideas. The landlords were the main obstacle to revolution. The peasants had first to be liberated, as the principal instrument by which the landlords would be overthrown (as the peasants were to be 'liberated' in Tibet twenty years later for the same reason). 'If the peasants do not rise and fight in the villages to overthrow the privileges of the feudal–patriarchal landlord class, the power of the warlords and of imperialism can never be hurled down root and branch.' Clearly this approach was fundamentally different from that being followed by the KMT, which considered Mao's ideas impractical, and it was also ideologically unacceptable to the Chinese Communist Party. But it closely followed Stalin's policy from 1927 when he set out to destroy the *kulaks*, richer peasants in Russia who employed other peasants as workers and who owned 'more than two cows'.

The Nationalist Revolutionary Army had many successes against the warlords, and Mao saw them also serving his own revolutionary cause. When the KMT army advanced, CCP members followed behind to consolidate new peasant associations and to foment revolt against the landlords. The leaders of the CCP began to change their minds and in November 1926 Mao was appointed Secretary of its Peasant Movement Committee. Now that Chiang was leader of the KMT, he moved its ideological position to the right, thereby allowing its left wing to be influenced by the CCP. However, the Communists kept a low profile so as not to antagonise the Nationalist leader.

A turning point came when in 1927 Mao took a month-long journey through the countryside in Hunan and wrote a 20,000-word report: 'I called together fact-finding conferences in villages and county towns, which were attended by experienced peasants and comrades in the peasant movement ... I listened attentively and collected a great deal of material.'[12] There was, he felt, no substitute for direct field research, supplemented by his own youthful experiences on his father's farm. Membership of peasant associations rose from 400,000 in mid-1927 to 2 million, and with the peasant uprisings in central Hunan the old feudal order there collapsed. Peasant associations became the sole authority in the countryside: 'The association actually dictates everything in the countryside ... whatever it says goes.' Against members of the KMT and CCP who complained of excessive violence Mao responded:

> If the peasants do not use extremely great force, they cannot possibly overthrow the deep rooted power of the landlords, which has lasted for thousands of years ... To put it bluntly, it is necessary to bring about a brief reign of terror in every rural area ... to right a wrong it is necessary to exceed the proper limits; the wrong cannot be righted without doing so. [This involved executing one or two landlords in each county.][13]

The leadership could point the direction, said Mao, but then it was up to the people to carry the revolution forward. In any revolutionary venture there would always be excesses: 'Only when disaster threatened, as in the end it almost always did, would the leaders have to slam on the brakes.' Use of the peasants to overthrow the landlords was a different mechanism from Stalin's, which depended much more on his close colleagues in the leadership and the military, but the ends were the same.

Mao put a proposal to the KMT's Third Plenum in March 1927: that village governments should be established, protected by peasant defence forces; that the death penalty or life imprisonment should be imposed on tyrannical landlords; and that land belonging to 'corrupt officials, local bullies, bad gentry and counter-revolutionaries' should be confiscated and redistributed. Mao then set about organising an All-China Federation of Peasant Associations.

All this was too much for Chiang. At 4.00 AM one foggy morning in April 1927, Nationalist troops, supported by 1,000 'labourers' – actually members of the notorious Green Gang – stealthily surrounded Communist pockets of supporters and attacked. Four hundred people were killed and many more wounded. Zhou Enlai, the senior Communist in Shanghai, ordered a general strike. Violence worsened and spread to Hunan and other parts of China; chaos ensued. Banks suspended dealings, tax collection ceased and money was printed without revenues to support it, sowing the seeds of inflation. Food ran short, and unemployment was severe. Foreigners became worried as trade ceased. The landlord militia then took revenge on the revolutionary peasants with the utmost cruelty. In all, some 300,000 people were killed – peasants, workers and other Communist supporters. In spite of warnings that Chiang was planning a purge of all Communists, they were not prepared. They had no clear policy and confusion reigned. Mao's position in the Communist hierarchy slipped to no. 30.

The one clear lesson from this disaster for the Communists was that force had to be met with force. Indeed, in May 1927 Stalin instructed the Chinese Communist Party to 'create your own reliable army', which was the only part of Russia's advice at that time that made sense. The left wing of the KMT collapsed, and all pretence of an alliance between the CCP and the KMT ceased. Russian advisors withdrew from the chaos. The following month Mao became Secretary of the Communist Party in Hunan – on the way up again. Ignoring Russian advice, Zhou ordered an uprising of peasants and workers in Nanchang, in Hunan province, which was successful. In August a force of some 20,000 people, largely peasants who did not, in reality, have much strength, headed south to find a new base in Guangdong province. Separate from this force, about 1,000 troops from the KMT defected to join the Communists. Thus was the embryonic People's Liberation Army formed.

Mao worked in Wuhan to prepare a Communist Party conference, assisted by a young member of the Secretariat seven years his junior called Deng

Xixian – later known as Deng Xiaoping. Under the influence of a new Russian advisor, Mao became an alternate member of the CCP's Politburo (the new name from Russia for the former Central Bureau). During an attempt to engineer an uprising in Changsha, the capital of Hunan, Mao took charge of the First Regiment of the growing CCP army, but was captured by loyal KMT militiamen. Assisted by some judicious bribing, however, he managed to escape. The expedition to capture Changsha was a ghastly failure; the First Regiment fell into an ambush and was almost wiped out. Other attempted uprisings also failed. Party membership collapsed. Only a few Communist strongholds remained, in the poorest and most inaccessible regions or where the authorities had no effective control. Mao was dismissed from the Politburo.

He was seen to be headstrong, stubborn and not easily controlled. He had his own ideas about everything, forged from his life experiences – and was a difficult person to work with unless one shared these ideas. He had tremendous energy, courage, imagination and a clear vision of the goal – a better China. He had thought through his position and had tested it against other views. Marxism did not, so to speak, spring from his upbringing, but if there was to be unity, peace and prosperity in China he could see no other viable option. He was a pragmatist, willing to serve with the KMT, for example, if that contributed towards the achievement of his Communist aims. Russia, too, could be used for support, but he was not to be told by them what to do – and often disagreed and did something else instead.

During the three years following these disasters, while the Communists regrouped and considered their future, Mao found himself responsible for a force consisting of 'an undisciplined band of [KMT] mutineers, armed workers and peasants, vagabonds and bandits'.[14] Somehow these had to be transformed into what he called the First Regiment, First Division of the First Workers' and Peasants' Revolutionary Army. This was a new experience. Typically, he brought new thinking to the task. The army would consist solely of volunteers (any man wishing to leave could do so and would receive money for the journey home). Soldiers' committees would be formed in each unit to ventilate and resolve grievances and to ensure that democratic processes would be followed. Officers were forbidden to beat the men for any reason. Soldiers would be required to treat civilians correctly. They had to speak politely, pay a fair price for what they bought and never take so much as a 'solitary sweet potato' belonging to the masses. Since most of his men were illiterate, Mao used folk tales and graphic images for their instruction. In truth, Mao himself was also on a steep learning curve about military matters. His instincts about how to manage troops were sound, although they had their origins in the

Han dynasty founder Liu Bang, 2,000 years before. What was new was that, following Russian practice, each squad had its Communist Party group, each company a Party branch, each battalion a Party committee, and all these were under the leadership of the Front Committee of which Mao was Secretary. These were unique organisational and managerial concepts at that time in China.

To avoid premature conflict with the KMT, Mao took his small force into the mountains around Jinggangshan, just over the border from Hunan, into Jiangxi province, where there were natural defences. It became the main operational base. Two groups of 'peasant self-defence' forces led by Communist Party members joined Mao and became his Second Regiment. Zhu De, an experienced man of action and the military expert of a local warlord in Sichuan, also joined, and with his men there were now four regiments of some 8,000 soldiers. Zhu, seven years Mao's senior, became the army commander, and Mao the Party representative. The army had many clashes with the KMT, although once a place was conquered and Communist forces left, KMT forces re-occupied it. Mao urged the leadership to concentrate on deepening the revolution in a single area before moving on. Then the KMT struck at Jinggangshan from five directions, and the stronghold was abandoned with many losses.

Mao's knowledge of military strategy and tactics was increasing fast. Mao and Zhu expounded many principles, based on *The Art of War*, such as:

> *When the enemy advances, we withdraw!*
> *When the enemy rests, we harass!*
> *When the enemy tires, we attack!*
> *When the enemy withdraws, we pursue!*

Mao was now in the ascendant again after his disobedience, because his earlier predictions had proved correct. A new General Front Committee was established to fight the war, with Mao as its Secretary. The committee was 'to act as the supreme leading organ of his own Fourth Red Army, the Fifth Army and a newly formed Sixth Army'. Mao was ordered by the Central Committee to attack key cities occupied by the Nationalists on transport routes. Since he had already been severely criticised for disobedience, he assented, but in fact did not carry the task out, believing the correct policy was to develop a series of rural bases from which to operate and to focus on Jiangxi province. In 1930 Zhou Enlai set down his policies in detail, seeking to win Mao's support by offering him the chairmanship of the new Military Commission, while Zhu De was made Commander-in-Chief.

As the Red Army advanced into Jiangxi with the aim of taking control of a single province, Chiang tried three times to encircle it and was twice defeated. The third time he amassed over 300,000 men. Mao and Zhu's forces avoided annihilation only by climbing over an undefended 3,000-foot mountain, the only escape route, with some 20,000 soldiers. It was thought by the Nationalist army to be unclimbable by an army. At this crucial time the Nationalists were distracted first by a split in allegiance by two generals who opposed Chiang's leadership and set up a separate government in Canton, and in September 1931 by the Japanese invasion of Manchuria to the north. Mao and Zhu, well hidden from view amongst rocks on the side of the mountain, watched with relief as the Nationalist forces withdrew. The third attempt at encirclement also had failed.

At the same time as these attempts were made to smash the Red Army, from early 1930 the Communist Party had started to arrest, torture and execute many in its own Party accused of 'counter-revolutionary' activities. Some Communists were thought to have belonged to a right-wing clique within the KMT known as the AB-*tuan*, or Anti-Bolshevik League. Many tens of thousands of Party members were accused. Rich peasants and landlords were similarly accused. The categories became confused. As those accused were expected to name other supposed AB-*tuan* members and were tortured for this purpose, so the numbers mushroomed. In some areas the Party members killed exceeded those lost in the battles against the Nationalists. There were no judicial proceedings, and many illiterate and uneducated peasants were given power to order executions. The procedure was to force the accused person to confess. If he confessed, he was to be believed and then killed. If he refused to confess, then he was simply to be killed. It was found later that there was no evidence against any of those accused of being AB-*tuan*, except admissions or accusations obtained under torture. There had been what was later called 'a mistake in terminology'. It was a tragic error – and a taste of what was to come. The executions were not thought to be in any way remarkable, although at one stage Mao thought that the AB-*tuan* killings might have gone too far.

The KMT used even more crude, brutal and barbarous methods. In areas where the Red Army had withdrawn, all the local men were killed and the women and girls sold into prostitution. Peasants who had risen up against their landlords were also killed. In Huang'an county, Hubei province, more than 100,000 villagers were killed, and in Xin county, more than 80,000. On the Hunan–Hubai border, once the home to about 1 million people, only 10,000 remained. Whole villages were razed to the ground. Mao's wife, Yang Kaihui, was beheaded on the orders of the KMT governor.

In 1930 Mao undertook a social survey of remarkable detail in a county at the corner of Jiangxi, Fujian and Guangdong provinces and in some 60,000 words described every aspect of life in that community. The survey, then repeated in another county, became the basis of a set of regulations about every aspect of the lives of the landlords, rich and middle rich peasants. Determination of a person's status became a matter of life and death. 'Land reform was a violent and ruthless class struggle the aim of which was to wipe out the landlords and to weaken the rich peasants,' Mao said. (Fortunately, his own father was dead by this time.) After 1933, in areas controlled by the CCP, class origin became the ultimate determinant of a person's worth and fate. This continued for half a century or more, as the children and grandchildren of landlords and rich peasants suffered because of their class background – more important than their ability, intelligence or work ethic. The lives of whole families were blighted with no possibility of reprieve.

In 1932 Chiang Kai-shek called in German aid and military expertise, and had himself named Chief of General Staff and Chairman of the National Military Council.[15] The principles of Clausewitz were instilled. Then, with German advice, he set up a Bandit Suppression Headquarters to defeat the Communists. Chiang became a leader independent of the KMT. The Germans made a DM100 million loan to Chiang for the purchase of arms and equipment for steelmaking, while China provided Germany with specialist ores for weapons-grade steel. Pressure now began to build up against the Communists in Jiangxi.

The Long March, from October 1934 to October 1935, was a defining event for the Communist struggle for survival and was the making of Mao as a military strategist and tactician. It was a strategic withdrawal of some 86,000 Communists from southern China, to the west and then to the north, to escape from the KMT. After several military disasters a new leadership troika was established: Zhou Enlai, Mao and Wang Jiaxiang. Mao became Zhou's chief military advisor and devised a dazzling display of his 'flexible guerrilla strategy', with lightning manoeuvres in unexpected directions seemingly without purpose. These totally disconcerted the Nationalist and warlord commanders in hot pursuit – and thoroughly confused his own side, too. But the Communists won victories and escaped from their pursuers. The leadership had little clear idea where they were going. By the middle of 1935 Mao had assumed undisputed control. The other leaders had to acknowledge that Mao had consistently been right on military matters, and they had been wrong.

During the dramatic and terrible year of the Long March, the Communist army occupied sixty-two cities and towns, broke through the armies of ten different warlords while outmanoeuvring the various forces of the largest of them – the KMT – and fought an average of one skirmish each day, with fifteen pitched battles in all. A large number of Communists were killed in the battles, but many people joined them on the way, attracted by the promise of an egalitarian society. There were also many defections from the KMT. Of the 86,000 people who started out on the Long March, only 5,000 survived; now there were some 15,000 men.

Their bravery, heroism and determination led them across the Dadu River on a chain bridge against Nationalist forces firmly entrenched on the other side; over 14,000-foot-high passes in the Great Snowy Mountains on the very edge of the Tibetan Plateau, where to stop was to freeze to death (two-thirds of their baggage animals perished); and across the vast swamp of the Songpan Meadows, stretching east from a bend in the Yellow River. By then they were down to 10,000 totally exhausted men. Mao's leadership was tested against that of the Communist Fourth Front Army, which had chosen a different route of escape and was three or four times the size of Mao's remaining forces, better equipped and physically in better shape. Mao was equal in seniority to Zhang Guotao, its leader, who was also on his home territory and supremely confident. Mao's leadership had been established with only half of the Politburo present, and his position with Zhang was most insecure. Suspicion and resentment increased, but Mao was patient and skilful and did not give in.

Mao and his forces then marched a further 600 miles into China's far north-west to Bao'an, a small village in Shensi, and into a desolate landscape – his base for the next two years. The leadership moved into a series of caves burrowed into the cliffs, with scanty furniture and brick floors. Mao settled in with He Zizhen, a gentle and unassuming woman half his age, who was looking after their fourth and only surviving child. She was also a tough, unyielding and intelligent person, and she loved Mao. But he had eyes elsewhere, and soon after she was pregnant yet again, she decided to leave. Despite his pleas to return, she stayed away. One year later Jiang Qing, an attractive young actress, came to Bao'an to live with Mao. She was eventually to play a larger part in Chinese politics.

'There is the desk at which Mao wrote his essays,' said a caretaker of the cave dwellings to the writer Colin Thubron in 1986;[16] here Zhou worked, over there was where Zhu (now Commander-in-Chief of the Red Army) had darned his socks on a spinning wheel, beyond were Liu Shaoqi's quarters. It was spartan accommodation and food was short, but it gave Mao time to think.

The first thing he did was examine the lessons from battles which the Red Army lost, and write about them. His appraisals were couched in the principles of Sun Tzu.[17] By the end of 1935 he had absorbed the military and political lessons. New pragmatic, flexible policies emerged which were 'designed to win maximum public support with a minimum of ideological baggage'. The land and property of rich peasants would no longer be confiscated. Shopkeepers, small capitalists and intellectuals would enjoy the same political rights as workers and peasants, and their economic and cultural freedoms would be protected. Mao also worked to win over those in the leadership who had opposed him.

Mao's diplomatic and strategic skills were successful in detaching Chiang Kai-shek's North-East Army in Manchuria under Zhang Xueliang, the son of a well-known bandit leader, to support his own stand against the Japanese. With the forces Mao had rallied to his own side and the remnants of Zhang Guotao's Fourth Army, he now commanded over 40,000 men. Zhang Guotao was finished as a political leader and submitted to Mao's will. (In April 1938 he defected to the KMT.)

By mid-1936 anti-Japanese feeling in China had hardened. Mao made continual overtures to Chiang to join with him against the Japanese. However, the Nationalist leader believed he was near to annihilating the Red Army, and resisted. Then fate stepped in. Zhang Xueliang, in Manchuria and now working with Mao, arrested Chiang and demanded that he forget the Communists and make resisting the Japanese his priority. Zhang, in turn, was arrested (and was not freed until his ninetieth birthday in Taiwan). In 1937 the Japanese, who already occupied about 20 percent of China, launched a full-scale invasion following the political defeat of the liberals in the Tokyo government. That changed everything. The Japanese remained in China until 1945.

Japanese forces concentrated at first in the north and east of China. Peking and Tianjing were quickly occupied. Then they penetrated as far south as Guangzhou (Canton). They captured Nanking (Nanjing), then the capital of China, before proceeding to capture Shanghai. The complete destruction of Nanking, the murder of some 200,000–300,000 Chinese[18] – mainly by bayonet and machine gun – and the rape of thousands of women and girls will never be forgotten by the Chinese. Mercifully a German businessman, John Rabe, created a Safety Zone and saved a great many lives.[19] But Japanese rape, murder and mayhem were also widespread in the countryside 'from Shanghai to Nanking and Wuhu ... all the other cities between here [Nanking] and Shanghai are as good as dead'.

Even when the Japanese had captured Peking and Tianjin and were attacking Shanghai, Chiang still resisted any kind of alliance with the Communists. To him the Japanese 'were a skin disease, while the Communists were a disease of the internal organs', and were by far the greater evil.[20] In September 1937, faced by the Japanese successes, the short-lived United Front agreement of April 1937 was revived, although with the Communists retaining their clear identity and control. But it, too, soon fell apart.[21] For Mao, the route to absolute power was unfolding. From his new headquarters in the more prosperous town of Yan'an, some sixty miles east of his cave dwelling, he mapped the future. This was to be his more luxurious headquarters until 1947.

The Japanese attack on Pearl Harbour in December 1941 changed the balance of power. The US saw China as an ally in its own fight against Japan, and supplied Chiang with huge quantities of armaments and cash.

In Yun'an, Mao read widely and worked hard at understanding Marxist dialectics more fully, developing in the process a distinct Chinese approach to the received wisdom, incorporating elements of ancient Chinese thought. Practice and knowledge became his watchwords. The power of human will, he believed, could achieve everything. In his essay 'On Contradiction', Mao wrote: 'The many are one, and change is permanence.' Determining the contradiction in any situation and its principal aspect, he learned, would lead to the best course of action. He took real delight in developing his philosophy and exploring the world of ideas, and read Clausewitz for the first time, concluding that 'politics is war without bloodshed, while war is politics with bloodshed' and that 'political power grows out of the barrel of a gun. The Party commands the gun and the gun must never be allowed to control the Party. Yet having guns, we can create Party organisations, create schools, create culture, create mass movements ...'. As he approached the age of forty-five his own distinctive ideology, set within the context of China, was now virtually complete.

(In January 1949, however, Stalin rather dismissively described Mao as a 'margarine Marxist'.[22] In December 1949, just after the formation of the People's Republic of China was declared by Mao in Tiananmen Square, he visited Stalin for several weeks in Moscow – the two did not get on well at all. During this time the Soviet foreign minister Viacheslav Molotov cross-examined Mao about his understanding of Marxism and later told Stalin that he was not a real Marxist – that 'he hadn't even read *Das Kapital*'.)[23]

Chiang took advantage of the frail alliance to try to damage the Communists. He saw them growing too powerful as more people rallied to their support. The Red Army ranks grew to 500,000 in number. Mao now had supreme power within the Party, and became Chairman of the Politburo. He launched the Yun'an Rectification Campaign to bring about a fundamental change in the way the Party thought, through the force of Confucian 'virtuous example'. Those who failed to see the light were subject to 'collective denunciation', the essence of the struggle sessions that featured so large during the Cultural Revolution much later. Reliance on torture and confession was the same as during the AB-*tuan* persecutions in 1930, although the death toll was lower. Mao was now Chairman of the whole party, Liu Shaoqi was no. 2, Zhou Enlai no. 3 and Zhu De no. 4. There was, by now, in 1947, a growing personality cult of Mao as much more than just the supreme leader. He began to act like a latter-day emperor, the founder of a new dynasty. The mythology of his continuous successes spilled over to the future; he could do no wrong. It was the beginning of his undoing.

But it was not the end of Chiang. The US, which had given total support to the Nationalists,[24] tried to negotiate a settlement with the Communists, and in January 1946 a ceasefire was signed. But it soon disintegrated as Chiang visited the US and tried to convince President Truman that unless the Nationalist armies could assert sovereignty over north-eastern China, the Communists would move in. The Red Army attacked the main Nationalist base in Changchun in the centre of Manchuria and occupied it. Large-scale clashes broke out, and soon the whole of central and northern China was engulfed in fighting. Mao had been unsuccessful in dealing with American politics, but now that the final battle had started he was, so to speak, on home ground.

In March 1947, when the Nationalists attacked Hun'an, the Communist headquarters, Mao laughed and withdrew, knowing that while losing Hun'an he would win China. The Red Army, now renamed the People's Liberation Army (PLA), steadily retreated on all fronts. Chiang proclaimed that he would have the Communists defeated by the autumn. But the PLA snipped off small Nationalist units wherever they had overwhelming power. The PLA withdrew further when the Nationalists were no more than one hour away, leading them in unexpected directions until they became exhausted and short of food. An American journalist travelling with Mao's column found his cat-and-mouse tactics 'terrifying'.[25] However, Mao's spies had penetrated the leadership of the Nationalist forces while Chiang had little idea of Mao's plans, which were all in accordance with Sun Tzu, while it seemed that Chiang was much more influenced by his German mentors and by Clausewitz.[26]

But the Nationalists had superior numbers, were better equipped and occupied a larger part of China than did the Communists. President Roosevelt saw in Chiang 'a champion of the "New Asia", a doughty fighter against Japan, and a Chinese George Washington who would be one of the post-war world's great statesmen – the undisputed leader of four hundred million people'.[27] British Prime Minister Winston Churchill was, however, unimpressed: 'very over-rated' was his blunt view of Chiang, and he denounced the notion of

China as a great power 'an absolute farce'. (He took a very different attitude to Chiang's wife Soong Mei-ling, whom he described as 'a most remarkable and fascinating person', clever, modern, brave and possessed of an almost terrifying charm.)[28] By midsummer Mao's forces halted and started to counter-attack. By December 1947, 640,000 Nationalist troops had been killed and more than 1 million had surrendered. All through the first half of 1948, the PLA pressed home their advantage. The US commander with the Nationalists called Chiang's officer corps 'incapable, inept, untrained, petty [and] altogether inefficient'. Moreover, Chiang's harsh treatment of his conscript army and of the civilian population in areas he controlled, together with blatant corruption in the leadership, turned people against the Nationalists.

In September 1948, Mao drew up the overall plan to annihilate the numerically superior Nationalist forces. There were to be three great campaign areas, and the outcome would be decisive for the future of China. Lin Biao won the first great battle to the north. The Nationalists lost the whole of Manchuria and half a million of Chiang's best troops. Many defected to the Communists. The other two campaigns went equally well. Liu Bocheng took control of the Central Plains and East China armies, while Chen Yi marched south. At the end of January 1949, just after Peking surrendered to the PLA, Generalissimo Chiang Kai-shek resigned the presidency. In four months he had lost 1.5 million men and control of all China's territory. Chiang himself, along with the Nationalist air force, the navy and the best remaining army divisions, fled to Taiwan with all of China's financial reserves, including gold, silver and foreign currency. Taiwan had been Japanese territory since 1895, and at the end of the Second World War it had been ceded to China. The population consisted largely of Han Chinese who had fled there early in the Qing dynasty to escape from the Manchus.

For the first time in the twentieth century there was the possibility of peace in China. It was unified. The Communists and Communism were popular amongst the people. The PLA behaved with honesty in dealing with them. The intelligentsia looked forward to working for a better future for China within an egalitarian society. But, while there was much genuine admiration for what Mao had achieved, many of those who were rich enough fled to Hong Kong and the US.

In March 1949 the victorious Mao embarked on a series of speeches to the Party hierarchy outlining his programme. Urban living standards must be raised, major industries and foreign-owned companies nationalised; China would be ruled by a coalition government headed by the Communist Party, with some small progressive parties of sympathetic non-communists from the bourgeoisie and liberal intelligentsia. The new system would be known as a 'people's democratic dictatorship'. There would be democracy amongst the people and dictatorship over the reactionaries. The judiciary would be an instrument of class violence. 'We should be capable not only of destroying the old world: we must be capable of creating the new,' said Mao. There was now much to be done.

So on 1 October 1949 in Tiananmen Square, facing a crowd of 100,000 or more, Mao declared the founding of the People's Republic of China (PRC) with himself as Head of State. 'We, the 475 million Chinese people, have stood up, and our future is infinitely bright,' he said. It was the beginning of a new era in the long and turbulent history of China.

It was also the beginning of the tragedy in Tibet. One year later, Mao unleashed the PLA into its territory and commenced a long, drawn-out campaign of destruction and dissolution in the name of 'liberation' of the peasants. It is doubtful that he really understood what kind of people or society he was attacking. Tibet, too, had a long history.

THREE

The Tibetan People and their Culture

'May all sentient beings enjoy happiness,
and the causes of happiness,
Be free from suffering,
and the causes of suffering.'
Traditional Buddhist prayer

Mao's direct experience of the Tibetan people at the time of the invasion was extremely limited. While escaping over the Great Snowy Mountains during the Long March, the rearguard of his bedraggled forces had been harried by the warlike Khampas; but other Tibetans had given Mao's forces some assistance, and he felt gratitude towards them. What perhaps he did not realise was that their daily lives were as different from those in China as could possibly be imagined. Tibet had a distinct and glorious history in the early years, much to the humiliation of China. According to Charles Bell, before the invasion their standard of living was higher than in China.

Since the second century AD, clans of people we would now call Tibetan – each under their own chieftain – came together for mutual support and to extend their influence and control northwards. As consolidation took place, the chiefs would choose a leader. Thus, by the fifth century the kingship system had developed. The people worked together, became increasingly warlike and powerful, and began pushing into north-west China. Inspired by King Namri Song-tsen and his more famous son, the Thirty-third Tibetan King Song-tsen Gampo, their armies fought with valour. Iron discipline was enforced by terrible punishments for misdemeanours. The people were organised efficiently on a war footing in their support. By the early seventh century they were set to become a great power in Asia.

In 641 AD young King Song-tsen Gampo, in a strategically strong position from military campaigns against China, demanded the Chinese princess Wen Cheng, daughter of the emperor T'ai Tsung (founder of the Tang dynasty) as his bride – and was successful.[1] This marriage secured the possession of a much-coveted bronze image of the Buddha, originally from India, as part of Wen Cheng's dowry.[2] Earlier, in 637, Song-tsen Gampo had married the Nepalese princess Bhrikuti (he already had three Tibetan wives) – in part so that he could secure a fine Buddhist image from Nepal. The two princesses also brought with them Buddhist knowledge and practices.

The Chinese today hold that the marriage to Wen Cheng laid 'a solid foundation for the ultimate founding of a unified nation', and that in the thirteenth century 'Tibet was officially incorporated into the territory of China's Yuan dynasty'. This 'solid foundation' never existed. It was Song-tsen Gampo who was dominant over China at the time, not the reverse – although China cleverly made it seem the opposite.[3] (The thirteenth-century claim of Chinese sovereignty does not hold water either.)

King Song-tsen Gampo had much influence on the subsequent development of Tibet, and later was considered to be the 'father of the nation'. The earlier bringing together of many nomadic and settled peoples was reaching its peak, and under his orders a Tibetan script was created, a code of law developed and histories written. Buddhist scripts were translated into Tibetan and the first Buddhist temples and chapels were built.

The Tibetan warriors did not have it all their own way: sometimes the Chinese struck back. Early in the eighth century Chinese forces invading Tibet were repulsed by King Tridhi Tsugtsen. In pushing the Chinese back, the Tibetans occupied several provinces of China. Seeing the danger of this, the Chinese Emperor, to prevent possible annihilation and the loss of his throne, agreed to pay a tribute to Tibet of 50,000 rolls of silk annually.[4] Eventually the Chinese failed to provide the tribute, so in retaliation, in 763 AD the Tibetans defeated a vastly superior Chinese force and captured the then Chinese capital, Xi'an, seat of the First Emperor. The Tibetans briefly installed their own emperor. Treaties did not, however, have a long-lasting effect on the restless Tibetan warriors. There were frequent battles with their Chinese neighbours – at least nineteen major conflicts during the 200-year Warrior King period, almost all initiated by the Tibetans. The first peace treaty with China was signed around 710 AD, when the king married the Chinese princess Jin Sheng. Between then and 784 AD there were a further six treaties.

The energetic and ambitious King Tri-song De-tsen (755–97 AD) further centralised and consolidated Tibet as a nation and extended its territories, eventually stretching from the boundaries of Persia in the west down into Burma in the south and east into China. As a result, by the end of the eighth century, Tibet had become the most powerful nation in central Asia – and a great problem for China. In 821 there was an attempt to bring the 200 years of conflict to an end. A treaty of friendship, inspired by a meeting of Tibetan *lamas* and Chinese monks, was signed by the Emperor and the King. To give it some semblance of permanence it was carved on three stone pillars: one in Lhasa, one in Xi'an and one on the border at Gugu Meru. In poetic and enchanting words, they describe the Chinese Emperor as 'uncle' and the Tibetan King as 'nephew',[5] pledge peace between the two countries and confirm the boundary between them:

> … all to the east of the present boundary is the domain of Great China. All to the west is totally the domain of Great Tibet. Henceforth there shall be no looting or ambushing and no making of war … Tibetans shall be happy in the land of Tibet, Chinese shall be happy in the land of China and the solemn agreement now made shall never be changed.

In an expression of complete harmony, it also referred to 'the two sovereigns, uncle and nephew, having come to agreement that their territories be united as one …' . The Chinese quote only the latter as part of their justification that Tibet is owned by China.[6] But that interpretation contradicts the whole sense of the treaty as between equals, seeking a peaceful resolution of their former enmity and an end to Tibetan aggression.

From the seventh century different forms of Buddhism had gradually been entering Tibet from India and from China. Amongst the nobility it had begun to displace the earlier Bon shamanistic beliefs and practices followed by the Warrior Kings as their state religion.[7] Lumbini (in modern Nepal) was the birthplace of Siddhartha Gautama, the historical Buddha Shakyamuni (c. 563–483 BC), and Buddhism first developed in India. In China, Buddhism had begun to take hold in the first century AD and was influenced by Taoism; lay people had begun to follow Buddhism from the fourth century AD,[8] and by the sixth century it was well established with many temples and fine stone images.[9]

Since two different versions of Buddhism had entered Tibet, during 792–4 AD a great debate was held before the Tibetan King as to whether to follow the Ch'an Buddhism of China or the Kamalashila school of Buddhism from India. Chinese Buddhists had to contend with the primacy of Taoism in their country and with Confucianism, and therefore had to adopt a sufficient number of these other spiritual practices to attract support. Also, Ch'an Buddhism gave emphasis to religious practices with less attention to Buddhist texts and doctrines – the *Dharma*. The Indians won the long debate, and the Chinese priests left the country. The Indian monk–philosopher Shantarakshita then wanted to establish Tibet's first Buddhist monastery at Samye, but it was said that local demons intervened. He advised King Tri-song De-tsen to bring the great saint Padmasambhava from India, who meditated for seven days and subdued the demons. Thus Padmasambhava is given the credit for building the first Buddhist monastery in Tibet. (Eventually there were over 6,000 of them in the country, for Buddhist monks and nuns.)

The path of Buddhist development was not smooth in either Tibet or China. In the ninth century its foothold in both countries almost gave way. The forty-first and last of the great kings of Tibet, Tsanpo Langdarma, was strongly pro-Bon and anti-Buddhist. He persecuted Buddhists ruthlessly but was, however, assassinated in 842 AD after a short reign. In China, in 845 AD, Emperor Wu Tsung believed that Buddhism had become too popular and threatened his supreme power (as would Jiang Zemin 1,100 years later, in Tibet). He destroyed 4,600 monasteries and 40,000 temples, and 260,000 monks and nuns were forced to live as lay people, bringing to an end the Golden Age of Buddhism in China which had begun in 581 AD under Emperor Sui. Buddhism became only a 'tolerated religion', but later recovered. In Tibet, Buddhism was again on the increase during the Kingless Age, and authority gradually shifted from lay warriors to religious *lamas*. It also began to flourish amongst ordinary people. Except in Kham on the eastern boundary of Tibet, where Tibetans remained more wild and warlike, nonviolence became the norm. No longer did people glory in the slaughter of enemies in all directions. Now they refused even to harm worms on the ground. It was a remarkable transformation.

Following the outbreak of a brief civil war in Kham in 869 AD, Buddhism again became decadent and corrupt, and it was the Indian scholar–saint Atisha who in 1042 AD came to Tibet to reform and revive it. He founded the great monastery at Sakya. The subsequent building of further monasteries began to shift the balance of power from the nobility to the heads of these fast-growing, rich and powerful institutions.

The great Mongolian leader Chingghis Khan, having been elected Khan of all Mongols in 1206, subjugated the Tangut Empire to the north of Tibet and threatened Tibet itself. However, the astute and nonviolent *lamas*, through their submission to the advancing armies, avoided invasion – but they had to pay tribute. When later the Tibetans failed to pay as agreed, Godan Khan

– the son of Chingghis – invaded Tibet in 1247 with 300,000 soldiers and caused much damage and many deaths. Godan then chose the most learned Buddhist scholar at the time, the sixty-two-year-old Sakya Pandita, a much-respected leader from the Sakyapa sect of Buddhism[10] and popular with the people, to rule Tibet on his behalf.[11] (Sakya Pandita had cured Godan of an illness and thus gained his confidence.) The soldiers withdrew. By 1249 the transition of the country to Buddhism was almost complete; but then again it lapsed. It was rescued in the late fourteenth century by Tsongkhapa, a monk from Amdo in north-eastern Tibet. Those who followed his reforms were known as Gelugpa Buddhists, or 'virtuous ones'. Thereafter, although not without an occasional struggle, the rulers of Tibet were either themselves *lamas* or required religious approval.

The spiritual relationships between the *lamas* of Tibet and the *khans* had already begun with Chingghis. He was much impressed by the young Sakya Pandita, and even invited him to teach Buddhism in Mongolia. The relationship deepened with Godan Khan and matured between Kublai Khan, Chingghis Khan's grandson, and Sakya Pandita's successor and nephew, Phags'pa, the then leading Sakya Lama and ruler of Tibet. (Both Godan and Sakya Pandita had died in 1251.) Kublai Khan was first Governor of the border territory between Tibet and China; then, in 1260, he conquered China and became Emperor. Phags'pa became State Tutor (or Preceptor), Kublai Khan's spiritual teacher and advisor.[12] One of the Emperor's first actions was to invite Phags'pa to devise a written version of the Mongolian language, completed in 1270, which became the script used in the Mongolian government. In 1271 the hereditary title was changed to Yuan. Phags'pa became Imperial Tutor (Preceptor) of the Yuan dynasty and remained so until his death in 1280.

When Kublai Khan became Emperor and Phags'pa State Tutor, on spiritual matters relating to Tibet the Emperor would defer to the *lama*. On political matters the reverse was the case – except that on very important matters concerning Tibet, the Emperor would act only with the consent of the tutor – an important constraint on the power of a potential aggressor turned protector. Thus, Phags'pa was the *khan's* spiritual teacher, the ruler of Tibet with the power to block important decisions of the Khan Emperor, and the declared head of the Buddhist world. The Sakya *lamas* ruled Tibet on behalf of all Buddhist sects, and the *lamas* would travel frequently to Peking, which Kublai Khan had chosen for his capital. In their meetings for spiritual transmission, the Emperor could keep an eye on the day-to-day decisions made by the *lamas* and mention matters of concern. Thus both the *lamas* and the Khan Emperors had constraints on each other's power in Tibet. They each had an interest in making the relationship work, and mutual trust developed.

However, in 1350, thanks to the leadership of a forceful ruler, Changchub Gyaltsen, Tibet regained its political independence from the Mongol empire and established its own distinctively Tibetan administration and laws. The spiritual relationship, however, continued between Tibet and Mongolia. It remained so, with modifications, well into the twentieth century.

The Mongolian Yuan dynasty fell in 1368. The first Ming Emperor, Ming T'ai-tsu, had been a Buddhist monk and so was sympathetic to Tibet. When his wife, Empress Ma, died in 1382, the Emperor sent for the Fifth Karmapa to conduct the Buddhist ceremonies. The formerly close relationships with Tibet were, however, discontinued.

The Dalai Lamas came on the scene much later when, in 1578, the Tibetan teacher Sonam Gyatso converted Altan Khan, a descendant of Kublai Khan, to Buddhism.[13] (By then, the *khans* had for over 200 years, no longer been the rulers of China.) In return, Sonam Gyatso was given the title of Dalai Lama – a Mongolian term often taken to mean 'Ocean of Wisdom'[14] – not only for himself but also for his two predecessors. Thus Sonam Gyatso became the Third Dalai Lama. The present Dalai Lama, Tenzin Gyatso, born 6 July 1935, is the fourteenth in the line.

The historical fact appears to be that the essential relationship throughout this long period was between Tibetan *lamas* and leading Mongolians, and it was largely spiritual. The relationship started early in the thirteenth century with Chingghis Khan, well before 1260 when his grandson Kublai conquered China, became Emperor and founded the Yuan dynasty. During the Yuan dynasty, the essential *khan* relationships with Tibetan *lamas* were personal and spiritual, and only partly political. The spiritual relationships with the Mongols also continued long after the Yuan dynasty fell in 1368. Tibet's secular administrative relationships with the Mongols, which also started before the establishment of the Yuan dynasty, were severed by Changchub Gyaltsen in 1350. So to argue, as the Chinese do today, that Tibet became part of China in the thirteenth century is a distortion of history.

Buddhism is at the very core of the lives of most Tibetans. It is, however, exceptionally complex. Here, all that is possible or necessary is to outline its principal dimensions. These are: the nature and training of the mind; rebirth (or reincarnation) after death; the principle of *karma*; the impermanence of everything; love, compassion and kindness towards all sentient beings; and nonviolence. They are all related, part of a complete and highly developed system for living and dying. The most basic spiritual principle is the quest for wisdom and happiness through the relinquishment of material values.

In Tibetan, the term 'Buddhist', or *Nangpa,* means 'insider', someone who seeks the truth from within: 'The nature of mind is the nature of everything.'[15]

At the heart of training the mind is meditation. There are, said the Buddha, 84,000 ways of meditating. At one level is simply 'stillness' and 'letting go'. After years of concentrated practice one reaches higher levels of consciousness, leading towards 'enlightenment', the ultimate goal. The training of Buddhists today in Namgyal Monastery in McLeod, the Dalai Lama's monastery, takes twelve years, and in the rebuilt Labrang Monastery in Xiahe, at the far side of Kham (in Gansu province), it is fifteen years; in truth, it never ends. Spiritual training requires continuous transmission with a master and learning; it is reckoned to take some twenty to thirty years to become a real Buddhist. Then, one's mind becomes extraordinarily powerful and can be directed towards self-control, affecting other people and making things happen. Labrang, now with some 2,000 monks, is an influential monastery both in Tibet and China and a centre of the Gelugpa tradition.

Reincarnation, or 'rebirth', is fundamental to Buddhism. In Tibetan the word for 'body' is *lu*, which means 'something you leave behind [when you die]', like baggage. Buddhists believe that what reincarnates is the most subtle level of consciousness, a 'special consciousness', the 'clear light' with its special energy – often referred to as the 'spirit' or the 'soul' by non-Buddhists.[16] When we die, Tibetan Buddhists believe, after three days all the other energies that kept the body alive gradually become dissipated. What continues is that subtle energy of consciousness, the true, primordial and uncluttered state of our mind. It is said that for about three weeks after death people still have strong impressions of the previous life, after which the future life becomes more dominant.

Buddhists believe that the average interval between the subtle energies' leaving the body of a deceased person and their entering the body of another person is forty-nine days. It could be shorter, much longer or might never happen – in which case those subtle energies may then manifest themselves as ghosts or spirits.[17] This intermediate period is called the '*bardo* of becoming'. There are four *bardos*, or states of mind, four continuously linked realities, which relate to: living; dying and death; after death ('becoming'); and rebirth. Meditation is the principal means by which one can access and begin to understand these higher states of mind.

Until about five hundred years after the death of Christ, Christians accepted reincarnation as a fact. The Catholic Church rejected it; Hindus believe in it today. As the Dalai Lama says, 'from a Buddhist point of view, whether the person who dies believes in rebirth or not, their rebirth exists'.[18] Believing in a past life and in rebirth changes one's attitude to living. Death is not the end. One is led to take a different and more responsible attitude towards moral behaviour, the environment and everything around us. It all becomes more sacred. If we desecrate the environment for present need or profit, for example, we are harming our future selves.

Karma (which means 'action') is the natural law of cause and effect. Every action of body, speech or mind has a corresponding result. It may be for good, resulting in good *karma*; for evil, resulting in bad *karma*; or neutral. It may be instantaneous, or take many years to become apparent. It may relate to the actions of an individual, a group of people or a nation. *Karma* is the truth and driving force behind rebirth. A surfeit of good deeds in one's lifetime will lead to a good rebirth. A preponderance of bad deeds will result in a painful rebirth, perhaps at a lower level than humankind. Good *karma* comes from practising love, compassion and kindness towards all sentient beings. 'My policy is kindness,' the Dalai Lama has said. Good deeds, positive action undertaken with a true heart, lead to the acquisition of merit. However, 'negative action has one good quality. It can be purified. So there is always hope. Even murderers and the most hardened criminals can change and overcome the conditioning that led them to these crimes.' Padmasambhava said: 'If you want to know your past life, look into your present condition. If you want to know your future life, look at your present actions.'

The impermanence of everything is a basic tenet of Buddhism. There is an old Tibetan saying: 'Tomorrow or the next life – which will come first, we never know.'[19] Buddhism holds that we are so busy leading our day-to-day lives, trying to cope with the way everything changes from one minute to the next, that we overlook – or do not wish to look at – the most basic change of all: the possibility of our own death. When it does come, most of us are completely unprepared. Buddhists, however, are taught what to expect and not to be afraid.

Spiritual persons, who, after many years of meditation and practice, can move towards enlightenment but have decided instead to remain in this world and do good for others and to teach, like the Dalai Lama, are called *bodhisattvas*. It is crucial for Tibetan Buddhists, therefore, to identify where the most highly evolved *lamas* have been reborn. To start one's life with an awareness gained from a past life, with received wisdom and experience in the intricacies of Buddhism or of any other complex discipline such as music, is invaluable in carrying it further during the present lifetime. The search for the reincarnations of the Thirteenth Dalai Lama and the Tenth Panchen Lama, leaders of the Gelugpa 'Yellow Hats', was a serious and important business. Likewise, finding the reborn Sixteenth Gyalwa Karmapa, who came from the Kargyudpa sect of Buddhism and died in 1981, was equally important. His lineage extended in an unbroken line of rebirths since the death of the First Karmapa in 1193 AD, the 'Black Hats'. To find the right child ensures that the wisdom-memory of a high *lama* who has died, and of his previous incarnations, will not be lost. As the child grows up, the deep understanding of his predecessors is revealed and enhanced, although not without years of study. The true teacher of Buddhism is therefore the one who brings through ancient wisdom from the rebirth of the masters.

The present (Fourteenth) Dalai Lama and others have described the processes involved in identifying the reincarnation of the Thirteenth Dalai Lama, who died in 1933.[20] The problem was where to find him. An early indication was given when the head of the embalmed body of the Thirteenth Dalai Lama inexplicably twice turned towards the north-east. He was seated cross-legged and facing south on his throne in the Norbulingka palace, dressed in fine clothes and on public display. When three State Oracles turned towards the east while in a trance, it seemed confirmed that the Thirteenth Dalai Lama would be reborn in that direction. Then, in the summer of 1935, the Reting Regent – a 'stand-in' governor, so to speak, who was appointed upon the death of the Thirteenth Dalai Lama – went to a sacred lake south-east of Lhasa called Lhamo Lhatso. Here a previous regent had seen visions that had turned out to be significant in locating the whereabouts of the child who became the Thirteenth Dalai Lama. Later, the Reting Regent announced to the National Assembly that he had clearly seen, in the lake, three Tibetan letters (*ah*, *ka* and *ma*), a monastery with a three-tiered building and roofs of jade-green and gold. From it, a twisting road led eastwards towards a bare pagoda-shaped hill. Near there would be found a small, one-storey house with oddly shaped guttering and turquoise tiles. The Regent felt sure that *ah* stood for Amdo, an area with many Tibetans but ruled by a Muslim warlord in the name of Nationalist China.

In 1936 three teams of about forty people, monks and lay government officials, each led by a high *lama*, set off to the north-east, east and south-east, charged with identifying two or three likely boys and bringing them back to Lhasa for a final selection. The search party to the north-east was led by the abbot of the Sera monastery, Kewtsang Rinpoche. They came to the Kumbum monastery and saw that it had a three-tiered, pagoda-style building with a path leading from it towards a bare hill. Did *ka* signify Kumbum, they asked themselves? Some ways down the path in the village of Taktser (which had about thirty small dwellings), in the middle of three houses and slightly raised above the others, they found a single-storey building with turquoise tiles and gnarled branches of juniper wood on the roof which served as guttering. It had Tibetan prayer flags fluttering from a thirty-foot-high pole in the courtyard; they decided to investigate.

It was now snowing hard, with some four feet already on the ground. The strangers who came to the door of the house said they were going to Sanho, and were lost. The residents of the house, a farmer and his wife, invited them to stay the night. The seekers did so, without revealing their purpose. The abbot of Sera, who spoke the local dialect of Tsongkha, a district of Amdo, pretended to be a servant of one of the others so that he could study the children of the family without formality. One child, aged two years (three by Tibetan counting), Lhamo Dhondrup by name, was the fifth child born to the family of sixteen, and quickly ran to the abbot and climbed on to his knee. Although disguised in simple clothes, the 'servant' was wearing a rosary hidden amongst his clothes which had belonged to the Thirteenth Dalai Lama. Immediately the young boy found it and asked for it to be given to him. He was told that he could have it if he correctly guessed the name of this 'servant'. Lhamo Dhondrup saw through the pretence and called out 'Sera *lama*, Sera *lama*'. The 'servant' then helped the farmer's wife stack the logs for the fire and carried round the young boy, who clung closely to him.

The next day the search party paid for their food and accommodation and left. Three weeks later they returned after visiting the Kumbum monastery near by, asking for directions for Tsongkha. Then, two weeks later they returned again as a formal deputation, bringing with them many objects – some of which had belonged to the Thirteenth Dalai Lama, and others not. The abbot, discarding his pretence, laid two walking sticks in a corner of the room. One was a walking stick of the Thirteenth Dalai Lama, which at first the boy rejected in favour of the similar-looking fake one – and then changed his mind. It turned out that the stick had been owned by the Thirteenth Dalai Lama, but he had given it away to a *lama* who in turn had given it to Kewtsang Rinpoche.

The young boy correctly identified all of the Thirteenth Dalai Lama's possessions while rejecting the others, calling out each time, 'It's mine, it's mine'. Of the two *damaru* drums offered to him, the boy chose the plain one, instead of one more ornate and imposing. Having chosen it, he refused to part with it and took it to bed with him. He then beat it exactly as monks do when calling for prayers. The young boy also had marks on his legs that looked like tiger stripes, and some other physical characteristics the search parties had been told were typical of previous Dalai Lamas. The abbot spoke to his associates in the Lhasa dialect, of which Lhamo Dhondrup's mother, Diki Tsering, did not understand a word – but the young boy understood perfectly, and responded in the same manner.

It later transpired that in 1909 the Thirteenth Dalai Lama, on his return from four years' exile in Mongolia, had rested at a small hermitage called Karma Rolpai Dorje on a hill above the village, and had remarked on the beauty of the scene. He would have seen the village, once occupied by nomads who had settled on the fertile soil with its rich pastures, the conifers on the nearby hills fragrant with scent and the berries which grew in the woods. He would have seen, too, the prayer flags fluttering in the breeze. When the Thirteenth Dalai Lama departed from this idyllic scene he left his boots behind, as if intending to return. It was then realised that most likely the *ka* and *ma* in the Regent's vision referred not Kumbum but to Karma, the first name of the hermitage. None of the search parties had found a more likely candidate who met all of the requirements. So this young boy, Lhamo Dhondrup, was chosen to become the Fourteenth Dalai Lama.

These great teachers are, of course, all human beings, in many ways just like the rest of us. When my wife Christina and I met the Dalai Lama, he seemed tired. While waiting for the audience, we had seen him besieged by an excited group of Japanese youngsters. They were overflowing with questions. They wanted his autograph. The Dalai Lama had had a long day giving many audiences. I wanted to ask him questions related to this book, which I was then writing, but Christina thought that what he really wanted was to put his feet up and have a cup of tea. So during a convenient pause she offered to play her flute for him. Rather bemused, he agreed to this. Being a professional musician and experienced at improvisation, she took her flute from its case, fitted it together, stood up, looked him in the eye, tuned in to the situation – and played. It was quite a short performance which she made up on the spot. The Dalai Lama leaned forward, enchanted by the pure and melodic sounds, and when it was over seemed overjoyed and rejuvenated, full of questions. A few days later when we were waiting in the Karmapa's anteroom we saw him through the window on the terrace outside his audience room surrounded by a dozen or so excited young Tibetan women. They were soon brought into line with the Karmapa in the middle for a photograph, himself grinning like any young man would in the circumstances.

In the West, the Buddhist belief system is gaining many adherents. The first edition of Sogyal Rinpoche's remarkable book *The Tibetan Book of Living and Dying*,[21] from which much of the above writing on Buddhism has been drawn, has sold over 1.5 million copies in ten years. In 425 pages, the author has distilled the essence of this complex, esoteric, ancient wisdom for our practical use and benefit in the modern world. He lectures in hospices the world over and helps the dying. In North America, the home of advanced science and capitalism, meditation and *Dharma* centres for the study and practice of Buddhism have been growing exponentially since the mid-1960s. By 1998 there were 1,062 of them, some with a very large membership.

Early accounts of the lives of ordinary Tibetans show how close most people there were to nature.[22] In many ways, nothing has changed. Tibetans are settled farmers or nomads, leading their animals to the best pastures as the seasons changed, year after year stopping at the same places, usually not travelling very far, taking their yak-skin tents and all their possessions with them. The land itself is precious – places of wild beauty, the homes of deities and spirits, some with very special meaning and significance like Mount Kailash, a holy place shared with Hindus, round which many thousands of people of all nationalities each year still circumambulate in pilgrimage.

Over the millennia, Tibetans found ways of surviving at high altitudes. The ubiquitous yaks thrive above 10,000 feet, nature's providers on the high plateau, carriers and hauliers whose bodies also provide milk and butter, cheese and yoghurt; fuel; insulation and fertiliser from dung; meat; skins and hair for clothing; shelter; coracles; blankets; ropes; and bones for building. The staple diet of Tibetans is *tsampa*, a loaf made from barley with perhaps oats and peas combined in many different forms. Buckwheat, potatoes, fruit and vegetables are grown at lower altitudes, and the staple drink, *chang*, is made from fermented barley.

The rhythm of Tibetans' lives is determined by the seasons and the state of their crops, and by annual celebrations such as Losar, the elaborate, fun-filled Tibetan new year festivities; a time for sweeping away the old and welcoming a new start, it is a much more extended celebration in Amdo and Kham than in Lhasa. The great religious Monlam prayer festival, of Buddhist remembrance and re-dedication comes next. Life continues with family events, births, deaths and marriages, occasional pilgrimages, visitors and recreational activities like picnics and kite flying.

External symbols and activities like chanting, dancing, music, butter lamps, prayer flags and so on are not the essence of Buddhism. They are reminders, outward expressions of belief, signposts to the faithful. The truth lies within the heart of each practitioner: secret, permanent, felt as deeply as their experience and understanding can allow. Prostrating full length on the ground, circumambulating religious sites and spinning prayer wheels mean nothing without inner intent and commitment. The Dalai Lama's mother has said: 'As peasants we did not have much understanding of religion, but we had great faith.'[23]

Arranged marriages, even amongst the peasants, were common, but only after consulting *lamas* or astrologers. Young Tibetan women often married at fifteen or sixteen, and were betrothed much earlier. Extended families were close, often with at least three generations. During the harvests everyone joined in, and there was much singing, joy and hard work. (Wool and salt were two of Tibet's main exports.) Children learned from their parents, and thus tradition was carried down the generations. As they grew up, they either followed in the footsteps of their parents or went into a monastery, the usual destination for at least one son of a family. It was estimated that more than one quarter of all males in Tibet were monks. This gave most families a direct connection with a monastery, which they helped support and which, in times of need, helped them. Monks would come and pray in people's houses; oracles would be consulted; astrologers would advise on auspicious days, on the suitability of young men and women for good marriages and when to conduct the ceremony; when to hold the rituals of birth, death and afterlife, when to be present during illness and when to contemplate travelling.

Some monasteries were quite small; others were the size of a large village or town.[24] They had their own lands and tenant farmers would pay in kind, each year, a required quantity of cereals, forage and so forth. Families who devoted themselves to rearing cattle paid their rent in butter, cheese, wool and dried cow dung for fuel, and the surplus produce also went to the monasteries. People were obliged to undertake certain labours, such as transport of the baggage of the *lamas* when they arrived. Close relationships would develop, as well as mutual trust and support. Monasteries raised money by sending out parties to distant places to perform rites, heal the sick and bring comfort to people in distress. In return they would receive gifts – animals, money, food, precious artefacts. They provided basic education for children and instruction in Buddhist doctrine as they grew up. Most also engaged in trading and in making loans to support economic activities. Thus the religious communities of Tibet formed little states within the state, of which they were largely independent.

The nobility were rich and lived in large houses, sometimes with forty rooms or more. They were well-represented in the government and tended to regard government posts as spots to be filled by themselves and their children, by rights. However, there was no barrier to commoners, the sons and daughters of the peasants entering into noble families through marriage or simply by being well-respected.

There is no doubt that some private landlords were cruel and oppressive, and lived away from their land. They were like many of the Chinese landlords whom Mao wished to eliminate. But in spite of the semi-feudal system and much poverty, few people in old Tibet starved. When families were in difficulty, because of bad harvests for example, the monasteries would give practical support. There were many holidays, most of them religious in character, and there was much fun.

Tibetans are by nature a happy people, smiling and laughing easily, enjoying many religious festivals, practising Buddhism, taking delight in everyday events. They tend to dislike change. Ordinary Tibetans have great respect for *lamas* with any kind of spiritual training and ability. They believe in magic, mysticism and divination. Strange occurrences are sometimes attributed to ghosts, spirits or other supernatural powers, but such things are considered normal, as well as the belief that thoughts and messages can be transferred over long distances and that objects can have special powers.

The discipline of years of training and experience in meditation which monks receive give them a truly remarkable degree of control over their minds and bodies.[25] Close observers of Tibetan monks describe the 'magic' they can do, unbelievable to Western minds. They become what the Falun Gong in China call 'supernormal people', although Buddhists generally disdain such descriptions. To them, the monks are simply being as Buddhists have been for over a thousand years, and are reticent in talking about such things. But Buddhists are also taught love and compassion, that the powerful minds of highly accomplished practitioners are to be used only for good, never for evil. The Dalai Lama recognises such powers, and has authorised scientific clinical research into certain practices for authentication.[26] As explained earlier, Tibetans – and many other people – believe that there are many levels of consciousness above the so-called 'gross' level of ordinary perception in touch, sight, sound, taste and smell. Connecting with higher levels of consciousness, which to some extent, it is believed, ordinary people can do, gives additional means of communication and other abilities. These can be accessed through long periods of meditation. Two monasteries in Lhasa taught *tantra*, esoteric ritual and occult science.

Foretelling the future was commonplace in the ancient world. From great leaders to humble peasants, all used systems of divination to find answers to questions about the future. Tibetans, from at least the twelfth century AD, had a system in use for ordinary people as well as the leadership, and it still in use today, through a special person – the oracle. (There were once many hundreds of oracles.) The Dalai Lama today may consult the State Oracle of Nechung on critical matters.[27] The oracle goes into a trance to access the unconscious world and gives answers relevant to the moment of asking.[28] Ordinary Tibetans, as well as consulting local oracles, also use three special elongated dice-like small bars to be thrown in the air one at a time, while meditating on the question asked. The resultant patterns when thrown correspond to the sixty-four sections of a book of wisdom that advise various courses of action. This system has very close parallels with the *I Ching* in China, a still more ancient book of wisdom and divination.[29] In Tibet, oracles are also protectors and healers and, normally as their principal function, they assist people in the practice of the *Dharma*.

Tibetan medicine is a distinctive aspect of Tibetan culture, originating over two thousand years ago. It is said to take several lifetimes to master. It is intimately connected to Buddhism and has close parallels with homoeopathy and *ayurvedic* medicine – both common today, especially in India.[30] All are holistic in approach, treating the whole person and not just the illness. Tibetans also integrate Eastern astrology with their medical system. (The main medical institute, formerly on a mountaintop in Lhasa until destroyed by the Chinese invaders and now in Dharamsala, is called the Tibetan Medical and Astrological Institute, the Men-Tsee-Khang.) They consider the medical implications of planetary configurations at one's time of birth, said to influence a person; in this system, astrology is important in both diagnosis and remedies. Likewise, Tibetan healers believe in the importance of *karma* from past lives in influencing the health of people today.

Education in Tibet pre-1950 was thoroughly out of date by international standards. The monasteries provided only very basic education, principally as preparation for becoming monks. Attempts by the Thirteenth Dalai Lama, who died in 1933, to modernise it were frustrated by the aristocracy and by traditionalists. They were afraid that exposure to the West would be corrupting and would undermine Buddhism. The regents also did nothing to improve education. Thus, after World War II, as the Dalai Lama laments, 'there were no people with the right educational background to master international diplomacy and to explore legal and diplomatic ways of securing our membership of the UN. We passed through this period of dynamic international change as though asleep.'[31]

It is, in general, a simple life that is portrayed in the literature and by elders who remember the past, but only in the sense that technology was unsophisticated, high-pressure consumerism did not exist and the pace of life was seasonal and slower; 'simple' must not be thought of in any derogatory sense. Many Westerners also yearn for the simpler life of previous eras. 'Simple' Tibetans also had their traumas, tragedies and frustrations. Many were poor in a material sense, but rich in spirit. Those who were poor or who suffered might have thought of their circumstances as the result of bad *karma*, due to bad deeds in previous lives and therefore to be borne with patience and forbearance in the hope that the next life would be better if they performed good deeds in the current one.

It was a unique feature of the governance of old Tibet that each high-level official would be paired with a high-level *lama*. They shared responsibility. Thus Buddhist thinking permeated all laws and executive actions, but not to the extent that Tibet was a theocratic state. Lay officials would have grown up with Buddhism all around them and so would understand the lama's point of view. Moreover, monasteries had large estates and engaged in finance and trading, so the *lamas* were not without business understanding and management practice and could comprehend the lay person's point of view. The Dalai Lamas and the abbots of monasteries, as well as other leading spiritual figures, were drawn not from the aristocracy but by the process of rebirth. It is remarkable how many of these were peasants, nomads, small farmers, lay people. While not exactly democratic, that system did ensure that the lowest in society could become the highest.

But there were also negative features. Below the Dalai Lamas, generally the aristocrats took the high-level government posts. These were often passed to the sons of the office holders; the question of merit was not an issue in their appointment. Moreover, the *lamas* came from the monasteries, which were powerful institutions with interests to protect, too. The aristocrats were also the guardians of the law. Until the Chinese occupation, the Tibetan legal system dated back to the great King Song-tsen Gampo in the seventh century. Three of the original sixteen legal clauses were removed in the seventeenth century, and the legal code then became known as the 'Thirteen Decrees'.[32] Capital punishment was, however, eliminated by the Thirteenth Dalai Lama, and he banned the use of inhumane punishments for misdemeanours. The laws were comprehensive in their coverage, appropriate to the circumstances of the time.

By early in the twentieth century it was widely recognised that drastic changes were needed in the governance of Tibet. The Thirteenth Dalai Lama modernised the army because he foresaw that in the not too distant future Tibet would be invaded by the Chinese. He was also a reformer, but all too often, as with education, the aristocrats blocked him.

The Chinese occupation in 1950 cut short the Fourteenth Dalai Lama's reforming zeal (he was then only fifteen years old). His priorities for change were the land ownership and tenure system, taxation and the practice of making loans to the poorer peasants. The Dalai Lama considered that Buddhism was incompatible with the unequal sharing of riches.[33] Abuses against the peasants were far greater from private landlords, especially absentee owners, than where land was owned by the monasteries. His plan was to purchase such land for the state and redistribute it to the peasants to achieve greater social equality. It never went further than experimentation before the Communist occupation. Between 1950 and 1959, when he escaped from Tibet, the Dalai Lama tried to introduce land reforms but was stopped by the Chinese themselves. They favoured their own extremely damaging reform policies instituted by Mao Zedong. The Dalai Lama recognised that some of his aims could be described as Marxist, and he thought of himself as half-Marxist, but his proposed methods of implementation were different. The changes he chose were neither revolutionary nor violent. A thorough reform programme for the governance of the Tibetan people had to wait until after 1959, when he had settled in India; however, it could then be applied only to those who had fled from Tibet into exile as a direct result of Mao's invasion.

Four
_____

The Invasion of Tibet and its Aftermath

'We are social revolutionaries, never reformists.'
Mao Zedong

In October 1950[1] Ngabo Ngawang Jigme, the newly appointed Governor-General of Kham, had a status equivalent to a member of the Kashag, the cabinet of the Dalai Lama's government. As the Chinese army – some 40,000 men in all – approached Chamdo, where he resided with his Tibetan army of under 1,000 men, Ngabo fled, evidently to Lhasa.[2] Some time after leaving Chamdo the small party reached a remote monastery in which Ngabo hid. But a column of Chinese troops soon reached it from a northern route, and he and his party were quickly discovered and captured.

The Tibetan military was unprepared for such a large onslaught or for such rapid advances by the Chinese troops over difficult terrain early in the winter, with ice and snow and no roads. Traditional Tibetan practice was for soldiers in the field to be accompanied by their families – women, children, babies cocooned on the backs of their mothers, together with their household effects: tents, pots, pans, carpets, butter-churns and bundles of clothes piled on to yaks and mules. The Tibetan army had no maps, and relied on local knowledge. It had declined in efficiency and effectiveness since the time of the Thirteenth Dalai Lama. With several lines of Chinese attack from different directions, serious defence was impossible.

While Tibetan Buddhists would engage in violence only in the case of self-defence, the Khampas had no such inhibitions. Their reputation was fearsome. Banditry was good sport. As they arrived in Chamdo to support the local Tibetans, they livened up the town by racing round on their horses, firing guns and brandishing their great swords. But when Tibetans fled Chamdo, the Khampas looted their homes. Kham did not fall under the direct control of the Dalai Lama and the Tibetan government in Lhasa and, not surprisingly, many Tibetans feared the Khampas more than the Chinese. They were, however, too few in number in Chamdo to make much difference. In parts of Kham where Chinese had long settled, Tibetans were used to them and so the Red Army passed through peacefully. The defence of Kham, and therefore of the whole of Tibet, was thus in some disarray, and individual bravery was not enough.

It must be recalled that it was the long-standing practice in the Tibetan government for each principal post to be held by two people, one of whom was a monk. Ngabo Ngawang Jigme was, in fact, junior to the leading monk, Khenchi Dawala, who wanted to arm some 500 monks from the monastery above Chamdo for their defence. But the monks themselves refused. They said that only the gods could deliver a Tibetan victory, and they were doing their bit by feverishly praying twice as often as usual. To go into battle would forfeit the recitation of several thousand prayers, which might be decisive.

News of a promised invasion to liberate Tibet from the grip of 'American and British imperialism' had been broadcast by Beijing in January 1950. According to the Chinese, the imperialists were planning to invade China through Tibet. There were no Americans in Tibet at that time and only three Britons. The Chinese mistakenly believed the British Mission in Lhasa was the centre of a spy ring, and that the two radio operators working for the Tibetan government – one of whom, Robert Ford, was captured with Ngabo – were British spies. There was, however, an American CIA agent in Urumqi (the capital of Xinjiang), about a thousand miles to the north of Lhasa, by the name of Mackierman. He was the US Vice-Consul, engaged in spying on China's nuclear developments and organising an insurrection of the Kazakhs in Xinjiang against the Russians. Early in 1950 he was ordered to go to Lhasa to talk with the authorities about organising resistance to an expected Chinese invasion. But in April of that year he and two of his four companions were killed as they tried to enter Tibet. The border guards, thinking they were bandits, had been warned too late of their expected arrival. The Chinese themselves had an extensive spy network and had perhaps misinterpreted – and exaggerated – American intentions.

As the likelihood of imminent attack became more obvious with widespread victories by the Communists against the Nationalist forces, the Kashag sought international support, appealing to Britain, the US and India. Tibet never became a member of the UN. It was *de facto* independent when the UN was set up in 1946, but not until December 1949 did Tibet seek support from Britain and the US for its membership application. Both governments advised that it would be vetoed in the Security Council by Russia and China, and refused help. India agreed that Tibet's application would be vetoed. The Indian ambassador to China, Sardar Panikkar, advised his government that India should 'wash her hands completely of Tibet'.[3] In November 1950, just after the Chinese invasion, an appeal for help by the Kashag and the Tibetan government to the UN was, on Indian advice, put to one side in anticipation of a satisfactory agreement with China (what became the Seventeen-Point Agreement). In 1948, however, India had offered military training – but the Tibetan army refused to subject itself to the disciplines required. Very late – in June 1949 – the Indian government supplied the army with some weapons, then increased this amount in March 1950. But the PLA had been hardened by some twenty years of continuous fighting against the Nationalists, other warlords and the Japanese occupiers. With about forty times the Tibetan military strength, its invasion in October 1950 was, inevitably, a walkover.

Heinrich Harrer (of *Seven Years in Tibet* fame) personally gave news of the attack to the Kashag in Lhasa, which was holding an annual picnic by the river. (Picnics were much loved by all Tibetans and could last all day.) Its members then held earnest discussions about what to do, while continuing with their outing. Reports of the attack did not make headline news internationally because practically on the same day American forces under General MacArthur and UN auspices crossed the Thirty-eighth Parallel from South to North Korea, and China declared that it was entering the Korean War (1950–3) on the side of North Korea. The attack on Tibet was well-timed to be obscure, although this seemed to be more a matter of chance than of clever scheming. The Indian government, supported by the British, protested to China about the invasion, and in November 1950 the Kashag protested to the UN. However, it did not publicise news of the attack locally or nationally for fear of causing alarm to the Tibetan people.

Following the advice of two oracles, the Kashag and the Regent called a meeting of the Tibetan National Assembly to accelerate the assumption of office, both religious and secular, of the Fourteenth Dalai Lama. He was then fifteen years old.[4] Normally this would have taken place three years later. But on 17 November 1950, with the government of Tibet in a state of manifest crisis, he was seen as the only person who could perhaps unite the country in its hour of need. It was too late, and unity was not sufficient. The Dalai Lama had been largely protected from the harshness and realities of the outside world, although Harrer had been instrumental to some extent in assuaging his thirst for such knowledge. At the time of the Chinese invasion, however, the Dalai Lama knew practically nothing about China or the Chinese, except, by his own account, what he had learned from copies of *Life Magazine*. By the time of the Dalai Lama's inauguration, the Chinese army had already crossed into his administrative territory and was poised to advance. He was faced with a hopeless situation. Dawa Norbu, a distinguished Tibetan historian, is harsh in his criticism:

> We Tibetans ourselves were responsible for our tragedy to a large extent. It would be unfair to condemn individual *lamas*, individual monasteries or individual aristocrats. The whole system was rotten to the core, and could not withstand twentieth-century pressures. It was ready to fall, and it fell disastrously.[5]

The system was certainly out of date, despite the best efforts of the Thirteenth Dalai Lama. Yet, even if Tibet had been modernised, the people would have remained dedicated to Buddhism and nonviolence, and thus easy prey. The era of the Warrior Kings was long gone. The Chinese were determined to capture ('liberate') Tibet and would have succeeded anyway.

What of the Chinese position? Over the years Mao Zedong had changed his mind about Tibet and other 'national minorities'. In 1931, in the constitution of the first Chinese Soviet Republic, in which Mao played a part, the following was written:

> The Soviet Government of China recognises the right of self-determination of the national minorities in China, their right to complete separation from China and to the formation of an independent state for each national minority. All Mongolians, Tibetans, Miao, Yao, Koreans and others living on the territory of China shall enjoy the full right of self-determination, i.e. they may either join the Union of Chinese Soviets or secede from it and form their own State, as they may prefer.[6]

At this time Mao and the Communist leadership were greatly influenced by the Russians, and Lenin had espoused such policies. They also reflected the views which Mao had been expressing in 1920 when Hunan was invaded by the warlords – 'Hunan for the Hunanese'. However Mao's ideas had shifted significantly by the time Edgar Snow interviewed him in Pao An five years later, on 23 July 1936. By then Mao had become the undisputed leader of the Communists:

When the People's Revolution has been victorious in China, the Outer Mongolian Republic will automatically become a part of the Chinese Federation, at its own will. The Mohammedan and Tibetan peoples, likewise, will form autonomous republics attached to the China Federation. The unequal treatment of national minorities, as practised by the Kuomintang, can have no part in the Chinese programme, nor can it be part of the programme of any democratic republic.[7]

In July 1949 the Kashag had expelled all Chinese residing in Lhasa who were representatives of the KMT government. These were principally the small number of *ambans* (local Chinese representatives) who had been in Lhasa since the Qing dynasty. The fear, probably justified, was also that Communist Chinese were infiltrating Tibet as spies. Both Communist and Nationalist leaders objected most strongly to the expulsions, and this may have made Mao all the more determined to attack Tibet when he assumed power three months later – especially if the Americans were becoming involved. Chiang Kai-shek had been prepared to consider independence for Tibet even as late as 1948, having had many conversations with the Dalai Lama's elder brother Gyalo Thondup (who had been educated partly in Shanghai and spoke Chinese fluently; in 1951 he had married a Chinese woman named Chu-tang). But now Mao was in charge.

By the time of the Communist victory over the Kuomintang in 1949, the policy had shifted further. To occupy Tibet was now a priority. Mao had said that 'we are securing our frontiers'. As the commander-in-chief of the PLA, Zhu De, said on 24 September 1949 – unanimously approved by the National People's Congress five days later:

> The Common Programme demanded the waging of the revolutionary war to the very end and the liberation of all the territory of China, including Formosa [Taiwan], the Pescadores, Hainan Island and Tibet.[8]

As soon as Zhu announced that the Chinese intention was to 'liberate' Tibet, the Tibetan government challenged Mao on its historical justification and requested negotiations to secure the return of territories in eastern Kham, which the Nationalists had occupied earlier. China responded by asking for Tibetan cooperation in releasing Tibet from 'foreign imperialists'. In September 1950 the Tibetan government, with Chinese agreement, planned to send a delegation to Hong Kong (via New Delhi) to negotiate. However, the British in India refused the Tibetans visas for entry into Hong Kong, as the stamps in their Tibetan government passports would have implied diplomatic recognition. Instead there were discussions with the Chinese ambassador in New Delhi. The ambassador made it clear that Tibet must be regarded as part of China, that China would be responsible for Tibet's defence and that all trade and international negotiations would be conducted by China. The Kashag in Lhasa did not accept the Chinese position.

In the Chinese mindset there was the deeply ingrained historical legacy and belief that Tibet had been part of China for over 700 years, with admitted occasional interruptions. As the Chinese saw it, Tibet had slipped from its grasp when the Qing dynasty disintegrated; while warlords fought each other; while the Communists fought the Nationalists; and while the Japanese attacked and occupied large parts of China. At long last, Mao had declared on 1 October 1949, 'the Chinese people have stood up!'. Taking control of Tibet was a historic mission and a symbol of China 'standing up'.

Mao himself had long believed that the Communist Party could achieve power only through violent revolution; such was his observation of Russia. If Tibet was to be brought within the great motherland of Communist China for its social transformation, then violence was inevitable. Premier Zhou Enlai saw the occupation of Tibet as a 'sacred duty'.[9]

Indeed, in January 1950 Choekyi Gyaltsen, the Tenth Panchen Lama, in a message to Mao broadcast over Beijing Radio and printed in the official newspaper *Xinhua*, had invited the Chinese to occupy Tibet. Some Chinese authorities still quote this as the reason behind the invasion. The Panchen Lama said:

> On behalf of the Tibetan people, we respectfully plead for troops to be sent to liberate Tibet, to wipe out reactionaries, expel the imperialists, consolidate the national defences in the south-west and liberate the Tibetan people. This assembly vows to lead the patriotic Tibetan people, to mobilise the Tibetan people in support of the liberation army and to struggle hard for the People's Motherland.[10]

At the time of this speech he was only eleven years old, and in September 1949 he had been seized by the Communist forces when they occupied Amdo in eastern Tibet while chasing the Nationalist army. He had been enthroned only the previous month at Kumbum monastery in Amdo, supported by the Kuomintang government. Clearly, he was subsequently manipulated by the Communists, of which the Lhasa government was fully aware. The words which he spoke were most unlikely to have been his own. Nevertheless, this discordant voice weakened the position of the Kashag in countering the Chinese threat, and the fact that the Tenth Panchen Lama was in the hands of the Communists was in itself a serious long-term concern.

The Democracy Wall Movement (also known as 'Beijing Spring') was begun in 1978 – with Deng Xiaoping's qualified blessing – to encourage freedom of expression, especially amongst China's intellectuals. The Wall, in Beijing, provided the people with the opportunity to express their thoughts and ideas. However, as contributors became more and more outspoken, the Party closed it down. Many of those who had written, and whose sharpest criticisms were directed against the Party, were arrested. *Photo: Inge Morath, Magnum Photos.*

Jiang Zemin visits the Tibetan Medical Hospital in Lhasa in 1990 as then-General Secretary of the Communist Party. (He is said to have a recurring heart problem.) The original Medical and Astrological Centre, on top of a hill near Potala Palace, was destroyed by the Chinese. However, Tibetan medicine has survived throughout the Chinese occupation, and there is now a University of Tibetan Medicine in Lhasa offering five-year degrees, with some shorter courses. *Photo: Tibet Information Network.*

The Serthar Institute in Sichuan (formerly Kham) before its destruction in 2001–2. Founded in 1980 by the late Khenpo Jigme Phuntsok, the institute gave the highest levels of instruction in Buddhism to all who sought it. By 2001 it had attracted 6–7,000 monks and nuns in roughly equal numbers from many parts of China and abroad. In June of that year, the Chinese authorities ordered some 80 percent of the students to leave immediately. *Photo: Tibet Information Network.*

By mid-2002 over 2,400 huts used as living quarters at Serthar had been destroyed. Jigme Phuntsok was arrested then released from a military hospital, and subsequently died. Many students who were forced to leave had no homes to go to, and all were prevented from joining monasteries elsewhere. Mental health problems became common, and at least one person committed suicide. *Photo: Tibet Information Network.*

It was Mao's policy in China to exterminate private landlords who had been exploiting the peasants, and he may have thought that the situation in Tibet was similar in this regard. Chinese forces would, then, liberate Tibetans from their oppressors too. But the private landlords were proportionally much less of a problem in Tibet, and the system could not be described correctly as 'feudal'.

Finally, there were the obvious military–strategic considerations. Tibet had a long border principally to the south with India and Nepal, but also with the rebellious Muslims to the north in Xinjiang (East Turkestan), Ladakh and troublesome Kashmir to the west. There were also Sikkim (the Chinese did not at that time accept Indian claims over that territory), Bhutan and Burma (later called Myanmar) – all part of China's outer defence and jumping-off points for possible future attacks. The passes over the Himalaya to India and Nepal were strategically important. Significantly, the policy of 'liberating Tibet' was being pressed by Zhu, the experienced military commander and Mao's close friend. The PLA stood ready to continue its battle for communism and national unity.

Mao's first military aim at that time was to invade and capture Taiwan. Stalin was pushing him to support Kim Il Sung in North Korea, who was attacking the South and had promised Mao practical assistance if he did so. It seemed that Mao, in his planned military escapades in Tibet, Taiwan and Korea, wanted to show the world that China was now a power to be reckoned with, fully united and, so to speak, ready for business. One might conclude that the attack on Tibet was part of much wider plan of national assertiveness based upon a perceived historical justification and a fear that American and British forces might be plotting to occupy Tibet and thus to threaten China.[11]

The Chinese forces wished to complete their occupation without having to fight more than necessary, thus avoiding the lasting hatred of the Tibetan people, the possible destruction of places that might be useful to them and the inevitable loss of life. After the initial attack and military success, China proposed negotiations with the Tibetans to complete the occupation of their lands peacefully. Exchanges of notes made the Chinese position clear and gave the Tibetans little room for manoeuvre. The situation was extremely serious.

In January 1951, after much heart-searching, the Dalai Lama left Lhasa and for nine months settled in Dromo, close to the Indian border – in case he needed to escape from Tibet. With remarkable foresight, he took with him gold dust, gold bars and silver from his personal treasury. This wealth was then transported on yaks south into Sikkim for secret safekeeping. There it rested for eight years, until the escape of the Dalai Lama to India in 1959. Sold in Calcutta, it proved crucial for the survival of Tibetans-in-exile and their governance.

The Chinese tactics were clever; in 1950 they had captured Ngabo Ngawang Jigme, who had a status equivalent to a Tibetan government minister and was senior enough to lead the Tibetan delegation. He sent a long letter to the Dalai Lama, followed by a telephone call, explaining what had happened in Chamdo and suggesting that he go to Beijing to negotiate with the Chinese (obviously a suggestion dictated by the Chinese themselves). The Kashag preferred the negotiations to take place elsewhere but accepted Beijing even though it would put their negotiators – quickly formed with Ngabo at their head – at a disadvantage. They were isolated in a hotel, and external communication was denied to them. The Chinese produced a draft agreement, which the Dalai Lama and his government had not seen, and which could not be communicated to them. The Chinese used the threat of force as a lever to secure their will. As soon as the Tibetan team left Beijing to return to Lhasa and report to the Dalai Lama, the Chinese announced publicly that the agreement had been approved by the Tibetans. It came into force immediately, they said.

The basic assumptions of the two sides were diametrically opposed. The Chinese began with the statement that 'the question of the status of Tibet was not under discussion and Chinese sovereignty over Tibet was non-negotiable'. Li Weihan, leader of the Chinese delegation, added that 'it was a historical fact that Tibet formed an integral part of China, and her claim over Tibet was internationally recognised', which was incorrect. The Tibetans assumed that since Tibet had been *de facto* fully independent since 1911, they would be negotiating from that strong position.

The pressure under which the Tibetan delegation negotiated is illustrated by a quotation from Tibetan historian Tsering Shakya:

> When Lhawutara [a senior Tibetan negotiator] asked what the functions of the commission [the military and administrative committee in Article 15] would be, Li Weihan stated that the commission would be responsible for the implementation of the agreement and would 'decide' all important political and military issues. Lhawutara pressed further, saying that this would contradict the assurance that the power and status of the Dalai Lama and the existing political system would not be altered. At this point Li Weihan got irritated and said, 'Are you showing your clenched fist to the Communist Party? If you disagree then you can leave, whenever you like. It is up to you to choose whether Tibet would be liberated peacefully

or by force. It is only a matter of sending a telegram to the PLA group to recommence their march into Tibet.'[12]

At the end of the face-to-face negotiation in Beijing was The Agreement of the Central People's Government and the Local Government of Tibet on Measures for the Peaceful Liberation of Tibet – the so-called 'Seventeen-Point Agreement' (which the Chinese call the 'Seventeen-Article Agreement') of May 1951. By this means the Chinese got what they wanted. The agreement included the following preamble:

> The Tibetan nationality is one of the nationalities with a long history within the boundaries of China and, like many other nationalities, it has done its glorious duty in the course of the creation and development of the great motherland ... In 1949, basic victory was achieved on a nationwide scale in the Chinese people's war of liberation; the common domestic enemy of all nationalities – the KMT reactionary government – was overthrown; and the common enemy of all nationalities – the aggressive imperialist forces – was driven out ... All national minorities are to have freedom to develop their spoken and written languages and to preserve or reform their customs, habits and religious beliefs ... Under the unified leadership of the Central People's Government ... all national minorities have fully enjoyed the right of national equality and have exercised or are exercising national regional autonomy ...

Selected references to the Seventeen-Point Agreement are given below:

> The Tibetan people have the right of exercising national regional autonomy under the unified leadership of the Central People's Government (Article 3);

> The Central Authorities will not alter the existing political system in Tibet. The Central Authorities will not alter the established status, functions and powers of the Dalai Lama. Officials of various ranks shall hold office as usual (Article 4);

> The policy of religious belief laid down in the Common Programme of the Chinese People's Political Consultative Committee will be protected. In matters relating to various reforms in Tibet, there will be no compulsion on the part of the Central Authorities (Article 11);
> The People's Liberation Army entering Tibet will abide by the above-

mentioned policies and will also be fair in all buying and selling and will not arbitrarily take even a needle or a thread from the people (Article 13);

In order to ensure the implementation of this agreement, the Central People's Government will set up a military and administrative committee and a military area headquarters in Tibet (Article 15).

The Tibetan negotiators knew that the Chinese troops had halted some way short of Lhasa, poised for an attack. The Dalai Lama and his advisors were appalled when they heard, over Beijing Radio, the terms of what the Chinese said had been agreed, and were strongly inclined not to accept them. The Americans, whose forces in Korea were being driven back by the Chinese in May 1951, telegraphed the Dalai Lama and said that if he renounced the Seventeen-Point Agreement then they would recognise Tibetan independence. They also offered the Dalai Lama asylum in the US. It seems likely that the motive for this deal was the expectation that rejecting the agreement accompanied by a declaration of Tibetan independence would precipitate a major attack by the PLA, thus drawing off some Chinese troops from the Korean front where they were rapidly advancing.

Now that the Chinese wanted the Tibetans to communicate with the Dalai Lama, a telegram from Ngabo a few days later repeated the Chinese broadcast and added that the 'Chinese Governor of Tibet', General Chiang Chin-wu, was on his way to Dromo. The Tibetan team knew that it did not have full plenipotentiary power to commit the Dalai Lama, although Ngabo said that it had. Since none of the negotiating team had been given the Seals of State (the Dalai Lama had deliberately kept them so that any agreement entered into could not be made final), the Chinese made up some personal seals for the Tibetan negotiators and used them to authenticate the agreement. Obviously, no negotiating team could agree to such an important document involving the future governance of Tibet without the approval of the Dalai Lama and his government.

What eventually persuaded the Tibetans to endorse the agreement was that refusal most probably would have led to a large loss of life and great destruction. The Chinese would occupy Tibet whatever was decided. At least with the agreement there was hope of winning something, whereas if there was a fight, inevitably the Tibetans would lose everything. So, on 24 October 1951, five months after the signature in Beijing, the Dalai Lama sent a telegram to Mao Zedong (which undoubtedly reflects the language of Zhang Jingwu, the most important Chinese person in Tibet at that time, to whom the telegram was shown in draft) saying:

The Tibetan local government as well as ecclesiastical and secular people unanimously support this agreement, and under the leadership of Chairman Mao and the Central People's Government will actively assist the PLA troops entering Tibet in consolidating national defence, ousting imperial influences from Tibet and safeguarding the unification of the territory and the sovereignty of the motherland.[13]

Two days after the sending of this telegram the PLA entered Lhasa. Although the agreement was negotiated under duress, which in international law would have rendered it null and void, in fact after much delay it had been approved by the Dalai Lama. But as he recognised that failure to agree would have brought much violence, it can also be said to have been accepted by him under duress. Many lawyers hold that if Tibet had been independent at the time, which it was, and if the agreement had been freely entered into by the Tibetans, which it was not, it would indeed have legally transferred the sovereignty of Tibet to the People's Republic of China.

Ngabo Ngawang Jigme himself was known previously to look favourably on the Chinese. He was also under extreme pressure, because he was now their prisoner and had undergone indoctrination in their policies. It was a classic example of 'Catch the Leader in Order to Win' (one of the Thirty-Six Strategies in Sun Tzu's *The Art of War*). After the negotiations, Ngabo returned to Chamdo, which by then was under the direct rule of China.

While the Dalai Lama was escaping from Lhasa in 1959, he was astonished to hear on the radio that the Chinese had dissolved the Tibetan government and were to replace it with the 'Preparatory Committee for the Autonomous Region of Tibet' (PCART). Ngabo had been appointed Vice-Chairman of the committee (previously, he had been its Secretary General). Later, in 1965, the Chinese appointed Ngabo as Governor, or head, of the newly formed Chinese People's Congress for Tibet. Then, in 1968, he was appointed a member of the Chinese 'Revolutionary Committee' in Tibet to help bring together the Communist Party, the cadres and the PLA. But he never attended a single meeting, preferring to live in Beijing. From there he wrote two reports critical of Tibet,[14] published by New Star Publications in Beijing, the state press. In May 2001 he reappeared in Lhasa as part of the Chinese delegation to commemorate the fiftieth anniversary of the signing of the Seventeen-Point Agreement. Ngabo was an enigmatic character, the illegitimate son of a Tibetan nun from one of the leading aristocratic families. This may explain why he felt set apart from other Tibetans and sided with the Chinese. Hugh Richardson described Ngabo as, 'after the Panchen Lama, the most important puppet of the Chinese in Tibet'.[15]

The thirteen-year-old year old Tenth Panchen Lama also played a part in Chinese public relations, giving support to the agreement. He had been brought by the Chinese to Beijing on 27 April 1951, and had participated in the banquet given by Mao on 23 May to celebrate the signing. He had a long conversation with Zhou Enlai, and at the end made a short speech saying:

> The issue of nationality in China and the Tibetan issue, left in abeyance for so many years, have been successfully solved under the leadership of Chairman Mao. The liberation of Tibet is a happy event in the great multi-racial family of China …

The Dalai Lama did not approve of this statement, but he understood that 'the Panchen Lama cannot be personally blamed. No boy who grew up under such concentrated, constant alien influence could possibly retain his own free will.'[16]

Although the Chinese had stated in 1951 that Tibet was then, and had been for 700 years, an integral part of China, they considered the Seventeen-Point Agreement an extremely important legitimisation of their occupation of Tibet. Their spectacular celebration in Lhasa of the fortieth anniversary of the agreement on 20 May 1991 was lauded by then Premier Li Peng in a speech the previous day, in which he said:

> The central government's policy towards the Dalai Lama has been consistent and remains unchanged. We have only one fundamental principle, namely, Tibet is an inalienable part of China. On this fundamental principle there is no room for haggling.[17]

On 19 July 2001 then Vice-President Hu Jintao, in a delayed speech in Lhasa to commemorate the fiftieth anniversary, repeated the Party line:

> With the abolition of feudal serfdom, under which the Tibetan people had long been suppressed and exploited, millions of erstwhile serfs who did not even have the minimum of human rights have now stood up and become masters of their own fate. Today people of all ethnic groups are fully enjoying political, economic, cultural and other rights and having complete control of their destiny. For the text of the full speech, see the Appendix.

As current conditions in Tibet demonstrate (see Prologue), every part of that statement is either misleading or incorrect. Hu Jintao had been seriously misinformed.

One may conclude that throughout the whole campaign to capture Tibet, the Chinese acted with consummate skill and subtlety, cleverly exploiting the two leading Tibetans – Ngabo Ngawang Jigme and the Panchen Lama – on whom the Chinese could exercise direct pressure while using a minimum of military force. As shown earlier, many of the ideas expressed in the Seventeen-Point Agreement were standard in the PLA and had been introduced by Mao when he first formed a military force in 1927 and a year later was joined by Zhu De, already an experienced military commander, in their war against Chiang Kai-shek and the Nationalists. Together they had worked on such principles of behaviour by the military. *The Art of War* was their bible, and the Second Emperor Liu Bang was a role model.

The Chinese began their occupation of Tibet after the agreement by showing respect for the Tibetan people, treating them well and allowing the Tibetan government to operate more or less as it had done previously. Mao's prime concern was that the army produce enough food to meet its own needs; otherwise, he warned, it would be impossible to win over the Tibetans, and eventually they would rebel. Within three years the mood had changed as more and more Tibetans began to resent the Chinese presence. The extra food required to feed them meant that Tibetans went short. Prices rocketed. Whereas initially the Chinese punctiliously paid for all the food they needed, soon they began demanding free food and lodging as a right – so much for Article 13 of the Seventeen-Point Agreement and the high-minded ideals of the PLA. By the mid-1950s power had effectively slipped from the Tibetans' grasp. The traditional structures of government under the Dalai Lama in U-Tsang remained the same, but the Chinese would not tolerate any opposition to their policies.

The Korean War ended in July 1953, with heavy losses to the Chinese. Now Mao was able to turn his mind to other matters. Following the full enthronement of the Dalai Lama in the Jokhang Temple, the next year Mao invited him and the Panchen Lama to visit Beijing. With some misgivings amongst the people, they did so in July 1954 (accompanied by the Sixteenth Karmapa and the Dalai Lama's mother, Diki Tsering), and were in China for one year. Zhou and Zhu (now Vice-President of the People's Republic) greeted them on their arrival, and soon they met Mao. They were lavishly entertained in China and were subjected to an exhausting tour of the country. (Diki Tsering pleaded illness many times to avoid these endless, boring excursions and factory visits.) During this arduous tour the Dalai Lama learned about two thousand characters of the Chinese language. As far as possible, the Chinese kept the two spiritual leaders apart.

Privately, Mao said to the Dalai Lama: 'Religion is poison. First, it limits the population because monks and nuns remain celibate. Secondly, it takes no interest whatsoever in development.' (Mao should have realised, however, that the celibacy of Tibetan monks and nuns was also a way of restricting population growth in the harsh climate and largely barren land of Tibet, and was more gentle than China's adoption a few years later of the 'one child' policy, ruthlessly and inhumanely enforced. Moreover, for Tibetans, 'development' had low priority because the spiritual life was more important.)

The collectivisation of agriculture at this time in the whole of China had now reached the eastern provinces, encompassing Kham and Amdo and their Tibetan autonomous prefectures. These attempts at collectivisation, including the first moves to settle the nomads, the destruction of villages and monasteries and the killing of Tibetan leaders, triggered an uprising called the Kanding Rebellion (after the main town in eastern Tibet). In 1955–6 they were supported by the US through the CIA, and some Tibetans were trained in Arizona and parachuted into Tibet. They did not affect the outcome. The remoteness of the Khampas from Lhasa had always afforded them a great deal of independence, and the Seventeen-Point Agreement did not include Tibetans in those areas. When the PLA moved in and defeated the rebels in 1956, groups of Khampas fled to Lhasa, which also began to become restive.

In May 1956, the Dalai Lama was made Chairman of PCART; the Panchen Lama became Vice-Chairman and Ngabo Ngawang Jigme became Secretary-General. The composition of the fifty-one-member committee ensured that China and its supporters held a majority.

When the Dalai Lama was just over twenty-one years old (in November 1956), he received an invitation from the Crown Prince of Sikkim to be present there at the 2,500th anniversary celebrations of the birth of Lord Buddha. To accept would also enable him to visit New Delhi. The invitation came at a crucial time. He wanted a break from the growing pressures in Tibet and the difficulties of dealing with the Chinese, who by then had wrested the power away from him and the Kashag. The Tibetan leadership had become mere figureheads in their own country. As the Dalai Lama has said, 'we desperately wanted sympathetic wise advice',[18] and he wanted to learn more, at first hand, about India's democracy. Accompanied by the Panchen Lama, after a long trek by pony, jeep and finally by car, the Dalai Lama was met in Sikkim by the Crown Prince and by all the Dalai Lama's family. In a small but significant incident the Tibetan flag, which flew alongside the Sikkimese state flag on the front of the government car in which the Dalai Lama was travelling, was torn down by a young Chinese person who dashed forward and replaced it with the Chinese pennant. After the joyous celebrations the two Tibetan leaders flew to New Delhi by air.

However, three days after he arrived there, Chinese Premier Zhou, accompanied by He Long, the general who had led the invasion of Tibet and was now responsible for its administration, arrived in New Delhi on their way to Europe. Since, in 1954, India had acknowledged Chinese sovereignty over Tibet, the Dalai Lama was now in a really difficult situation. His strong inclination was to stay in India indefinitely, and he was also being urged to do so. But in New Delhi, Indian prime minister Jawaharlal Nehru – with whom the Dalai Lama had several personal discussions – urged him to return to Tibet and work with the Chinese on the basis of the Seventeen-Point Agreement, saying also that 'India could not support you'. The Dalai Lama knew Zhou well, recognised his charm and honeyed words and thought him deceitful. At the first meeting in New Delhi the Chinese Premier gave the Dalai Lama a letter from Mao, which stated that communist reforms in Tibet 'would not be conducted during the Second Five-Year Plan period [1958–62]; whether reform should be conducted after six years would be decided by Tibet according to its own situation and conditions then'. (This assurance was rescinded after the Tibetan uprising of 1959.) At a second meeting with Zhou in New Delhi a week or so later, the Chinese Premier said that 'the situation in Tibet has deteriorated and the Chinese authorities are ready to use force to crush any popular uprising'. In March 1957 the Dalai Lama returned to Lhasa to face the crisis, with more fighting in the east and open warfare soon to come in Kham and Amdo as the Tibetans sought their freedom from Chinese control.

What precipitated a mass exodus of some 20,000 Khampas into U-Tsang was the flight of Chime Youngdong. As their king, he governed some 200,000 people around Jyekundo, to the far north-east of Lhasa. After Chinese atrocities against his people, he made the difficult journey to Lhasa with about a thousand followers to explain their plight to the Dalai Lama and to ask for help. He was described as 'sitting straight as a ruler on a large tan-coloured horse; a man of almost incredible beauty and taller by a head than any of the bodyguards clattering at his heels'. He arrived in Lhasa in February 1959. As the news of the Chinese atrocities in the east filtered through to the leadership and to ordinary Tibetans in Lhasa, which was already tense because of Chinese oppression, it stirred further unrest there and in other towns and villages. The situation in Tibet was beginning to get out of hand.

At the end of 1958 the Dalai Lama, after successfully completing the final stage of his examination – a series of gruelling debates – for the degree of Doctor of Buddhist Studies, left Lhasa in a splendidly colourful procession for the Norbulingka Summer Palace, four miles west of the capital. Politically, matters were coming to a head. Early in 1959 the Dalai Lama had, in response to a casual invitation from China's General Chiang Chin-wu, expressed an interest in seeing the performance of a Chinese dance troupe that was due to arrive shortly in Lhasa. The only place with a proper stage and footlights was the Chinese military headquarters. He was asked by the Chinese to choose a date for the performance, which he did, in two days' time. Shortly before the due date, the Chinese insisted that no Tibetan soldiers should accompany him, that his bodyguards should be unarmed and that the whole affair should be conducted in absolute secrecy. However, the news of this performance and the unusual arrangements quickly spread amongst the Tibetans. There was immediate alarm, fearing that the Dalai Lama was about to be kidnapped. Senior Tibetans attempted to persuade him not to attend, which at first he resisted. Rumours were rife. Tibetans poured out of Lhasa, headed for Norbulingka and surrounded all the entrances to the Jewel Park. In all, according to the Dalai Lama, some thirty thousand people (the Chinese put the figure at about two thousand) came with the aim of preventing him from leaving the Summer Palace and falling into the hands of the Chinese. Personal assurances from the Dalai Lama himself did not satisfy them.

General Tan Guansen, recently arrived in Lhasa, and Ngabo Ngawang Jigme, now openly sitting alongside the Chinese, then separately tried to lure the Dalai Lama into staying at the military headquarters 'for his own safety'. Additional letters made clear that the Chinese intended to attack the crowd and shell the Summer Palace. The Dalai Lama sent conciliatory and time-delaying replies. The State Oracle, having earlier advised the Dalai Lama to stay in Lhasa and pursue a dialogue with the Chinese, now upon second enquiry said: 'Go! Go! Tonight!'

Although a decision to leave Tibet had been made in the latter part of 1958, the right time had not yet come. There were no detailed plans. But now they were hurriedly put together in the utmost secrecy by Phala, the Dalai Lama's Court Chamberlain. On the evening of 17 March 1959 there was bad weather in Lhasa and poor visibility. At 10 PM the Dalai Lama, dressed as an ordinary soldier with a rifle slung over his shoulder, his cap pulled down over his eyes and a scarf covering the lower part of his face, walked in the dark through the gates of the Summer Palace into the crowd, with a small party of relatives and senior officials. The Tibetan who led them out said that they were going for a routine inspection. Earlier, as darkness fell, the crowd had been told not to use their torches (in case the Dalai Lama was recognised). The Dalai Lama's mother had left a short time before, dressed as a man with a toy rifle over her shoulder.

It was an extremely dangerous journey. The weather at first provided valuable cover. They were to travel by little-used, difficult and hazardous routes to evade detection. They surmounted two 17,000-foot mountain passes, the second during a blizzard with screaming high winds, when the Dalai Lama's eyebrows froze. The Chinese made frantic efforts to capture him. Spotter planes were sent out, but often the party was wrapped in clouds and for some time remained undetected. Then they were pursued from behind, and there was danger of being cut off at the front. There were some very narrow escapes. Once the Chinese were on the trail, they had to be delayed. Only great heroism from the Khampas saved the Dalai Lama's party. They were the long-range protectors, fearless for their own lives, many of which were lost in clashes with the pursuing Chinese. On 31 March the exhausted party, with a very ill Dalai Lama, crossed the border – into freedom.

Back in Lhasa on 20 March, with the demonstrations still active, the PLA was ordered to retake the city. They prepared thoroughly. At the same time the Khampas, now in Lhasa in large numbers, were moving arms and ammunition from secret stores in Potala Palace and from beneath Jokhang Temple. The Khampas had been enraged by the cruel behaviour of the Chinese in Kham, and this was their revenge. They had no fear. They would fight for the cause of saving Tibet and defeating the Chinese. The battles were extremely fierce, but uncoordinated. There were many heroes who displayed inspiring leadership. The Chinese were routed time and time again, their tanks put out of action and whole groups wiped out. But eventually, the PLA gained the upper hand. Suddenly, all was quiet. The Khampas packed up and left to fight another day. Probably between ten and twenty thousand Tibetans were killed, along with much greater numbers of Chinese. The shelling destroyed most of the Summer Palace, and the Tibetan bodies there were all examined by the Chinese to see if the Dalai Lama was amongst them – they did not realise that, by then, he was well away on his epic journey to the south. On 23 March the Chinese hoisted their flag over Potala Palace.

When later Mao was in Moscow, briefing Soviet premier Nikita Khrushchev on the successful Chinese crackdown of the 1959 'rebellion', Khrushchev asked, 'And what happened to the Dalai Lama?' 'He escaped,' replied Mao, with an air of 'good riddance'. 'Then you lost the war,' said Khrushchev.[19]

The Panchen Lamas were the most senior religious figures in Tibet after the Dalai Lamas – the 'moon' to the Dalai Lamas' 'sun'. The Fifth Dalai Lama created the position for his revered teacher, the abbot of Tashilhunpo monastery near Shigatse, in 1642, and invested it with spiritual but not secular authority. The Panchen Lamas were of the Gelugpa tradition of Tibetan Buddhism and thus, with the Dalai Lamas, consolidated spiritual leadership. The Dalai Lama was the administrative head of all of U-Tsang, with its capital Lhasa, except for the small part around Shigatse administered by the Panchen Lama.

After the Dalai Lama fled to India in 1959, Choekyi Gyaltsen, the twenty-one-year-old Panchen Lama, became the most senior religious person in Tibet. He was quickly appointed Chairman of the PCART (with Ngabo as Vice-Chairman) and therefore head of the Tibetan government. In 1960 he was also appointed Vice-Chairman of the Chinese People's Political Consultative Conference, which gave him the rank of a Chinese national leader. The Chinese had begun to see him as the successor to the departed Dalai Lama, for he was now the key figure in Tibet.

During 1959–62 the Panchen Lama travelled a great deal in U-Tsang, Xinjiang (East Turkestan to the north) and the Tibetan areas in Qinghai, Sichuan and Gansu provinces, and started writing a major report on his observations. In May 1962 he completed his work (123 numbered pages of Chinese characters in the Chinese version) and sent it to Mao through Premier Zhou. It was a devastating criticism of Chinese behaviour in Tibet during that period, and revealed in agonising detail the tragedy of a people under threat of survival. His report, known as the Seventy Thousand-Character Petition, was suppressed. Some of the criticisms were said to be so severe that the translators from Tibetan into Chinese refused to include them, finding them too dangerous. Few, if any, outside the narrow circle of the Chinese leadership had seen it. Mao later described it as 'a poisoned arrow aimed at the Party by reactionary feudal overlords'. Deng Xiaoping was, however, impressed by it. In 1980 Hu Yaobang, the Communist Party Secretary, had a meeting with the Panchen Lama at which no doubt Hu was informed of the Petition. Eventually, after thirty-four years, its secrets were revealed. In 1996 a copy of the Chinese translation from the Tibetan was unexpectedly delivered to the Tibet Information Network office, an independent news reporting agency in London led by Tibet specialist Robert Barnett. It was translated into English by three teams checking and cross-checking each other's work, and checked again by a series of readers; in 1997 it was published. It is an extraordinary and revealing document and a major contribution to understanding the truth. As Professor Dawa Norbu says in an introduction to the published work:'His [the Panchen Lama's] Petition is based on a fearless confrontation with the realities of contemporary China and Tibet, on first-hand experience, on on-the-spot observation and on rigorous empirical analysis.'

The report, titled 'A Report on the Sufferings of the Masses in Tibet and Other Tibetan Regions and Suggestions for Future Work to the Central Authorities Through the Respected Premier Zhou',[20] began diplomatically in its second paragraph with honeyed words in praise of China, no doubt to encourage Mao to a favourable frame of mind:

In the vast land of our beloved, holy and pure Great China with beautiful mountains and rivers, where there are all things above earth and rich resources hidden beneath, the great and glorious Chinese Communist Party, saviour of people of all nationalities, and the great leader of the people, the great, correct and wise Chairman Mao, led the broad masses of the working people with the Chinese working class in the vanguard, caused the great wave of the Great Proletarian Revolution to surge up to the heavens, fought a series of class battles with reactionary cliques at home and abroad ...

As for our region of Tibet, under the radiant illumination of the Party and of the Great Thought of Chairman Mao, it formally obtained peaceful liberation in 1951 ... Tibet returned to the great family of the motherland. Since then, the people of Tibet have affirmed their wish to walk along the glorious road of democracy and socialism, together with people of all nationalities in the motherland ...[21]

And so it continues, in fine declamatory style. The devastating criticisms which followed were balanced against statements of the right things that had been done within the context of the high-level policies for China as a whole. Thus, on the 'suppression of the rebellion' in 1959:

The rebellion in Tibet was counter-revolutionary in nature, being against the Party, the motherland, the people, democracy and socialism. Its crimes were very grave. Thus it was entirely correct, essential, necessary and appropriate for the Party to adopt the policy of suppressing the rebellion. But later it emerged that the cadres were at fault. They wanted to suppress the people so they attacked them by falsely accusing and slandering them. People chanting Buddhist scriptures were regarded as counter-revolutionaries, suppressed and attacked. The cadres did not carry out investigation and study but just believed groundless rumours that 'a rebellion has taken place'.[22]

On other matters criticisms are made followed by acknowledgments that something is being done to rectify the situation. The whole report was a *tour de force* description of the terrible sufferings of the Tibetan people, their starvation due to the forced collectivisation of agriculture (inhabitants of many whole villages died), oppression, the attempted eclipse of Buddhism by destroying the monasteries, the expulsion of 93 percent of monks and nuns, the forced abortions (which began in Tibet in 1955) and enforced sterilisations of young women, the severe disruption to the lives of ordinary people, the attempts to destroy their culture, the mistakes of the Chinese cadres ... The words 'errors and mistakes' appear regularly on most pages, also 'not done in accordance with the policy', 'was not carried out properly' and 'this was very bad and should not have happened'. There were, however, a few 'slight turns for the better'. The whole report seemed to be leading to the conclusion that much more genuine autonomy should be granted to the Tibetan people to manage their own affairs, but that proposal was not made explicit.

Premier Zhou's comments on the document were complimentary, and he asked for suggestions. But when the Panchen Lama started making speeches drawn from his findings, finishing with 'Long live the Dalai Lama!', he was arrested. Then, two years after completion of the report, in September 1964, the Panchen Lama began a fifty-day series of 'struggle sessions' – interrogation by the Chinese, abuse and humiliation in front of an audience of thousands of people. He was branded 'an enemy of the Party, an enemy of the people and an enemy of socialism'. Confessions were demanded. Accusations were repeated time and again: 'Confess! Confess!' He was imprisoned in China for over nine years, and then was under house arrest. He was released in 1978 but did not return to Tibet until 1982.

The Panchen Lama then set up the Tibet Development Fund, the first NGO started from within Tibet, to attract funds for its economic development. He launched the Ganggyen Corporation, a model of entrepreneurial organisation some of whose profits supported the Tashilhunpo monastery, and a school for senior *lamas* in Beijing. He was also instrumental in setting up the Tibetan University in Lhasa. He lobbied for and succeeded in introducing a law making Tibetan the official language in Tibet and he set the timetable for introducing Tibetan medium education from primary school to university. Much earlier, when he was only eighteen, he had set up a school in Shigatse for 300 students selected from his estates with an unconventional curriculum. Thus, in a practical way he was an innovator and a natural organiser who also understood well how business worked, using these talents in support of the Tibetan people.

He also continued his criticism of the Chinese rule in Tibet. In a public address on 17 January 1989, he affirmed that most of what he had written in 1962 remained true and in some respects had worsened. He repeated his criticism to Hu Jintao, the newly arrived Party Secretary in Tibet, declaring that the Chinese occupation had brought more destruction than benefit to the Tibetan people. Four days later on 28 January, at the age of fifty-three, the Panchen Lama died from a heart attack under rather mysterious circumstances. Many Tibetans believe he was poisoned. After his death, in the mid-1990s, much of what he had initiated on behalf of the Tibetan people was systematically reversed by the Chinese. Hugh Richardson's earlier remark that the Panchen Lama was the foremost puppet of the Chinese was premature, but at the time he wrote his history of Tibet he was unaware of the Panchen Lama's Seventy Thousand-Character Petition. The Panchen Lama was a brave and heroic supporter of the Tibetan people.

Superficially the matters reported in 1962 were similar to the International Commission of Jurists' (ICJ's) fact-finding report of 1960 based on the Universal Declaration of Human Rights, but the detail is much greater and the means of collection used by the Panchen Lama – because of his authority and position of trust – were not available to the ICJ. It is tragic that this detailed indictment of Chinese behaviour in Tibet could not have been made available to the UN at the time it was written. There is no doubt that it could have strengthened the resolution of the General Assembly in coming to its conclusions and might well have changed subsequent UN policy.

FIVE

The Great Helmsman: Disaster

> 'Heaven and earth are ruthless;
> They see the ten thousand things as dummies.
> The wise are ruthless;
> they see the people as dummies.'
> *Lao-tzu*, Tao Te Ching,[1] *Chapter Five*

In 1950 there were still approximately a million bandits marauding through the countryside in China, creating havoc and misery. Industry was in ruins. There remained only about 13,000 miles of extremely damaged railway.[2] Unemployment in the cities was vast, and in parts of China there was famine. Even Beijing was short of food. Many people with money, fearing what communism and the promised egalitarianism might mean for them, had already left China. Many were welcomed in the US where, from 1945, Senator Joe McCarthy had been fanatically spreading the message of anti-communism. Others fled to Taiwan, now restored to Nationalist control after the defeat of Japan, and many more fled to Hong Kong. However, recovery was helped by the immense enthusiasm amongst vast numbers of people remaining in China, young and old. The military was self-disciplined, polite and helpful, as Mao and Zhu De had trained it to be. There was a great sense of relief and euphoria at the prospect of a more equal society in conditions of peace and stability.

Mao and the Communist Party leadership were very aware of the importance of effective public administration if anything was to be done well.

Even before Chiang Kai-shek was defeated, they had established government administrations in Manchuria and northern China as the Nationalists were driven south. In 1950 the Communist leadership in Beijing worked as a team with the military, which initially played a large part at higher levels in government administration, with Party leaders and others. (Most of the leadership had two roles, in government and the Party.) Zhou Enlai, Liu Shaoqi, Zhu De and Deng Xiaoping were all Mao's long-standing friends. They and others less senior had worked with him over many years and had the self-confidence to argue about policies without fear, although there were rivalries, jealousies and some plotting. At lower levels of administration in the provinces, some 2 million cadres from the defeated Nationalist government were retained because the CCP could not muster even half this number. At this time Mao appreciated the importance also of an appropriate legal framework applicable to the whole of China. In 1949 he set up a law commission and in 1954 transferred it to the Bureau of Legislation. During the first ten years of the PRC, 1,581 laws, regulations and codes of practice were issued, of which one half were economic in character.[3]

After more than half a century of conflict, destruction, dislocation, upheaval and unrest in China, a period of peace and calm under a wise and compassionate administration of good men and women with virtue would have been a good idea and appeared to be possible. But it was not to be.

In 1950 Mao's military priority was to launch an invasion of Taiwan. Chiang had taken refuge there the previous year, and it had been governed by the Nationalists since 1945. In 1949 Chiang had declared Taipei the provisional capital of all China, an extreme insult to Mao. Exploratory attacks had been made by capturing Hainan island from the Nationalists in April 1950 and there were preparations for attacking Quemoy prior to the main assault on Taiwan.

But in June 1950, with the approval of Stalin, North Korea under Kim Il Sung attacked South Korea with the aim of reunifying the two Koreas. It was an ill-judged venture, and soon Kim was in trouble. He appealed for help from Mao, who was at first most reluctant to become involved. China had colonised Korea for 400 years (first to third century AD) and had exercised suzerainty over that country prior to the Japanese occupation. To help Kim Il Sung control the whole country over which China itself had historical claims was not very appealing. However, Stalin half-promised air cover and munitions if Mao would enter the war. The PLA calculated that if it went to Kim's aid it would lose around 60,000 soldiers with 140,000 wounded in the first year alone. This would have been a considerable sacrifice for perhaps little direct benefit to China. But when the UN endorsed the US's aim of supporting

South Korea (in effect a US protectorate) to reunite the two Koreas from the south, the situation became extremely serious. A majority of the Politburo was still against intervention, but Mao decided to go ahead with or without Russian support. His position as the supreme authority was such that he could overrule the majority even on matters of war or peace. China entered the war on 19 October 1950, and all told committed some 2.3 million troops to it.

Using well-tried tactics of flexibility, surprise and withdrawal until enemy supplies became overstretched and the men exhausted, the Chinese People's Volunteers – as the Korean military force was called – won great victories. They advanced down the peninsula, across the Thirty-eighth Parallel, to capture Seoul, the South's capital. It was a triumph for Mao and his wise and experienced commander-in-chief, Marshal Peng Dehuai. Even Stalin was impressed. The US then seriously considered using the atomic bomb against the Chinese invaders.[4] In December 1950 the British prime minister, Clement Attlee, flew to Washington to persuade President Harry S. Truman against this plan.

The Americans themselves had begun to have doubts, but they need not have worried; Mao's pride and political wisdom then overcame his military sense. He overrode Marshal Peng's judgment in the field, and catastrophe resulted.[5] It was mid-winter, and the Chinese were ill-equipped for such cold. American reinforcements hastened to the front, and were too strong. The Chinese withdrew in disarray; Mao's eldest son, Anying, was killed. It was a vast setback for the new regime and a personal tragedy for Mao. The war ended in stalemate, and China lost 148,400 men with some 250,000 wounded. There were huge anti-American demonstrations across China. The war also led the US to use its fleet to police the Taiwan Strait in order to discourage a revival of the earlier planned invasion. The other war, against Tibet, had begun on 7 October 1950, the day before Mao issued the decree to create the Chinese People's Volunteers for Korea. Militarily it was a small affair, almost a side issue against the huge Korean commitment.

Social engineering, political and ideological indoctrination, persecution and the attempted enforcement of moral behaviour are characteristic of Chinese history. The Legalist rules of the First Emperor in the third century BC were the model, and Mao had taken them to heart. First, in the winter of 1950, came the 'Campaign to Suppress the Counter-Revolutionaries'. In six months some 710,000 people were executed or driven to suicide. More than 1.5 million disappeared into the newly established 'Reform Through Labour' camps. Most of these casualties were, or were thought to be, connected in some way with the Kuomintang.

Then, in the autumn of 1951, there was the 'Three Antis' campaign: anti-corruption, anti-waste and anti-bureaucratism. It was designed to prevent the 'corrosion of the cadres by the bourgeoisie'. The writer Jung Chang describes the effects, as her father saw them, as creating a new attitude towards public property.[6] Cadres would no longer treat the public's money as their own or abuse their positions. Even ink in offices, when used for private purposes, came from one's own pen. There was a good side to this campaign, to some effect.

This was followed early in 1952 by the overlapping 'Five Antis' campaign (known colloquially as the 'Anti-Five Poisonous Creatures'): anti-bribery, anti-tax evasion, anti-fraud, anti-embezzlement and anti-leakage of state secrets. This was aimed at the capitalist classes, especially factory owners and merchants. Many such persons had been engaged in the bribery of cadres, tax evasion and other inappropriate behaviour. Since, at this stage, Mao needed these people for economic reasons, the punishments were usually fines and few were imprisoned.

Even though the work teams that implemented these campaigns had been vetted and trained, the downsides were considerable. Activists set up 'tiger-hunting' teams to drag out presumed offenders for humiliation before massed meetings. Workers denounced their bosses, cadres exposed each other, children informed on their parents, wives turned against husbands. Several hundred thousand died, mostly by suicide. The human, social and economic costs were huge. A vast number of people were traumatised by these experiences, and families broken up. Deep unhappiness, mistrust and dislocation of long-standing social relationships resulted. The entire population was involved in the machinery of control. This created divisions in society which did not exist before, and a climate of terror developed. By mid-1953, however, the two campaigns had wound down. Inevitably some of the worst effects were long-lasting – trauma, distrust, hatred and social dislocation.

Next, in 1952, came the 'Thought Reform Movement' – again following the First Emperor – designed to remould urban intellectuals to enforce conformity and eradicate bourgeois ideas. Anything incompatible with Mao's orthodoxy would be condemned and eliminated through self-criticism in small groups.[7] It was the first attempt to influence these important people, who are not by nature readily responsive to such manipulation. Worse was to follow later.

By 1956 the government had begun to buy out private businesses – to 'clean up inside the house' as Mao declared. They were valued by committees of three: a government official, a worker in the factory and the owner. Owners were overruled by the other two, and low valuations were set. Even then, owners received only about one-third of what was decided, supposedly paid in instalments over seven years. Many owners became labourers in their own factories, their self-respect dissipated, their skills wasted, and their health often fatally undermined.

Help from the Soviet Union was crucial at this early stage, especially material help. But the Soviet so-called planning system, while it focused priorities through Five-Year Plans, was a dead end in terms of managing the economy. Production programmes were issued from the top and prices were determined from central authorities, which suited Mao's style. But a Soviet-style 'command economy' was useless to China – the basic circumstances of the two countries were very different, and it did not work in the Soviet Union anyway.[8] Public ownership was central to both the Soviet and Chinese systems, and ensured protection from foreign competition. All these – command economy, public ownership and protection – created massive inefficiencies and corruption, which had long-lasting deleterious effects.

Parallel to the two 'antis' campaigns was the drive for small cooperatives and collectivisation in agriculture with the elimination of landlords and rich farmers. This had started in Manchuria and north-east China after the Nationalists retreated from these areas in 1948. Collectivisation was developed in stages. By the end, the results were Agricultural Producers' Cooperatives, which were usually part or all of a village, later called 'production teams'. Groups of these teams formed brigades and by 1958 brigades were grouped into communes. It was, in fact, 'a long, drawn-out, increasingly bitter and devastating struggle to fend off a type of serfdom under Party control'.[9] The individual farmer found himself under a hierarchy of six levels of administration. There were eventually some 70,000 communes, under which were 750,000 brigades and under them some 5 million production teams. On top of this, the state established a centralised grain monopoly to create central stockpiles, with each family allocated amounts for their own consumption according to circumstances. By the end of 1956, only about 3 percent of peasants still farmed as individuals. This campaign destroyed centuries of tradition and ways of working which had been found the most effective in the widely different circumstances in which crops are grown in China.

In Tibet the attempts at collectivisation also had devastating effects. In 1955 there was serious fighting between Tibetans and Chinese, first in Kham and Amdo to the east: the Kanding Rebellion. Kanding was the demarcation between Tibetan and Chinese culture, where collectivisation was most resisted. Chinese officials and others were killed. However, the rebellion was put down by the PLA and land was redistributed to the peasants. Many Khampas and others fled to central Tibet. For sound practical reasons of altitude and climate, Tibetans grew barley, not wheat, but it was the latter which China wanted and enforced. Also, in Kham and Amdo, attempts were made to herd nomads together, and their survival techniques were overridden. Hunger and then starvation resulted.

However, many survived the process of collectivisation in China, as in Russia, by cheating: keeping two sets of team books, under-reporting, padding expenses, keeping new fields hidden from brigade inspectors and using many other devices. The new relationships and procedures were a breeding ground for corruption. Collectivisation sapped the energies of the countryside for a generation to come,[10] causing a levelling of rural society that stifled independent initiative, de-motivated the most productive, rewarded the least able and replaced the rule of the landlords and intelligentsia with rule by the Party – whose members enjoyed power and privilege unconstrained by the fear of banditry and rebellion that, for centuries past, had kept their predecessors in check.

In April 1955 Mao set off for the countryside to assess progress. Of course, officials said what they wanted him to hear, which often bore no relation to reality. The livelihood of cadres was bound up with the appearance of success. Mao thought collectivisation was a huge success. But after his death twenty-one years later, it was abandoned.

In 1955 Mao declared that the bourgeoisie in the cities should be dealt with 'once and for all. Our aim is to exterminate capitalism, obliterate it from the face of the earth and make it a thing of the past.'[11] By 1956 all private businesses had been taken over by the state.

There seems nothing in modern China that does not have its forerunner in the mists of time. 'Let a hundred flowers blossom and a hundred schools of thought contend' was a slogan to encourage free speech in the Han dynasty some two thousand years previously (when it also became popular to assign numbers to important campaigns or events).[12] In May 1956 Mao revived this entreatment (so did Jiang Zemin, in July 2001), but intellectuals waited a year before responding; they knew the dangers. However, in May 1957 they let loose a barrage of complaints that the Party had turned into a new privileged bureaucratic class which monopolised power and had alienated itself from the people. It had become the new aristocracy. There were hundreds of thousands of criticisms. As the movement gathered momentum, Mao himself was increasingly criticised. Appalled, he retired to his bed, depressed and apparently immobilised, to plan a counter-attack: 'We want to coax the snakes out of their holes. Then we will strike. My strategy is to let the poisonous weeds grow first and then destroy them one by one. Let them become fertiliser.'[13]

In June the 'Hundred Flowers' movement was closed down, and in the ensuing Anti-Rightist Campaign around 500,000 leading intellectuals and cadres were arrested and sent to labour camps. Many died from ill treatment. Mao said that about 5 percent of cadres were 'rightists', and so many local Party secretaries set a target of 5 percent to be arrested and many innocent people had to endure years of imprisonment. All told, some 6 million people, most of them Party members or low-level officials, were criticised and harassed for allegedly opposing Mao's policies. Suicides were common.

'Blooming and contending', as the policy became known, was controversial from the start. Cadres at all levels feared what might be revealed. Many intellectuals were worried that Mao's public assurances – he went around the country speaking in its favour and bludgeoning the press to support it – were opposite to his private thoughts and plans. Perhaps he wanted to smoke out potentially dangerous opposition, they suspected. They were right.

That Anti-Rightist Campaign, strongly supported by Deng Xiaoping – then General Secretary of the Communist Party – was severely damaging to China's future. The people arrested were mainly those who made the whole machinery of government work, and who understood the problems of administration in the vast country of China. The intellectuals had access to foreign publications and had worked with university-trained and experienced leading cadres. Since the Soviet-style Ministry of Higher Education was set up in 1952, specialised foreign – mainly Soviet – textbooks had become available. These were the people who should have been conducting policy analysis, giving impartial advice to the Party leadership and then taking the lead in implementing whatever was decided. But they were gone. Others were, for example, leading doctors and surgeons, so the quality of medical care – which had increased during the warlord era – began to decline. Many were teachers, so the quality of education was eroded.

At the beginning of the 'Great Leap Forward' which then followed, with the economic aim of modernisation, Mao and the whole leadership needed such people, experts in a wide range of disciplines and the experienced administrators. But now they were working as manual labourers under strict discipline and supervision in the countryside, or dead. Those who replaced these leading cadres were 'fundamentalists' in Marxism–Leninism–Mao Zedong Thought. They lacked knowledge of the outside world, were anti-intellectual and inexperienced, with only a minimal understanding of China's problems of modernisation. The scene was set for disaster.

In 1949, shortly before the Nationalists were defeated, Mao said: 'We shall have to master what we do not know. We must learn to do economic work from all who know how, no matter who they are … We must acknowledge our ignorance and not to pretend to know what we do not know.' So he called in the Russians, who drew up a Five-Year Plan in their own manner and built more than 100 large heavy-industrial plants which became the core of Chinese state enterprises. The remaining private businesses were to become partners with the state. In 1952 Gao Gang, an able senior Politburo member who had the confidence of Mao, was appointed head of the new State Planning Commission, set up along Soviet lines. But Gao had ambitions to replace Mao, who had begun to talk of retiring from the top position, to leave the running of the Party and the economy to younger men. Gao developed a secret conspiracy to oust Mao. He was unmasked and committed suicide.

It must have been extremely disconcerting to the Chinese leadership in 1956 to hear Khrushchev's outspoken denunciation of Stalin as a 'brutal psychopath ... with a persecution mania of unbelievable dimensions ... whose personality cult had concealed a capricious, despotic rule ... whose "military genius" had brought Russia to the verge of defeat by Germany ... and whose sickly suspicion and mistrust had sent millions of innocent men and women to cruel and unnecessary deaths'. Not only had the CCP leaned on Russian advice and expertise for so long, but there were uncomfortable parallels with Stalin already beginning in China at this time. Mao was furious with Khrushchev for this public condemnation. Even though Mao, too, hated Stalin, Khrushchev had been disloyal to Stalin and to Mao disloyalty amongst revolutionaries was a major sin.

In 1956 Mao launched what was later called the 'Little Leap Forward' to jump-start the economy. According to Marxist theory, economic development came before and led to social change. The Little Leap failed because local cadres set impossibly high targets, and peasants and factory workers went on strike. Targets were taken from thin air and were ill-matched to capacity and material supply. In yet another 'campaign', to help agricultural production and promote good health, 'Four Pests' had to be eliminated. This would make China a country of 'four nos' – no rats, no sparrows, no flies and no mosquitoes. The whole population was mobilised. Mao was told that eliminating all the sparrows would lead to a plague of caterpillars, advice he ignored. However, after the massive destruction of sparrows and the consequential infestation of crops by caterpillars that devoured everything, the target was changed to bedbugs.

By 1957 the Chinese leadership had begun to realise that the Soviet system was quite inappropriate to Chinese conditions. China's population was four times bigger than USSR, while its standard of living was only about one half. Moreover, Chinese collectivisation had not increased agricultural production, and urbanisation had outstripped industrialisation; unemployment had also risen. So Mao adopted the dual approach – 'Walking on Two Legs' – the simultaneous development of agriculture and industry.

He tried again. China would obtain the highest crop yields in the world. Steel production would increase by four times (to 20 million tons). Later, in 1957, he promised to overtake Britain's steel production to 40 million tons annually by the 1970s. The same bullish targets were set for cement, coal, chemical fertilisers and machine tools. To find out how to achieve these, Mao set out to seek 'truth from facts' in a four-month tour of China. As before, he was shown only what the provincial authorities wanted him to see. Peasants were mobilised to tend crops that had been transplanted alongside miles of railway track so that Mao could see the appearance of a bumper harvest, whereas in fact it was a disaster. He ended with the illusion of being well-informed which was far more dangerous than ignorance.[14] In fact, Mao was not quite as ignorant as has been supposed: Hua Guofeng, who was to be Mao's chosen successor, had told him of the deception.[15] But, as a result of Mao's 'findings', targets were raised: 60 million tons of steel by 1960, 100 million tons by 1962, then 700 million tons by the 1970s. The 1958 grain target rose first to 300 million tons (a 50 percent increase on the previous record), then to 350 million tons. It would come about through technical revolution and correct socialist policies. Mao's credo at this time was: 'Go all-out, aim high and build socialism with greater, faster, better and more economical results.'[16]

Those remaining amongst technical staff following the Anti-Rightist campaign, and who urged more caution, were in great danger of being called 'anti-Marxist' and labelled 'rightist', so they kept quiet. But they were right. It was all completely unrealistic, not based on understanding of what was required. Mao had been to only one country abroad, Russia, and then not to observe steelworks, cement works or fertiliser plants in operation or to talk with their managers. He did not appreciate the huge inefficiencies of the Russian manufacturing and agricultural systems. At that time only one person was prepared to ask awkward questions – Chen Yun, a Politburo member since 1934 – and he was quickly sidelined. (Later, under Deng, he was to become crucial to economic policy.) Many top-echelon cadres and leading intellectuals who had breadth of experience and enquiring minds had all been arrested. But, it was thought, Mao could do no wrong. No one dared to challenge him.

There were primitive iron foundries all over China, at the peak at least 600,000 of them. Pots and pans were taken away in triumph by Party members, and iron railings, locks on doors, radiators for heating and many other metallic objects were despatched to primitive, steaming, red-hot cauldrons. People were given quotas for finding them, and children were enlisted. Public canteens were set up so that no time would be wasted cooking at home, and cooking utensils disappeared from people's homes into furnaces. One commune leader explained that he had learned steelmaking from a newspaper article. Factories, government offices, universities, schools and even writers' associations all had their own foundries. Steelmaking went on twenty-four hours a day, seven days a week. At the peak of the Great Leap some 90 million people – about one quarter of the active population – had given up their normal jobs, including farming, to participate. It was a remarkable demonstration of the enthusiasm of the people for Mao's leadership, and of their willingness to make sacrifices.

Mao had come to believe that ordinary people, especially the peasants – if well-motivated – could achieve anything. Intellectuals were simply not needed. For all this immensely dedicated effort and enthusiasm, most of the so-called steel was unusable.[17] When Mao was shown ingots alongside a 'model' furnace during a visit from his special train, they had in fact been brought specially from a conventional steel plant. Also, backyard furnaces had been built for one *li* (about one-third of a mile) on either side of the rail tracks to create the impression of vast numbers. When people were told to start cooking their own meals again, the woks and the pots and pans had gone. In 1961 the decision was taken to scrap all these furnaces.

In other ways the Great Leap Forward achieved remarkable results, which had a lasting impact – the construction of new roads, dams, dykes, lakes, new cities and factories, more afforestation and land cultivation. There was a fervent application of manual effort by millions of peasants in which all levels in society took part including the leadership, and even Mao himself for one hour – a labour that was photographed for the nation's newspapers. (As Mao's physician, Dr Li Zhisui, remarked: 'Never in humankind has such a symbolic gesture galvanised a nation to such a frenzy of enthusiastic, backbreaking work.') These projects were useful to society, and Mao wanted the whole nation to see how good and worthwhile was the manual labour on which the new China would be built.

In 1958 seven administrative regions had been established, each required to build its own 'Independent Industrial Structure'. Most of the smaller central government state-owned enterprises were transferred to local government administrations; only the largest remained with the centre. The institutional framework was there to establish 'Five Small-Scale Industries' (including mining, cement, mechanical engineering and steel). Everyone felt the excitement of rebuilding China. It was a remarkable demonstration of national unity and effort. Also, in 1958, there began a long campaign to 'sweep away illiteracy', which was beneficial to women.

While the steel fiasco was a horrendous waste of resources, the most tragic consequences occurred in agriculture. The harvest in 1958 was above average, but most of it could not be collected because so many peasants were working on Great Leap Forward projects elsewhere. Grain allocation and distribution had been centralised. Grain yields and production had been grossly overstated by local cadres in efforts to show with pride how successful the policies handed down from above had been, and how deserving of praise and rewards. But the reported doubling of output led to corresponding increases in grain allocation from the centre, and the cities received more grain to meet the rising urban population. Since in fact output was down the following year – bad weather in 1959, the adverse effects of collectivisation, the continuing loss of agricultural labour on the projects, all together with rural migration to the cities – what was left for the peasants was a fraction of that required for subsistence, less than half of their minimum needs. Monthly ration coupons were severely cut. Malnutrition and starvation resulted. Between 1958 and 1960 some 20–30 million Chinese died along with a further 5 million in 1961, when grain imports began to ease the shortages. Cannibalism in the countryside was widely reported. Tibetans suffered alongside the Chinese, especially in Kham and Amdo, the eastern provinces. Whole families starved to death. It was a vast, Mao-induced human tragedy, the worst ever in China's long history, which no amount of government propaganda could long conceal.

What went wrong? Mao's roots were in the countryside and amongst the peasants. There he felt most at home and at his most confident. But after October 1949 he faced an entirely different range of problems in the military and political spheres in which he excelled. He thought there was more to learn about development from history than from textbooks of modern engineering.[18] So much was now unfamiliar, including many technical questions (scrap metal, the basis of the Great Leap Forward, is useful in properly designed steelworks and under quality control, as in American 'mini-mills', but obviously has its limits). People who knew the answers were never consulted. Mao 'accepted only with the greatest reluctance the need to call upon the services of a modern intellectual elite for which he felt an instant and almost uncontrollable mistrust and dislike'.[19]

To try to recover the ground lost in agriculture and industry, and to correct the mismanagement of the whole economy, the government adopted a Legalist (First Emperor) approach to uniformity and change. In 1961–2 it issued 'Seventy Codes of Conduct for Industries, Sixty Codes for Agriculture, Forty Codes for Commerce and Six Codes for the State Budget'.[20] The low degree of literacy, especially amongst the peasants, and the need for cadres to interpret these codes and to implement them conferred considerable power and opportunities for corruption.

Social change would follow economic development, according to Karl

Marx. A classless society was the aim. This would involve the repression of the ruling classes – all except workers and peasants. The six-year period leading up to the Cultural Revolution was one of economic revival largely through investment in new state enterprises and their growth in employment; massive forced population transfer from the cities to the countryside, where small-scale enterprises developed; rectification of local cadres through the 'Four Cleanups' campaign; and a new approach to political education.

But the leadership was in complete disarray. Mao's close-knit supporters had found his judgment lacking, first in launching the Hundred Flowers campaign against their advice and then in the panic measure of the Anti-Rightist campaign. They had to get him out of the hole he had dug for himself. Then the disasters of the Great Leap Forward revealed his absurd and disastrous attempt to solve China's technical problems of modernisation by returning to those he trusted and knew best – the common people of the land. Not only had he alienated the intellectuals, but now he had failed the common people – and they knew it. Mao was on a slippery slope. He now 'lived a life of total exclusion, suspicious of everyone, never attending official meetings and rarely dealing directly with the Party apparatus'.[21]

At the Wuchang Conference in December 1958 he was forced to relinquish his position as Head of State in favour of Liu Shaoqi. But Liu was a loyal and obedient servant to Mao, who therefore effectively retained the power. However, at the Lushan Conference of July–August 1959, there was a direct attack on Mao and his policies – especially the Great Leap Forward – led by Marshal Peng, who voiced the concerns of many others in the leadership. He had been with Mao for thirty years, was a member of the Politburo, fourteenth in the Party hierarchy, a successful leader during the Long March, Minister of Defence, tenth in seniority in the PLA and its leader in Korea and extremely popular with both the army and the people. In other words, he was a well-informed heavyweight (although Philip Short describes him as 'an irascible, pig-headed old soldier'[22]). But criticism from him was taken to mean outright opposition. He was accused by Mao of being a 'rightist' and anti-Party, and in this condemnation Mao was supported by Deng. To trump Marshal Peng's card, Liu, as the new Head of State, was given real power. Liu knew that Marshal Peng was right and that Mao had to be restrained, but to save the regime he had to condemn the marshal and safeguard Mao's prestige. So Peng and his two supporters were stripped of all their positions, although they retained their titles and Peng his membership of the Politburo, which he never again attended. His long and distinguished career was finished. Apart from these massive indignities, none of them was punished physically. However, good and loyal men were lost to the government, and the former unity of the

Politburo was undermined. No member of it was ever again openly critical of Mao.

The marshal's supporters and Liu's strengthened team tried to ensure that Mao became 'a sort of ancient totem: everyone genuflected to him but he was completely powerless in his wooden immobility'.[23] Liu wooed some intellectuals back to help with reconstruction after the many disasters, but discarded them again in 1962 when their help was completed. Mao remained partly in the background until 1965. He was constantly criticised, often in clever parables with references to historical figures from China's past. There was a serious attempt to destroy his political existence forever. A dossier of his errors was prepared, but never used for fear that the whole regime would fall. Liu saw himself as Mao's successor.

Mao began to plot his own rehabilitation. The period of the Cultural Revolution (1966–76), has often been described as 'China's ten lost years', but in truth they had started in 1957 and were twenty lost years. From 1957 the Communist leadership under the firm hand of Mao had made mistake after mistake on a vast scale, and millions of people had died.

His supporters were the ever-loyal Zhou Enlai and Marshal Lin Biao. Lin was a very competent military strategist but was consumed by desire for political power. He had led the denunciation of Marshal Peng and, as his reward, was given the marshal's former post of Minister of Defence. Lin used this to develop some military initiatives, including the formation of 'elite companies' which were to play a large part in the Cultural Revolution. Mao himself tried several initiatives, but they were all thwarted or ignored. Lin formed 'departments of political work' in the army and transferred some 200,000 troops into civilian life for purposes then unclear. Officers took over important propaganda functions from the Party.

Frustrated in Beijing, Mao cultivated the propaganda machine in Shanghai through his wife, Jiang Qing, the Shanghai actress he had married in Yan'an. Shanghai became the pace-setter for the Cultural Revolution. The Party's Central Committee sent a Group of Five there to investigate the cultural purge against feudal and capitalist thinking that Mao appeared to be initiating – and they fell into the trap he had prepared. Then Mao planned to corner his rivals by setting out to destroy the Party and to sink the whole regime – for the reinstatement of his own personal power.

That anyone should even contemplate such an awesome strategy to be inflicted on his own people, to destroy what he had been instrumental in creating all his adult life, seemed a bizarre insanity. Yet that is what Mao did. At the highest level of political ambition was his absolute priority to make China a realm of 'Red virtue', a socialist paradise, a classless society the whole world would admire and ultimately copy. 'Spiritual regeneration,' as Mao put it, 'was to take precedence over economic development.'[24] To be poor in a socialist utopia was better than to be rich in a capitalist hell. To smash the 'Four Olds' – old thought, old culture, old customs and old practices – would get rid of the past with its bourgeois tendencies and leave the people like a blank sheet of paper on which the new orthodoxy could be inscribed.

Mao also saw the effects of 'revisionism' under Khrushchev in the USSR, where a new ruling class was emerging with the downgrading of egalitarian principles. At a practical level he was also deeply concerned that the rural cadres had become the new privileged class in China and were highly corrupt – the main message from the Hundred Flowers movement. At a personal level he was clearly outraged and frustrated at the persistent attempts by many of his colleagues in the leadership to keep him as if under lock and key where, as they saw it, he could do no more damage. He had fought to save China once by being cunning and courageous, and by 1949 had been supremely successful. Now he had to be equally cunning and courageous to save the revolution.

His ally in bringing this about was Marshal Lin and the army, with its civilian wing. In August 1966 the university youth, largely the children of the Party elite and intellectuals – the Red Guards as they became known[25] – were mobilised to lead the new revolution. Ultimately there were some 10 million youths caught in this network of violence. They were the 'angry young men and women' of their time. With the hormones of youth rushing round their bodies and rebellion against parents on their minds, they were ideal to lead a fight. They were first unleashed on their teachers, who suffered unbearably, many dying in the most cruel manner. Next, they and older revolutionaries were to attack the Party, the cadres and everyone in authority including supposed counter-revolutionaries. Havoc was unleashed. Mao, then seventy-two years old, had escaped from his enemies, and through many devious, well-plotted and brilliantly executed manoeuvres, regained power. The Great Proletarian Cultural Revolution was, however, not truly 'proletarian', because it was conducted principally by school teenagers and young university students who for these purposes were considered 'workers'. It had nothing to do with 'culture', except in the purely destructive sense, and was not a spontaneous 'revolution' – the class conflicts were created as policy. It was, in truth, a vast power struggle in the name of socialism, and was described as such in the official newspapers from the beginning of 1967.

The events of the Cultural Revolution have been written about many times, by historians and by those who suffered and survived.[26] The accusations, indescribable tortures and deaths – it is estimated that some 400,000 people died as a result of maltreatment – directly involving some 100 million people, started with the teachers and then spread to anyone seemingly in authority. Condemning teachers was a spectacular departure from the past – since the time of Confucius, teachers had always been shown the greatest honour and respect. About 60 percent of Party officials were purged. The killings, the ruining of the lives of so many innocent people, the tearing apart of families, the wanton vandalism and destruction of China's cultural and artistic past (to 'burn the books and bury the scholars alive', as had been done under the First Emperor two thousand years before), were all a form of collective insanity.

Love and compassion evaporated. People were divided into either the 'Five Reds' who could obtain the Little Red Book, or *The Quotations of Chairman Mao* (factory workers, poor and lower-middle class peasants, soldiers and officers of the PLA, Party officials and revolutionary martyrs) or the 'Five Blacks' (former landlords, rich peasants, counter-revolutionaries, rightists and former capitalists), the 'shit-smelling class who exploit the workers'. The Blacks were subject to terrible persecution. Amongst the evil horrors of the time there was cannibalism, at least in many towns and villages of Guangxi and Guizhou provinces, southern China, in the late 1960s.[27] The compulsion was not hunger or deprivation but ideological fervour. 'At some high schools, students butchered and roasted their teachers and principals in the school courtyard and feasted on the meat to celebrate a triumph over "counter-revolutionaries". One woman was forced to identify and denounce the mutilated corpse of her husband, who had been killed, stripped of his flesh, and mostly eaten. As punishment for having loved a "counter-revolutionary", she was then forced to sleep with his severed head beside her.' Students aged, say, eighteen in 1967 were fifty-five in 2004, many therefore now in senior positions. They live with their memories.

Then there were the 'Greys', children of shopkeepers, office clerks and some elementary and middle school teachers. Many of these were persecuted and beaten to death, while others were not, and some became a kind of second class of revolutionaries called the Peripheral Red Guards. 'What is your class background?' was the defining question which divided the nation. There was incredible confusion as university children of the cadres and others in the new elite with a revolutionary background organised their own Red Guards to protect themselves from the original Red Guards, the university children of the intellectuals and the leadership.

The top leaders of the Party were themselves also decimated. Liu, Head of State, chosen by Mao to be his successor and to be given time to learn the job while Mao was still alive, was identified in 1966 as 'the biggest person in authority taking the capitalist road'. In August 1967 he and his wife suffered prolonged 'struggle sessions' after which he resigned, was held in solitary confinement and then expelled from the Communist Party; he died the next year but was posthumously rehabilitated in 1980 after Mao's death. Deng, since 1956 the Party's General Secretary, was dismissed and put under house arrest. He was reinstated as Vice-Premier in 1973, rehabilitated, dismissed again in January 1976 just after the death of Zhou and returned to power in September 1976. In December 1978 he became the paramount leader. Lin, Minister of Defence, had helped launch the Cultural Revolution, reviewed a major Red Guard rally alongside Mao and praised their nationwide beatings, lootings, burnings and killings – 'the direction of your action has always been correct,' he had said. As the fighting between factions in 1967, called the 'Red Terror', went out of control, Mao brought in the PLA with Lin at its head to steady the nation. On Mao's recommendation, the Ninth Party Congress nominated Lin as his successor. But later, Lin was himself accused of plotting to assassinate Mao and take power. An Anti-Lin Biao Movement was launched. In 1971, the plane on which Lin was fleeing from China with his wife and son crashed in Outer Mongolia, having run out of fuel; all the passengers were killed. This whole affair greatly saddened Mao, and his doctor dated the onset of his major illnesses from this time.[28] Zhu De, at first protected by Mao because of their long and successful military collaboration and their personal friendship, was called 'an old swine, a black commander and a big warlord' and dismissed. (Dr Li, who knew Zhu well, described him in 1956 as 'a kindly old man with thick black hair and a ready smile … who devoted his time to inspection trips and to raising orchids in his Zhongnanhai greenhouse'.[29]) Yang Shangkun, the army veteran, head of the Communist Party's General Office, later President of the PRC (and who, as a 'Party Elder', was to play an important part during the Tiananmen Square disaster), was dismissed. Thus did Mao treat his friends and close associates who helped him achieve his successes.

The two institutional pillars of a well-ordered society – education and the law – also suffered greatly, with long-term effects. For about six years (1966–72) virtually all schools were closed. Formal education ceased. Millions of youngsters became illiterate philistines. Exams were condemned as being the products of bourgeois teachers and were 'unfair surprises'. Cheating was encouraged. University standards fell because their entrants had none of the right qualifications, and the whole curriculum was skewed towards political education.

Another casualty of the Cultural Revolution was the law. Mao boasted that he 'lived without regard for the law or heaven'. All laws and regulations were labelled 'capitalist and reactionary handcuffs'. The slogan in 1966 read: 'The legislative and procuratorial system must be thoroughly smashed!' Legislative institutions and even criminal courts were closed down; law professionals were sent to the villages to farm, or had to adopt another activity. China became lawless, which gave the Red Guards a completely free hand. However, after the nightmare, the education system recovered more quickly than did the legal system. Respect for the law has not, even now, been re-established.

After February 1967, the Politburo ceased to function. Mao himself was deified, the god who could do no wrong, whose every word was the revealed truth, the First Emperor of the Communist dynasty. Zhou, the great survivor, summed it up: 'Whatever accords with Mao Zedong Thought is right, while whatever does not accord with Mao Zedong Thought is wrong.'[30] However, not all that Mao said or thought was Mao Zedong Thought, and so there was considerable confusion, compounded by the twists, turns and reversals of Mao's policies. In Mao's presence no one could be quite sure what the right thing was to say, in case yesterday's orthodoxy was today's heresy. A perceptive summary of Mao's tactics was written by a group formed to protect the position of Lin, led by his son:

Today he uses this force to attack that force; tomorrow he uses that force to attack this force. Today he uses sweet words and honeyed talk to those whom he entices, and tomorrow he puts them to death for some fabricated crimes. Those who are his guests today will be his prisoners tomorrow.[31]

The Cultural Revolution – which was largely an urban phenomenon – officially ended in April 1969, but since many of its most barbaric acts continued, especially in the countryside, while supposed reactionary groups were persecuted with torture and killings, it was not brought to an end until Mao died in 1976. The long-term psychological and physical effects of these terrible events on the people compounded those sustained during the earlier purges. For the vast majority it was one trauma after another from 1950, for twenty-six years, as their lives, families, friends and livelihoods all suffered agonies.

The effects of such prolonged trauma – Post-Traumatic Stress Disorder, in today's terms – may have been underestimated. Unless properly treated it can blight people's lives until they die, and damage succeeding generations. Trying to block off the pain of the past may simply drive the hurt more deeply into the body. Physical illnesses may result. The pernicious influences will only gradually subside of their own accord. The present leaders of China were children or young adults of an impressionable age during these terrible times. Of course many will have been affected, and their lives distorted. The only question is one of degree and form.

Another personal consequence of these tragic events is that a large number of people must have become brutalised. Participating in 'struggle sessions', being prison guards or prisoners, cadres on low incomes with power over other people's lives, forcing others to do things which their basic instincts will have told them is wrong, because that is their job – all such actions demean their spirit and accustom them to cruelty. That, too, would affect their own children and their children's children. Thus, in so many ways, the tragic legacies of the era of Mao Zedong continue to blight Chinese society and institutions.

There were three ways in which Tibet was affected. First, in 1959, the postponement of applying Chinese policies in Tibet was cancelled. The policies were then applied fully. The Red Guards wreaked havoc in Tibet, destroying all but a few of the remaining monasteries and stealing their contents; confiscating the wealth of the bourgeoisie; collectivising agriculture; engaging in forced labour; causing malnutrition and even starvation; destroying Tibet's ancient but valuable legal system; disrupting society; and a lot more. Second, many of the Chinese cadres who came to Tibet might have been brutalised in China, which showed them the way to treat Tibetan 'splittists' and others. Third, the families and friends in China of most Chinese cadres in Tibet would have suffered greatly under the terrible events described above, and the cadres could do nothing about it. They were stuck in Tibet amongst a hostile population who spoke a language they did not understand, at altitudes and in a climate they were not used to. So they vented their frustrations on the people who were the 'prime cause' of their distress. These reasons account for much of the suffering in Tibet.

In January 1976 Premier Zhou died of cancer. There was a great outpouring of spontaneous public grief. Mao was too ill himself to attend the funeral. The vast crowd mourning Zhou's death reacted angrily when the police removed the piles of wreaths placed there by the million or so people who passed through Tiananmen Square. Each night trucks would remove the wreaths, only for them to be replaced the next morning. In April 1976 some 10,000 police, militia and soldiers clashed with mourners in the Square. Thousands were beaten and hundreds arrested. This expression of anger was called a 'counter-revolutionary incident'. Deng was blamed; Mao stripped him of all his posts, and he went into hiding.

In July 1976 Zhu, the great military leader, founder of the Red Army and its successor the PLA, died aged eighty-nine. For almost fifty years he had worked closely with Mao – so closely that many Nationalists thought they were one man, 'Zhu Mao'. Eventually he became Chairman of the National People's Congress, the legislature. During the Cultural Revolution he, like other loyal supporters of communism, suffered the indignities of criticism and dismissal. Shortly after his death there was a great earthquake (measuring 8 on the Richter Scale) which hit Beijing, Tianjin and Tangshan. The last of these was virtually a newly built city and great industrial centre to the east of Beijing. It was completely destroyed, with over 242,000 deaths resulting. Jiang Qing refused all offers of help for the survivors from the UN and various countries. With the deaths of Zhou and Zhu and now the immense earthquake, whatever would follow next? In September 1976 the Great Helmsman himself, Mao Zedong, died after a long illness and many strokes, aged eighty-two.

His was a life of extraordinary achievement in defeating the Nationalists and unifying China after the chaos and turmoil of earlier years, to wide and justifiable acclaim in his own country. However, he leaned too much on Lenin and Stalin. Henry Kissinger said of him: 'I have met no one, with the possible exception of Charles de Gaulle, who so distilled raw, concentrated willpower … Mao emanated vibrations of strength and power and will.'[32] But his great victory was followed by disaster upon disaster in running the country he had created. It was characteristic that very soon after Mao founded the People's Republic of China in October 1949, he began to talk of retiring to leave younger men to run the country. He was the right man to have defeated the Nationalists, unified the country and fired it with inspiration and zeal, but the wrong man to have led it from then on. He had turned his energies in other directions.

Mao's private life followed the example of most emperors of old. They all had their concubines, and when discussing the day's meals with the head of their household they would also decide which concubine would be on the menu that night. Mao was addicted to sex; he missed important state business because of his latest young women, did not read the state papers he needed to and would keep important guests waiting while he savoured his latest delights, four or five of them at a time in his vast bed.[33] Many women felt privileged to be his lover, for it conferred a certain prestige. This behaviour did not, however, endear him to his closest associates, who were well aware of these activities, nor gain their respect. Morality and 'virtue' ceased to be a concern. He became completely self-indulgent and did not care for the suffering of others.

Hua Guofeng was Mao's chosen successor as acting premier and head of the State Council instead of Deng Xiaoping, who was First Deputy Premier. Mao thought Deng placed too much emphasis on improving living standards and not enough on the class struggle. He was thought to be abandoning the Cultural Revolution and its values. Mao had met Hua in 1959 when visiting his own birthplace, Shaoshan, and was much impressed. Two years later, when Mao was visiting the countryside and saw the 'bumper harvest' from his railway carriage, it was Hua who had the courage to tell Mao: 'The people are losing weight, the cattle are losing weight, even the land is losing weight. How can we talk about increases in food?' 'No one tells the truth like Hua Guofeng,' said Mao to his accompanying doctor, Li.[34] Years later, the friendship deepened. Hua was widely liked for his sincerity and integrity and was genuinely loyal to Mao. Just before his death, Mao, in Hua's presence, wrote down (as he could no longer speak): 'With you in charge my mind is at ease … Act according to the decisions laid down … Don't be nervous. Take it easy.' These three brief written notes legitimised Hua's succession.

Jiang Qing (alias 'Li Chin', alias 'Lan P'ing', alias 'Li Yun-Ho', originally 'Luan Shu-meng'[35]), Mao's wife and a hypochondriac[36] scarred by an impoverished childhood, had been seeing herself for some time as Mao's successor when he died – she aimed to become the Party's chairperson, the 'Red Empress'. She would follow the precedent of Empress Lu of the Han dynasty, two thousand years earlier, who had succeeded the founder of the Han dynasty upon his death. Jiang planned that when Mao died, Zhang Chunqiao would be her prime minister and Wang Hongwen the head of state. But Hua, with his newly endowed authority as acting premier and then as First Vice-Chairman of the Communist Party, plotted against them. Four weeks after Mao's death Hua summoned Zhang, Wang and Yao Wenyuan – three of the 'Gang of Four', as this group (along with Jiang Qing) came to be called – to a Politburo meeting in the Great Hall of the People. As they entered, they were arrested: 'You have entered into an anti-Party and anti-socialist alliance … in a vain attempt to usurp the leadership of the Party and to seize power. Your offence is serious. The Centre has decided that you shall be taken into custody for a full examination.' It was Hua's moment of glory. One hour later Jiang was also arrested, by armed guards who forced their way into her bedroom on Deng's orders. He had suffered under her harsh words and deeds and had called her 'rotten through and through'. This was his triumph, too.

SIX

Policy Developments After 1959: In Exile and in Tibet

'On my face there is always a smile,
but in my heart there have been tears for fifty years.'
Elderly Tibetan woman, Lhasa, 2001

About 85,000 Tibetans followed the Dalai Lama in his escape from Tibet in 1959. From his temporary accommodation in Mussoori, Uttar Pradesh, in northern India, he re-established his friendship with Jawaharlal Nehru, the Indian prime minister, who was immensely helpful, and set up a government-in-exile later called the Central Tibetan Administration. But Mussoori was too hot, humid and unhealthy. The next year he moved to McLeod Ganj, once a place for British colonial officials and their families to escape the heat of the summer, set amongst the wild and beautiful 17,000-foot Dhauladar mountains above the busy Indian town of Dharamsala, Himachal Pradesh. McLeod had few buildings or shops, and a couple of dusty roads. Many Tibetans followed. Acting swiftly, in 1960 the Dalai Lama also established the Assembly of Tibetan People's Deputies, responsible for making the first laws for his exiled community. The first elections were held in September 1960.

In 1961, 1963 and 1991 the Dalai Lama presented drafts of a democratic constitution and instituted major reforms.[1] In 1963 the Assembly annulled all hereditary titles and prerogatives granted to the aristocrats under the old system in Tibet. The practice of appointing both a monk and a lay person to each senior position was abandoned. The monasteries of old Tibet began to be replicated in India and Nepal, although without their former vast estates or indentured labour. Within four years of the escape from Tibet the old semi-feudal system, which had existed for centuries, was entirely eradicated amongst the exiled community. The Dalai Lama had freedom to develop the system of governance as he would have done had the Chinese not invaded, and he set about the changes with youthful vigour. It gives the lie to the repeated Chinese accusation that the Dalai Lama would have continued with the former feudal system and that the Chinese 'liberated' Tibetans from this.

The democratic system continued to evolve. In 1975 candidates for the Assembly were for the first time chosen in primary elections. In 1990 the size of the Assembly was increased (forty-six members from Tibetan exiles now living in thirty-four countries). Exiles numbered in all about 130,000 and all persons over eighteen years formed the electorate. There was also provision for establishing Local Assemblies in all Tibetan settlements with at least 160 persons. They can pass laws relating to their own settlements and have contact with the Central Assembly in Dharamsala. There is scope for further development.

The government-in-exile is led by ministers in charge of government departments – the Kashag. Since 1990, government ministers and the new Kashag are appointed by the Assembly, not the Dalai Lama. In September 2001 the leader of the Kashag, the Kalon Tripa (prime minister) was for the first time directly elected by the people from a wide selection of candidates. Anyone could stand. Following the primaries, the person with the overwhelming majority of the votes was Professor Samdhong Rinpoche, a distinguished monk, Chairman of the Assembly (its Speaker) and Director of the Buddhist Higher Institute at Varanasi, India. He was well-known, highly respected and suitably experienced. His election was confirmed by the Dalai Lama in accordance with the new charter. He then chose his own ministers, reducing the number to four, to head the government departments and to form the Kashag, ratified by the Assembly. None was a monk.

The Kalon Tripa is tall, distinguished, clever, determined and courteous, with his finger on the pulse of events. (I have known him well for over ten years and spoken with him many times.) Since most Tibetans are Buddhists (there are some Muslims), one would expect the Assembly and the government-in-exile to follow Buddhist principles. It could not, however, be described in any way as a theocratic system. The monasteries, for example, do not have special representation in the legislature, and the constitution guarantees religious freedom.

In 1990 the Dalai Lama set up a Constitution Redrafting Committee. This resulted in two documents: a draft constitution for a free Tibet and a charter for the governance of Tibetans-in-exile, with 108 articles. The latter covered the judiciary, the legislature, the executive and a number of institutional bodies. It was widely discussed by the people, and returned to the Redrafting Committee; a final version was put to the Assembly of People's Deputies and to the Dalai Lama in 1991, and it was duly passed in June of that year. Thus has the democratic system amongst Tibetans-in-exile evolved, reflecting a growing confidence about their own capabilities and a maturity in thinking about democratic processes. It has taken over thirty years to develop, and is a radical transformation of the ways in which Tibetans (in exile) want to govern themselves.

There are, however, at present, no political parties between which the electorate can choose (although there is a small Tibetan Communist Party in India). People decide who is best from amongst their local candidates on the basis of primaries. Also, Tibetans-in-exile are a people without their own territory or state. They are refugees residing in India who therefore come under Indian law – and, for those living elsewhere, under their relevant state laws. While that is undoubtedly a constraint on parliamentary action, the extraordinary and sustained generosity of the Indian authorities in allowing Tibetans to establish their own parliament and administration on Indian territory, and to protect their right under Indian law to do so, is widely understood and appreciated.

Observing the systems of governance in other states around the world, it is obvious that apparently similar-sounding ways of doing things (a parliament for lawmaking, a government for the execution of laws and policies and a judiciary) are, in fact, all different. History and culture are the prime causes of variety. Tibetans have to follow their own path.

In the 1963 constitution all executive power was vested in the Dalai Lama, and he was also Head of State. In 1987 he clarified his own role:

> When we say that the Dalai Lama office is the head of both temporal and religious activities, this does not indicate any sort of rigid role in either secular or religious spheres. The role in the religious sphere is not like that of a Pope. It is more nebulous and abstract. It is just a general title meaning that the Dalai Lama is respected as a religious teacher while having a voice in Tibetan political affairs. I am free to express my opinions openly on both political and religious matters, and do not have to voice the viewpoints of any specific religious or political institution. So I think that when we Tibetans say 'combining religious and secular functions', it does not mean what Western people think of when they say 'combining church and state'.[2]

He then added: 'Of course, as a refugee, my function in both spiritual and temporal activities is quite different from what it would be in a free Tibet.' The last point was clarified in the 1992 Guidelines for Future Tibet's Policy and Basic Features of its Constitution (reprinted unchanged in December 2000). What the Dalai Lama now says is this:

> Personally I have made up my mind that I will not play any role in the future government of Tibet, let alone seek the Dalai Lama's traditional political position in the government. There are important reasons why I have made this decision. There is no doubt that Tibetans, both inside and outside Tibet, have great hope in, and reverence for, me. From my side, too, I am determined to do whatever I can for the well-being of my people. The fact that I am in a position to do this is due to my *karma* and prayers over past lives. However, in future I will not hold any official position in the government. I will most likely remain a public figure who may be called on to offer advice or resolve some particularly significant and difficult problems which could not be overcome by the existing government or political mechanisms. I think I will be in a better position to serve the people as an individual outside the government.

In April 2004 the Dalai Lama formally handed over all his residual powers to the Assembly of Tibetan People's Deputies, which they accepted. Thus closed the long history of Dalai Lama rule.

After the initial exodus of Tibetans who followed the Dalai Lama in 1959, many others have braved the journey in rising numbers over the high Himalaya. The Office of Reception Centres of the government-in-exile in McLeod has an important outpost in Kathmandu, Nepal, supported by the UNHCR, for those who have just escaped, and there is one in New Delhi. In McLeod one can see refugees arriving in various states of distress – men, women, children and babies, usually with just the clothes they are wearing, many with bandages from injury or frostbite, looks of bewilderment and disbelief on their faces. The young women have the pink cheeks of those who live at high altitudes in the sun. There are many tears and, at first, little laughter. All will talk with the Dalai Lama. Debriefing and record-keeping are thorough. Medical and psychiatric services are on hand. Tuberculosis, which can be brought on by prolonged grief amongst other causes, is common. The Transit Centre near Dharamsala gives two years of basic education and training for those aged eighteen to twenty-five; many then to return to Tibet, urged to do so by the Dalai Lama.

Over the years, fifty-four settlements have been constructed as Tibetan villages in India, Nepal and Bhutan, most with their own primary health care centres, and there are even more groups of 'scattered communities'.[3] There are also many large and small communities in Sikkim, Ladakh, the US, Canada, Switzerland, Austria, Britain, France, Germany, Finland, Liechtenstein and other places. There refugees will join others, if possible from the same general locality from which they came in Tibet. Settlements are charities, registered under Indian law in India. This restricts but does not prevent the possibilities for earning cash for their own benefit through manufacturing and trading, but some prefer to work outside the settlements. Unemployment is above 18 percent in Tibetan settlements in India. Now, however, there is a growing number of training schemes which teach both traditional disciplines such as carpet-weaving and tailoring, and more modern ones like electronics and computer technology. About half the refugees in settlements work in agriculture.

In 1997 the Promotional Agency for Development of Micro-Enterprises (PADME) was set up under the Planning Council (now the Planning Commission) to help Tibetans start their own businesses.[4] A revolving fund of soft loans was made available through local committees (PALCOs) and Regional Project Support Officers have been trained to provide help. The secretary of the council asked me to review these schemes. (I felt that the period before loans had to be repaid was unrealistically short, which would discourage applicants and could result in bad debts, that equity capital should also be available where the business prospects looked good and the applicants were suitable, that 'mentors' or experienced consultants should be available at low cost – or for free, initially – to offer advice and help and that the whole scheme was too bureaucratic. But there was much enthusiasm and determination to make it successful, and it could play an important part in helping Tibetans to become self-sufficient and regain their self-respect.)

The Dalai Lama gave modern education a high priority. The first school, with Indian support, was set up in 1959 in Mussoori by Tsering Dolma, his elder sister. Then, in Dharamsala, she set up the Tibet Children's Villages (TCVs), which now take in everyone from tiny babies wrapped in swaddling clothes to eighteen-year-olds. Older children help the younger ones. When Tsering Dolma died in 1964, Jetsun Pema, the Dalai Lama's younger sister (then aged twenty-four), took over.[5] Under her inspiration the school system developed in McLeod with many countries funding boarding houses for the children, each with Tibetan 'house parents'. They take Indian exams and score consistently high marks, and some then go to university. Throughout all Tibetan settlements there are TCV schools. In 1985 Jetsun Pema established an Educational Development and Resource Centre to produce Tibetan books and teaching manuals. Had the Dalai Lama remained in Tibet there is no doubt that he would have developed a modern educational system such as this to replace the role of the monasteries.

From my early visits to Dharamsala it was clear that many new arrivals from Tibet had been tortured. I had some previous experience in successfully treating, with homoeopathy, several Somalis in Africa with severe trauma caused by the horrifying events witnessed during the civil war there.[6] I found that some Tibetan survivors of torture whom I met in McLeod had the same symptoms of trauma; I recognised the psychological and psychosomatic effects, separate from their bodily damage.[7] I felt that many of them, too, could be treated homoeopathically – but doing so was beyond my capabilities. Simultaneously, I was introduced to an experienced Swiss doctor and homoeopath, Dr Beate Knapp, who was working in a clinic near Dharamsala. She had been treating Tibetan nuns from the nearby Norbulingka monastery, who had been tortured by the Chinese. We compared notes, and found that the basic remedies for trauma that we used were the same. She agreed to set up and run a Homoeopathic Centre for the Treatment of Survivors of Torture.[8] In July 1999 Christina Michell (now my wife) and I conducted a review of the first year's work of this centre.

Dr Beate's experience was that many Tibetans were very reluctant to admit they had been tortured. They somehow blamed themselves, their parents or their bad *karma* for their condition. Of the 255 patients whom Dr Beate treated in the first year, most with several visits, a significant number admitted only later that they had been tortured. But she found it divisive amongst the Tibetan community in Dharamsala to separate them from others who also asked for treatment.[9] She could not turn them away because they had not been tortured physically. Their tortures were of the mind. Many of their lives had been blighted. Our funders did not want to extend the project to include all Tibetans, and Dr Beate wanted to return home to Switzerland, so the project eventually folded. There was, however, another programme in Dharamsala to help 'torture victims' using more traditional methods, including antidepressants and counselling, funded by the Danish government. Their programme, called DANIDA, included both rehabilitation and training. Also, the *geyshe* (principal) of a Tibetan University at Sarah, near Dharamsala, was conducting 'small group therapy' with several survivors of torture amongst his students, with some success.

Tibetans who were born in Tibet naturally look towards that country as their homeland, to which they will return one day, some armed with new skills. Yet, after nearly fifty years, many Tibetans wonder in their hearts whether they will ever return. Those born in India and other countries where their parents have settled as refugees are citizens of those countries; they are more ambivalent about 'returning' to Tibet when it is free.

NGOs proved more supportive than had many governments earlier. In July 1959, shortly after the 10 March uprising and the flight of the Dalai Lama into India, the International Commission of Jurists (ICJ) based in Geneva published a preliminary report on Tibet. It concluded that:

> The evidence points to a *prima facie* case of a systematic intention … to destroy in whole or in part the Tibetans as a separate nation and the Buddhist religion in Tibet … On the basis of the available evidence it would seem difficult to recall a case in which more ruthless suppression of man's essential dignity has been more systematically and efficiently carried out.[10]

In September 1959, six months after he had arrived in exile in India and with his report in hand, the Dalai Lama appealed directly to the UN. While many UN members considered Tibet part of China and therefore an internal matter beyond the scope of the UN, a majority of the General Assembly voted for a resolution. This referred to Tibet's 'autonomy which they have traditionally enjoyed', called for 'respect for the fundamental human rights of the Tibetan people' and referred to 'its belief that respect for the principles of the Charter of the UN and of the Universal Declaration of Human Rights is essential for the evolution of a peaceful world order based on the rule of law'. But this declaration (December 1948) is not a legal instrument and therefore states (including, of course, China) are not bound by it. Nor are UN General Assembly resolutions binding on the states referred to. The indirect effects are, however, considerable, and the UN tends to regard the declaration as part of its own policy.

Meanwhile, the Legal Inquiry Committee of the ICJ had been working on a detailed fact-finding report on Tibet, although the Chinese had refused them permission to visit. Their 340-page report was presented to the ICJ in July 1960, and published. It used the Universal Declaration of Human Rights as its framework, and conducted many interviews with Tibetan refugees, including the Dalai Lama. Its findings were devastating. It listed sixteen separate articles that the Chinese had violated in Tibet. They included murder; rape; arbitrary arrests; indoctrination by turning children against their parents; denial of freedom of movement within, to and from Tibet; forcing monks and nuns to marry; denial of the right of free assembly; denial of a democratic government; denial of the right to a reasonable standard of living and of a liberal education in accordance with the choice of parents; the attempt to eradicate Buddhism in Tibet ... It was a list behind which lay human tragedy and suffering on a gigantic scale. It concluded also that Tibet was 'at the very least a *de facto* independent State' prior to the Seventeen-Point Agreement.

These findings were presented to the UN. In December 1961 a further General Assembly resolution was passed which called for the 'cessation of practices which deprive the Tibetan people of their fundamental human rights and freedoms, including their right to self-determination', and it expressed the hope that 'Member States will make all possible efforts, as appropriate, towards achieving the purposes of the present resolution'. As explained in Chapter Eleven, 'self-determination' means the freedom of a 'people' to determine their political status and thus to freely pursue their economic, social and cultural development as they wish.

A third report from the ICJ in December 1964 said that 'the domination and persecution of the Tibetan people at the hands of the People's Republic of China and its army of occupation in Tibet is continuing unabated ...' and that there was 'a continuance of ill-treatment of many monks, *lamas* and other religious figures, resulting in death through excessive torture, beatings, starvation and forced labour'. It concluded that the previous General Assembly resolutions 'have had no effect on Chinese policies or action in Tibet'. In a further resolution, in 1965, the General Assembly reaffirmed its earlier resolutions and renewed its call to the Chinese government 'for the cessation of all practices which deprive the Tibetan people of the human rights and fundamental freedoms which they have always enjoyed'.

At this time in the mid-1960s, Mao was subdued by the disasters of the Hundred Flowers revelations and the Great Leap Forward. He had smashed China's entire legal system. His personal position was being eclipsed and his scheming mind was plotting the Cultural Revolution. China was still represented in the UN by the Nationalists in Taiwan. The ICJ and the General Assembly resolutions on Tibet must have meant absolutely nothing to him.

Two years after Mao's death – in December 1978 – Deng Xiaoping, then Vice-Chairman of the Central Committee of the Communist Party, was more receptive and said that the Dalai Lama could return to Tibet 'in his capacity as a Chinese citizen'. This, of course, was not acceptable to the Dalai Lama. The crucial question of authority over the Tibetan people if he did return was not mentioned. In March 1979 Deng, having met with Gyalo Thondup, the Dalai Lama's elder brother, said that 'the problem is whether Tibet is to start a dialogue with the Central Government in its capacity as a country, or to discuss things with the Central Government in its capacity as a part of China. This is the realistic question.' The Dalai Lama could not accept that Tibet was 'a part of China'. Deng would not accept Tibet as a 'country'. However, an opportunity to explore what each meant by these phrases, and thus perhaps to make progress, was missed. Tibetans took the Chinese position as absolute, whereas most likely Deng saw it as an invitation to negotiate (see Chapter Twelve).

Nevertheless, at the meeting with Gyalo Thondup, Deng invited the Dalai Lama to send people to Tibet to investigate the true situation. The Dalai Lama agreed, and the first investigating team left in August 1979 for a tour which lasted six months. They visited Tibetan communities both inside and outside the Tibet Autonomous Region (TAR) and wrote a devastating report. The second team left in May 1980 and was expelled in July after talking with the press (at a meeting the Chinese had arranged to take place) about their enthusiastic reception by Tibetans and the appalling conditions they found. The third team started in June 1980, primarily to investigate education in Tibet. It was led by Jetsun Pema and lasted four months.[11] All reported back on the conditions they observed in Tibet and the bad behaviour of the Chinese. This is not what the Chinese leadership had expected to hear, for evidently they had believed their own propaganda regarding how happy, prosperous and better-educated the Tibetans were after their 'liberation'.

To his credit, Deng – who in December 1979 had become the 'paramount leader' – took swift action. In May 1980, following the report by the returning first investigating team, Hu Yaobang – soon to become General Secretary of the Communist Party and a strong Deng supporter – led the 'First Forum on Work in Tibet' and visited the country. Hu was dismayed by what he saw and recommended some fundamental changes in Chinese policies. He acknowledged that the Communist Party had failed in Tibet: 'We feel that our Party has let the Tibetan people down.' He compared the situation the Chinese had created in Tibet with 'colonialism'. The Dalai Lama wrote to congratulate Hu on his initiatives. However, the Chinese cadres in Tibet were greatly angered at hearing their thirty years' work in a hostile Tibet described as 'a failure'.

After his return to Beijing, Hu issued a six-point recommendation regarding autonomy for Tibet, defining autonomy as 'having the right to decide for oneself' – but to decide exactly what was the crucial question, which no doubt was negotiable.[12] There followed a period of significant relaxation of Chinese policy, especially in agriculture, while thousands of Chinese cadres (not as many as planned) were transferred back to China and the vacancies filled by Tibetans. By 1981 the number of Tibetan cadres had increased fourfold over 1965 and the proportion of Tibetan cadres amongst the total had risen from one-third to over half. Religious practices were also permitted, and cadres were told to respect them. Tibetans felt reassured that these liberalisation policies would not be reversed because Hu himself came to Tibet to announce them, thus also making sure that the Chinese cadres in Tibet understood. Nevertheless, decisions were still taken by the Chinese, and some of the new policies were slow to be introduced.

A year later (May 1981) Hu put five proposals to the Dalai Lama which focused on the latter's personal status; one of these was that he should not live in or hold any position in Tibet. It ignored the conditions of the people of Tibet which, though improved, were still unsatisfactory. Consequently the Dalai Lama rejected the proposals, though again, they might have been negotiable. Then, in 1982, he himself put two proposals to the Chinese: the unification of all Tibetan areas – U-Tsang, Kham and Amdo – into a single political and administrative entity and the granting to Tibet of the same status as that offered to Taiwan and Hong Kong. The Chinese rejected them. This mutual rejection of proposals in 1981–2 created a negative atmosphere amongst the Chinese leaders, who seemed to lose interest in Tibet. In 1983 wall posters appeared in Lhasa calling for independence and many Tibetans were arrested for 'counter-revolutionary propaganda'. (The former prisoner of conscience Palden Gyatso was arrested at this time, and was released thirty-three years later.)

In March 1984, at the Second Forum on Work in Tibet, held in Beijing and presided over by Hu Yaobang, the second phase of liberalisation was announced: the opening up of Tibet. This would allow more Chinese to enter Tibet for commercial opportunities and encourage more tourism and investment from abroad. 'To get rich quickly' was the catch-phrase; the liberalisation was in line with Deng's policies for all of China. While many Tibetans were still extremely poor, a situation from which they would welcome relief, 'getting rich' was not in accordance with their religious beliefs – although younger people found the idea attractive. Moreover, many who reaped surpluses from their produce were criticised by the Chinese because they did not expand their farms or businesses or purchase more consumer goods but instead used the extra cash to help rebuild monasteries. These differences in attitude revealed that, at the deepest spiritual level, the Chinese did not understand the Tibetans.

Then, in May 1984, First Secretary of the Communist Party in Tibet, Yin Fatang, who was a moderate leader and a strong supporter of Deng, attacked the Dalai Lama, accusing him of treason. The tide seemed to be turning. In October 1984 the Dalai Lama sent a three-man delegation to Beijing which argued for the unification of all three Tibetan areas and for the demilitarisation of Tibet, making it a 'zone of peace'. The Chinese responded with a repetition of their earlier proposals for the future position of the Dalai Lama, which he himself had already rejected.

There was, however, some relief in 1985 when Beijing announced that the local authorities in Tibet could disregard those central government instructions and regulations which did not conform to the specific conditions in the region. Also in 1985, then Premier Li Peng visited Lhasa to celebrate the twentieth anniversary of the TAR's creation and announced that the policy of loosening control and increasing flexibility in Tibet would remain unchanged 'for a long time to come'. Also, Wu Jinghua, the new First Party Secretary, further reduced restrictions on the monasteries and in 1986 permitted the Tibetans to hold the Great Prayer Festival (Monlam Chenmo) in Lhasa immediately following Losar, the traditional celebration of the Tibetan New Year – the Monlam had been banned since 1967. Also in 1986, Tibetan was adopted as the main language of administration (in spite of most Chinese cadres being ignorant of it) and all primary schools were to adopt Tibetan as the language of teaching. There were still many problems – in particular there was still no freedom of speech – but the mid-1980s were good for most Tibetans, and optimism was in the air. The TAR seemed at last to be moving towards 'genuine autonomy'.

The programme of relaxation bore a remarkable resemblance to the positive proposals which the Panchen Lama had made in his Seventy Thousand-Character Petition. By 1985–6 improvements in Tibet were palpable. But the policy of opening up Tibet for economic development resulted in a large influx of Chinese people, which began to cause problems as immigrants took all the best jobs. Hu's policies were, however, criticised in China for encouraging nationalism rather than alleviating discontent.

In January 1987 came disaster. Hu was dismissed as General Secretary of the Chinese Communist Party for his self-confessed 'mistake' – he had been too sympathetic to the Chinese democracy movement and had organised many study groups to consider democratic alternatives. He had conceived and masterminded the relaxation of restrictions in Tibet and was a champion of reforms in China. The hard-line Chinese cadres in Tibet who had opposed his reforms were delighted at his downfall. Tsering Shakya remarks that with the departure of Hu Yaobang 'there was no single leader in the Central Committee of the Communist Party who had the power and imagination to solve the problems in Tibet'.[13] There was also deadlock on the question of negotiation with the Dalai Lama. Worse still, Hu's more liberal policies for Tibet soon began to be reversed. It was time to appeal to the wider world community for support.

During the Dalai Lama's visits to the US in 1979, 1981 and 1984 it was clear that Tibet had many supporters amongst ordinary Americans and their leaders. In 1985 ninety-one members of Congress sent a letter to the president of the Chinese People's Assembly expressing support for direct talks between the Chinese government and the Dalai Lama's representatives. It was ignored. In June 1987 Congress passed a bill which declared that Tibet was an occupied country and supported many of the claims made by Tibetans about Chinese behaviour. With a stalemate in negotiations, a sudden worsening situation in Tibet and growing support in the US, a letter of invitation to the Dalai Lama from the Human Rights Caucus of the US Congress to give an address was a welcome opportunity to raise the profile of the Tibetan cause. This took place on 21 September 1987. He outlined five 'basic components' of a solution to Tibet's problems.

1. Transformation of the whole of Tibet into a zone of peace. The Dalai Lama used the term *ahimsa*, a Hindu word meaning 'a state of peace and non violence'. To achieve this would require the withdrawal of Chinese troops and military installations in Tibet. The presence of troops in Tibet after 1950 had disturbed historically peaceful relations with India, which for the first time had had to station troops along the border. A buffer zone of peace would give reassurance to both Indians and Nepalese.

2. Abandonment of China's population-transfer policy, which threatens the very existence of the Tibetans as a people. By subsidising the transfer of Han Chinese into Tibet, Chinese people already began to outnumber Tibetans. This is the Chinese 'final solution' to the Tibetan problem. It follows similar policies in Manchuria, where only 2–3 million Manchurians in 1987 faced 75 million Chinese. In East Turkestan (Xinjiang) north of Tibet the Chinese population had grown from 200,000 in 1949 to over 7 million, more than half the total population in that area, and in Inner Mongolia the Chinese now numbered 8.5 million against 2.5 million Mongols. Unless the policy of Chinese population transfer into Tibet is reversed, said the Dalai Lama, 'Tibetans will become no more than a tourist attraction and relic of a noble past'.

3. Respect for the Tibetan people's fundamental human rights and democratic freedoms. Human rights violations by the Chinese in Tibet are extremely serious. 'Segregation and assimilation' is their policy. 'Tibetans exist under a colonial administration in which all real power is wielded by Chinese officials, the Communist Party and the army,' said the Dalai Lama.

4. Restoration and protection of Tibet's natural environment and the abandonment of China's use of Tibet for the production of nuclear weapons and dumping of nuclear waste. Prior to the Chinese invasion, Tibet was an unspoilt wilderness sanctuary in a unique natural environment. In the last few decades the wildlife and forests of Tibet have been significantly reduced by the Chinese. Tibetans have a great respect for all forms of life. The use of Tibet for nuclear purposes must cease. (Only on 19 July 1993, according to a *Xinhua* news report, did the Chinese officially reveal that they had a nuclear waste dump in the Haibei Tibetan Autonomous Prefecture near the shores of Lake Kokonor, the largest lake on the Tibetan Plateau.)

5. Commencement of earnest negotiations on the future status of Tibet and of relations between the Tibetan and Chinese peoples. 'It is my sincere belief,' said the Dalai Lama to the US Congress, 'that if the concerned parties were to meet and discuss their future with an open mind and a sincere desire to find a satisfactory and just solution, a breakthrough could be achieved.'

This 'Five-Point Peace Plan' was visionary, but asked for the impossible.[14] The Dalai Lama wanted to give his supporters a clear focus for their concerns and to help the Chinese to see a way forward for Sino–Tibetan relationships. He saw the plan as contributing to world peace through regional peace.

The response from China was extremely negative. They regarded the Dalai Lama's speech simply as a call for a Tibet separate from China. An immediate and intensive media campaign by the Chinese denounced 'US interference in China's internal affairs' and accused the Dalai Lama of wanting to 'split the motherland'. Tibetans were furious at this negative response, and on 27 September and 1 October 1987 there were serious riots in Lhasa led by monks and nuns which resulted in over 2,000 arrests and at least nineteen deaths, twelve of which were confirmed by the Chinese. The riots and the harsh police actions were observed by foreigners in Lhasa at the time and received worldwide publicity. The Chinese moved in special torture teams for those arrested, using new methods not seen before in Tibet. They then started a massive programme of 'political re-education' in Tibet. In November and December there were riots outside Lhasa. The Chinese moved over 1,000 armed police into Lhasa in advance of the 1988 Monlam Great Prayer Festival, and on 5 March clashes occurred; Chinese shops were burnt down and over 2,500 Tibetans were arrested. These also received wide publicity. Tibetans had been forced to attend the festival in an attempt to show the outside world that everything was now normal in Lhasa. Their refusal to cooperate was in sympathy with those who remained in prison following the earlier riots.

The speech to Congress was followed in October 1987 by a resolution in support of the plan by the European Parliament, which also urged the Chinese government to respect the rights of the Tibetans to religious freedom and cultural autonomy. Thus, within a short period, there were two high-profile international political events and much international media attention. Now the pressure was on China.

Wu Jinghua, Hu's appointee as First Secretary of the Communist Party in Tibet, lifted more controls over the monasteries. His plan in 1985 was to train 15,000 Tibetan professional and technical personnel to enable the proposed economic development to take place without large numbers of Chinese being brought into Tibet. These were, however, details which, though valuable and much appreciated by the hard-pressed Tibetans, did not match the higher-level policies urged by the Dalai Lama. In January 1987 Hu was sacked and by September, without his support, the future looked bleak. Thus there were good reasons to appeal to the highest political level in China for new policies. At that time Premier Li was in favour of recognising the special circumstances in Tibet but he had two absolutely firm policies: he would not tolerate the use of religion or religious institutions to undermine the 'unity of the motherland'; and there could be no impediments to the path of economic development.

Monks and nuns were leaders in the riots following the Chinese dismissal of the peace plan. The records show that through 1987 until September, Tibet was generally peaceful.[15] Then, from October, there were riots and protests through to December, resuming in March 1988 at the Monlam celebrations and in later months. (In April 1988 the Venerable Bhagdro, a Tibetan monk from Ganden monastery, was arrested; he was later to become a leading advocate for Tibetan independence and a widely read author of his experiences.) In December 1988 a group of Tibetans demonstrated in Tiananmen Square, a very public act of protest in the heart of Beijing. Wu was dismissed for his failure to curb the protests and Hu Jintao, China's future leader, replaced him. Then, on 5 March 1989, the largest anti-Chinese demonstration in Lhasa since 1959 was held, involving some 10,000 Tibetans. The authorities in Beijing ordered Hu to impose martial law in Lhasa. At the end of three days of exceptional violence, Hu did what he was told. The military regime was extremely harsh and lasted for thirteen months.

In April and May 1988 the Right Honourable Lord David Ennals, formerly a minister of health in the British government and then a member of the House of Lords, was in Tibet on a fact-finding mission for International

Alert, a UK-based human rights NGO, assisted by Rikki Hyde-Chambers and Yeshe Tsultem. They found irrefutable evidence of torture and physical abuse of those arrested at the earlier demonstrations and considered that there was a crisis in Tibet that required immediate response. They were passed, in secret, a great many notes by Tibetans appealing for help.

(By that time I had already been writing reports for the Tibetan government-in-exile, and when I met David Ennals on his return from Tibet we began to work together, continuing to do so until his death in 1996. He had tremendous energy, compassion and a wide circle of friends in high places who supported his work. His first love was Tibet, then Kurdistan, then mental health and other causes which touched his heart.)

Less than one year after the Five-Point Peace Plan speech to the US Congress, the Dalai Lama shifted his attention to Europe. He told a private meeting at the European Parliament in Strasbourg on 15 June 1988 that:

> The whole of Tibet known as Cholka-Sum (U-Tsang, Kham and Amdo) should become a self-governing democratic political entity founded on law by agreement of the people for the common good and the protection of themselves and their environment, in association with the People's Republic of China ... The Government of Tibet should be founded on a constitution of basic law which should provide for a democratic system of government entrusted with the task of ensuring economic equality, social justice and protection of the environment. This means that the Government of Tibet should have the right to decide on all affairs relating to Tibet and the Tibetans.

The self-governing democratic entity would be made up of a 'popularly elected chief executive, a bicameral legislative branch and an independent judicial system'. China would retain responsibility for foreign policy and it could 'retain a restricted number of military installations in Tibet for defensive purposes'. The Dalai Lama added also that a regional peace conference should be called to ensure that Tibet becomes a genuine sanctuary through demilitarisation. Later he clarified the phrase 'in association with the People's Republic of China'. He has repeatedly stated that he is not seeking independence for Tibet but some form of 'genuine autonomy' for the Tibetan people within China. Indeed, he had first formulated the idea of Tibet being in some form of federal relationship with China as early as 1978, and now it was at the forefront of his policy.[16]

The Chinese totally rejected the Strasbourg proposals, saying: 'China holds indisputable sovereignty over Tibet [which the British government did not accept]; it will not do for Tibet to be independent or semi-independent or independent in a disguised way.' Nevertheless, in September 1988 an offer to talk with the Dalai Lama was made.[17] The message said that the talks could be held in Beijing, Hong Kong, any Chinese embassy or consulate abroad; or, if the Dalai Lama found these inconvenient, he could choose any place he wished. The Chinese were now ready to designate 'one official with certain rank' to have a direct dialogue with the Dalai Lama. Under pressure they appeared to have given in.

There were, however, conditions attached. No foreigners could be involved; the Chinese would not receive any delegation or fact-finding group designated by the 'Kashag government' (for that would give it some legitimacy); the Strasbourg proposal could not be considered as the basis for the talks because it '[had] not at all relinquished the concept of the independence of Tibet'; the Dalai Lama himself would have to give up the idea of independence and place himself 'in the great family of the unified motherland and join the Central Government, the People's government of Tibet and the Tibetan people in discussing the major policies concerning Tibet'.

An offer of talks with the Dalai Lama, however hedged around, was in effect the first stage of a negotiation and thus not necessarily to be taken at face value. The Chinese regard negotiation as a psychological game. To have the first meeting between the Dalai Lama and 'one official of certain rank' would appear to have downgraded the Dalai Lama to that of an official in the Chinese government, and needed clarification. In 1989 the Chinese leader said that he wanted to open communications with the Dalai Lama or with his brother Gyalo Thondup, whom Deng Xiaoping knew well, to speak on his behalf.[18] Setting the agenda for subsequent talks would have been the second crucial stage in a negotiation, for that would have determined the boundaries. It appeared to the Dalai Lama that the Chinese were willing to discuss not only his personal position but also the matter of Tibet itself.[19]

The response to the invitation came not from the Dalai Lama but from a minister of the Tibetan government-in-exile. It stated that the meeting would be held in Geneva in January 1989, named the delegation members led by Tashi Wangdi (a distinguished and experienced minister in the government-in- exile) and added that Dr Michael van Walt van Praag, the Netherlands-based legal advisor to the Dalai Lama, would be one of the advisors to the Tibetan team. It soon also emerged that the Dalai Lama would not be attending the meeting personally. This response made the Chinese furious. It must have seemed to them not only to have breached the normal courtesies of international diplomacy by announcing the time and place of the negotiation without first checking with the Chinese side but, more importantly, it completely ignored the conditions the Chinese had set. They accused the Tibetans of not being 'sincere' and 'seeking cheap publicity'. January 1989 went by, and there was no meeting – or even the prospect of one.

On the Chinese side, the problem was partly that an earlier act of openness by Deng had mushroomed and was now out of control. The Democracy Wall Movement had set out in Beijing from 1978 to encourage freedom of expression, and there had been flurries of protest accompanying this relaxation, calling for some form of democracy in China. From April 1989, following the death of Hu Yaobang, the pro-democracy protests in China had increased sharply and were causing great concern to the leaders. Moreover, they were seriously concerned about the rise in corrupt practices and 'antisocial' behaviour in the Communist Party amongst cadres and ordinary people. There was also unrest in the military. Deng now had more immediate problems on his mind than Tibet, and much closer to home.

The Tiananmen Square tragedy of June 1989 was soon to show what the Chinese leadership thought about calls for democracy. They were prepared to run tanks over their own people. With such an attitude, a meeting between the Chinese and the Tibetans was unthinkable. Then, in December 1989, the awarding of the Nobel Peace Prize to the Dalai Lama for his 'unwavering non violence and tireless search for peaceful solutions based upon tolerance and mutual respect in order to preserve the historical and cultural heritage of his people' highlighted the contrast in approach. To Tibetans this was a huge victory and a great boost to their morale and their cause. To China it consolidated their opposition to Tibetan proposals.

The Strasbourg statement has been much criticised by Tibetans and others for not claiming independence from China, thereby acknowledging implicitly that Chinese sovereignty would continue to prevail over Tibet. For many, a 'self-governing entity' did not go far enough. The Tibet Youth Congress (TYC) retained the clear objective of independence. The Senior Convening Member of the Rangzen Alliance,[20] Thubten Jigme Norbu, Professor Emeritus at Indiana University in the US, stated:

> For many years I have said that only Tibetan independence can serve as a safeguard for the preservation of our heritage, culture and national identity. Talk of 'autonomy' masks a sad defeatism and an acceptance of the inevitability of China swallowing our country; it is unworthy of the descendants of the great *Dharmarajas* who made Tibet a powerful and enlightened state.

The case for independence (*rangzen*) was powerfully argued by Jamyang

Norbu in the Rangzen Charter,[21] in which he said that 'the hope for any kind of autonomous status under China is not realistic because it assumes that the Chinese system is flexible enough or tolerant enough to accommodate different political or social systems within it' (presumably notwithstanding the special case of Hong Kong). He argued that 'the Chinese leaders are as much victims as their people of a long and oppressive cultural and political legacy … which has paralysed the possibility of positive and fundamental changes'. Furthermore, he pointed out that China itself has fundamental weaknesses: 'Social unrest in China has no legitimate outlets except insurrection and violence.' Tibet's opportunity for independence, Norbu believes, will arise out of the resulting chaos and as Chinese in Tibet lose heart and decide to return home.

It is ironic that Mao himself, in arguing the case for a united front with the Kuomintang against the Japanese occupation (see Chapter Two), put independence for China as the top priority:

> If our country is subjugated by the enemy, we shall lose everything. For a people being deprived of its national freedom, the revolutionary task is not immediate socialism but the struggle for independence. We cannot even discuss communism if we are robbed of a country in which to practice it.[22]

Most probably, the truth is that practically all Tibetans would dearly love to be completely free of Chinese rule. But the Dalai Lama is a realist. He knew that under the leadership then in China, independence was a non-starter. Autonomy and some degree of self-government within a state is widespread internationally; the Dalai Lama understood this well and thought it could be a stage towards independence. Of the sixteen foreign countries he had visited by June 1989, five had federal systems of government. His legal advisor was a much- respected international lawyer to whom such matters were extremely familiar. But Deng appeared to be totally ignorant. His longest visit abroad had been to France, a unitary state centred on Paris with some overseas colonies which are part of greater metropolitan France – not a good model for China.

On the question of making Tibet a demilitarised zone, the PLA is a powerful constituency in the governance of China, with Li Peng its constant supporter. Its presence in Tibet is important in terms of China's military strategy because of its long international border, especially with India and Nepal. For Tibetans to have sovereignty over Tibet and to leave the long border to the south with no military presence would not be negotiable. The continuing presence of the military in Tibet could also ensure that overall control would remain Chinese.

Hu Yaobang had inspired the first two National Work Forums in Tibet, in 1980 and 1984, to give new policy direction and leadership. Now he was gone, and his policies unravelled. By the early 1990s, with the collapse of the Soviet Union, Chinese policies under President Jiang Zemin focused on 'stability' and the fight against corruption. The situation in Tibet deteriorated. In May 1993 there were exceptionally large demonstrations by lay people in Lhasa against increasingly high food prices, unaffordable medical fees, school charges and increasing taxes on Tibetan traders. Too much money was being spent on the massive Chinese bureaucracy and at the periphery the squeeze was felt acutely. Political protests had grown in rural areas, and in Lhasa about fifty members of an underground movement in support of independence were discovered and arrested. A reassessment and new focus were needed in China.

At the Third National Forum on Work in Tibet, in July 1994, the Party leadership in Beijing recognised failures on two fronts: the international propaganda to win adherents to China's position on Tibet, and their ideological campaign to convert Tibetans, especially Buddhists, to socialism. The Work Forum heralded policies – some for later development – for a 'Second Cultural Revolution' in Tibet to reverse Hu's policies and was in part a response to the demonstrations in May 1993.

The tone and purpose of the Third Forum is indicated in a document by the Propaganda Committee of the TAR Communist Party, dated 1 October 1994:

As the saying goes, to kill a serpent we must first chop off its head. If we don't do that, we cannot succeed in the struggle against separatism … it is not a matter of religious belief, nor a matter of the question of autonomy, it is a matter of securing the unity of our country and opposing separatism. It is a matter of antagonistic contradiction with the enemy, and it represents the concentrated form of class struggle in Tibet at the present time. It is the continuing struggle of the Chinese people against imperialism, the struggle against the invading force of the imperialists … any separatist activities and convictions must be continuously crushed, according to the law … Whoever sabotages the solidarity of the nationalities and wants to separate China will be completely opposed by the Tibetan people and the people of the whole country, and will definitely be smashed and will become criminals who have committed the most heinous crimes.[23]

This statement of hysterical fantasy could be dismissed as crude propaganda if it were not so serious and accurate in intent. It emerged that 'separatism' and 'splittism' were to be redefined such that any activity, attitude or belief different from those of the Chinese were to be eradicated. All differences between Tibetans and Chinese, which formerly were accepted as justification for calling Tibetans a minority people, were to be extinguished. Tibetans were now to become Chinese. The attempt to achieve this had become very serious.

While religious belief, which is taken to be a state of mind, is protected under Chinese law, all religious practices or displays of any kind were under threat. Chen Kuiyuan, Communist Party Secretary in Tibet (1992–2000), proposed to the central government that 'an all-out effort must be made to eradicate Tibbetan Buddhism and culture from the face of the earth so that no memory of them will be left in the minds of coming generations – except as museum pieces.' He also said:

> We must teach and guide Tibetan Buddhism to reform itself. All those religious laws and rituals must be reformed in order to fit in with the needs of development and stability in Tibet, and they should be reformed so that they become appropriate to a society under socialism.[24]

The teaching and guidance was to come from Communist Party cadres, who are officially atheist. 'Atheism is necessary,' said Chen, 'to promote economic development in the region and to assist the struggle against the infiltration of the Dalai Clique.' (Atheism is thus China's 'religion'.) But Chen's actions in Tibet were so unpopular with the people that he soon preferred to live in Chengdu, capital of Sichuan, and to visit Lhasa only when his presence was absolutely necessary. Thus he cut himself off from direct contact with the Tibetan people, as had Hu Jintao.

The Dalai Lama himself came under his direct attack: 'One of the important tasks in facilitating the Spiritual Civilisation drive is to screen and eliminate Dalai's influence in the spiritual field. If we fail to accomplish this task, we cannot claim to have attained any great results in facilitating the Spiritual Civilisation drive.' So said Chen on 23 July 1996. This idea of building a 'socialist spiritual civilisation' had been initiated by Deng Xiaoping in 1986 in order to correct bourgeois ideological and moral thinking amongst the people of China. Its appearance ten years later in Tibet seems likely to have been Chen's way of legitimising his actions in wanting to destroy Buddhism.

Monasteries and nunneries became the first targets of the Patriotic Education campaign because they had become 'the breeding ground and hotbed for the Dalai Clique's splittist activities in Tibet' (Chen again). As mentioned in the Prologue, Democratic Management Committees and Patriotic Education Work Units, with a myriad of restrictions, were established in every monastery and nunnery. A Ten-Point Disciplinary Code for all monks and nuns was issued in July 1997. Between 1996 and 1999 more than 11,000 monks and nuns were expelled from their institutions, and over 500 were arrested. Once expelled, it is almost impossible to find employment. By March 1998, 35,000 monks and nuns in more than 700 religious institutions had been supposedly 'rectified by patriotic education'. A high proportion of the most senior and experienced *lamas* were compulsorily retired and the transmission of high spiritual knowledge was thus severely restricted.

Chen left his post as Party Secretary in Tibet in September 2000. Robert Barnett gives a balanced appraisal of his achievements. While Chen dismantled the 'gradualist' approach towards Tibet's incorporation into China and so was extremely unpopular, he achieved much in the economic sphere. He was replaced by Guo Jinlong. After Chen's harsh and repressive policies, it was difficult to believe that the situation in Tibet could become worse.

Generally, the Fourth National Forum on Work in Tibet in June 2001 endorsed and extended the radically new policies put forward at the Third National Forum. Economic development – 'to improve living standards to win the hearts of Tibetan people so that they will not depend on the spiritual influence of the Dalai Lama' – was to be implemented through 'leap-over development'. There were to be 187 extra investment projects, two-thirds for infrastructure construction, funded by the central government. Others, at proportionately lower cost, were to be funded by Chinese provinces and municipalities. Tibetans had no say in what these were to be. This supposed 'carrot' was to be accompanied by the 'stick' of renewed and more intensive attacks on the Dalai Lama, and more efforts to promote a 'Marxist outlook' on culture and religion. The elimination of corruption amongst officials seemed now to take second place to political considerations – that Party officials should be atheist was seen as crucial to the maintenance of 'stability' (having observed Buddhism in the course of their duties, many had become attracted to it).

President Jiang and Premier Zhu Rongji also put forward what might be termed the 'We must ...' directives: 'We must resolutely promote ...'; 'We must closely seize upon ...'; 'We must strengthen ...'; 'We must attach great importance to ...'.[25] In a mesmerising speech, Jiang put forward at least twenty-three of them, some with many items, and Zhu added nine more. It was, presumably, left to the Party Secretary in Tibet to translate these into action plans. With their local responsibilities also for the 187 investment projects, cadres in Tibet seemed likely to be burning much midnight oil. An unclear distinction was also made between 'basic stability' and 'long-term stability'. Most likely, basic stability is to be achieved through repressive measures whereas, so the theory goes, long-term stability will come about naturally as Tibet develops, prosperity increases and the people become happy. However, between these two policy meetings in 1994 and 2001, a dramatic event occurred which upset China's plans for the future of Tibet.

At 10.30 on the bitterly cold night of 28 December 1999, when all was still at the Tshurphu monastery in Tibet, a window was quietly opened. Two men in laypersons' clothes slid silently over the sill and dropped on to the roof below. They waited, alert but without movement. A voice said, 'Have you seen my driver?' A brief conversation was heard between a person waiting below and a monk who had unexpectedly appeared. The monk went inside and the two men jumped some ten feet on to the ground below, and slipped silently inside a waiting vehicle. It started with a noise that cut through the stillness – it was late at night, but not so late as to arouse suspicion. It left the precinct of the monastery and turned away into the frozen wilderness of the Tibetan Plateau, then west towards Mustang in Nepal.

So began the 900-mile secret journey to freedom of Ogyen Trinley, the Seventeenth Karmapa, leader of the Kagyu 'Black Hat' sect of Tibetan Buddhists.[26] In 1992, this six-year-old child from a nomadic family – he was now fourteen – had been recognised by both the Dalai Lama and the Chinese religious authorities as the reincarnation of the Sixteenth Karmapa who had died in 1981. ('Karmapa' means 'man of action', a master of *karma*.) The Seventeenth Karmapa was accompanied by two of his followers, Lama Tsewang and Lama Nyima, his chamberlain Drupngak and two Tibetan drivers. The two *lamas* had carefully explored the route earlier and, by various deceptions, obtained the right permits.

The dramatic and dangerous journey – dangers were posed by the Chinese, who would soon be searching for them, from the bitterly cold winter and from the hazardous route, which included many detours to escape attention – is well told by Mick Brown, who later interviewed the Karmapa, Drupngak and Lama Tsewang. They had extraordinary luck in escaping detection – though 'it was [they believed] the blessing of His Holiness' the Karmapa himself which ensured their safety, not luck. After eight days' travel in their Toyota four-wheel-drive, on horseback, on foot (the highest pass they had to cross was at 20,000 feet), by helicopter and in several taxis, they arrived in Dharamsala. There the Karmapa was welcomed with a warm embrace by the Dalai Lama.

The escape was as much a surprise to the Tibetans-in-exile as to the Chinese. After anxious negotiations, the Seventeenth Karmapa was granted asylum by the Indian authorities, although his movements were restricted. Then he was granted full refugee status, but was not permitted to visit either the principal Kagyu monastery at Sherab Ling in India, a couple of hours' drive from Dharamsala, or the monastery at Rumtek in Sikkim, where the

Sixteenth Karmapa had settled after his escape from Tibet in 1959. The Seventeenth Karmapa moved into the Gyoto monastery near Sidbhari, a fine monastic Tibetan-style building with great mountains behind it, to the south of Dharamsala. There he continues with his studies and receives visitors (including my wife and myself, in October 2001). The monks' living quarters were still under construction, ready for a great expansion.

The Seventeenth Karmapa's defection from under the very noses of the Chinese was a bitter blow to them. Their hope had been that he would become the leading *lama* in Tibet, highly respected by the people because of the Dalai Lama's recognition of him as the rebirth of the Sixteenth Karmapa. The succession of Karmapas since the twelfth century has been by identification of rebirths and the passing on of the potential for great progress towards enlightenment. Their oral tradition has meant that only by hard work with their teachers could they evolve. The Seventeenth Karmapa had several times been refused permission to travel to Rumtek and Dharamsala to be with his teachers, one of whom was the Dalai Lama, and with the increasing restrictions at Tshurphu he felt that leaving Tibet in secret was his only option.

After the September 1988 public offer of talks with the Dalai Lama there was a pause of ten years. In June 1998 there was another offer of talks (following US President Bill Clinton's visit to China and the exchange of words with President Jiang about Tibet and the Dalai Lama). 'The door to dialogue and negotiation is open,' said Jiang. The conditions this time were that the Dalai Lama had to make a statement and commitment in public that Tibet is:

> ... an inalienable part of China, he must recognise Taiwan as a Province of China and accept that the People's Republic of China is the sole legal government representing the whole of China. Also, the Dalai Lama must truly abandon his proposition on the independence of Tibet and stop all activities to split China.

The response from the government-in-exile (again, not from the Dalai Lama personally) was rather negative. The first question was a matter of history (whether or not Tibet is an inalienable part of China), it said: 'Nobody can change the past ... but we should not be encumbered by it.' The Dalai Lama has stated 'very unequivocally' that he is not seeking independence. On the question of the status of Taiwan, as the Dalai Lama had already said during his visit to Taiwan in March 1997, 'this is a matter to be discussed and decided between China and the Taiwanese people. Confrontation and the use of military force will help neither China nor Taiwan.' The Chinese response was that 'Tibetans are not sincere. They have refused our offer.' Again, the Tibetans took these demands at their face value rather than as the opening gambit in a negotiation.

The Chinese made yet a further offer of negotiation in June 1999. Beijing would send an official at the vice-premier level to negotiate with the Dalai Lama himself or his family members as his representatives on condition that the Dalai Lama no longer insisted on Tibetan independence and refrained from pursuing 'splittism'. If he agreed with this, then he would be allowed to return to Tibet any time he liked. If the Dalai Lama agreed that Tibet was well-administered, he could live in the region. He would be free to come and go. The phrase 'refraining from pursuing splittism', as something different from 'no longer insisting on independence' (which the Dalai Lama had not even mentioned for well over ten years), could now be construed as covering any degree of 'autonomy'.

An official at the Foreign Ministry's news briefing on 31 October 2000 reiterated that 'the Dalai is a splittist in exile attempting to split China and destroy national unity'. He said:

China's policy towards the Dalai is very clear. As long as the Dalai openly declares that he thoroughly gives up the proposal on Tibet independence, stops his activity to split the motherland, openly recognises that Tibet and Taiwan are inseparable parts of Chinese territory and that the People's Republic of China's government is the only legitimate government representing [all of] China, the Chinese government will conduct open talks with him – the gate for talks is wide open at all times.

He added that 'the talks will mainly involve the Dalai's future'. Obviously this spokesman was not aware that in 1992 the Dalai Lama had already made clear that he would not play any role in the future government of Tibet. When Per Gahrton, head of the European Parliament's Committee on Relations with China, spoke with Li Peng, the latter suggested that the Dalai Lama might become the governor of Tibet. The usual conditions for any progress were then repeated by Li, to which he added that the Dalai Lama must also take Chinese nationality.

In October 2000 the Dalai Lama's elder brother Gyalo Thondup visited Beijing at China's invitation. On his return to India, the Dalai Lama requested that he send a delegation to Tibet. The Chinese repeated the same conditions. On 9 March 2002, following a direct appeal by US President George W. Bush to President Jiang to open negotiations with the Dalai Lama, the Chinese responded in almost the same words and the spokesman added that the Dalai

Lama 'was a feudal lord who helped keep the people of Tibet in serfdom'. Early in July 2002 Gyalo Thondup again visited Lhasa, and on 14 July the Chinese repeated that talks could not commence until their conditions were met. They also said that the Dalai Lama's Strasbourg speech calling for autonomy 'was not enough'.

However, in September 2002, just before Jiang's retirement, two envoys from the Dalai Lama – Kasur Lodi Gyari[27] and Kelsang Gyaltsen – visited Beijing and Chengdu with two assistants 'on a sightseeing trip' to see the Great Wall and the Forbidden City. They also visited Lhasa, without publicity, and met Ngabo Ngawang Jigme and local Chinese leaders. This was an unexpected positive development. The preconditions for advancement were, however, the same: the Dalai Lama must agree that Tibet and Taiwan are part of China, and all 'splittist' activities must cease.

But in May 2003, with Hu Jintao now in charge, and without having agreed to any of China's conditions, the two envoys again visited Beijing, and a third visit took place in September 2004. Lodi Gyari reported that this was 'the most extensive and serious exchange of views on matters relating to Tibet so far … but it was apparent that there are major differences on a number of issues, including some fundamental ones'. Evidently there was discussion about the possibility of the Dalai Lama's returning to live in Potala Palace in Lhasa, with important freedom of movement and the right to appoint abbots of Tibetan monasteries. Both sides agreed that more substantive discussions were needed. The Chinese side was represented by the United Front Work Department (UFWD) of the Central Committee of the Communist Party, its highest-level committee. The UFWD is headed by Liu Yandong, who is also a member of the Leading Group on Tibet, which is responsible for developing policy on Tibet; the foreign minister, Li Zhaoxing, is also a member. While the Central Committee *approves* policy, it is the Politburo Standing Committee under Hu which *decides* policy. Thus the route through to Hu and the Standing Committee from the UFWD is not simple.

In October 2004 the Dalai Lama, in an interview with *Time* magazine, repeated his much earlier statement, to which I had responded back in 1988, that 'Tibet might benefit more by remaining within the People's Republic of China, provided the culture and the environment of the Himalayan region is protected'. I still do not believe that Tibet needs to be a part of China to promote its economic development. Moreover, the mechanism by which Tibet's culture and environment would be protected is a major problem (addressed later in this book). In any event this statement was rebuffed by a Chinese foreign ministry spokesperson repeating the usual mantra that 'he [the Dalai Lama] must genuinely give up his stance on Tibet independence, should publicly declare that Tibet is an inalienable part of China and that Taiwan is an inseparable part of China. He should stop all activities that aim to split the motherland.'

The publication on 23 May 2004 of the 8,500-word White Paper on Regional Ethnic Autonomy in Tibet, published by the Information Office of the State Council of the PRC in Beijing, has also been negative. It was an updated version in five chapters of the earlier White Paper on Tibet published on 24 September 1992, also by the State Council. The new White Paper is unconvincing because it tells only half the story and repeats the myths on which China's policies in Tibet are based. But at the end it has one possibly redeeming feature.

The May 2004 White Paper argues in its Chapter I that after Tibet became part of China in the thirteenth century, its administration was left largely in the hands of the existing ruling body, the 'upper-strata ecclesiastic and secular' people, with extensive decision-making powers. This meant that 'even in the first half of the twentieth century Tibet remained a society of feudal serfdom under theocracy even darker and more backward than medieval Europe'. Thus, so the argument seems to run, giving independence or extensive decision-making powers to Tibet today would throw away all the benefits China brought after the 1951 Seventeen-Point Agreement, and would open doors to imperial aggression while Tibet would revert to feudal serfdom with all its supposed cruelty and oppression.

But this reasoning is totally undermined in Chapter V, where it is stated that 'since ancient times Tibet has been an inseparable part of Chinese territory, where *the Central Government has always exercised sovereign jurisdiction*' (my italics). They cannot have it both ways. Moreover, it is claimed that the 10 March uprising in 1959 was staged by the upper ruling strata in Tibet to preserve feudal serfdom against the Tibetan people who were demanding democratic reform. This is manifestly absurd. Thus illogicality rules, and history is turned on its head.

Chapter II argues that Tibet already has the 'full political right of autonomy' to 'implement the laws and policies of the state in the light of the existing situation'. But of course the Tibetan people cannot make their own laws in major policy fields. That is the principal issue. Nor has the leading administrative authority in Tibet, the Communist Party Secretary, ever been an ethnic Tibetan. Then, in Chapter III, it is said that the TAR has a tax rate three percentage points below the rest of China, and farmers are exempt from taxes and administrative charges while the state and other regions of China support economic development in the TAR on a massive scale. But Tibetans have no control over whether or where such developments take place or how they are managed. However, as a result of this development, say the Chinese,

GDP per capita has risen dramatically. As stated earlier, such a statement is extremely misleading so far as Tibetans are concerned.

Chapter IV concentrates on Tibetan culture and religion. Tibetan is stated to be the major language in schools and the 2002 law requiring the use of both languages throughout the official TAR, including street names and in other public places, appears to have been already implemented – which cannot yet be true. Government money is renovating Potala Palace and the Norbulingka and Sakya monasteries. On religion there is no mention of Democratic Management Committees in monasteries with their many restrictions, nor of the significant contraction of the Serthar Institute ordered and executed by the government. Indeed, the Karmapa escaped from Tibet in December 1999 because of the increasing restrictions placed upon him and his monastery. Chapter V admits that the regional ethnic autonomy in the TAR needs to be improved and developed. But 'historical facts indicate that without the unification and prosperity of the country and without the unity and mutual aid of different ethnic groups in China there would have been no new lease of life and no rapid development for Tibet … Only by adhering to the leadership of the Communist Party, the socialist road and the system of regional autonomy can it be possible to truly make the Tibetan people masters of their own affairs and guarantee them this status.' The Tibetan wish for a high degree of autonomy after the model of Hong Kong and Macao is 'totally untenable' on historical grounds. The White Paper concludes, 'it is hoped that the Dalai Lama will look reality in the face, make a correct judgment of the situation, truly relinquish his stand for a "Tibetan independence" and do something beneficial to the progress of China and the region of Tibet in his remaining years.' But what he could do best, to speak words of wisdom in his unique style to audiences of thousands of Chinese about peace, compassion and solutions to the ethical and moral dilemmas of the twenty-first century, most likely would not be permitted.

The White Paper exemplifies a well-known tactic in Chinese negotiation (see Chapter Twelve). Before a negotiation starts the Chinese often issue a statement of policy or principle which appears to be unalterable, set in stone for all time (as at the commencement of the 1951 negotiations). They use this to pre-empt the other side, to throw them off balance and to have the negotiation conducted entirely on their terms. But experience shows that if it suits them, they will simply disregard such policy and principle and carry on as though they had never said it. They negotiate as if it were a psychological game. Thus, in spite of these negative statements, the significance of the White Paper is that it may indicate they are prepared to negotiate, and this is in line with the September 2004 discussions, which seem set to continue.

SEVEN

Deng Xiaoping: Recovery, then Tragedy

'Not exalting the gifted prevents quarrelling.
Not collecting treasures prevents stealing.
Not seeing desirable things prevents
confusion of the heart.'
Lao-tzu, Tao-Te Ching, *Chapter Three*

Tibet became a long-term concern for Deng Xiaoping, and he was responsible for its best times (1980–7) under Communist rule. He was a committed Communist and a believer in socialism 'with Chinese characteristics', and he changed the course of China's history. He set it on a viable path of economic and social recovery and embraced large measures of economic democracy. He believed in, but did not introduce, political democracy – that was supposed to come later when the country was better educated and more prosperous. Towards the end of his life his reputation became tarnished by the brutal oppression in the Tiananmen Square demonstrations for which he was blamed, but what is probably the true story shows him in a different light.

Born on 22 August 1904 in the countryside near the remote town of Guang'an in Sichuan, Deng was the son of a prosperous landowner with ten hectares of land. His father was deeply interested in politics and his mother was illiterate but shrewd and capable. When he was sixteen his father paid for him to become a 'student worker' in France, as eventually were 1,600 other Chinese. There he met Zhou Enlai, who converted him to communism, and they became lifelong friends. After five years in France, the organisation that had arranged these visits went bankrupt, and Deng took menial jobs to survive. (When he was short of cash he lived off milk and croissants, which he adored.) He left for Moscow, and for nine months studied at Sun Yat-sen University, which was set up to train personnel for the revolution in China. He came home briefly in 1927 for the last time.

After a short term in prison in 1933 for refusing to follow the Russian-inspired Communist leadership on military tactics, Deng took part in the Long March. In 1937, at the onset of the Japanese invasion, he became political commissar of the highly successful 129th Division of the Eighth Route Army and then the political commissar of the Southwestern Military Region; amongst his other responsibilities, he was in charge of devising the CCP's policies towards Tibet.

Deng left the military, and in 1952 moved to the bigger stage as Vice-Premier. In 1956 he became Party General Secretary and a member of the Politburo Standing Committee. From his official position, and as a loyal supporter of Mao, he took an active part in the 1957–8 Anti-Rightist Campaign against China's intellectuals.

However, early in the Cultural Revolution, Deng was purged by Mao as being the 'number two Party person in authority taking the capitalist road', and lost his position. Quietly rehabilitated in March 1973 as Vice-Premier to Premier Zhou, in 1975 he became Vice-Chairman of the Communist Party but was again purged in 1976 by Mao. In July 1977, after the Gang of Four was arrested, Deng recovered his positions, then moved to centre-stage in December 1978 at the Third Plenum of the Eleventh Central Committee. He was confirmed as Vice-Premier. Hua Guofeng was shown to be a true follower of Mao's policies, but had made some early mistakes in administration; Deng did not find it difficult to push him aside. Deng's ideas for the future of China were totally different. As paramount leader for more than ten years, he remained in a commanding position. In 1989 he dismissed Zhao Ziyang and gave Jiang Zemin the reins of power. He led the 'Party Elders' (also called the 'Party Central'), who authorised the military to clear Tiananmen Square. In 1992, at the age of eighty-seven, he made his 'Southern Tour' to rejuvenate the economic reform movement, evidently dissatisfied with progress under the Jiang Zemin–Li Peng team. He also pointed the finger at Hu Jintao as Jiang's successor and had him promoted to the Politburo Standing Committee. Deng died in 1997.

Through 'socialism with Chinese characteristics', Deng cast aside one of Mao's basic aims by which Mao had attracted such a large and devoted following – egalitarianism. Deng preached that socialism would succeed only if it made people rich, and that some people could get rich quicker than others. While he was willing to see the growth of economic democracy – more and more individuals and businesses making their own economic decisions – he was implacably opposed to 'bourgeois liberalism', by which he meant any form of Western political democracy. However, Deng said that he was not against fundamental political change for all time. In December 1978, when he came to power, he declared:

> Democracy has to be institutionalised and written into law so as to make sure that institutions and laws do not change whenever the leadership changes, or whenever the leaders change their views or shift the focus of their attention ... these laws should be discussed and adopted through democratic procedures.[1]

There was, he thought, a proper sequence in which change should be made. It would be dangerous to have political democracy before economic recovery, because China's low standard of living and high degree of illiteracy would lead the Party to lose power in an election, from which defeat it might never recover. To try to bring about simultaneous reforms in both economic and political spheres would be too difficult and would lead to chaos. (Soviet leader Mikhail Gorbachev, on a visit to China in June 1989, had as a central theme to advise China that real economic reform would be impossible without political reform. They did not agree with him; Gorbachev was soon to find that combining *perestroika* [economic reform] and *glasnost* [political reform] was simply not feasible, especially against determined opposition. Russia had got it wrong.) So Deng's plan appeared to be: get the economy on the right path first, which, after the Great Leap Forward and the Cultural Revolution, would be difficult enough. Educate the people; then, when everyone could see how successful the Party had been in improving their livelihood, democracy would lead to its survival. So his mind seemed to run.

Thus reform began by 'opening' China to the world economically. Diplomatic recognition from the US paved the way for American investment in China. Deng also saw that the Chinese in Taiwan were far in advance of China itself, and he wished to encourage their trade, investment and the transfer of technical know-how (at first achieved mainly through Hong Kong). Overtures in 1981 to bring Taiwan back into the Chinese fold were, however, repulsed.

Not only did Deng want foreign investment and technology, but he also wished to make the best use of China's own intellectuals, their ideas, capabilities and support. In 1978–9 the Democracy Wall Movement (the 'Beijing Spring') encouraged many people around the country to express their thoughts and ideas in public. In 1979 Deng, who had been supported by the movement to oust his opponents, at first gave qualified blessing to it. However, in yet another rerun of history, as its contributors became more and more outspoken against the Party, he soon moved to close it down. Many of those who had written, especially those who appeared to be the leaders of dissent, were arrested. They included Wei Jingsheng, a talented and persistent critic of the government and supporter of Tibet.

In 1980 Deng promoted his two protégés. Hu Yaobang became General Secretary of the Party (in place of Hua Guofeng) and Zhao Ziyang became Premier (in place of Zhou Enlai). They were both caring and compassionate leaders, open-minded and responsive to the people and to new ideas. They reflected Deng's own deeper instincts. In human rights circles, he and Hu should be remembered for ratifying five international conventions relating to the 'rights of peoples' (see Chapter Eleven), a major step in joining the international community, charged with high ideals.

Deng's economic policies had a large effect on Tibet, although not in the way he had hoped. He was no economist and did not understand what made capitalism work on behalf of the people. The secret he missed was the central role of competition and the discipline on companies that it created, while strong economic and financial regulation was also necessary to maintain effective and fair competition and benefit consumers. Without strong regulation, producers would grab too large a share of the benefits. Deng was also naive in his understanding of development economics, not recognising that culture and history play the largest part in how relatively poor communities respond to external endeavours to lift them out of poverty. Yet, later, his instinct led him in the right directions.

From 1973, when as Vice-Premier Deng had charge of the economy for the first time, he re-centralised the central planning bureaucracy and unwisely followed the unworkable Russian practice that had fallen apart during the Cultural Revolution. The Ten-Year Plan of 1976–85 contained many gigantic (and unattainable) projects. The 'Four Modernisations' launched by Deng in December 1978 were in the fields of industry, agriculture, defence and science and technology. (Wei Jingsheng then took a step too far, demanding what he called the 'Fifth Modernisation' – democracy.) The means by which the modernisations would succeed were 'opening' to foreign practice; material incentives; market forces; and a resurrection of the law and some private ownership. Deng then authorised 122 major investment projects, including twenty-two complete industrial production units from abroad, costing over US$ 12 billion.[2] They were to be paid for with oil exports, but despite feverish searching, no significant amounts of oil were discovered. Chen Yun, a man of unusual talents and a member of the Politburo Standing Committee since 1934, became head of a new Economics Leading Group and promptly cancelled all the foreign contracts except, at Deng's specific request, the Baoshan steel complex near Shanghai awarded to Nippon Steel. This proved to be a wake-up alarm call for the Chinese when confronted with Japanese technology, control processes and management systems. In steel plants of similar output, for each man employed by Nippon, China employed about thirteen men.[3]

In 1971 the PRC took over China's seat on the UN Security Council from the Nationalists now centred in Taiwan. The first visit by US President Richard Nixon to China in February 1972 was a turning point, following twenty-two years of isolation. But by then Mao was eighty-three and seriously ill, so it was left to others to carry forward this initiative. Mao had operated within a virtually closed economy. 'Self-reliance' was the watchword.[4] It was not until 1979 that formal diplomatic relations between China and the US were established, when Jimmy Carter was President and Deng in the ascendant. The way was now clear for 'opening' to take effect, with much capital and technology from the US, Japan and elsewhere. International trade began to flourish.

China then had ten years of stability (until the interruption of Tiananmen Square in 1989) in which to develop policies and gain experience. There was no blueprint, no preconceived theory or ideology. Ideas were taken from the West, from Taiwan and elsewhere and tested in the circumstances of China.[5] Some worked, some did not. (One Chinese official said of this pragmatic approach, with tongue in cheek, that those that worked were called 'socialism' and those that did not were called 'capitalism'.[6]) Baoshan was thus a socialist project using capitalist technology, designs, materials, management systems and ideas.

In April 1979 an idea was mentioned to Deng by a visiting group of officials from Guangdong for attracting foreign investment and technical know-how. Deng's imagination was fired. 'Draw a boundary,' he said. 'Name it a special zone ... but since the central government is short of money, you will have to run the special zone with local resources.' A wire fence was duly put in place by the PLA construction corps enclosing a small village called Shenzhen in Guangdong province – thus were a new city and a new era born. Deng personally ensured that the best planners, builders and craftsmen were engaged on the work and that sufficient funding was available. In 1980 delegations were sent round the world to investigate export-processing zones, but the best models were found on their own doorstep, in Taiwan – which had had three successful zones since the 1960s – and in Hong Kong and Macau. (Jiang Zemin was one of those sent to investigate.)

Central to the remarkable success of China's economy at this time was the development of these Special Economic Zones (SEZs), as they were called. These were designated areas free of import duties for industrial manufacturing and commercial development, principally for the export of Chinese-made goods through joint ventures between Chinese and foreign firms. SEZs were provided with all the necessary buildings, facilities and infrastructure (airports, roads, railways, electricity, gas, etc.) for rapid occupation and growth. Incentives were offered to foreign firms, and preferential policies and regulations were set. The first four SEZs were set up in August 1980. Then the general idea of special designations to provide a focus for development spread rapidly.[7] In 1988 Hainan Island was designated as China's largest SEZ. These initiatives formed the basis for China's remarkable export-led economic growth. During 1980–95 China's Gross National Product was said to have grown at an astonishing average 9.8 percent per annum (although one should deduct perhaps about 2–3 percent or even more to arrive at somewhere near the truth).[8] Premier Zhao Ziyang was continually making speeches to explain and to promote China's new policies, and his role in making these opportunities a reality was crucial.

Joint ventures required a framework of government institutions and of business law. The first law on joint ventures was introduced in 1979. After thirteen years without law, and with the disappearance of China's lawyers, this was a first step towards normality. But they were, so to speak, still scraping the mud off their boots, and the inadequacies of the Baoshan contracts with Nippon Steel were the result. Contract law was needed – it came in 1985 – along with patent law and a host of others. By the end of 1987 there were about 200 laws and regulations relating to foreign investment in China, and they were constantly found to need revision as experience revealed their deficiencies. In 1986 Zhao said that 'though criminal law and civil law are important, the most important is economic law'.[9] It was this low priority accorded to civil law in China, especially in the field of human rights, that permitted so many violations to occur in Tibet.

Sharp and experienced multinational enterprises, supported by their lawyers to protect their interests and to exploit loopholes in China's laws, at first ran rings round the Chinese. With China's complete lack of modern experience in this area, and with its legal profession still in disarray and unversed in the wily ways of foreign enterprises seeking profit, it was not surprising that mistakes were made. Many Chinese enterprises found themselves seriously disadvantaged by less-than-scrupulous multinationals. Mistakes notwithstanding, the SEZs proved extremely attractive to foreign enterprises and were immensely to China's benefit.

Town and Village Enterprises (TVEs) also grew far beyond the expectations of those at the centre who had authorised this decentralisation of the smaller state-owned enterprises. Some borrowed too much and had to be rescued or closed down, but again, growth was remarkable. At the higher level, the ten 'Independent Economic Regions' that had been established in 1972, each with their own investment plans, resulted in much duplication – each wanted to have its own car manufacturing plant, its own plant for TV sets, refrigerators, etc., and many were too small for efficiency. There was enormous waste. Also, in 1979, over 60 percent of China's manufacturing enterprises were equipped with machinery dating from the 1930s and '40s. Production processes were equally antiquated. The need for modernisation was acute, and Baoshan was the beacon.

Agriculture quickly recovered once Mao's policy of collectivisation was abandoned in 1979. By 1984, some 98 percent of agricultural production was from independent economic units operating under the new 'responsibility system' for leasing of land to individuals or groups (many families registered themselves as 'groups') for up to fifteen years – the leases were renewable. Contracts could be passed on to the children of the original contractors, and other transfers were possible. Tibet also benefited from this nationwide liberalisation.

The pace of change from 1979 was hectic. China's economic progress amazed the world. These ten years under Deng, Zhao and, until January 1987, Hu Yaobang, can sound a long time, but in relation to what was needed to transform China into a modern industrial state with efficient agriculture, a well-balanced and regulated economy, a reduced military burden and an appropriate set of institutions and laws, it was very short. There were a great many experiments in applying, for example, the incentive of profit to state-owned enterprises, in taxation, shareholding, removing price controls, applying subsidies. Much more time was needed, but the gains made were for others to take forward. The groundwork had been laid.

There was, however, a most important downside to these amazing developments. During the 1950s and '60s it seemed that corruption had lessened. However, in the 1980s, with the delegation of much economic control to regional levels and as the prevalence of central planning and state price determination began to decline with the development of free markets, the discrepancies widened. Corruption filled the gap and began to increase again – on a vast scale. Those in China who had access to goods sold at low prices fixed by the state then made millions by reselling on the free market at much higher prices, a simple process of profiteering called *guandao*. In the early years there were shortages of practically everything. Those who controlled supply, distribution and the issue of permits also made millions. *Guanxi*, or political connections, were extremely important, and the use of these connections meant 'going through the back door', for a consideration – gifts, elaborate banquets, returned favours. The children of top Party officials made the most because they had the best connections. But the people without *guanxi* – the overwhelming majority, including the Tibetans – felt cheated and resentful. If all the best jobs and business contracts went to those with connections, what chance had they in this highly unequal world? Corruption seriously undermined society.

The leadership was well aware of these destructive developments. In September 1982, Hu Yaobang had reported to the Twelfth Congress of the CCP:

> A grave problem at present is that in quite a number of organisations Party discipline has slackened, right and wrong are confounded, rewards and punishments are misused and there is a failure to criticise and punish where necessary ... Party commissions for discipline inspection have met considerable, and in some cases shocking, obstruction in their work.[10]

In 1982 Deng launched a campaign against 'economic crime'. The difficulty was that some of the children of the leaders were involved. In 1986 the children of three top officials were executed for corruption. Many were imprisoned. In 1987 the Ministry of Supervision, which had been abolished in 1959, was resurrected with a staff of 15,000 to investigate corruption, and a 'hotline' for reporting misdemeanours. In 1988 a new campaign was launched. Forty-two companies run by the children of high cadres – the 'princelings' – were closed down, including the export–import trading subsidiaries of a charity – the China Welfare Fund for the Handicapped – run by Deng's eldest son, who was a paraplegic (having been thrown out of a window at Beijing University by Red Guards during the Cultural Revolution). This ceaseless campaign against corruption was continued under Deng's successor, Jiang.

The persecution of intellectuals during the Anti-Rightist campaign of 1957, the closure of schools and universities during the early part of the Cultural Revolution and the persecution and killing of so many teachers were major setbacks for the education of China's young people. Most foreign textbooks were called 'poisonous weeds', and foreign literature was unobtainable. Many students in schools and universities were sent to the countryside, where there was little or no appropriate education. The late development of science in China also meant that much catching-up was needed.

Within a month of Deng's return to power as Vice-Premier in 1973, he began to reform the university entrance system. Hitherto, anyone who had been employed in a work unit for two years and had the appropriate recommendations could enter a university without taking entrance tests. They were called Worker-Peasant-Soldier students. Now, candidates had to sit examinations – although 'political correctness' would also be a consideration. Until the examination system was properly established, many children who had not even finished elementary school were admitted, and some who gained admission were almost illiterate. Also, there was still an anti-academic atmosphere. 'Better Red than Expert' was a common slogan, and many teachers, in the words of one student, 'would rather have us walk out of the campus as revolutionaries than as slaves to knowledge'.[11] Foreign books and magazines became obtainable, although there were warning posters: 'Read with Caution against Bourgeois Perspectives'. Postgraduate schools were, however, not restored until 1978, after Deng's return to power.

The tragedy of Tiananmen Square was triggered by an untimely death. At a meeting of the Politburo at 9.00 AM on 8 April 1989 to discuss education, Hu Yaobang, former Party General Secretary – his face suddenly ashen white – began to rise to request permission to leave the meeting. Suddenly he slumped back in his chair and collapsed. 'It's probably a heart attack – don't move him,' someone said. 'Anyone have nitroglycerin?' Zhao asked urgently. 'I do,' said Qin Jiwei, who himself had a heart condition. Ten minutes later Hu was rushed to hospital. On 15 April he died.

Hu and Deng had met in 1941 when Hu was assigned as a twenty-six-year-old army political commissar to work under Deng in the Eighteenth Red Army Group operating in the arid Taihang Mountains. They served together for eight years, and 'the two men became practically inseparable' (they were also good bridge partners.)[12] Hu became General Secretary of the Communist Party in 1980 and Party Chairman in 1981. He was relieved of his position as General Secretary in January 1987, accused by Deng of supporting 'spiritual pollution'. He was described by many students as the 'soul of democracy', although he did not believe in Western-type democracy.

Since 1952, when Hu became First Secretary of the Youth League, he had been quietly encouraging independent political thought. He had a reputation for openness to new ideas and a willingness to listen. During the Cultural Revolution he was accused of being a 'capitalist roader', 'anti-Party' and 'anti-socialist', and was paraded through the streets in a dunce's cap. He spent two and a half years in a 'cow-pen', a general term for a makeshift prison.

In 1973 Deng made Hu Vice-President of the Chinese Academy of Sciences, and in 1977 he became Vice-President of the Central Party School, the training centre for high officials, where he set up a Theory Research Office. Hitherto unthinkable ideas were allowed free expression.[13] In 1977 Hu was elected to the Party's Central Office and became head of the Organisation Department. He then sought to right the injustices of the Cultural Revolution. Hu was instrumental in securing the release of over 3 million officials, scientists, intellectuals and skilled workers, and returning them to public life.

Under his active protection many groups had been studying, arguing and producing ideas for a democratic China, and some had had a very difficult time. But for this protection many would have been in prison. He had a large personal following, especially in the universities, and had become the centre of a substantial network of like-minded intellectuals, deeply patriotic but wanting something much better for China. Late in 1986 student protests began to give public expression to the lack of progress towards democracy, and by December had spread to 150 campuses in seventeen cities. The Party Elders and their associates began to use these protests as an excuse to crack down on Hu Yaobang. Hu gave instructions to Jiang Zemin, then the mayor of Shanghai, to persuade some 3,000 students at the Jiatong University to return home. Jiang was booed and hissed. In January 1987 Deng ordered Hu to suppress the demonstrators, but he refused. He also refused to purge Fang Lizi, Wang Ruowang and Liu Binyan from the Party because they had provoked the demonstrations. Then Deng himself ordered the students to return home, which they did, peacefully. The Party Elders strongly criticised Hu; Deng was receptive, and on 16 January 1987 Hu was forced to resign as General Secretary. These demonstrations were a forerunner of the catastrophe of Tiananmen Square in 1989.

Hu was a courageous and sympathetic reformer. In Tibet, where he reversed the existing policies of repression, he was hailed as 'China's Buddha'. His death, a tragedy for Tibet, also brought many students on to the streets in Beijing. They flooded into Tiananmen Square to express their deep sorrow and grief, with a huge demonstration on 22 April 1989, the day of Hu's memorial service.

Thereafter, the demonstrations in Tiananmen Square grew larger day by day, and the students were joined by many ordinary people.[14] By 25 April the protests had spread to over twenty large and medium-sized cities. Detailed reports were coming in to the Party Standing Committee all the time – but they were long on description and short on analysis. The leadership was becoming extremely worried. Deng remarked:

This student movement shows that we haven't been thorough enough in our political thought work. We've talked about the Four Principles, we've talked about political thought work and about opposing bourgeois liberalism [Western democracy] and spiritual pollution [Western cultural influences], but we haven't followed through. We haven't carried these things out.[15]

In the absence of Party General Secretary Zhao, on a state visit to North Korea, Premier Li gave his summary of the situation: 'A small minority is manipulating the students ... some protest posters and slogans were anti-Party and anti-socialist.' Deng agreed that 'they want to confuse the people and throw the country into chaos. This is a well-planned plot whose real aim is to reject the Chinese Communist Party and the socialist system at the most fundamental level.' Li suggested that *The People's Daily* publish an editorial to repeat what Comrade Xiaoping said. The editorial was published the next morning, and badly misfired. Further demonstrations broke out in at least twenty towns and cities. The headline alone enraged people: 'The Necessity for a Clear Stand Against Turmoil'. 'Turmoil' implied an 'antagonistic conflict' which would constitute a political crime, rather than an expression of dissatisfaction and agitation by a crowd of people. It was Deng who altered the draft editorial to include the word 'turmoil'. Li set up a high-level committee, the 'Small Group to Halt the Turmoil'. The students said they were loyal to China and not trying to overthrow the government, but they wanted it to take action.

The leaders of China, perhaps because they were unelected, were prone to 'conspiracy theories'. Fear of being overthrown was a deep worry during times of crisis. In Tibet, the Dalai Lama was constantly being accused of masterminding riots, supporting 'splittist' movements to disintegrate the state of China and aiming to re-introduce feudalism into Tibet. Such thoughts occur in the minds of a leadership in China that does not owe its positions to popular support.

The student calls for democracy, on which they were extremely vague as to detail, were shorthand for the need to address a wide range of problems. As already mentioned, by the late 1980s corruption, crime and a decline in moral standards generally had become so widespread and deep that they were a threat to both society and the economy. 'To get rich is glorious,' Deng had said, and many people were not too scrupulous about how they went about it. Inflation was the highest since 1949, when it had reached dizzy and disastrous heights. State-owned enterprises were grossly overmanned and were still price-controlled. Many were corrupt on a gigantic scale. Not surprisingly, most state-owned enterprises in China were incurring huge losses. Also, the bureaucracy of the Chinese government was overblown and inefficient. Riots had been breaking out in prisons against the appallingly brutal treatment prisoners received from the authorities. There was so much wrong that students could only blame the system which gave rise to it.

There was also some confusion about political ideology and the high-level aims of government. Deng constantly emphasised the 'Four Basic Principles' and the need for reform and 'opening'. The Four Basic Principles were: adherence to Marxism–Leninism–Mao Zedong Thought; socialism; dictatorship of the proletariat; and the primacy of Communist Party leadership. While there was no disagreement between reformers and conservatives in the leadership on the importance of these matters, there were heated debates about what they really meant.[16]

By 'the need for reform' Deng appeared to mean principally making a clearer distinction between the powers of the Communist Party and the government. He had said about new laws on assembly, association and other rights, which had been planned before the demonstrations, that they should be crafted carefully to avoid 'instability'. However, on 31 May 1989 he said that 'some people understand "reform" to mean movement toward liberalism or capitalism. Capitalism is the heart of reform for them, but not for us. What we mean by reform is different and still *under debate*' [my italics]. All the leaders were clear that 'reform' did not mean importing bourgeois liberal democratic ideas from the West. Ideologically the Party seemed very unclear and disunited about what they stood for – it was much easier to say what they were against.

In Shanghai, Jiang Zemin – the Communist Party Secretary – had already taken a tough line against student demonstrations, and on 27 April he 'rectified' plans by a leading newspaper, *The World Economic Herald*, to publish a sympathetic memorial article on Hu Yaobang. This newspaper had become a forum for Hu's network emphasising the need for political reform. The Communist Party's 'Leading Group for Discipline' entered the offices of the newspaper and 'signed off' for the publication of a different version of the article with deletions required by the political leadership in Shanghai. This provoked further demonstrations throughout the country. Jiang came to the notice of the leadership in Beijing for his firm handling of the situation.

Then, on 30 April, Zhao returned from the state visit. He was a moderate, and stressed the need to respond to the students' 'legitimate concerns with accelerated reform', but Li argued that the restoration of order had to come first. Zhao's conciliatory speeches pleased the students, and tensions eased. He felt that the Shanghai Party Committee had moved too hastily and made things worse, and wanted to develop a form of socialist democracy based on law but not a Western multiparty system: 'We must make the people feel that under the leadership of the Communist Party and the socialist system they can truly and fully enjoy democracy and freedom.'[17] The previous year he had argued that local leaders should engage in a process of 'consultation and dialogue' with local citizens,[18] which sounded like grassroots democracy. Zhao was more open to political reform than Deng, and he assumed Hu's role as protector of the intellectuals. The leadership became polarised between the supporters of Zhao the moderate and of Li the hardliner, which exposed a bitter division at the highest level in government and the Party.

Tension was rising fast. On 4 May the students issued a significant 'Declaration on the Seventieth Anniversary of the May Fourth Incident'. The declaration brought tens of thousands of students from fifty-one campuses around the country on to the streets to call on the government to accelerate political and economic reform, guarantee constitutional freedoms, fight corruption, adopt a press law and allow the establishment of privately run newspapers.

The hunger strike by students in Tiananmen Square started on 13 May 1989. The reasons were to protest against the government's indifference towards the motives behind the student uprising and against labelling 'our patriotic, democratic student movement as "turmoil"'. For the leadership, the hunger strike was a double disaster. The strike was bad enough in itself but it was made worse because the world press (with full television coverage) was just arriving in Beijing to cover the state visit of Mikhail Gorbachev on 16 May. The leadership's every response quickly became world news. Zhao wanted to separate the broad mass of students from the 'tiny minority' who were causing all the trouble; 'getting rid of corruption is, however, the most urgent task,' he said. Deng emphasised yet again the need for stability to achieve the goal of democracy. There were fears that the Gorbachev visit would be disrupted. In spite of leadership appeals and some dialogue with the students, the hunger strike spread. Soon over 700 students collapsed from weakness and exhaustion and were taken to hospital. The government estimated that there were now 1.2 million protesters.

By 17 May imposing martial law in Beijing was now on the agenda. Five members of the Politburo Standing Committee voted: Zhao plus one were against, Li plus one for, with one abstention. At this impasse, by an earlier agreement, the matter was referred to the Party Elders, led by Deng.

At 5.00 AM on 18 May began a momentous two weeks in the history of China. Zhao spoke to some hunger strikers now in the Xiehe hospital (other leaders went to other hospitals):

Your enthusiasm for democracy and the rule of law, for the struggle against corruption and for furthering reform, is extremely valuable. The Centre takes your reasonable opinions and demands very seriously and will study them immediately and carefully ... The aims of the Party and government are the same as your aims; there is no basic conflict between us. You and we can stay in touch in many different ways and can solve problems together. So please don't continue fasting. You're young and you've got a long time ahead of you for making contributions to the nation and people, so you should take care of your health first.[19]

He then went to his office and wrote out his resignation. Eighty-two-year-old Yang Shangkun, a veteran of the Long March, now Head of State and a Party Elder, persuaded him to withdraw it. At 8.30 AM the same day, eight Party Elders met with the Politburo Standing Committee (Zhao was absent, ill) and the Military Affairs Commission. Li strongly criticised Zhao's policies and actions. There was increasing alarm. The majority decided to impose martial law from midnight 21 May. Including the armed police, there would be 180,000 troops in Beijing. (Later it became clear that this was to ensure that all significant units would be represented to reduce the likelihood that any one unit or leader could stage a coup.)

At 4.00 AM on 19 May, Zhao and Li entered Tiananmen Square, each accompanied by a supporter. Wen Jiabao (of whom more later) went with Zhao to speak with the protestors.[20] 'We have come too late,' said Zhao, and he begged the students to protect their health, to end the hunger strike and to leave the square before it was too late. He was sure that the demands they had raised would be dealt with. He said that he was old and didn't matter – almost as though he was no longer the country's leader. He was in tears, as were many of those who heard him. When Deng heard the details, he criticised Zhao for flouting Party principles and being 'very undisciplined'. To his close friend Yang, he said:

When economic reform reaches a certain point, you have to have political reform to accompany it. You know, I've never opposed political reform. But you have to consider the realities, you have to think how many of the old comrades in the Party can accept it now ... I have to give the nod on every important decision. I carry too much weight, and that's not good for the Party or the state. I should think about retiring [he was eighty-five], but how can I right now?

That day more than 1 million people came to support the students. In twenty-one provinces there were massive demonstrations; in seventeen provincial capitals, crowds of 10,000 or more had gathered.

That evening Li said:

> Anarchy is growing … we're headed for nationwide turmoil if we don't put a stop to this soon … a tiny, tiny minority of individuals are trying to use the turmoil to reach their political goals to deny the leadership of the Chinese Communist Party and the socialist system, they challenge our opposition to bourgeois liberalisation and they oppose the Four Basic Principles, now they have directed their spear at Comrade Deng Xiaoping … their goal is to subvert the leadership of the Communist Party, to overthrow the government and to repudiate the people's democratic dictatorship … there will be no hope nor future for China.

The next morning Li Peng signed the martial law order and made the necessary announcements. Immediately students and other citizens started erecting barricades throughout Beijing to block the passage of troops, and the military began to move to their pre-determined positions. The countdown to violence had begun.

Then the Institute for Economic Reform in China, part of Zhao's 'think tank', wrote:

> Li Peng's speech on the evening of 19 May recklessly distorted the truth, inverted right and wrong, stirred up disturbance, intensified conflicts, ignored appeals of all kinds of people, rejected the spirit of a series of correct speeches by General Secretary Zhao Ziyang beginning 4 May, seriously worsened the situation and brought society to the brink of 'turmoil'.

Li's speech was widely praised by Communist authorities in eleven major cities. 'Martial law hasn't restored order,' said Deng at a crucial meeting of Party Elders on the evening of 21 May. Some 300,000 people crowded into Tiananmen Square; the military manoeuvres had been only partly successful. Eight Party Elders had assembled at Deng's house; the two eldest were eighty-seven and the average age was eighty-three. They had taken command of the situation. Deng said:

> Other than those of us here tonight, nobody seems even able to describe the problem correctly … the last two General Secretaries didn't hold up, but that wasn't because they weren't qualified. There was nothing wrong with them at the start. Later they stumbled over the fundamental issue

of sticking to the Four Basic Principles. The keys to the Four Principles are Party leadership and socialism. The opposite of the Four Principles is bourgeois liberalisation ... In the recent turmoil Zhao has exposed his position completely. He obviously stands on the side of turmoil, and in practical terms he has been fomenting division, splitting the Party and defending turmoil. It's lucky we're still here to keep a lid on things.

It became obvious that Zhao had to go. Candidates for his replacement were discussed but Deng had already made up his mind, and had briefed two of his colleagues to propose Jiang. Li was hardly mentioned as a serious possibility, although being the Premier he was next in line. Zhao and his close supporter on the Politburo Standing Committee, Hu Qili, were relieved of their duties the very next day, 22 May 1989, and were placed under house arrest.[21] Zhao remained there until his death at eighty-five years, in January 2005. Thus was wasted another fine man who could have led China in a more liberal direction.

The protests spread. Then, late in the night of 29 May, students in Tiananmen Square assembled a thirty-foot-high plaster statue of the Goddess of Democracy with flowing hair, holding a torch. Made by the students, it was modelled on the Statue of Liberty in New York. Amongst a leadership consisting of men (apart from 'Sister Deng', as Deng called the eighty-five-year old Deng Yingchao, a Party Elder, widow of Zhou Enlai and foster mother to Premier Li), it was doubly offensive to the authorities. The Beijing municipal government considered that the act violated its regulations, and bitterly opposed it. On 1 June, in a report to the Politburo ordered by Li from the Beijing Party Committee called 'On the True Nature of the Turmoil', the unarmed students and ordinary citizens who supported them were described as 'terrorists who were preparing an armed seizure of power', and referred to a supposed 'counter-revolutionary riot'. It was almost as though Li believed that the Goddess of Democracy in Tiananmen Square was a Trojan Horse filled with armed terrorists.

Furthermore, also on 1 June, a second report ordered by Li – this time from the State Security Ministry and addressed to the Party Elders – hit hard at the US for trying to convert China to democracy and American lifestyles: 'The aim is to make China dependent on the United States economically and, eventually, politically as well,' it said. (Zhao was known to be strongly pro-US, so this was a further nail in his coffin.) 'These [foreign influences] have only one goal: to annihilate socialism.'

At a fateful meeting of six Party Elders led by Deng and three members of the Politburo Standing Committee on the morning of 2 June, Li summarised and quoted from the two reports, preceded by the recitation of slogans:

We do allow reform but on one condition: that the Four Basic Principles are upheld ... The nature of this turmoil is extremely clear: its bottom line is death to our Party and state ... Stability must take precedence over everything.[22]

After a long discussion the fateful decision was taken based on a proposal from Li to clear Tiananmen Square by military force. At 10.00 PM that evening Martial Law Command ordered units in the suburbs to enter the city. The crowds reacted violently. Buses with darkened windows full of soldiers and guns were surrounded; roadblocks were set in place. Military vehicles were seized by the crowd, soldiers were beaten and army units were scattered. It was chaos. At an emergency meeting of the leadership Li called it a 'counter-revolutionary riot'. The military desperately needed moral support and guidance, although 'the political thought people are working hard to keep things calm'. Li urged that 'we must be merciless with the tiny minority of riot elements'. The final act had begun.

The next day the military met with stiff resistance. The people showed no fear. Their actions were spontaneous. Some soldiers lost their self-control and fired haphazardly. People were rushed to hospital on all sorts of makeshift transport. Deng wanted two things: that the square be cleared before dawn the next day, and to be reasonable with the students, 'to make sure that they see the logic in what we are doing'; but there was to be 'no bloodshed within Tiananmen Square'. During the night of 3 June, independent eyewitnesses such as Kate Adie of the BBC and *New York Times* correspondent Nicholas Kristof (who was in Tiananmen Square from about midnight), saw many bodies riddled with bullets.[23]

In the small hours of the morning of 4 June, students began to organise a peaceful withdrawal from the Square. Then the lights went out, and they were unsure what was happening. When the lights came back on at 4.30 AM, troops were everywhere. The students were hemmed in; soldiers pressed towards them with swinging batons, and the tanks came closer. A corridor was left for students to withdraw. They began to move more and more quickly. By 5.40 AM Tiananmen Square was clear. The number of deaths there that night is still uncertain.

However, once outside the square, the scene was different. Soldiers opened fire; tanks drove straight at people. At several places the confrontation was direct and bloody, and casualties mounted. More than 500 army trucks were set on fire at different places. Many soldiers were killed by angry crowds – some were burnt to death in their vehicles. On 4 June, an atmosphere of terror pervaded the city. Trucks were still burning, and there was sporadic gunfire. In sixty-three cities across China over the next few days there were major demonstrations, mostly nonviolent, and roadblocks disrupted normal life. Wreaths were carried, along with many banners and placards condemning Li and the leadership, demanding vengeance. Chinese living abroad in many countries joined the protests. Governments abroad, especially in Europe and the US, condemned the Chinese government and some imposed sanctions. In all, it was thought that about 400–800 people had died, 90 percent of them civilians, and some 7,000 were wounded. Of the mass of students from Beijing universities, thirty-six died.

Thus ended one of the most catastrophic failures of government in modern times. Almost every single action the leaders took made matters worse. There were many lessons to be learned. Deng himself thought that their greatest mistake was in education.[24] By this he meant not a failure in reading, writing and arithmetic but in political education – teaching everyone the Four Basic Principles and the policies of reform.

Li was seen by Andrew Nathan, one of the two authors of *The Tiananmen Papers* and a China expert, as 'perhaps the most capable, certainly the most resolute, politician on the scene in 1989 …'.[25] Li emerges from the documents as vengeful, judgmental, politically rigid and committed to Party dictatorship as a principle. He was certainly not popular, and became known as 'the Butcher of Beijing'. When much later Chris Patten, in his role as Governor of Hong Kong, met Li, he found him 'ploddingly unimpressive'.[26]

But on 21 May the Party Elders made a provisional decision, confirmed on 27 May, to pass him over as the next General Secretary – the top job in the country – which no doubt Li considered his by rights. He must have been devastated with disappointment, frustration and anger. Perhaps those two reports were also intended to show how strong, loyal, well-informed and perceptive he was, and how suitable to lead the country.

In criticising Zhao and the way he consulted a number of 'think tanks', one of the Party Elders said: 'Our Communist Party doesn't have think tanks – never has. This is pure bourgeois stuff.' This may account both for the vast amount of information collected at the centre during this crisis, with so little impartial analysis, and for the absence of truly independent studies and reports. Li's two reports, which proved so influential, came from the Beijing Party Committee and the State Security Ministry, over which he could exert pressure.

The very notion of a 'loyal opposition' was – and is – foreign to the Chinese leaders. Opposition to the government is tantamount to being an enemy of the state. Therefore, except for the brave souls who risk torture and imprisonment, opposition has to be kept hidden, secret and – a small step – conspiratorial. Conspiracies were common in imperial China, for few dared to tell an emperor that he was wrong. Those who expect there to be conspiracies will find them.

Deng, as the paramount leader, had the ultimate responsibility. Regardless of his advanced age, once the Party Elders assumed ultimate leadership it was his authority that counted above all others. But he was gravely misled by Li and the two partisan reports produced under his authority. There was no independent source of analysis and no proper dialogue with the protest leaders. The '2 June Hunger Strike Declaration', written by the students to explain their actions, was forthright and essentially moderate in tone but, evidently, it never reached the leadership. There was a vast and unbridgeable gulf between this document and the alarmist rhetoric of Premier Li.

It is easy to understand how preoccupied the leadership was in China during 1989, and why the hardliners in Tibet felt they had free rein. At the top, Tibet was seen as having the potential to cause serious unrest. The fear of 'instability' was at the forefront of Jiang's mind as he occupied the highest office in China.

EIGHT

Jiang Zemin: A Lot for China, Little for Tibet

'In caring for others and serving heaven,
there is nothing like using restraint.'
Lao-tzu, Tao Te Ching, *Chapter Fifty-nine*

Jiang Zemin (*zemin* means 'benefit the people') was born in Yangzhou, a city of culture in Jiangsu province, on 17 August 1926, to prosperous parents in a wealthy neighbourhood.[1] But he had a disturbed childhood; China was in its most chaotic period of internal conflict, and in 1937 – when he was ten – the country was invaded by the Japanese. His school became a stable, and all the books were burnt for fuel. At age thirteen he was adopted by the widow of his uncle, a Communist revolutionary martyr who had been killed by bandits. Adoptions within an extended family were not uncommon, although those outside the family were rare and considered to be 'fetching water with a bamboo-woven basket'.

Jiang joined the Communist Party in 1946 aged twenty, and trained in electrical engineering at the prestigious Jiaotong University in Shanghai. He later trained further at the Stalin Automobile Works near Moscow. (Stalin's death in 1953 had led to improved relations between China and Russia.) Jiang worked as an electrical engineer in various state enterprises in China, became Vice-Minister of the newly created First Machine-Building Ministry and then head of the Power Equipment Department. For the next six years he was in China's First Automobile Works at Changchun, to the north in Jilin province, during its construction, and became the plant's director.[2] (In 1994

I visited that plant on a consultancy assignment, saw the FAW trucks rolling rhythmically off the very labour-intensive, nuts-and-bolts production line and talked with the director about his relationships with the government, trying to discover where his responsibility began and where the state made decisions. The lines were unclear.)

At the beginning of the Cultural Revolution Jiang came under suspicion because of his background, but argued persuasively that he was a dedicated and long-standing Communist. (At University he had been one of only 180 Communists out of some 3,000 students.) He argued further that he was not rich, pleading that his sole possessions were an old leather suitcase, a kerosene stove and a transistor radio – although he realised, just in time before the interview, that he needed his hair cut (long hair could have signified a bourgeois background.) However, members of his family suffered and were bullied by the Red Guards.

In 1980 he led a team that visited Sri Lanka, Singapore and Mexico to investigate their export-processing zones, and became Minister of the Electronics Industry. Then he turned to serious politics, first as Mayor of Shanghai (1985–7), then as Party Secretary, the most senior position (1987–9). He is a good linguist and a natural all-round musician, bursting into song at banquets, playing all manner of musical instruments, reciting poetry and being rather jolly. At a banquet in Russia he sang 'Doleko, Doleko', a well-known Russian song, after which Russian President Boris Yeltsin was heard to remark: 'We have been deprived of a great opera star.' Jiang would later say (quite rightly) that 'it's not good if people know nothing about Beethoven's Ninth Symphony'. When Jiang was appointed General Secretary of the Communist Party in May 1989, the tragic events in Tiananmen Square and around the country were reaching their peak. Abroad, the years 1989–91 marked the end of Soviet communism, the disintegration of Communist Eastern Europe and the dramatic destruction of the Berlin Wall. In December 1989 Nicolae Ceausescu – a friend of China and a frequent visitor to Beijing – was executed, and Romania rejoiced. In February 1990 the Soviet Communist Party fell apart and in August 1991 Gorbachev was arrested; Yeltsin came to power from the turret of a tank. These were truly awful warnings to the new leadership in China, mesmerising and terrible events to be avoided at all costs. The Soviet Communist Party's heroes, Marx and Lenin, were cast aside. Thus it was that Jiang saw the absolute need for 'stability' in China. Also, when the states of the Soviet Union became independent, many adopted flawed democratic systems, which reinforced Jiang's hatred of multiparty democracy.

Jiang was now leader of the third generation of the Communist dynasty. From 1989 he was General Secretary of the Communist Party and Chairman of the Central Military Commission with responsibility for the armed forces. In 1993 he became President of the People's Republic of China, and could thus more appropriately represent China's interests abroad. He assumed the mantle of an emperor; all power resided with him. He, not the Pope, would ordain bishops of the Patriotic Catholic Church and be responsible for Beijing Cathedral; he, not the Dalai Lama, would appointnew Buddhist spiritual leaders such as the Panchen Lama; he, not international law, would decide what human rights meant in China.

In July 1990, two months after lifting martial law in Lhasa – imposed by Hu Jintao, the Party Secretary there, on Jiang's orders – Jiang visited Tibet. Reportedly he wanted to 'do something that will really help the Tibetans out, rather than offering cheap words of support'.[3] This turned out to mean principally a new airport for Chamdo, and more technically qualified Chinese cadres, very different from and significantly less useful to Tibetans than Hu Yaobang's reforms a decade earlier.

Jiang also travelled widely abroad in his role as the president, but his lovely smile did not always win him friends. Governments and heads of state gave him the welcome due to the president of a country in which many leaders see business possibilities for their industries. However, often people were not so diplomatic, especially supporters of Tibet and branches of Falun Gong abroad. He criticised those countries for not keeping better control over protestors, and did not appear to understand what freedom of speech and of assembly meant in practice. Indeed, the reality of these freedoms was tested during his visits – and, in Britain at any rate, was found wanting. At home, however, in 1989, Jiang had a number of very difficult problems to resolve. The students had emphasised democracy and corruption, but many other issues were awaiting his attention.

In October 1997, in an interview with *The Washington Post*, Jiang said that 'elections are impossible in a country with a population of nearly 1.3 billion, of whom 100 million are illiterate.'[4] Surely he was aware that India, his neighbour, has a population over 1 billion, and all adults over eighteen – about 680 million – have the vote. Almost half the population there is illiterate, and democracy is increasingly popular. At each of the thirteen elections so far held, a higher and higher proportion of those eligible to vote do so, and has now reached 65 percent (which exceeds many Western countries).

India is a federal republic, originally with twenty-five states and seven union territories, each with its own elected government and legislature – so democracy is decentralised.[5] In November 2000 the Indian government created three new states within the federation (Uttaranchal was carved out of Uttar Pradesh, Jharkhand from Bihar, and Chhatisgarh from Madhya Pradesh). The Indian view was that smaller states, being nearer to the people, can respond better to their needs, and offer less opportunity for corruption, while new developments can be accelerated and made more useful to the people. (Within China's centralist system, in 1988, Hainan Island was separated from Guangdong and became a new province; in 1997, Chongqing, with a population of 31 million, was separated from Sichuan to become a new province, so that orders from the centre could better take local conditions into account.)

Chinese Communist leaders have all rejected multiparty democracy. No doubt they remember that democracy in the Chinese Republic (from 1911 to the mid-1920s) resulted in 130 different political parties, and chaos. Indian parliaments have been dominated nationwide by two political parties, and there are several smaller ones – some in only one state arguing for local issues. Coalitions are sometimes necessary to reach a majority on which power is based.

That, however, is not the only model. In Nepal there was for a time a 'partyless *panchyat* system'. People were elected not on the basis of party allegiance, but according to who was thought to be the best person to represent the people at the local level, from whom regional and national representatives were then elected. When I was in the high Himalaya in 1987, I interviewed many heads of remote small villages, high in the mountains. The local people, who quickly gathered round to hear our talks on such matters, nodded in general approval of that system. National politics were simply too far away and communications so bad in the mountains that they wanted the people whom they knew best and trusted most to be their representatives. The system was, however, abolished in 1990.

China is so big in terms of population and land mass and so extremely diverse, that some kind of federal democratic system seems appropriate. Throughout history, as a degree of anarchy settled upon China, provinces and even counties began to adopt a kind of informal federation. It was this development that finally brought the Ming and Qing dynasties to an end. Left to its own devices, federalism would develop naturally in China. Guangdong province virtually manages itself already. The policy of 'stability' keeps these movements towards formal autonomy in check and supports centralism.

There are many countries with federal democratic systems, and thus many real-life examples to scrutinise. In 1975 Eric Blaustein published a looseleaf book, *Constitutions of Dependencies and Territories*, which is kept up to date.[6] It is possible therein to identify all the constitutions that have federal characteristics, and therefore to conduct in-depth enquiries about how they work and what would be most appropriate for China in the twenty-first century. Also, several authors have made lifelong studies of the subject, including Daniel J. Elazar of the Jerusalem Institute for Federal Studies in Israel and Hurst Hannum of the Fletcher School of Law and Diplomacy, Tufts University, in the US.[7]

In 1994 a meeting of Chinese dissidents in San Francisco drew up a draft constitution for a federal/confederal system in China (I later attended their London meeting). Tibet was seen as an 'autonomous state', rather like a Swiss canton, within China. Then, in June 2000, the Foundation for China in the Twenty-first Century, a democratisation think tank, held a meeting in Boston with Han Chinese, Mongolians, Uyghurs, Tibetans, Taiwanese and guests from Europe and the US.[8] 'With the high-handed repression practised by the Communists in China, sooner or later there will be an explosion and collapse,' said Wang Lixiong, a well-known author who had come from Beijing. 'That's why people should concentrate on peaceful political transformation.' The meeting proposed the creation of a confederation in China and an even more decentralised form of federation in Xinjiang, Hong Kong, Macau, Inner Mongolia, Taiwan and Tibet, to replace the Communist central authority.

For democracy to work effectively for the benefit of the people and for world peace also requires freedom of speech including freedom of the press, broadcast media and internet.[9] It does not exist in China today. There is also no equivalent of a Freedom of Information Act. An open society in which people can learn the truth is a prerequisite for a truly democratic system. At present, political indoctrination starts in primary school in China. Patriotic songs are still sung, such as 'We Must Liberate Taiwan' and 'Without the Communist Party There Will Be No New China'.[10] Democracy also requires willingness to accept a degree of social conflict according to the prescribed rules of the game, in which the majority, voting without harassment and by fair calculation, wins. Losers must also be accepted by society, permitted to contest a later election if they choose. What is unacceptable and damaging to the practice of democracy is the blatant rigging of polls (as, for example, in March 2002 in Zimbabwe and in November 2004 in Ukraine). The 'first past the post' system of voting in both the US and Britain has led towards a 'democratic dictatorship'; some form of proportional representation would be fairer and less extreme. No democratic system is guaranteed foolproof, but with good intentions and popular support it can be made to work.

Well before democracy could be planned and introduced in China there would have to be a sustained period of education and training nationwide both for government and people. Experience in democracy at the rural village level has already started.[11] Most villages now elect their local leaders, and they and their deputies represent them in township People's Congresses, the next level up. But there is no standard system for doing so, and some are deeply flawed. Candidates must be approved by Party officials and politically loyal to the state; a list of six or seven candidates are selected by the Party and the people vote to elect, say, five of them, or local clans would make sure that they got control. In other villages there are secret 'primaries' in which all the people write down the name of their chosen candidate; then, in a second round, villagers vote from the shortlist of the most popular – a method called *haixuan* – and many non-Party members have been elected. Even so, the leaders have little real power. Developing democracy 'from the bottom up' is a feasible strategy.

To introduce a democratic system in China starting from the country's current situation would be a vast undertaking, and would demand the full assent of the Party and the people. Already China has studied the experience of Taiwan in introducing a multiparty democracy, but it would require a long period of research and feasibility testing into possible structures and voting systems in a country as vast as China. In particular, globalisation is seen to be damaging to democracy by restricting the area for democratic choice, because many important economic decisions would be made by head offices abroad.[12]

Corruption, a major complaint of the people, found its critics in Tiananmen Square. There were wall posters, originating in Qinghua University in Beijing, listing the names of thirty leading members of the Party and their sons, daughters and other relatives who had been appointed to top positions in government and business. It showed a vast web of nepotism, and was seized upon as the focal image of a corrupt regime with its resonance at much lower levels where ordinary people could see and feel the injustices. The leaders had set the example and the followers had adopted their corrupt ethics.

At Jiang Zemin's first meeting of the Politburo following the tragedy in Tiananmen Square he took action banning the children of senior cadres from engaging in business operations. The children of the leadership – the 'princelings' – had become the first to benefit from the *de facto* privatisation of part of the economy under Deng Xiaoping, acquiring wealth beyond imagination; in 1992–3 Jiang issued regulations designed to bar all officials from employing relatives. Cadres had to report all sources of their income to their respective personnel departments. Yet these directives, which had barely begun to meet the students' demands, proved to be ineffective. They were virtually ignored – there was, for many of those concerned, too much to lose.

In 1997 Wei Jianxing, known as a 'graft-buster', a role in which he had a good reputation, was appointed to the Politburo Standing Committee and became Secretary to the Party's Central Commission for Discipline Inspection. This body was charged with purifying the Party's ranks of corruption at all levels. Then began a long campaign of arresting people engaged in embezzlement, extortion, theft of state property and other corrupt practices. Reporting on work carried out in 1998, the Commission estimated that some US$ 10 billion of state money had been embezzled that year, but only 3,970 Party members at the level of county magistrate or above had been penalised.[13] Investigators had looked at 1.6 million cases, investigated 120,000 and recovered US$ 560 million. Yet corruption persisted.

Reporting on a further 'Strike Hard' campaign in mid-2001, Amnesty International reported that 'at least 2,960 people have been sentenced to death and 1,781 executed in the last three months ... [and that] more people have been executed in China [during this period] than in the rest of the world in the last three years'.[14] Tens of thousands of arrested suspects were assigned to *laogai* camps for 'reform through labour', 'education through labour' or 'forced job assignments'. Introduced by Mao in the 1930s, they are the equivalent of Stalin's *gulags*. There are some 990 such camps, with a high concentration in remote Qinghai and Xinjiang.[15]

The Chinese authorities have stated that one of the purposes of Strike Hard was to 'tackle the serious economic crime situation before entry into the World Trade Organisation (WTO) and the challenge of globalisation'. In areas such as Tibet and Xinjiang the campaign has been extended to 'strike hard' against so-called 'separatists' in the monasteries and elsewhere. Most executions take place after sentencing rallies in front of massive crowds in sports stadiums and public squares. Rallies in Shaanxi were reportedly seen by 1,800,000 people. Some were broadcast live on television. The Amnesty International report was based on monitored public reports, and the organisation believes that only a fraction of death sentences and executions are publicly reported – the true numbers may be much higher.

To process such an enormous number of cases in a short space of time, police and prosecutors were told to 'cut corners and not to get entangled in the details' so as to achieve 'quick approval, quick arrest, quick trial and quick results'. In Hunan province, Amnesty International reported that during a 'Spring Thunder' operation (23–5 April 2001) police boasted of 'solving 3,000 cases in two days'. In Sichuan province police reported that they had 'cracked' 6,704 cases in six days (19–24 April), apprehending 19,446 people. Shandong province reportedly held an average of sixty-five criminal trials every day from 10 April to 25 May 2001. Amnesty International commented that 'curtailed procedures plus great pressure on police and judicial authorities mean that the potential for miscarriages of justice, arbitrary sentencing and the execution of innocent people is immense'. It would appear that the due processes of the law, which were inadequate anyway, had become once again subservient to political expediency.

Party members had thought themselves almost guaranteed immunity from prosecution, especially senior officials and those related to them. In December 2000 there were newspaper reports that the minister of justice himself, with his mistress, had been arraigned for embezzlement, and that a vice-minister of the Water Resources Ministry had been arrested on corruption charges.[16] In February 2002, the former governor of the Bank of China, Wang Xuebing – a protégé of Premier Zhu Rongji– disappeared after allegedly embezzling almost US$ 1 billion.

In January 2002 the government announced that it was investigating the alleged embezzlement of some 6 billion *yuan* (US$ 723 million) from the Bank of China in Guangdong.[17] About 160 billion *yuan* (US$ 19 billion) was allegedly embezzled by Chinese officials from the Bank of China during 2001. Moreover, Jiang's own son Jiang Mianheng became the chairman of the fast-growing telecom business China Netcom. In 2001 he allowed Rupert Murdoch's News Corporation to take an illegal 12.5 percent stake in China Netcom (although China then planned a change in the law).[18] This has big implications for the development of internet services in China, and of China's first broadband telecom network. Jiang Mianheng also obtained an exclusive licence to construct a national fibre-optics network.[19]

Although no doubt most people at all levels are entirely innocent, as corrupt practices pervade the whole of society – including Party members and cadres – it is likely that many of those charged with investigating, arresting, conducting trials, sentencing and punishing are themselves corrupt. Who will punish these authorities? Who will apprehend those who gave orders to 'cut corners and not get entangled in the details'? And who can be sure that there are no 'hidden agendas' amongst the accusers, people whom they wish to see suffer for reasons quite other than their alleged crimes, if the details are not thoroughly investigated?

The 'impact effects' of Strike Hard will be considerable but it is the long term that matters. By June 2002, responsible observers believed that 'corruption is now worse than in 1989'. Institutionalised corruption has become so entrenched, so pervasive, so long-standing, and benefits to individuals so large, that a different approach may be required. The problem is one of ethical behaviour and is, at its core, spiritual. Yet Mao himself had said that 'first, every human being and every society must have a moral compass, if not Confucianism then something else that fulfils that role'; and he urged the primacy of 'right thinking', which Confucius called 'virtue'. Preaching to the Chinese of the need for a 'moral compass' and of 'virtue' today, as Jiang did in his major speech of 1 July 2001, would most likely not convert their ways of thinking and behaving. Chris Patten believes that the best way of dealing with corruption would be through increasing democracy and 'asking damned awkward questions in a legislative body'.[20] In China more questions are indeed now being asked in the National People's Congress, the supreme lawmaking body,[21] but not enough.

Jiang also saw the need to reform the bureaucracy. The reduction in the 'command economy' under Deng, the introduction of more 'openness' in foreign investment and the gradual introduction of market mechanisms since 1979 all created organisational redundancies. Many planners, controllers, ministries, commissions, bureaus and offices became unnecessary. Moreover, boundaries between ministries had become blurred, and there was weak coordination between them. There was no legislative framework for important institutions and areas of policy, no administrative law.

In short, the machinery of government no longer corresponded to the needs of government, the economy or the people. It was in a muddle, hugely overstaffed and extremely corrupt. In March 1988 the National People's Congress voted to cut the number of central government ministries from forty to twenty-nine and to lay off 8 million civil servants. By June 1991 this had led to the beginning of a three-year major reform programme for reducing the size of and restructuring the Chinese government to be more responsive to local conditions. In the process of restructuring, it was hoped to reduce the number of people employed in government by a more modest 2 million overall.

At that time the central government in Beijing had forty-one ministries and commissions (eighty-one if the subordinate bureaus and offices were included). At the second level down in the administrative hierarchy were twenty-two provinces, five autonomous regions and three centrally administered cities (Beijing, Tianjin and Shanghai), each typically organised into fifty or sixty departments or bureaus broadly corresponding with those in the central government. At the third level down were 1,919 counties (rural areas) and 447 municipalities. County governments, headed by county magistrates, each typically had some forty or so administrative departments, and the municipalities – headed by mayors – each typically had some fifty-five departments. At the fourth level down were 56,497 towns and township administrations – in total a vast and ill-assorted bureaucracy of alarming proportions.

It was right that during the major economic innovations introduced by Deng in the 1980s, especially because the changes were at first cautiously experimental, there should have been stability in the machinery of government; otherwise, the administrative chaos would have been even worse. Whatever the reasons behind the timing of the structural reform programme in the government, it was a bold step forward for Jiang, and change was much needed. It was, however, Premier Li Peng, continuing as head of the government, who was directly responsible for administrative reform. He sought help in this formidable task from outside.

In 1991 the UNDP (United Nations Development Programme), on contract to the Chinese government, produced a three-year programme for the 'Administrative Structural Reform at Central and Local Government Levels' to give effect to these needs.[22] In April 1994, towards the end of the three-year period, I was a member of a ten-man UNDP 'team of international experts' charged with observing and commenting on the progress that had been made. After a conference at which we all presented papers to the assembled ministers, bureau chiefs and academics,[23] two teams of five conducted field investigations. One group went to Nanning in the south of China, and I was in the team which flew north to Jilin province (in what was once Manchuria), to talk with the Jilin provincial government, the Jilin municipal government, the Changchun municipal government and officials of a pilot county-restructuring project near Changchun.

We five experts from Australia, Hong Kong, Thailand, the UK and the US all had experience in management and public administration and connections with universities (in my case as Professor of Economics at the London Business School and as a former senior civil servant, Chief Economist in the British Board of Trade, a large government department). We had a formidable task. The Changchun Municipality alone had eighty government agencies and employed 7,400 people at the time of our visit. Any substantial reduction would raise such questions as: what will happen to the functions performed by the eighty agencies [abandonment, transfer, restructuring]?; what will happen to their redundant staff?; how appropriate has the training given to local officials in their new tasks and in the management of change as the role of the central government been, both above (in the Jilin provincial government) and below? There seemed to be no systematic monitoring of such changes in Beijing, and therefore no clear picture at the centre of what was happening at the periphery – with no resource centre there, either, which puzzled officials in the provinces charged with reducing numbers could refer to for advice and help. The five senior cadres who were sent on training courses in France, Germany, New Zealand and the US, whom we interviewed, found it difficult to relate their experiences in those countries to the problems they faced in China. We produced a sensible report with six recommendations.

What happened to administrative reform? Instead of the number of officials working for the government falling by 2 million as planned, or by 8 million as earlier agreed, they subsequently *rose* by about 1 million.[24] Also, the number of officials working for the Communist Party's central organs rose by 61 percent. By the time Zhu took over from Li as Premier in 1997, the number of central government bodies had risen to 200, and an astonishing 60 percent of central government revenues were spent on staff costs of the bureaucracy. In March 1998 another attempt was announced to reduce the size of the bureaucracy – to more than halve the number of central government staff to 4 million – and the number of official organisations, the tenth such attempt to reform the bureaucracy since 1949. One of Wen Jiabao's first actions on being appointed Premier in November 2003 was to restructure most of the central executive bodies.

Such a large proportion of government revenue is absorbed by administration costs that, at the periphery of the system, and especially in rural areas, there is little money left over for the people. This has had two effects. First, essential social organisations like schools and hospitals have had to earn a proportion of their own costs. Many children and teachers became employees of local firms. In 1987 China's schools had a combined turnover of some 9 billion *yuan* (US$ 1.1 billion) and made profits of 1.7 billion *yuan*. To some extent, the practice continues. For example, in March 2001 it was reported that children in class at a school in Jiangxi province were assembling fireworks for sale when an explosion occurred, killing at least forty-five of them along with their teachers. The local Party secretary had agreed that the headmaster could take on this work for a local company in order to help cover the school's financial deficits. Parents had complained to the township government about the time taken on such mandatory classwork and the dangers, but they were ignored.

The second consequence of under-funding was that local officials imposed illegal taxes and fees to raise money. Taxes were imposed on everything from the slaughter of pigs to 'hanging objects from the ceiling' and, in Tibet, for a time, even circumambulating religious objects or sites. In 1998 the central government in China abolished 973 different 'taxes' that had yielded 45 billion *yuan* (US$ 5.4 billion) and local governments had promised to abolish 26,710 'random fees' which had yielded some 98 billion *yuan* (US$ 11 billion).[25] To give instruction on 'correct' Party policies and to strengthen control from the centre, in 1999 some 600,000 senior cadres were sent to rural areas to give talks, and a further 15 million rural cadres attended training courses to improve their understanding of Party policies. But, as a local Party chief said to Jasper Becker in 1999: 'We have the power here, we do what we like.'[26]

In China itself some rural communities have rioted against continuing taxation. In August 2000 there were protests at villages in Jiangxi province, and in April 2001 the People's Armed Police raided the village of Yuntang in Jiangxi province, where villagers had been protesting for years.[27] The villagers, whom the security forces called a 'criminal gang', had refused to pay illegal and impossibly high local taxes and fees. For the peasants, the tyranny of the former landlords from which Mao released them has been replaced by tyranny from local Party officials.

In Tibet, at the periphery of the Chinese empire, the arbitrary, punitive, discriminatory and blatantly unfair taxes and the lack of public money for social services and development can now be seen as a consequence of the cost of China's huge bureaucracy, which leaves too little cash for all other purposes. In spite of the 1998 policy initiative from the highest level, in the year 2001 Tibetans were still being subjected to excessive and arbitrary taxes[28] (see Prologue).

Historian Merle Goldman observed that at the close of the twentieth century:

> Party directives and ideological exhortations on such matters as rampant corruption, accelerating social and geographic disparities, regional protectionism, agricultural stagnation, increasing lawlessness and worsening environmental pollution are generally ignored or only heeded superficially.[29]

The Falun Gong[30] has become another problem for the government of China. It is a popular spiritual movement which, in 1992, emerged from relative obscurity. Its principles and practices are drawn from Taoism, Chinese Ch'an Buddhism and the more obscure Chinese Qimen school. It is based on ancient Chinese methods of cultivating mind, body and spirit, collectively called *xulian*. Falun Gong has a moral code and way of living that emphasise truthfulness, compassion and forbearance. It promotes the cultivation of these principles to achieve high spiritual levels. Falun Gong's physical practices are drawn from ancient Chinese *qigong*, which cultivates the body's vital energy (*qi*) for healing and fitness. Meditation is also a key feature.

Formerly, Falun Gong consisted of a rather low-key, private set of beliefs and practices passed from master to pupil, but in 1992 Li Hongzhi made it a public movement. (He was exiled from China in 1996 and now lives in the US.) Anyone can participate. It has no official membership, no subscriptions, no hierarchy, no temple, church or designated places of worship, study or practice. It is a 'formless' organisation, as evoked in *The Art of War*, and thus difficult to eliminate. According to Falun Gong, there are about 70 million followers in China and about 30 million abroad. There are some forty countries with groups of Falun Gong followers. (I have met many in the UK.)

Falun Gong is totally opposed to killing, and maintains that 'attachment' to material things interferes with the cultivation of a person's higher being, and is deplored. The cultivation of these principles and practices through meditation, Falun Gong believes, leads as a byproduct to the development of 'supernormal' abilities, including clairvoyance, precognition and retrocognition. (Such observations have also long been claimed by Tibetan monks and nuns.) It also leads to mental and physical healing, followers say, which could help overcome trauma from the era of Mao. Falun Gong is dedicated to small-scale activities so as not to disturb 'the state of human society', and is no threat to the Chinese state.

However, Jiang considered it to be a serious political problem outside his control. The Chinese authorities were alarmed when, in April 1999, without their prior knowledge or permission, some 10,000 Falun Gong followers conducted peaceful *qigong* exercises outside the Communist Party Headquarters in Beijing. In July 1999 Luo Gan, in charge of security in China, set up the 'Leading Small Group to Deal with the Falun Gong' and banned it (except in Hong Kong, where there are more liberal policies). He called it 'an anti-humanity evil cult … spreading fallacies, hoodwinking people, inciting and creating disturbances and jeopardising stability' which 'aims at achieving a vicious political objective at the expense of its followers … to split the motherland and subvert the Chinese government'.[31] It was seen as a 'reactionary force bent on sabotaging socialist China in league with various foreign enemies' – invective familiar to Tibetans, and especially the Dalai Lama. The authorities also condemned meditation as being 'anti-science'. They claim that more than 1,600 people have died from suicide or from lack of medical care as a result of following Falun Gong. Beijing television reported that if Falun Gong had been allowed to continue, all economic reform would have been stopped.[32]

The European Falun Gong Information Centre said in August 2004 that over 100,000 Falun Gong members have been arrested in China, and many have been sent to labour camps for periods of three years, without trial. Many have been beaten and suffered torture. In July 2001 Falun Gong appealed to the UN to investigate the allegation that fifteen women followers were tortured to death at a labour camp in the north-eastern province of Heilongjiang, and that others had attempted suicide when their period of detention was extended for engaging in a hunger strike. The followers of Falun Gong feel so strongly about the rightness of their movement that some have committed suicide publicly in Tiananmen Square rather than give it up. These tragic and high-profile suicides publicise their plight internationally. Just four days after President George W. Bush took office in 2001, the State Department issued a statement condemning the Chinese persecution of the Falun Gong. In 2002 even foreigners in China who showed support for Falun Gong were being arrested.

Falun Gong shows every sign of being a spiritual, peaceful and highly beneficial movement. Truth, compassion and forbearance make for a good credo. But the great Taiping Rebellion (1851–64) is still seen as an awful warning. It began as a Christian fundamentalist movement with hymns and Christian rituals, preaching a moral life and austere puritanism. Converts in the 'God-Worshippers' Society' believed the Old Testament urged people to rise up against their oppressors. The Society became militant, then military; the devastation and loss of life were huge. In China today there are many religious groups, mostly Christian, some with fundamentalist practices and beliefs: 'Spread the Gospel', 'Eastern Lightning', 'Principal God Cult', 'Spirit-Spirit Church', 'World Elijah Evangelical Mission' and others. Buddhism, once widespread in China, is currently experiencing its 'best period in living memory'.[33] Falun Gong is, however, Chinese – and different.

The foundations of economic development in China and control of the economy had been laid by Deng Xiaoping. His encouragement of foreign investment in China led to an influx of famously named global corporations seeking their fortune in this supposedly vast market. But by 1989 the difficulties of operating in China had become apparent.[34] Even negotiating with the Chinese took most companies into uncharted territory. Nothing ever seemed to work out quite as planned. Promises, or what were thought to be promises, were not kept. Licences were necessary but elusive, and when obtained were unexpectedly restrictive. Costs escalated. Profitability receded towards the distant horizon. Most worrying of all, where was this vast market? Was it real or was it a statistical illusion? Dismay set in. Many companies withdrew and a few persevered, believing that all would be right in the end. An even smaller number were successful – the Chinese loved the fast food chain McDonald's, for example; it was a new experience to them.

Deng's most successful organisational initiative, the Special Economic Zone (SEZ), was carried forward by Jiang. But the burst of energy generated in the 1980s and the euphoria of foreign enterprises had dissipated under Premier Li, who was opposed to SEZs. In 1991 Deng decided to intervene personally. His famous Southern Tour, on which he was accompanied by his wife and children and by his close friend Yang Shangkun (then President of China) and his family, started at the Shenzhen railway station on 19 January 1992 – a date entered into the annals of history. It was billed as a family vacation (Deng was then eighty-seven years old), but there was a deeper motive. With Deng's force of personality and through massive media coverage at all the places visited, he single-handedly raised the whole profile of development. It was an astonishing achievement. Jiang and Li no doubt looked on with amazement and some discomfort as the old man upstaged everyone. At the time, Deng's only formal position in China was Honorary President of the Chinese Bridge Association.

As a result, there was a further burst of foreign investment, and the SEZs took off. At the beginning of 1992 there were about 100 of them. By the end of the year there were 8,700 of them, and by March 2001 there were some 12,000.[35] In April 1990 the Shanghai Pu Dong New Area, across the Huangpuat River at the mouth of the Yangtse, had been inaugurated as an open economic zone, set to be the largest SEZ of them all. Deng passed through Shanghai on his tour and excited local officials sufficiently to bring new life to the city and lift it to a high pitch of enthusiasm. He also made Zhu Rongji, then the tough Party Secretary in Shanghai, Vice-Premier under Li. Shanghai had always had a cosmopolitan lifestyle since becoming the major Treaty Port in the nineteenth century, and now it has been endowed with freedoms unheard of under Mao or Deng. Shanghai's economy is booming to an extraordinary extent. Literature and art flourish there, and lifestyles amongst younger people have become more Westernised.[36]

The year 1992 saw the 'Five Fevers': the astonishing growth of the SEZ; the stock exchange fever; a real estate fever; 'government cadres getting into business' fever; and the fast-growth fever. The banks were called upon to lend, lend, lend. In 1992 the central government lost all control of bank credit (the banks were all state-owned, and the four biggest accounted for about 90 percent of all credit in the economy); but 1992 and 1993 were remarkable years, and they showed what one ageing patriarch could achieve.

In March 1999 the National People's Congress recognised the private sector as an 'important component of the socialist market economy'. This was a far cry from the era of Mao, who had large placards made proclaiming: 'Strike hard against the slightest sign of private ownership!'. It went further than Deng, who saw the private sector only as a 'complement' to the socialist market economy. Now the private sector accounts for about 45 percent of non-agricultural Gross Domestic Product (GDP). But, ominously, in May 2000 President Jiang called for all private companies to have Communist cells within them 'to guarantee the healthy development of the [private] sector'.[37]

This painting depicts Sun Tzu giving military instruction to the concubines of King Ho-lu of Wu. Sun Tzu's *The Art of War*, written at the end of the sixth century BC, is the world's most enduring book of military and negotiating strategy, which informs Chinese tactics and is used in the present day even in the West by military, diplomatic and business strategists. *Painting by Yukihiko Yasuda, 1938; copyright: Ken-ichi Yasuda and Reiyukai.*

Lhasa's Potala Palace, a seventeenth-century reconstruction of the original seventh-century structure, was the home of the Dalai Lama (and his predecessors) until he fled to India in 1959. Discussions between Chinese authorities and two Tibetan envoys of the Dalai Lama in September 2004 included the possibility of the Dalai Lama returning to live at the palace, with freedom of movement permitted outside China and to Tibetans living within China, and with authority retained over the publication of all religious texts and the appointment of abbots for all monasteries in Tibet. *Photo: Ian Cumming, Tibet Images.*

A new dam on the road between Gyantse and Nagartse, Tibet – an example of the intense, Chinese-driven changes wrought on Tibet's environment and infrastructure. Chinese Premier Wen Jiabao, who is very environmentally aware, has put 'on hold' for further investigation an ambitious plan by the Yunnan provincial government to construct a multiple dam system on the River Nu in a World Heritage Site area – also opposed by NGOs and many individuals, including Tibetans, who would have to be relocated. *Photo: Tibet Images.*

Two views of Lake Lhamo Lhatso, southeast of Lhasa. By tradition, search parties seeking the reincarnations of Dalai Lamas and Panchen Lamas consult the lake for magical properties that assist the quest. Chanting and other rituals may be conducted for several days before signs are revealed as to where the reincarnations are to be found. *Photo: Chrysalis Books Archives.*

Public space and shrine just below the Dalai Lama's residence in Dharamsala, India. *Photo: John Heath.*

A Tibet Children's Village (TCV), in Dharamsala. Conceived by Tsering Dolma, the Dalai Lama's eldest sister, and later run by Jetsun Pema, his younger sister, the village system comprises boarding houses for children up to eighteen, each with Tibetan 'house parents'. Throughout all Tibetan settlements there are TCV schools. (The buildings at right are for instruction in science.) The children take Indian exams and score consistently high marks, and some then go to university. *Photo: John Heath.*

Chinese shop in Lhasa's main street, with fluorescent plastic palm tree, in 2001. Old Lhasa has been largely destroyed and replaced by modern buildings out of keeping with Tibetan traditions. Tibetan lifestyles are also changing, especially in Lhasa. *Photo: Tibet Information Network.*

By late 2003, however, protests by UNESCO against the destruction of World Heritage Sites in Lhasa led to a change in Chinese policy. The plastic palm trees were removed, and a number of plain-looking Chinese buildings had their facades 'Tibetanised' by Chinese workers. *Photo: Tibet Information Network.*

Scenes from a life on the railways. Building railways has become one of China's top priorities. In 2001, Jiang Zemin initiated the vast project of constructing a rail link between Golmud and Lhasa in Qinghai (formerly Amdo), as part of the Western Development campaign motivated by defence, economic and political considerations. Tibetans fear that Chinese immigration will greatly increase as a result. The Golmud-Lhasa line is 695 miles long, and mostly above 13,000 feet (the highest point is 16,600 feet); more than half the route runs over unstable permafrost, and temperatures can drop to -40 degrees Celsius in winter. *Photos: Department of Information and International Relations, Central Tibetan Administration.*

Monks gather in March 1990, in Dharamsala, to protest Chinese policy in Tibet. Such demonstrations against the Chinese are rare on Indian soil, as Tibetans are mindful of the sensitive diplomatic relations between China and India; the latter could come under increasing pressure to expel Tibetans. If such demonstrations were held in Tibet (very rare nowadays), experience shows that arrests would certainly follow, with tragic consequences. *Photo: Tibet Images.*

Street protest in Lhasa in 1987. Such demonstrations used to be common, especially in the capital. But monks and nuns, who were the main protestors because they could meet more easily in secret, gradually began to ease off. The tortures and long prison terms they were forced to endure eventually discouraged such actions; but occasionally they still occur, outside Lhasa. *Photo: Tibet Images.*

Happiness amongst young and old: Tibetans-in-exile in Dharamsala, India. *Photos: John Heath.*

If that order were ever implemented, it could have the opposite effect.

In June 1999, with an immense fanfare of publicity, Jiang launched a broad plan for Western Development (considered in more detail in Chapter Nine). It was seen as being of major significance for the future prosperity of the country and of the Communist Party's 'long reign and perennial stability'. Development was seen as the most pressing need, not democracy. To begin with, there would be massive extraction of a wide range of minerals in the western regions of China that would enable the east coast industries to grow faster and more efficiently; then, later, the secondary manufacturing industries would spread towards the west itself in large industrialisation. The areas for Western Development embrace in all 56 percent of China's territory and 23 percent of its people: something really big, it is safe to say. If successful, it will be part of Jiang's historical legacy.

There were two previous ambitious epoch-making attempts to take a giant step into modernity: Mao's Great Leap Forward in 1957–8 and, in 1978, Deng's ordering from abroad 122 large-scale investment projects. Such bold initiatives, coming, as it happens, roughly every twenty years, do not have a good record in China.

The main problems for Western Development, especially in Tibet, if it is to be anything like 'epoch-making' in scale, will be management and funding. Both large and small businesses need professionally trained managers, accountants and business lawyers, and many will need professionals in engineering, chemistry and other disciplines. Both management and financial accountants are necessary, for decision-making and for internal and external audit. In China they are in extremely short supply. Without them there will be waste, inefficiencies of all kinds and corruption. Chinese managers are seen as autocratic and non-participatory.[38]

In China only about 3.5 percent of schoolchildren in the relevant age group go to university (compared, for example, with 6 percent in India). Large numbers of China's best students receive their higher education abroad, and only a modest proportion return (about 10–30 percent). The first professionally trained accountants in China graduated in 1996, and postgraduate management training did not begin until the mid-1990s.[39] Even the largest management school (Fudan University School of Management in Shanghai) graduated only 270 people in 1997. Such persons will need many years of practical management before they can enter senior positions. Meanwhile, many bad mistakes will be made. There are, however, a great many graduate engineers, and in the West many civil engineers turn out to be good general managers.

Joe Studwell has made a detailed study of banking and finance in China.[40]

The banks, all currently publicly owned, account for about 90 percent of financial assets and lend heavily, mainly to state-owned enterprises (SOEs). They see this as a duty in part because SOEs have to carry many social costs for their employees, used sometimes as an excuse for incurring losses. Already in 2001, loans outstanding in the Chinese financial system were probably in the order of 120 percent of GDP and rising fast. This is unsustainable. While the World Bank will undoubtedly assist with funding, it does not come as free money, and the domestic banking system will be heavily involved.

Government revenues rely heavily on taxes paid by the SOEs, but most SOEs are unprofitable and remain afloat only through heavy borrowing from the banks, who see their primary job as being to respond to their needs. Revitalising SOEs and Western Development will need much capital, which will come mainly from the banks. The Organisation for Economic Cooperation and Development (OECD), in a study in 2002, described this as a 'severe vicious circle'. Government money is given out by the state banks with one hand and returned as taxes with the other. The whole system is kept afloat by the huge savings of individuals in China in the banks, the continuation of which depends on the confidence of the people that their savings are safe. 'Household savings deposits' are over 70 percent of GDP. SOEs are overburdened with debt – their debt/equity ratios are collectively about 500 percent, which leaves little margin for risk – except by means of further borrowing. Foreign observers see that China has a 'dangerously weak banking system'.

At the end of 2003, however, some US$ 45 billion was transferred from China's foreign reserves to bail out the debt-ridden Bank of China, the country's largest foreign-exchange bank, and the China Construction Bank. China's big four banks between them had bad debts ('non-performing loans', where recipients cannot even pay the interest, let alone repay capital), arising from past lending in the order of US$ 188 billion at the end of 2003, a high proportion of their total loans. Lending practices of China's banks will have to change. This will be difficult if major non-commercial projects such as the Golmud–Lhasa rail link (see Chapter Nine) are to be funded.

All this means that there is much sleight of hand in the Chinese financial system, and deliberate obfuscation. The International Monetary Fund, of which China became a member in 1980, would normally place resident experts in the central bank and the Ministry of Finance who would ferret out the truth, but the Chinese government refused them permission. China does not adhere to the standard reporting criteria of the 'Basel Committee on Banking Regulations and Supervisory Practice', in spite of a 1993 government decree to do so. So the truth has to be pieced together by specialists from abroad.[41] It appears that if China were to embark on Western Development on any significant scale, foreigners with their eyes on China's precarious financial position might take fright and cause a major crisis. The whole financial system could unravel. The key year for getting China's financial house in order is 2006, when financial services must adhere to the WTO free-trade commitments. Foreign banks can then compete for China's huge personal savings market.

On 1 July 2001 Jiang made a significant policy statement in some 13,500 words[42] in the Great Hall of the People, commemorating the eightieth anniversary of the Chinese Communist Party. He declared that the Party was 'upholding the guiding role of Marxism' and 'cherishing dearly the memory of Mao Zedong, Zhou Enlai, Liu Shaoqi, Zhu De, Deng Xiaoping and Chen Yun ... [the Party has] realised a high degree of unification of the country and unparalleled unity of all ethnic groups.' Marxism–Leninism, Mao Zedong Thought and Deng Xiaoping Theory were summoned many times in aid. 'Our Party made mistakes and even suffered serious setbacks in some historical periods', was all he said about Mao's horrific disasters. Not to confront the past openly makes people feel that their suffering was in vain, and blights the future.

Jiang then concentrated on the future, declaring the need to:

> ... correctly understand and fulfil the requirements of the 'Three Represents' ... We [the Communist Party] must always represent [or 'champion']:
>
> (1) the development trend of China's advanced productive forces;
>
> (2) the orientation of China's advanced culture in:
>
> (3) the fundamental interests of the overwhelming majority of the people in China.

These comprise, Jiang said, 'the foundation underlying all our efforts to build the Party, the cornerstone for exercising political power and a source of strength of our Party'. This significant shift in policy was masterminded by Zeng Qinghong, now in Hu Jintao's Politburo Standing Committee.

Speaking of the first 'Represent', Jiang said:

> science and technology are the primary productive forces and a concentrated expression and hallmark of advanced productive forces ...[43] All comrades in the Party, no matter what posts they are in, should check and review their work regularly to see whether it conforms to the requirements of the development of advanced productive forces. If it does, hold on to it

without wavering. If it does not, correct it where necessary. Only by doing so is it possible for Communists to give a full expression to their advanced nature and to the spirit of the times ...

This absurd and meaningless instruction to the Communist Party leaves out everybody else. Jiang continued:

Also, we must, under the guidance of the Party's basic theories, basic line and basic programme, stick to and improve the basic economic system with public ownership[44] as the main body and the common development of the main sectors; we must hold on to and improve the socialist market system ... we must hold on to and improve the people's democratic dictatorship led by the working class and based on worker–peasant alliance[45] ... and the system of regional autonomy of minority nationalities ...

In 2001, after twelve years in office, socialist ideology was still the driving force. What about private ownership? Speaking of the second 'Represent', Jiang continued:

We must persist in taking Marxism–Leninism, Mao Zedong Thought and Deng Xiaoping Theory as the guide, base ourselves on the practice of building socialism with Chinese characteristics ... we should persevere in arming the people with scientific theories, guiding the people with correct public opinions, moulding the people with noble minds and inspiring the people with superior works. We must stick to and consolidate the guiding status of Marxism ... have firm belief in Marxism and socialism ... and let a hundred flowers blossom and a hundred schools of thought contend.

'Blooming and contending' (revisited) must have made all thinking Chinese gasp with incredulity. Regarding the third 'Represent', the object and purpose of developing China's advanced productive forces and the orientation of China's advanced culture is to serve the fundamental interests 'of the overwhelming majority of the people in China' – not *all* the people in China. The 'Three Represents' are a linked series of interdependent events, and may be called 'Jiang Zemin Theory'.

Internationally the policy was, Jiang said, 'to seek an early solution to the question of Taiwan and to accomplish the great cause of national reunification. While we do have the greatest sincerity to work for a peaceful reunification, we cannot and will not undertake to renounce the use of force. We are fully capable of checking any attempt to split China by seeking Taiwan's 'independence' ...

the complete unification of China represents the aspirations of the people and is a historical trend that no one and no force could stop.'

A surprising omission in this speech was China's population. The 'one child' birth policies have not achieved stability[46] (officially it is thought to have reduced the otherwise expected population by 200 million in the last twenty years[47]). With limitations on numbers, girl babies are generally not wanted. Ultrasound scanners are widely used to identify whether a pregnant woman has conceived a boy or a girl, and if the latter, except perhaps for a first child, an abortion is likely to be procured As a result, instead of the normally expected 105 or 106 boys born per 100 girls, in at least five provinces of China the ratio has risen to about 120.

Also, the omission of China's ratification of the International Covenant of Economic, Social and Cultural Rights (ICESCR) on 27 March 2001 is puzzling. Perhaps Jiang just forgot. It was a major event for China and all its peoples. Article 1 reads: 'All peoples have the right of self-determination. By virtue of that right they freely determine their political status and freely pursue their economic, social and cultural development.' 'All peoples' would most likely include the Han Chinese, Tibetans and Muslims of Xinjiang.

An even more surprising omission was any mention of China's expected accession to the WTO due to take place five months after Jiang's speech, on 11 December 2001, after thirteen years of negotiation. How did it fit within his ideological framework? Gordon Chang,[48] in *The Coming Collapse of China*, believes that the admission of China to the WTO will have devastating effects. No longer will global enterprises have to establish manufacturing plants in China to supply the market; direct exports will be possible. No longer will the Chinese have to put their savings into China's state banks. Chang argues that China's economy and finances will not be able to withstand these pressures. Many large SOEs have not been restructured. Without state protection and financial support they will probably suffer severe losses.[49] SOEs employ over 110 million persons (possibly as high as 200 million), about 41 percent of the urban workforce.[50] The Baoshan steelworks example (see Chapter Seven) shows the possible scale of concealed unemployment in China. The weakest sector is agriculture, and here already the poorest peasants suffer greatly. Tibet's rural economy is also vulnerable.

Jiang can be credited with many positive achievements during his time as Party General Secretary and President, in particular China's amazing domestic and international economic performance; but the negatives are also great. They have arisen mainly from fear of the collapse of communism, fear of democracy and fear of political opposition. There is much unfinished business, now in Hu Jintao's hands.

NINE

Hu Jintao: A New Beginning?

'Force is followed by loss of strength.
This is not the way of Tao.
That which goes against the Tao
comes to an early end.'
Lao-tzu, Tao Te Ching, *Chapter Thirty*

Hu Jintao is a quiet, unassuming, rather secretive man born in December 1942 and brought up in Taizhou, Jiangsu province. His ancestors were tea merchants, and his father ran a tea shop. Hu's mother died when he was six years old, and he is believed to have been brought up by his aunt, Liu Bingxia.[1] During the Cultural Revolution he spent two months undergoing 'reform through labour' in the countryside, refusing to join the Red Guards. He became a civil engineer at the elite Qinghua University in Beijing, and then spent fourteen years building dams at the edge of the Gobi Desert. Building dams and bridges seems not to have satisfied him – he really wanted to help build a new China. He then became Party Secretary, first in the mountainous province of Guizhou and then, in January 1989, in the even more mountainous Tibet, where he replaced the more liberal Wu Jinghua, the appointee of Hu Yaobang. Evidently the altitude gave him headaches, and he spent nearly half his time living in Beijing. His son and daughter were not 'princelings', and had to make their own way in the world (his daughter worked in a bar to pay for her education at Columbia University, New York). He appeared to be an orthodox thinker, and to have made little impact in the areas for which he was responsible. He has, however, a wide network of friends and admirers, is said to be an incorruptible ascetic and is very good at finding consensus amongst colleagues.

He was appointed to the Politburo Standing Committee, the youngest member by eight years, in 1992 at the instigation of Deng Xiaoping. In November 2002 he became General Secretary of the Communist Party, the country's most powerful position; and in March 2003 he succeeded Jiang Zemin as President. He is also Vice-Chairman of the Central Military Committee and President of the Central Party School, which specialises in doctrinal matters. In this, amongst other matters, he has encouraged study of the development of social democratic parties in Europe.

In June 2000, in a speech to Party cadres, Hu said:

> Leading officials must at all times be on their guard against the plots of Western hostile forces to split us up or to Westernise us and against the danger of bringing about our own metamorphosis. There must be absolutely no hesitation or wavering in our commitment to Marxism and the pursuit of socialism with Chinese characteristics.

However, this was before he had been appointed to the top position, and following the Party line was a necessity. He believes that authoritarian single party rule is best for China, but also that the political system needs reforming while social democracy needs widening.[2] He wants the Communist Party to 'undertake a sweeping systemic project' to increase public participation in government and to enforce the rule of law. He wants a political process to emphasise 'decision-making transparency, the public's right to know, official accountability and responsiveness to meet the needs of the Chinese people'. These high ideals are being translated into action through the establishment of a 'scientific decision-making network' including the appointment by the people of local officials and direct elections, pioneered in Jilin. Also, there is a new public-relations section of the Chinese foreign ministry to solicit the views of its citizens. By February 2005 one third of the owners of businesses had become members of the Communist Party, which has far-reaching implications. The Counsellors' Office of the State Council, China's highest-level 'think tank' comprising mostly non-Party members, held its first-ever press conference in March 2004. These forward-looking ideas, reiterated in Hu's speech on 22 August 2004 at the centenary of Deng's birth, are hopeful of more to come.

Hu is also very concerned about the widening gap between rich and poor in China and, with Premier Wen Jiabao, he has travelled widely to see people and places left behind by the booming east-coast cities. He speaks also of needing a new legal framework to keep pace with the growth of private businesses and the need for property rights. (In March 2004 the Chinese constitution was amended to add the clause: 'Private property obtained legally is inviolable'.) He has approved plans for restructuring the central executive bodies. In Qinghai, which has close links with the TAR and where over 1 million Tibetans live (it covers most of Amdo), he has appointed a new governor (head of the executive) from the TAR who, encouragingly, is said to have adopted some Tibetan children and sent them to school in China. The young and energetic Party Secretary, Zhao Leji, was also appointed Chairman of the People's Congress and to a seat on the Central Committee of the Communist Party, which increases his standing and authority. They both have close links to Hu Jintao.

On the other hand Hu has discouraged reformist discussion in universities and research institutes, which suggests that he wants to control the process (to avoid another Tiananmen Square, no doubt). Clearly there is caution about pushing ahead too fast with a radical political agenda, and he is concerned that Hong Kong may elect a non-Party member as Chief Executive in 2007. Hong Kong's Basic Law was re-interpreted in April 2004 to prevent this. Jiang has his supporters on the Politburo Standing Committee and their influence remains to be seen.

President Hu's first public statement about Tibet was in January 2004, in Paris. He is reported as saying:

As long as [the Dalai Lama] abandons his stand on Tibetan independence, stops activities aimed at splitting China and recognises Tibet as an inseparable part of Chinese territory, the channel for contact between the Chinese government and the Dalai Lama is always open.

Apart from the obvious exclusion of Taiwan, there are subtle differences between these words and the previous references by Jiang to Tibet's being 'an inalienable part of China'. Tibet as 'part of Chinese territory' is different from being 'part of China', which is all-embracing. Thus, control over territory may now be seen as separate from control over its people.[3] Perhaps this change is a result of Hu's visit to the UK in 2001, when he went to Scotland and saw its elected parliament. It has a population of over 5 million, and he will have been told that Scotland has its own legal system and laws, police force, education system, national health service and religious beliefs and practices (in the Scottish Presbyterian Church) and national flag – not to mention its own football, rugby and other sporting teams.[4] In many respects the elected Scottish parliament pursues different policies from the government in

Westminster. It has 'autonomy' within the UK in the sense meant by the Dalai Lama. In 2002 Hu went to the US, which is organised on a federal basis. California, for example, like all other states in the Union, has an even greater degree of autonomy than does Scotland, yet the territories remain within the sovereignty of the UK and the US respectively. If this interpretation of Hu Jintao's intentions is correct, it is an important new development.

Jiang's initiative to permit two envoys of the Dalai Lama to visit Beijing and Tibet in September 2002 and the second visit in May 2003 authorised by Hu should, however, also be seen in the context of the deadline set by the European Parliament for negotiations between the Tibetans and the Chinese to have started by 5 July 2003 – otherwise EU member states would be urged to recognise the Tibetan government-in-exile as the legitimate representative of the Tibetan people. The commencement of talks prevented this. July 2003 was also the time when, if there were no concrete outcome to the Tibetan issue, Tibet support groups throughout the world would ask the Tibetan government-in-exile to rethink its position on Tibetan independence. Talks have indeed been held, but there has been no hint of negotiation. The Dalai Lama has expressed the hope that many further meetings will take place. 'The best way to eliminate suspicion is to meet face-to-face,' he has said.

Hu's team[5] has been through a thorough and professional process of scrutiny by the Organisation Department, and comprises persons who, as judged by the criteria set (which do not appear to include human rights), have earned high merit for their achievements (very much along Confucian lines). But there are no women on it, and all members except one have had significant experience as professional engineers before entering politics (there are no lawyers). The exception is Wen Jiabao, the new premier.[6] He qualified in geology at the Beijing Institute of Geology, and held geology posts from 1968 to 1985. He was a supporter of Zhao Ziyang (whom he accompanied into Tiananmen Square to plead with the students, and for whom he helped formulate wide-ranging political reforms). Earlier he was appointed by Hu Yaobang, then Party General Secretary, as director of the Central Office coordinating and managing the daily paperwork of the Party leadership, including the Politburo and the Secretariat, in order to 'water down the influence of the hardliners in the central leadership'. Thus, in some respects, he would appear to have been cast in the mould of both Hu Yaobang and Zhao. As Vice-Premier to Zhu Rongji, he has also had experience in many of China's most difficult problem areas – the state-owned enterprises; the rural economy; managing Western Development; environmental protection; and sustainable development. He is renowned for his scrupulous fairness and attention to detail. Like Hu Jintao, he does not favour a Western-type democracy with competing political parties.

A major problem for him is revealed by the husband-and-wife team of Chen Guidi and Wu Chuntao in their 460-page book *A Survey of Chinese Peasants*, published in January 2001 following a three-year investigation in the agricultural province of Anhui.[7] Local cadres imposed high taxes on farmers, which caused great poverty. Many such taxes were retained by the cadres. Peasants who complained were severely punished, and some died. False reports were being passed upwards, which led Zhu Rongji to issue unattainable directives and made matters worse. In March 2004 Wen Jiabao announced that over five years all agricultural taxes will be abolished. The financial implications will be huge.

Zeng Qinghong, now Vice-President, is also a powerful member of Hu's team and was Jiang's chief political aide.[8] Zeng is also seen as 'the leader with the boldest ideas and the greatest potential to steer China in new directions … with the strongest network of political allies and contacts and the most political skill'. He wants 'more efficient, less corrupt and more democratic government' and follows Hu in believing that a good job has been done in Tibet. He is reported as saying:

> Everyone can see the advancing development in Tibetan society. In pushing forward the modernisation of Tibet and opposing the separatist activities of the Dalai clique, China has followed the trend of the times and has won the hearts of the people.[9]

Zeng urged more propaganda work to correct distortions and misunderstandings about Tibet. In July 2001 he spoke to 136 cadres selected by the central government about to work in Tibet (out of 685). He urged implementation of the 'Three Represents' and of the Fourth Forum on Work in Tibet, which was extremely anti-Dalai Lama.

China's international situation is crucial to peace and stability both within China and in regard to the future of Tibet. In particular there are large issues between China and the US, issues of war and peace, competition and cooperation, which will command Hu's attention. Early in 1994, in the Great Hall of the People, there was a gathering of Party secretaries and propaganda chiefs from all of China's twenty-nine provinces and regions, with delegates from other major central government agencies.[10] Its main purpose was to announce that the US was now China's main global rival.

Hu, speaking for the Politburo, said that 'according to the global hegemonist strategy of the US, its main rival at present is the PRC. Interfering in China, subverting the Chinese government and strangling China's development are strategic principles pursued by the United States.'[11] General Zhang Wannian, Chief of the General Staff of the PLA, responded by saying that 'we must reinforce our armed forces more intensively'. Li Peng was then still Premier, and this policy accorded exactly with his statements to the Party Elders on that fateful day of decision in June 1989, with similar rhetoric. This hard line, as it emerged in 1994, was a policy which Deng roundly opposed, but by then he was eighty-nine years old and no one listened. However, Noam Chomsky, a leading American intellectual, agrees with Hu that 'China is regarded as a prime potential enemy by Washington hawks, and much military planning is geared to that contingency'; President George W. Bush sees China as a 'strategic competitor'.[12] Moreover, China possesses weapons of mass destruction, is alleged to have passed nuclear military technology abroad, lacks democracy, is ruled by a Communist oligarchy, has disregarded human rights law – and opposes Tibetan autonomy and the Dalai Lama. With Bush's policy of pre-emptive strikes, China might seem a likely future target.

It seems likely that, with the threat from Russia greatly diminished, with a treaty of friendship signed between that country and China and with Russia a friendly supplier of military weapons, Chinese policy is to keep the US out of the way in Asia so that China can come to be the undisputed power to which all other states would have to defer. China has been trying to make clear that it will not tolerate US interference in its sphere of influence. An accidentally leaked internal Chinese document saw that after 2000 the 'Asia–Pacific region is likely to gradually become an American strategic priority'.[13] It came more quickly than had been foreseen.

Since the tragedy of 11 September 2001, the US has established or strengthened long-term military bases in Kazakhstan, Uzbekistan, Kyrgyzstan and Tajikistan, all independent states formerly part of the Soviet Union. But China considers these countries within its sphere of influence and has expressed concern – especially about Kazakhstan, with its major oilfields. With Turkmenistan, these four countries form the Shanghai Cooperation Organisation (SCO), initiated by Jiang Zemin. Strategically, these former Soviet territories are part of an outer defence ring to China's west. The world's second-largest reserves of natural gas are in Turkmenistan, on the borders with Afghanistan and Uzbekistan.[14] Trade and influence are growing between China and these countries, and will be enhanced when the new Urumqi–Kashgar rail link in Xinjiang, opened at the beginning of 2000, is extended to Kyrgyzstan and Tajikistan across the border and to Kazakhstan from Urumqi through Yining. The US spy-plane incident in April 2000 and the bugging of the new Chinese presidential Boeing 767 in September 2001 will have infuriated the Chinese and helped unite the people against the US. They will also have provided evidence to support the attitudes expressed at the 1994 meeting in the Great Hall of the People.

The urgent desire by Bush and the British prime minister Tony Blair in the autumn of 2001 to bring China into the campaign against terrorism put it in a strong negotiating position. In October 2001 the State Council decided that China would join the international campaign against 'terrorism, splittism and fanaticism', thus hijacking the campaign against terrorism for its own ends. In return it wanted US support for its policies against so-called 'separatists' in Tibet, Xinjiang and Taiwan. Bush has agreed that some of the separatists in Muslim Xinjiang are 'terrorists', which seems to legitimise further action.

Apart from all this power-politics and military muscle, China remains linked to the US in more peaceful ways through a dense network of professional and personal bonds. Annually over 200,000 Americans visit China, and over 50,000 Chinese students are granted visas to study in the US. It is the preferred country for Chinese exiles to settle in abroad. Also, China had a surplus on its balance of trade with the US in 2003 of US$ 13.5 billion, and some of the dollars it earned are returned through China's investments in US Treasury bonds – thus, ironically, helping to keep the US government afloat – and in the purchase of IBM's PC business by the Chinese computer manufacturer and distributor Lenovo for US$ 1.75 billion in December 2004.

The US is a strong supporter of the Dalai Lama and of a dialogue between him and the Chinese government. The State Department has a 'Tibet Coordinator', and it publishes an annual 'Report on Religious Freedom' which, in its fifth report in December 2003, contained a lengthy description of religious suppression in Tibet; in its February 2004 annual 'Country Report on Human Rights Practices in Tibet' the State Department again found serious human rights abuses. On 2 February 2004 the House of Representatives in Washington unanimously passed a resolution that all Tibetans held as 'prisoners of conscience' should be released. China's patience finally gave out. On 1 March 2004 the authorities hit back with a detailed catalogue of human rights abuses by the US in Afghanistan and Iraq (not to mention Guantánamo Bay), highlighting the US's vast military expenditure (larger than that of the rest of the world combined), its sales of conventional weapons to developing countries (48 percent of the world total) and its catalogue of domestic social ills and abuses. They also suspended bilateral human rights dialogue and exchanges with the US.

A related issue for Hu's attention is Taiwan. China's attitude towards Taiwan under Jiang Zemin was a threat to peace in East Asia, and perhaps beyond. Violence seemed just around the corner. Guns, missiles, ships, aircraft and the PLA were ready. Almost all the people of Taiwan are Han Chinese and descendants from China. The conflict of wills has its roots in history.

In the mid-seventeenth century many Chinese fled to what was then Formosa ('Beautiful Isle', so named by the earlier Portuguese invaders), when the Manchus gradually took control of the mainland. The Japanese attacked and took control of southern Manchuria in 1894, and with the Treaty of Shimonoseki the following year Japan acquired Formosa as part of the settlement. They rapidly modernised and developed their new colony, and even held local elections in the 1940s that allowed the Taiwanese some say in running their own affairs. However, all the top positions were occupied by Japanese.

At the end of the Second World War Taiwan was returned to Nationalist China, and Nationalist troops from the mainland were received with rapture. But this soon turned to dismay and disillusionment as the newcomers seized power and regarded the earlier Chinese settlers almost as enemies because of their long association with the Japanese. Their achievements were belittled, and the Nationalist administrators from the mainland treated them with contempt. There was an uprising in 1947 against the newcomers. Some 10,000 troops from the mainland savagely suppressed the revolt, resulting in about 30,000 deaths. Two years later, when Chiang Kai-shek was defeated by Mao, Chiang and the best of his military fled to Taiwan. Also some 2 million civilians, many of them the cream of Chinese intellectuals, joined the defeated Nationalists to escape the Communists. The population was then some 7.3 million and had a high proportion of well-educated Chinese. Now, with a population of 22 million, all but about 380,000 are ethnic Chinese.

In 1950 it had been Mao's military priority to attack Taiwan and to extinguish the Nationalist forces there, but the war in Korea postponed that ambition. It also led the US to make moves to defend Taiwan. Between 1954 and 1979, under a Mutual Defence Treaty, Taiwan effectively became a protectorate of the US. With defence security, a good basis of industry established by the Japanese, new investment and technical know-how from the US, and with a well-educated population, the Taiwanese economy took off. It became a major supplier to the world and the largest foreign investor in mainland China.

The Nationalists long dominated Taiwan's political affairs, at first under the dictatorship of Chiang and then his son, Chiang Ching-kuo. In 1971 the Republic of China lost its seat in the UN to the PRC, and the international status of Taiwan fell into limbo. Losing that seat was a bitter blow to Nationalist political ambitions to return to the mainland as the legitimate rulers of China. Then, in 1979, the US and the PRC established diplomatic relations and, as part of the deal, the 1954 US defence treaty with Taiwan was terminated.

Chiang Ching-kuo was no liberal, but he brought some leading Taiwanese into his government and introduced limited democratic reforms. Shortly before his death in 1988 he allowed the formation of an opposition, the Democratic Progressive Party. Lee Teng-hui took the leadership of the Nationalists and skilfully steered Taiwan towards a more open society, forced the retirement of ageing Nationalist leaders and introduced local elections. In national elections in 1994 the KMT just retained its majority and in 1996, as Taiwan's first elected President, Lee came to power. The military threats and the firing of Chinese missiles just off the coast of Taiwan prior to the elections may have been counter-productive. The US aircraft carrier *Independence* and its battle group were only 200 miles away, and in response to the threats President Clinton ordered a second aircraft carrier, the *Nimitz*, with its own battle group, to the region. Clearly, the US would not stand idle if China carried out an invasion.

In the elections of 2000, the Democratic Progressive Party (DPP) of Taiwan won power and Chen Shui-bian, Mayor of Taipei since 1994, became President – this in spite of renewed, highly visible military threats from the mainland and a possible invasion if such an event were to happen. The KMT rule of fifty-five years in Taiwan was ended. President Chen was, however, more cautious in power than during the election campaign, in seeking formal independence for Taiwan. He launched a new peace initiative with China, and introduced direct trade, transport and postal links with the mainland – and refused to be browbeaten into accepting Taiwan as a province of China. However, in the December 2004 elections for the legislature the KMT won by a small majority over the DPP.

To have Taiwan return to the warm embrace of the Chinese motherland as one of its provinces was Jiang's burning ambition. His speech of 1 July 2001 specifically referred to this, with the use of force if necessary. Earlier threats to use military force led Taiwan to purchase military aircraft from the US and France in 1992. During 1997–9 Taiwan was by far the world's largest importer of conventional weapons, although by 2004 this had slackened.[15] To some extent there had been competitive purchases of armaments as each side saw the other as increasing its weaponry. During 1995–8, China increased its domestic government expenditure on armaments by some 34 percent, although this is probably an underestimate because the PLA used some of its own business income on weaponry. In June/July 2001 China conducted several weeks of military manoeuvres, war games and a simulated invasion on and around Dongshan island, off China's south-eastern coast. Miliary experts think that the capture of one or more small Taiwanese islands might be the first stage leading to an invasion. By 2004 China had some 500 missiles in place aimed at Taiwan's strategic targets, increasing at about seventy-five per annum.

Such threats worry the US and the Philippines (where the US has bases), and concern the South Korean government.[16] Two bilateral organisations, the Straits Exchange Foundation (SEF), set up by Taiwan in 1990, and the Association for Relations Across the Taiwan Straits (ARATS), set up by China in the same year, do not appear to have dampened the Chinese government's desire to possess the island.

China seems to be living out one of its own proverbs: 'what is false will turn into truth after being repeated a thousand times'. On every possible occasion, Jiang reiterated that 'Taiwan is a province of China' and attempted to persuade others, such as the Dalai Lama, of its truth. Hu has followed the same line. It is difficult for Westerners to see why China does not accept that Taiwan is *de facto* independent and warmly embrace it as a friend. As Chris Patten has said, 'free societies make the best neighbours'.[17] A friendly Taiwan could provide protection strategically for China's southern coastal provinces. China does not have to own and control Taiwan to receive such benefits. Taiwan would be seen by all as *de jure* an independent state with strong economic, social and ethnic ties to the mainland.

Strategically China appears to have been trying to isolate India from India's friends, especially Nepal and Bhutan, and to support its enemies, especially Pakistan. China has now softened its line. However, it would like India to expel all Tibetans from Indian territory, thus weakening the effectiveness of Tibetan opposition to China's occupation of their homeland. The Indians are not forthcoming on this matter. They regard the Dalai Lama as 'theirs' and treat him with utmost respect. (Many Hindus consider the Buddha to be an avatar of the god Vishnu.)

Tibetans are extremely sensitive to their position on Indian soil. Tibetans run their own schools, learn Hindi, take Indian educational examinations and attend Indian universities. They ensure that Indians are employed in building work for them and even employ them to guard the Dalai Lama. Where settlements engage in commercial or manufacturing activities, Tibetans ensure that Indians are not harmed by such activities. McLeod is a major centre of spiritual tourism from which the Indian treasury and local shops benefit. A joint cost-benefit study was undertaken to ascertain whether Indians benefited from these activities; there were costs, but there was a clear net gain to them. So China, which from time to time has tried to persuade the Indians to expel all Tibetans, makes no progress.

India and Tibet have a long history of relationships, until 1947 also involving the British in India. The Simla Convention in 1914, never ratified by China (which was in some disarray following the collapse of the Qing dynasty), was about trade but also demarcated the 'McMahon Line' border along the Himalayan peaks between India and Tibet, some 1,175 miles, but parts of the border remained disputed. By 1962 China had been quietly infiltrating Indian territory east and north of Ladakh called Aksai Chin, the Western Sector, and there had been skirmishes elsewhere. Mao decided to teach 'that representative of the reactionary national bourgeoisie', India, a lesson, and on 20 October China invaded. Aksai Chin quickly fell, and in a month so had most of what is now the Indian state of Arunachal Pradesh in the Eastern Sector. The Chinese then withdrew from that sector, which thereafter they claimed was their territory, but not from the Western Sector, which India still claims as its own. In June 2003 Atal Bihari Vajpayee, then India's prime minister, and Premier Wen agreed to have senior envoys from both countries consider the issue of border sovereignty along its whole length. There has been little progress.

In 1954 India, China and Burma initiated the 'Five Principles of Peaceful Coexistence' which became known as the Pansheel Agreement. It included 'mutual respect for each other's territorial integrity and sovereignty', non-aggression and peaceful coexistence. As a result India had, in effect, accepted that Tibet was part of China. Subsequently, these principles have been called upon by many other countries, and the agreement is considered to rank alongside the UN Charter. Although it lapsed in 1962, both India and China – as part of a new rapprochement – agreed to celebrate its fiftieth anniversary in 2004. China would not give Tibet any degree of control over its internal policies unless the true friendship of India were secured, so these current events are of great importance.

Kashmir is a flashpoint for the interests of India, Pakistan and China. In 2002 India and Pakistan came near to war, but in 2004 a settlement looked possible following a visit of the Indian prime minister to Islamabad. The situation remains serious.

Alongside India to the east, adjoining the southern flank of Tibet, is Nepal, which has a continuing crisis. Since 1996 the 'Communist Party of Nepal (Maoist)' has been bombing and killing the Nepalese police force; many innocent people have also suffered. The Maoists have worked their way steadily towards the capital, Kathmandu, leaving behind large areas to the west under their control. They blame 'imperialists' (the CIA) and 'hegemonists' (in India) for all the country's ills. Up to February 2005 over 10,000 people had been killed, mostly Nepalese. Prachand, the leader of the Maoists, has said that 'our policy is to attack the anti-national murderers and fascists belonging to the [King] Gyanendra–[Prime Minister] Girija caucus' in the Nepalese government. Their political aim appears to be to establish a Maoist republic. The army, which is under the direct control of the king, has been fighting back.

The tragedy in Nepal was compounded by the killing in June 2001 of all the leading members of the royal family in what appears to have beeen an internal family matter. Crown Prince Dipendra shot the king and queen (his parents) along with seven other family members. The newly enthroned King Gyanendra (aged fifty-five) and the unpopular seventy-eight-year-old prime minister, Girija Koirala, who the Maoists claim are in league with the 'imperialists' and the 'hegemonists', have a terrible problem, which was made worse when, in 2002, the king replaced the formerly democratic system with one that supported the monarchy.

Tibet has an 870-mile border with Nepal, and China has been consolidating its close relationships the Nepalese government. Jiang visited the country in 1996, and General Fu Quan-you, Chief of the General Staff of the PLA, visited Nepal for a week in April 2000. He met King Gyanendra and Prime Minister Koirala. With the visit of King Gyanendra to Beijing in August 2002 and his agreement not to allow any 'anti-China activities' (unspecified) in Nepal, cemented by many Chinese infrastructure projects in Nepal, the position of the Tibetans who have settled in Nepal is precarious. Now there is a much more restrictive attitude towards Tibetan cultural and religious events in Nepal. For example, photographs of the Dalai Lama cannot be publicly displayed (they would be 'making a *de facto* political statement'), and gatherings of Tibetans are prohibited.

One other result of these visits is that harsh policies have been introduced to try to prevent Tibetans escaping over the Himalaya into Nepal and to discourage others from trying. Those who succeed may be robbed and severely abused by the Nepalese police and returned to China, where they will be punished. Also, Tibetans wishing to return from India to Tibet through Nepal without the necessary documentation (because they escaped over the mountains originally) have to pay impossibly large sums of cash to the Nepalese authorities. Failure to pay, which is normal, results in long prison sentences. The UNHCR in Kathmandu, which has long assisted escaping Tibetans medically and in other ways, now has been denied access to some border areas with China and been restricted access to others, which has hindered their work.

It may be thought odd that China wishes to prevent Tibetans from escaping the persecution in their country – the Chinese should be glad that they leave;

the more the better, one might think – but of course escapees provide a huge amount of first-hand information about the true conditions in Tibet, which the Chinese wish to conceal. It is then eagerly pounced upon by human rights organisations and the Tibetan government-in-exile.

Another problem for Hu Jintao is Xinjiang, which means 'New Frontier', a huge, largely desert area rich in minerals that borders north-western Tibet.[18] The Chinese claim that Xinjiang has been a part of China since 60 BC, but it has been their long-standing practice to regard a territory they once occupied as having being theirs ever since (and that early invasion was a military disaster). The Tang dynasty made brief inroads into the territory in the seventh century AD, and the Mongols swept into it in the thirteenth century as they did into China itself. In 1731 Emperor Yongzheng of China was set upon expanding the Manchu empire to the far west.[19] He wanted the territory but, being a practising Buddhist and a fair-minded man, he was against an aggressive approach towards the Muslims. It was his fourth son, Emperor Quianlong, who completed the occupation, and the territory was given the name 'Xinjiang' in 1768. (The Emperor had Iparhan, the legendary Fragrant Concubine who became the love of his life, taken from Kashgar for the imperial harem.) It became a province of China in 1884, but not ruled by China until Mao occupied it in 1949. The present-day Uyghurs, one of the many Turkic tribes and now the predominant (Sufi) Muslim indigenous group, are their eighth-century descendants. They still consider Xinjiang as their homeland and the Chinese as occupiers.

In 1933 local Muslim reaction to earlier Chinese pressure was to set up the Republic of East Turkestan ('East and West Turkestan' predated the name 'Xinjiang').[20] It was short-lived, but they tried again in 1944 and this lasted until 1949 when Xinjiang was absorbed into the PRC. (Early in 1950 the pro-autonomy Muslim leaders of the East Turkestan Republic were all killed in an air crash on the journey to Beijing to negotiate; many Uyghurs think the crash was contrived.) The PLA moved in, and a Han immigration programme was inaugurated in 1950. A quasi-military organisation, the Xinjiang Production and Construction Corporation – which the Chinese call 'Bing Tuan' – then predominantly a Han organisation of demobilised PLA men, former KMT soldiers and resettled Han Chinese, was instrumental in establishing control from 1954.[21] It is, however, more a coloniser than a company, and it maintains a 100,000-strong militia. It also controls prisons and the *laogai* system of labour camps. Some of its produce is exported. Its 2.38 million employees make up 14 percent of Xinjiang's population. The corporation is directly accountable to Beijing and is run by the PLA.

Xinjiang has two autonomous regions. The Xinjiang Uyghur Autonomous Region was set up in 1955 with autonomous Mongol, Kyrgyz, Kazakh and Hui prefectures and counties reflecting their predominant nationalities (the Hui are Han Muslims – 'Hui' means 'Muslim') loyal to Beijing, and 80 percent of Uyghurs are in the Altishahr region of Xinjiang bordering Pakistan and Afghanistan. Secondly, the Ningxia Hui Autonomous Region was carved out of Gansu Province in 1965. But, as in Tibet, the designation 'autonomous' was misleading. The Chinese took complete control, though with many local cadres at lower levels.

Mao's 'Great Leap Forward' was designed to eliminate ethnic and class differences as well as to promote rapid economic progress. But in 1962 persecution by the Chinese led to a rapid exodus of some 80,000 Muslims, many of them Kazakhs, across the western border in search of food and shelter. The Red Guards then arrived and created chaos. Direct military control was imposed in 1971, but some semblance of order was not established until the death of Mao in 1976. Meanwhile immigration of Han Chinese into the area continued, and Chinese control tightened. Han Chinese immigrants continue to arrive.

In 1980, although there were severe riots that year, Hu Yaobang considered that Xinjiang was less of a problem than Tibet because it had no leader of international stature and no comparable foreign support. Nevertheless, modified reforms were introduced. When Hu was dismissed as Party General Secretary in 1987, the more liberal policies in Xinjiang were soon reversed. The Chinese had long had their eyes on the rich oil, coal, mineral and non-ferrous metal deposits in Xinjiang, especially in the huge Tarim basin to the north-west of the area, part of which was Tibetan territory. Exploitation for the benefit of China is deeply resented locally. Also, Chinese nuclear-weapons testing in Lop Nor in northern Xinjiang was the focus of protests. There has been growing militancy against the Chinese occupiers and a rising sense of Muslim national identity and unity of purpose. This was exacerbated by the Chinese ban on the use of the Uyghur Turkic language – universities teach only in Mandarin – and local Muslim cadres are not permitted to practise their religion. All mosques must be registered and are monitored.

The 1980s were, however, a hopeful time for the Uyghurs, as for Tibetans. They watched their formerly oppressed cousins in Kazakhstan, Uzbekistan and Kyrgyzstan break away from the Soviet Union and become independent and wondered, could this happen to them too? Serious riots followed in 1990, when the Kyrgyz Muslims called for a *jihad* against the Chinese and demanded an independent East Turkestan state. Thereafter, there have been bombings and riots in many parts of Xinjiang, the most serious in 1996 when the Chinese 'Strike Hard' campaign included the attempted destruction of the Muslim independence fighters. Police infiltrated mosques, rounded up suspected 'splittists', held them for long periods and executed 190 people. The situation was rapidly getting out of hand. Militant Muslims from Uzbekistan and other nearby Islamic countries began to influence those who sought independence in Xinjiang. In October 2002 George W. Bush accepted the Chinese claim that the East Turkestan Islamic Movement is a terrorist group.

Since 1996 there have been annual meetings between Russia, Kazakhstan, Kyrgyzstan, Tajikistan and China – known as the 'Shanghai Five', the first meeting having been held in Shanghai – to discuss border issues, security, trade and economic relations. When Turkmenistan joined the Five, the name was changed to the Shanghai Cooperation Organisation (SCO), mentioned earlier. It has taken a more political turn, towards preventing ethnic peoples from these areas in Xinjiang escaping to their home territories and trying to stem the flow of Muslim fundamentalists in the opposite direction. The foreign governments of the SCO have agreed to assist China in stemming 'splittism' in Xinjiang. Following the 11 September tragedies, the subsequent attacks principally by the US in Afghanistan have greatly complicated the situation.

The Xinjiang Production and Construction Corporation has become a powerful force in the development of agricultural and industrial projects, and effectively manages many towns in the Autonomous Regions. It exercises even more control than the regional administration, and discriminates against the employment of Uyghur labourers, in spite of their being relatively well-educated. In 2001 the Lanzhou Military Region, which includes Xinjiang, Ningxia and part of Qinghai, was placed on a war footing. The mid-2001 surge in executions in China during the 'Strike Hard' campaign spread to Xinjiang. Amnesty International reported that Chinese authorities in the Xinjiang Uyghur Autonomous Region aim 'to deal a decisive blow to separatist forces, eliminating separatism and illegal religious activities'. Many more Uyghur and other political prisoners have been executed.

The June 1999 Western Development programme (see Chapter Ten) has the same approach in Xinjiang as in Tibet. The transfer of large numbers of Han Chinese into Xinjiang will completely swamp local people and their Muslim culture, aided by the rail extension to Kashgar in 2002. Although the Chinese settlers now comprise 40 percent of the population in Xinjiang, whatever happens they will not be able to extinguish Islam from the hearts of the people. Like Tibetan Buddhism, the Muslim faith is practised in many parts of the world by about 1.3 billion followers. Xinjiang may cause as much concern to the new leadership as does Tibet – indeed, there are many parallels between Tibet and Xinjiang. The Chinese leadership needs to address these causes of injustice to the Islamic people in Xinjiang.

One of Jiang Zemin's legacies was a solid foundation of participation in international fora. Multilateralism is helpful in learning about experiences in other countries, resolving problems and keeping the peace. China is a member of the UN Security Council with the right of veto.

ASEAN (the Association of South-east Asian Nations) was set up in 1967 by five nations in South-east Asia deeply concerned about the military strength and eccentricities of China under Mao. By 2002 it had ten members, and the EU has had a formal relationship with it from 1980. In 1993 ASEAN formed a Regional Forum, which China joined and in which the EU participates. China is expected to become a full member in 2010 and India in 2011. The formation of a Free Trade Area between members from 2003 with maximum tariffs of 5 percent has been slow in implementation.

Chris Patten, at that time the EU's representative in ASEAN, was impatient with the lack of progress and urged a more results-orientated approach based on modernising the original contractual basis of the EU's association.[22] He wanted be able at least to discuss human rights, economic governance, environmental issues and the fight against terrorism.

APEC (the Asia-Pacific Economic Cooperation organisation) was formed in 1989, and now has twenty-one member nations including China, Taiwan, Hong Kong, Russia, Japan, South Korea and the US. Meetings of their political leaders began in 1993 in Seattle and were attended by Jiang.

ASEM (the Asia-Europe Meeting), with ten Asian members including China and with the EU, has so far proven to be a good forum for developing relationships both at the highest political level and through working groups of experts. Topics of discussion range from human rights, Tibet, the causes of terrorism and the balance between security and civil liberties, to problems of false documentation of migrants. The first ministerial summit was held in 1996, and there have since been five more.

Thus, Hu Jintao faces many delicate and tough issues which will affect China's position in the world, and has an important network of international relationships to assist him. In China's relationships with the US, Taiwan, India, Nepal and Xinjiang, Tibet is directly or indirectly involved.

TEN

Tibet's Ecology and Economic Development

'When the stallion of progress ...
is bound tightly ...
When the white yak of freedom
is chained by the nose ...
When the sheep of peace ...
are exploited ...
and sheared again and again –
Oh – how tears of regret flow
uncontrollably from my eyes!'
'Tears of Regret Flow Uncontrollably',
by Lhagyal Tsering, translated by Janet L. Upton[1]

Tibet is a land bountifully endowed with nature's gifts. An amazing variety of flora, fauna and minerals exist there. It is the source of ten of the greatest rivers in Asia. To the human eye Tibet is a place of great beauty, and to the heart a sacred land. All are precious to its people who, for generations, have been its custodians. Its gifts are to be used sparingly and, as far as possible, sustainably.

China has a deep antipathy towards forests and trees. With the Chinese occupation came the destruction of vast areas of forest, at first mainly in the east, to serve China's needs – booty was carried away in an endless stream of trucks. The result has been a fall in the forest cover of the TAR from about 9 percent of the territory in 1950 to about 5 percent in 1985 and even less today. The land was clear-felled, and although reafforestation was required by law, it was the exception. Where possible, previously forested land was used for grazing cattle. State enterprises charged with timber felling were given quotas and had to sell the produce to other state enterprises at below market prices, sometimes even at below cost.[2] To compensate they would fell even more timber for sale on the free market, unrecorded. The gigantic scale of this operation was such that it had two unforeseen consequences.[3]

First, removing the tree cover over large mountainous areas caused the topsoil to slide into the rivers. Unprecedented silting and flooding downstream in China, India and Bangladesh were the tragic consequences. In 1998 Yangtse floods killed 3,656 people, affected 5.6 million households and caused about US$ 37.5 billion worth of damage – the worst since 1954. The Chinese authorities admitted that deforestation was responsible, after initial denials. Following earlier toxic contamination of the Huai River in 1994, the Yangtse floods triggered a fundamental change in policy. The authorities set up the 'National Natural Forest Protection Project', which called a halt to further logging and promoted reafforestation in the upper reaches of the Yangtse and Yellow Rivers. The Three Gorges Dam, now filling with water, is intended to solve the problem of periodic flooding, as well as generating electricity. Great concern was expressed by Jiang Zemin for the need for ecological regeneration and environmental protection and they were given high priority. The difficulty will be to develop appropriate policies within the wider context of Western Development, and to secure their correct application at the periphery of China's bureaucratic system where bribery and corruption are rife. Since 2002–3 there have been many small, localised reafforestation projects in the TAR, but the administrative system for ensuring that new planting will be nurtured to ensure growth requires attention before the policy can be claimed a success.

Second, it now seems likely that cutting down about one half of the tree cover in Tibet has delayed melting the winter snows. Snow on flat ground reflects the spring sunshine, and melting is less rapid than when it is caught in the treetops. This delays the updraft of warm air in the mountains of Tibet, which sucks in the moist air over India from the ocean, and so the monsoon may be delayed. Indian and Bangladeshi agriculture would be adversely affected.

With the destruction of so many forests and with hunting for sport, much of the wildlife has disappeared. The wanton killing of wild animals upsets the balance of nature and demeans the spirit. Then there is the extraction of minerals, which at first occurred only on a comparatively small scale. Now there is a major programme of bending nature to the will of man.

In June 1992 Jiang launched China's ambitious programme of Western Development on a scale which could earn him a place in China's history. It is a broad strategy of economic development that could affect the whole of China and is reminiscent of the First Emperor's remarkable infrastructure developments in the third century BC. The 'West' referred to covers 56 percent of China and some 23 percent of its population. Territorially, Tibet – including its traditional lands in Amdo and Kham – covers nearly half the 'West'. The remainder includes Xinjiang, the Ningxia Hui Autonomous Region, the Chinese provinces of Gansu, Shaanxi, Sichuan, Guizhou and Yunnan and the newly formed Chongqing province.

The economic motives for Western Development are to provide physical resources to sustain and develop China's manufacturing centres, largely in eastern China, and to enable agriculture to feed the ever-increasing population, with an overall economic growth rate of about 9 percent per annum. Self-sufficiency is a major aim and demand has already outstripped domestic supply. Hydroelectric power generation and transmission and natural gas and oil pipelines (China is now the world's second-largest importer of oil) will transfer energy to the eastern cities, accompanied by new waterways, more rail and road construction and the extraction of gold, copper and many other valuable minerals. The arid lands of Tibet's high plateau and the deserts of Xinjiang contain huge, untapped reserves of such minerals, and they are needed urgently. The problem is that commodity imports (as a percentage of GDP) have more than doubled since 1999, and from mid-2003 have been driving up world metal prices dramatically. China consumes 36 percent of the world's steel and 55 percent of global cement, both high energy users. Coking coal for steelmaking, which was exported by China, is now being imported, driving up world prices. About 71 percent of China's electricity is generated from coal, and demand is increasing faster than supply. Three tributaries of the Yangtse, arising in traditional Tibetan areas, will be channelled to feed into the upper reaches of the Yellow River, the most westerly of the new waterways. (The Yellow River has had so much water extracted that since 1985, at some time each year, it has failed to reach the sea.) Part of the 2,500-year-old Grand Canal is to have its flow reversed by fifteen giant pump stations to take water uphill from the south to Tianjin in the north. Water shortage is a huge problem in China.[4]

The economic aim is also to develop the West for the sake of its people. Primary mineral extraction will come first, then intermediate processing (to capture more of the 'value added' and to create more employment) and, finally, local manufacturing with new towns and cities.

There are also powerful political motives. Prosperous Tibetans and

Uyghurs will then, it is hoped, gratefully accept their place in a united China, abandon their religions and truly embrace atheism, the Communist Party and democratic centralism. Ethnic and national unity will then be assured. 'Splittism' and the threats of instability will recede into the past. Also, the success of the Communist Party in enriching the whole country will ensure its election if democracy is introduced in the distant future.

Western Development will, however, raise in acute form a number of potential conflicts between large-scale development and the sustainable use of the environment, and between the interests of local people whose livelihoods may be adversely affected (mineral extraction seldom achieves lasting solutions to poverty reduction) and the traditional desire for self-sufficiency in China when confronted by the obligation for free trade under the WTO. In general, one may say that if there are five separate objectives, then to be successful in all of them five specific and well-targeted policies may be needed. One should not expect that a single bold policy such as 'economic development' will achieve success in several different ways. Some objectives may conflict with the achievement of others. The initial doses of infrastructure investment and mining may bring short- and medium- term benefits to those engaged in Tibet and Xinjiang but in the long-term they will not be sustainable. Ethnic and national unity, even if they do result, are also very long-term.

A major conflict of policy arose in June 2003 concerning the Yunnan authorities in southern China, supported by Western Development agencies in Beijing, about the proposed building of thirteen dams on the Nu ('Angry') River to supply electric power for Yunnan's development and for China's eastern provinces, especially Guangdong. Deals had been signed with a new development corporation in spite of protests from many Chinese and foreign experts from relevant NGOs, China's own National Environmental Protection Bureau, the 100,000 or so people (including Tibetans) who would be displaced from their homes and downstream governments of Cambodia and Vietnam whose water supplies would be adversely affected. Complaints were also based on the fact that the Nu is part of the Three Parallel Rivers (with the Mekong and the Yangtse) World Heritage site, the largest in China.[5] In April 2004 Premier Wen Jiabao stepped in to halt the development, saying that it had become too controversial. He called for a more extensive investigation and for more involvement from the scientific and environmental communities.

Former Premier Zhu Rongji, who headed the 'Leading Group to Develop Western Areas', reported three main obstacles to Western Development: poor infrastructure, ecological degradation and an unsatisfactory quality of cadres.[6] To correct the first two will be a gigantic and costly task but is feasible. More serious is the perceived low quality of local cadres. This can frustrate the proper execution of plans, lead to inefficiencies and mistakes and result in corruption. Costs will increase and development times lengthen. There is, however, a fourth cause for concern: shortsightedness. The likely long-term effects on sustainable development and on the environment may not be fully appreciated. Much of the Yangtse flooding was brought about by decimating the trees in Tibet and restricting the areas for safe flooding by the construction of dams and artificial lakes for hydroelectricity. Warning voices were ignored. The effects were unanticipated. There are already some brave and outspoken Chinese critics of the whole Western Development plan on the basis of its damaging ecological and environmental effects and the destruction of ethnic cultures. Premier Wen Jiabao, who was Zhu's Vice-Premier, is now responsible for it all.

The unemployed in China are quite 'footloose' about where they go, and there is less direction by the authorities than there was. There will be a large migration of Han Chinese settling in Western Development territories. Many will be highly qualified and skilled in construction and manufacture; others will be specialised in trading, finance and other support services. Inevitably, the indigenous peoples in these areas will be further marginalised because they lack the relevant skills and experience. Also, there are many poor and unskilled Chinese people entering Tibet, taking low-level jobs away from Tibetans. The real danger is that a general increased prosperity for Tibetans and Uyghurs will not be forthcoming, because it has not been sufficiently targeted, while the influx of Han Chinese and their adverse social and cultural consequences will be all too successful. In spite of rapid growth in the east, to stem the flow of internal migrants – assessed at around 150 million persons – and to absorb some of the continuing population growth running at perhaps 13 million per annum, Western Development will provide habitable living space and work. To the Chinese, this is highly desirable. To the indigenous inhabitants, it foretells disaster.

Project decisions are made in Beijing, and some are financed wholly from the centre. While there are normally consultations with local officials and many 'on-site' visits from the planners and experts, there have been no reported consultations with the Tibetan people about their needs or the likely effects on them although now they may put forward their own projects and approval will now be given to projects which will benefit them.

The grand strategic plan for Tibet's development is predicated largely on the construction of a new railway starting from Golmud, an existing railhead in Qinghai province, to Lhasa. Directly south of Golmud are the Kunlun mountains, a great wall of rock and ice behind which lies the even higher, rugged, barren, mountainous plateau of Tibet. The railway will demand a feat of engineering that would have caused even Isambard Kingdom Brunel[7] to scratch his head. Most of the 695 miles will be above 13,123 feet, about one half over permafrost, frozen in winter and slushy in summer; 118 miles of this is 'not stable' and 62 miles is 'not at all stable'.[8] The land rises and falls unevenly by nearly four feet or more between seasons. The route will tunnel through great mountains and cross the least populated, highest, coldest (down to -46° Fahrenheit) and most arid part of Tibet. Fierce winds, landslides and earthquakes are frequent. The highest of the five passes is 16,600 feet and trains will ascend the steepest gradients anywhere in the world. New engines are being designed. Passenger trains will be pressurised, like aircraft. The line's capacity is said to be 5 million tons of cargo per annum into Tibet and 2.8 million tons of mineral resources in the reverse direction. Work has started at Golmud, the track climbing to around 9,800 feet, roughly following the existing road south-west. The San Chahe bridge at nearly 12,500 feet has been completed. Already some Tibetans are at work on the project, including some who have been arrested for attempting to escape from Tibet into Nepal. Over 170 Tibetans are being trained in China as 'railway engineers and administrators' for the project. It is expected to take six to ten years to complete.

In September 2002 the 'Qinghai–Tibet Railway Company' was established as a State-Owned Enterprise, administered directly by the Ministry of Railways. The Chinese News Agency reported that the company 'will be held responsible for its own profits and losses'. This sounds inconsistent with its being administered by the ministry. The financial arrangements are at present unclear. The cost, according to the Chinese, will be about US$ 2.3 billion (thought by experts to be a considerable underestimate), funded entirely by the central government. Chinese economists believe that the railway will yield a negative rate of return. (The returns will not even cover the current paying-out costs, let alone a return on capital.) If they are correct, it will require continuing subsidies to keep going, so the company cannot be held fully responsible for its own profits and losses. With such an uneconomic project, most of the benefits must be in non-monetary terms.

These may include the ability to bring in military personnel and weapons swiftly in case of a foreign attack, possibly supporting aggressive policies along Tibet's southern border and suppressing an internal uprising. China has both a Rapid Reaction Force, highly mobile and able to fly anywhere within twenty-four hours, and a Rapid Deployment Force armed with missiles and tanks – in total, some 300,000 men – which could be carried by rail. Also, as a result of subsidising the movement of people and freight both into and out of Tibet, the fear of Tibetans is that the movement of Chinese workers and settlers into Tibet will be made easier. Over 11 million surplus rural labourers live in Sichuan province next to the TAR.

Golmud was once part of a vast, pastoral land inhabited only by a few hundred Tibetan nomads. Today it is the second-largest town in Qinghai with some 200,000 inhabitants, of whom only 1.8 percent are Tibetans. With the building of the road to Lhasa it became a trading post.[9] Kazakh and Tibetan nomads and traders still roam its dusty streets; trucks are parked haphazardly. Muslim traders and travellers mingle with Han Chinese arriving at the railway station from the east to catch the bus to Lhasa. Trucks from Tibet unload yak skins and frozen meat and take on goods brought from China by rail for the return journey.

From Golmud, an existing railway goes east to the main junction at Lanzhou, a busy (and highly polluted) city of oil refineries and manufacturing industries. From Lanzhou it goes to the industrial centres in the east and north to Beijing. At Lanzhou it is also joined by a long branch line that snakes through mountains and desert north-west to Urumqi, the capital of Xinjiang. This line was opened in 1960, and the place has since become a Chinese city. Uyghurs find it hard to obtain work; they have to be able to speak Chinese. Also, it is difficult for them to obtain visas to trade over the borders in the former Soviet republics, as has been their practice for generations. Border security is being tightened. The people who benefit most from cross-border trade are the Chinese, who are also steadily infiltrating those countries as traders. Xinjiang is mainly desert. The arable land can no longer support the burgeoning population, so more land reclamation will be necessary – or more trading.

Another railway, completed early in 2001, goes from Urumqi 620 miles south-west, a thirty-hour journey through the Taklamakan Desert, to the hitherto remote Silk Route oasis town of Kashgar at the very edge of Chinese-claimed territory. Moreover, as part of the Western Development scheme, there are plans to extend the railway from Kashgar into Osh in neighbouring Kyrgyzstan and to Tashkent in Uzbekistan.

The new railway station at Kashgar and the trains there from Urumqi suggest what may be in store for Tibetans in Lhasa. Neither station nor trains give any indication that the territory is the heartland of the Uyghur people who have lived there for generations. Everything is in Chinese. The station is designed for a Chinese clientele: Chinese kiosks, Chinese signs and Chinese staff predominate. There is one Uyghur restaurant in the far corner of a forty-strong café complex (Uyghurs do not like eating amongst Chinese, whom they still consider to be foreign occupiers). The trains also have Chinese signs, Chinese staff, twenty-four-hour piped music, Chinese announcements and Chinese food. The effects of opening this rail link to Kashgar were an immediate loss of employment for Uyghurs and more Chinese immigrants.[10]

The new line to Lhasa is planned for completion in 2007, just in time for the Olympic Games – a southern showpiece for tourists. However, many experts think it will take much longer. For many years after completion, the Golmud–Lhasa rail link will be the most powerful force affecting Tibet's future, directly and indirectly. However, three other railway links are planned to link China with Tibet.[11]

Complementary to these and other rail developments, there has been a US$ 65 billion road programme underway in China over the last ten years, according to the State Planning Commission. Now, during the Tenth Five-Year Plan (2001–5), as part of Western Development, some important highways in Tibet are intended.[12] There are plans to upgrade the existing road to Lhasa from Lanzhou through Xining and Golmud to become a four-lane, all-weather highway. This will complete the Chinese National Trunk Highway System, modelled on the US Interstate Highway System. It would be as heroic a venture as the rail link. While parts of this route may well be improved, especially Xining–Lanzhou in connection with the Tsaidam Basin mineral projects, one doubts when – and even whether – the whole route will become a reality. Either the road or the railway to Lhasa can only be a dream and since the railway has been started, for some time the four-lane highway must surely remain in the imagination. Evidently the regional authorities are counting on the central government for investment funds, no doubt a cause of much delay. The four-lane highway starting in Urumqi in Xinjiang will head west for 165 miles to Kuitun, where the road forks to two major oil and gas fields at Karamay and Yining. The World Bank is contributing US$ 300 million. The Lanzhou–Lhasa highway may also be a toll route.

There is another great project affecting Tibet. The Tsaidam Basin (Qaidam Pendi in Chinese),[13] is a large group of dry salt lakes in the traditionally Tibetan northern area of Amdo, now part of Qinghai province, spreading out 100 miles or so to either side of Golmud. Geologically it is a remarkable area, rich in deposits of oil, natural gas, chrome, lithium, plutonium, boron, gold, salt – and potash, now the key mineral. The project's purpose is to alleviate China's crisis in agriculture, especially the output of grain.

For thousands of years the fertility of China's agricultural lands were sustained by the application of human and animal waste, highly effective but labour-intensive. Even in 1974 schoolchildren collected dung for use on the land and the schools paid them for this.[14] Then came chemical fertilisers and tractors. In the 1980s, with the flight of people seeking a better life in the eastern cities under Deng Xiaoping's new freedoms, there was a drive for greater agricultural productivity. The use of nitrogenous fertilisers suddenly exploded throughout China. Tibetan farmers, for example, were paid by the state for their produce partly in fertiliser, which they were required to use. As the fertility of the soil in China fell, more nitrogenous fertilisers were applied. The soil was further degraded. Scientists said that more phosphorus and potassium were needed in the form of potash for a better balance;[15] the Tsaidam Basin is the only major source in China. But the development of phosphate production has been slow in spite of its almost uniquely simple form of extraction. Part of the problem was the legacy of unplanned extraction of salt and other minerals on a small scale over many years. Only the easiest and richest minerals were taken, including boron and lithium, a practice called 'high grading'. It was a free-for-all. Chinese people flooded the area; towns grew up almost overnight. Large parts of the remaining forests in the Tsaidam Basin were destroyed. As a result, desert sands have spread. Most food has to be brought from afar.

The early response to the perceived need for potash was met by imports, from Israel and, latterly, Canada. Until 1995, potash imports were subsidised by the government to encourage their use. Then, corruption and smuggling to avoid import duties grew apace. A major factor behind these bewildering changes in policy was the accepted political necessity of achieving self-sufficiency in food production. This has been a traditional aim since the time of Mao and his experience on the land in Hunan, constantly threatened by enemy blockade.

Small potash plants were caught in a squeeze between state-fixed prices and rising costs. Many were closed down. China's Ministry of Chemical Industry formed a joint venture (the Qinghai Potash Fertiliser Plant) with Israeli Chemicals, to exploit the latter's experience in potash extraction from the Dead Sea. Production from the large new plant of 1 million tons' capacity was due to commence in 2000, but was delayed.

There are also plans for constructing a west–east gas pipeline 592 miles from the Tsaidam Basin to the industrial complex in Lanzhou through Zining. Some 10 percent of all China's reserves of natural gas are in this area, estimated at 1,500 billion cubic metres. Oil reserves in the area are estimated at 42 billion tons, and there are already over 100 oil wells there (if only Deng had known!). Thus, the potential for development in the Tsaidam Basin is vast. British Petroleum (BP) took a shareholding stake and signed a US$ 8.5 billion contract with PetroChina to construct the pipeline and for this BP was targeted by the British-based Free Tibet Campaign; BP has now sold its stake. There is concern that with China's accession to the WTO and cheaper imports, it may be less expensive and more flexible to import the liquefied natural gas than to pipe the raw gas a vast distance across land.

For generations gold has been extracted from Tibet. There are now thousands of prospectors and mines, almost all small-scale and most illegal. In 2002 there were still about 20,000 illegal gold prospectors entering Qinghai annually, and there is illegal mining in the TAR and Tibetan prefectures in Sichuan. For local cadres, prospectors provide ready cash 'under the counter'. However, mercury and/or cyanide may be used in separating the gold, and arsenic may be released. These dangerous toxins may then enter the waters of many rivers. The official policy is to concentrate gold extraction in two large state-owned mines and to close all small extraction processes.

Also in the TAR is the vast Yulong copper belt stretching for hundreds of miles, mainly in Chamdo prefecture with Chamdo, formerly the regional capital of Kham, at its northern end. Copper is scarce in China, and as the eastern industries expand, imports are rising fast. As the TAR National Land Specialist Plan (1996–2020) acknowledged, 'copper is a greatly superior mineral in Tibet' (excavating for the new railway has uncovered further deposits). But its concentration is low, only some 0.35–0.90 percent, so vast tonnages have to be mined to extract small quantities. Infrastructure developments, roads, housing and power are being developed, and the Chinese Western Mining Company in Qinghai has been awarded two major contracts for copper extraction.

Many state-owned mines in China employ compulsory labour and use *laogai* prison labourers, with some schemes dating back to 1956; Falun Gong members incarcerated in such prisons are also engaged. However, in spite of all these developments taking place, many in areas traditionally occupied by Tibetans, it is not reported that Tibetans have featured widely in employment. But constructing the Golmud–Lhasa railway is expected to employ 67,000 Chinese technicians and labourers all year round, with some 16,000 labourers employed locally on a seasonal basis.

How much of Western Development is really necessary? The lodgepole pine, when it becomes aged and unproductive in its growth, puts out an audible noise – a signal which can be heard by the mountain pine beetle. It arrives and begins to eat and break down the tree. Humus is then created for the next generation of trees. How many industrial processes mimic this process? Will modern manufacturing in China and the disposal of the waste it creates, both from production and the disposal of its products, result in yet more toxic waste? Will it demand the extraction and use of more and more non-renewable basic materials? This is a global problem, addressed at the 2002 World Summit on Sustainable Development.

The path of least resistance for resource-hungry industries is to exploit nature's bountiful gifts, to dig more basic minerals out of the ground, tap into deposits of oil, natural gas and coal. It seems not only the easiest but also the most obvious way. The future can look after itself, some will say. In a free market, as those precious natural reserves come into short supply, their prices rise. This will have the effect of making natural deposits, which were uneconomic to exploit when prices were lower, suddenly become worthwhile. Thus, oil reserves increase when prices rise even though no more has actually been found. The 'carrying capacity' for nature depends on the demand for its reserves and how long they take to be regenerated. As soon as extinction of even the least of economic materials becomes a real possibility, clever scientists will have invented an alternative, say some commentators from the comfort of their armchairs. Perhaps.

The crisis is highlighted in a report by the Worldwide Fund for Nature (WWF) International for the World Summit on Sustainable Development in August 2002. Since the beginning of the 1980s, the total biologically productive capacity of the earth has been exceeded at an increasing rate by its consumption. 'Unless governments take urgent action to encourage a more sustainable way of life, human welfare will go into drastic decline by 2030 with falls in the average life expectancies, lower education levels and a shrinking economy.' Within fifty years, says the WWF, there is little doubt that average standards of living will be falling. This sounds alarmist, but undoubtedly there is a problem. China is a big player in these global concerns. It should use its yet-unexploited reserves in Tibet and other areas of 'the West' sparingly or it, too, will be vulnerable in the longer run.

'Sustainability', the key concept for finding a way out, may be defined as an economic state where the demands placed upon the environment by people and commerce today can be met without reducing the capacity of the environment to provide for future generations. This is a powerful general principle. It cannot be fully achieved in the rich societies in North America, Europe and Australasia, but there is enormous progress in this direction. China is in the early stages of Western Development and will have opportunities to incorporate sustainability into its plans from the very beginning.

What are the strategic options? There are several possibilities. One is to switch to those materials which are more sustainable, through the use of timber only from sustainably managed forests (not clear felling), for example, or through the development of plant-based materials as substitution for those based on oil. This has always been so amongst indigenous peoples.[16] Now, many large Western manufacturers have adopted these principles – and they find that it is good business. Organisations as far apart as The Body Shop (cosmetics and health products), Nike (sporting goods) and IKEA (household goods) are at the forefront. Another is to maximise the re-use of waste, at both the manufacturing and household levels. Local authorities need to be geared to the collection and separation of different materials for onward processing.

There is, however, a more fundamental approach. Paul Hawken has been arguing for years in, for example, *The Ecology of Commerce*, that something more radical is now needed by breaking with tradition in building and product design. Ecologically designed houses have been around for a long time, but not in mass quantity. Ecologically designed offices, warehouses and factories are of interest for their rarity. Now it seems that 'lift-off' is becoming a reality in product design, in the US, Germany and Japan.

The Ford Motor Company in the US is redesigning its cars so that at the end of their useful lives they can be disassembled, the parts used again. It is planning to use waste arising from all its activities so that it is no longer waste at all – a 'cradle-to-grave' industrial system of responsibility. BMW in Germany already has a disassembly plant to recycle parts of its older cars, and newer models are designed with disassembly in mind. In Japan, 1992 legislation requires manufacturers to establish resource-recovery centres for their products at the end of their useful lives. A big effort is going into redesigning products. Matsushita's newer washing machines can be disassembled with a single screwdriver, and many parts used again. Moreover, if waste products from one industry can become valuable inputs into another totally different industry, and if there is some local planning to assist the near-location of such interconnected enterprises, the 'metabolism' of one industry can be more easily linked to that of another and many sectors of the economy will benefit.

At the level of self-managed poverty reduction, 'community-based sustainable development' has become a watchword for the development of poor, remote communities. Although helping rural people to develop and use new technologies that give them more control over their own lives would have political implications, in Tibet and Xinjiang access to these ideas would help them achieve their own poverty relief. The World Summit on Sustainable Development in Johannesburg, August–September 2002, attended by then Premier Zhu Rongji, took these matters further. Community-based sustainable development can be seen in action in the southern part of Ladakh, in remote Jammu and Kashmir, northern India, which is most relevant to rural Tibet.

The Ladakh Project was started in 1980 under the inspiring leadership of Helena Norberg-Hodge. In 1991 the International Society for Ecology and Culture was formed, based in Leh, the ancient capital. Ladakh is a plateau of 10,000–13,000 feet sweeping up to high pastures at 18,000 feet and separated from the TAR to the east by even higher and forbidding Himalayan mountains. Its people were in origin mainly Mongolian nomads, and they are Buddhists who recognise the Dalai Lama as their spiritual leader (there is a Muslim area further north). Tibetan medicine is widely practised, as in Tibet, with astrology an important component. Shamanism is also followed for healing and divination. The area is sometimes called 'Little Tibet'. So Norberg-Hodge's twenty-two-year development experience of Ladakh is very relevant to the development of 'big' Tibet.

The essence of her practical findings is that the Western model of development, which China has in effect followed, is inappropriate to the Ladakhi people and to many other rural indigenous peoples. The answer is more decentralised technology, small-scale for local needs, based on renewable resources. Thus there are solar panels and efficiently designed solar cookers and dryers in use. Traditional mudbrick walls are adapted to give more insulation during the bitter winters and for cooling in summer. Hydraulic 'ram' pumps use the energy from local streams to pump water without using external sources of fuel, and micro-hydroelectric and wind power are used for electricity and for milling. There are training schemes in Ladakh to widen the employment base, to keep the young people contented and reduce their outward migration, and to have money to spare.[17] As Hawken remarks, 'you could almost define the restorative economy as one that turns its attention in a big way to the small things.'[18]

In China, small local Township- and Village-Owned Enterprises (TVOEs) have mushroomed since the 1980s, and by 1991 there were about 550,000 of them.[19] Many are, in effect, local private cooperatives, although for political reasons they have to appear owned by the town or village authorities. Their technologies and equipment were often 'cast-offs' from the SOEs and labour-intensive in character. Most labour came from agricultural families as productivity increased. Their export performance has been remarkable. No doubt the large number of secondary schools and training establishments in rural areas in China has much to do with this economic growth.

The Chinese have not appeared to be truly interested in helping Tibetans to prosper, except on their own terms, but perhaps that policy will now change following the rural visits by Hu Jintao and Wen Jiabao. While there are already several Western NGOs engaged in poverty relief, education, health, orphanages and other good works in Tibet (some also include poor Chinese in their constituency), only a few are supporting the development of new businesses.[20]

There is a wider institutional issue relevant to development. The 'right to development' is enshrined in the International Covenant on Economic, Social and Cultural Rights (ICESCR), Article 2, which says that 'all peoples may, for their own ends, freely dispose of their natural wealth and resources without prejudice to any obligations arising out of international economic cooperation, based upon the principle of mutual benefit, and international law'. The Chinese government, having ratified the ICESCR in March 2001, is legally bound by this provision.

On 4 December 1986 the General Assembly of the UN adopted 'The UN Declaration on the Right to Development'. In ten articles, this made more specific the above ICESCR Article 2. It confirms that the right to development is an 'inalienable right' and the prerogative 'both of nations and of individuals who make up nations'. A nation is a distinct race or people, such as Tibetans. However, since General Assembly resolutions, although influential, are not binding on states, the ICESCR is the operative treaty in relation to China and Tibet.

In March 1999 the Constitution of the People's Republic of China was amended in Article 9 to state that 'All mineral resources, waters, forests, mountains, grasslands, unreclaimed land, beaches and other natural resources are owned by the state, that is, by the whole people, with the exception of [those natural resources] that are owned by collectives in accordance with the law.' Thus, if Tibetans are a 'people' within international law, a matter considered later, there is a direct conflict between the ICESCR and the constitution of the PRC, in which international law as ratified by the PRC takes precedence.

The Chinese 'Guidelines for Investment in Tibet' in 2000 pay no regard whatsoever to any possible interests of Tibetans.[21] They consist of privileges which investors in Tibet would receive at the expense of Tibetans, such as 'free funds' to purchase land at 50 percent of its value, first priority authorisation to develop land and underground resources in the construction of railways or rail stations, and exemption of income and operating taxes for projects such as infrastructure, transportation and energy development.

The Tibetan government-in-exile has also issued its 'Guidelines for International Development Projects and Sustainable Development in Tibet'.[22] These set out the basic ethical principles for development in order to protect Tibetan culture, promote rural development, secure land rights and encourage Tibetan participation in the local economy. They encourage the use of Tibetan managers, the provision of loans and credit for Tibetan entrepreneurs, skill training and other forms of technical assistance – following broadly the PADME and related programmes which already exist for Tibetans-in-exile.

Both Chinese and foreign enterprises engaging in development should have environmental guidelines and principles which take full account of the impact on local people and on the wider environment. They should be required to write 'environmental impact statements' to force them to consider whether there are disadvantages that might arise to indigenous peoples and the environment, and if so what actions they should take. Current Chinese laws and regulations provide for such environmental impact assessments.

Traditionally in the West, only private costs and benefits (revenues) to the enterprises concerned would be considered in a new project, on the basis of ratios such as the return on investment. The expected costs and benefits to society not otherwise included have normally been ignored. The social costs might include injuries and deaths from industrial processes (a serious problem in China);[23] land, water and air pollution (another serious problem); noise; traffic congestion; environmental damage; and loss of social amenity. Costs can be estimated for some of these. A planning authority can impose restrictions to protect people and the environment, or to pay compensation to those adversely affected with funds from the polluters.[24] 'Green taxes' encourage conservation and reduce pollution. They might cause enterprises to plan new projects with environmental concerns built in so that their exposure to such taxes would be eliminated. Revenues could be used to reduce other taxes, starting with the most disadvantaged people, so that they are national-budget 'revenue neutral'. From a national welfare point of view there are two net gains: a better environment for all, and income enhancement for the most needy. In OECD countries there are already at least eighty-five levies that attempt to address environmental issues in this way.[25]

In 1996 China was admitted as a member of the World Conservation Union (formerly the International Union for the Conservation of Nature). It has over eighty other member states and over 700 NGOs. It meets every three years, has high standards of environmental protection and conducts investigations, wielding influence but no power. For China, it signifies a step in the right direction.

Environmental protection was not a feature of Western Development until the great Yangtse floods of 1998. Now it is said to be top priority. The National Environmental Protection Agency has a daunting task. One problem is that local cadres have been given the task of implementing China's environmental protection laws, and they are the same people who corruptly take money to permit the laws to be broken. The agency should have its own field staff, trained and dedicated to their tasks with powers of enforcement.

Environmental NGOs are beginning to emerge in China. Most operate through the state Environmental Protection Agency and can become useful 'whistleblowers', although more seek greater freedom by registering as private companies. Then they have to raise private money to survive. Some NGOs have taken money from well-respected organisations such as the Ford Foundation, but others have incautiously been funded by big corporate environmental polluters. Even so, they have to be careful not to criticise government policy or they will be closed down and the offenders arrested. In 1999 a planned peaceful demonstration in Lhasa to express concern about damage to Tibet's ecosystem and to promote awareness about environmental issues was stopped by the police before it even started.

PART TWO

Bringing about Change

ELEVEN

Human Rights Law

'Why are the people rebellious?
Because the rulers interfere too much.
Therefore they are rebellious.'
Lao-tzu, Tao Te Ching, *Chapter Seventy-five*

Human rights are universal but not all countries value them in the same way. Some argue in favour of 'Asian values', as distinct from 'Western values'. The Chinese foreign minister at the 1993 World Conference on Human Rights in Vienna put the issue most concisely: 'Individuals must put the state's rights before their own.' Singapore's foreign minister also argued that 'universal recognition of the ideal of human rights can be harmful if universalism is used to deny or mask the reality of diversity.' To which Warren Christopher, the US Secretary of State, responded: 'We cannot let cultural relativism become the last refuge of repression.' It was argued by China that to foist Western values and standards on Asian countries with deep roots in Confucianism would be damaging to progress and would lead to all the social ills evident in the US, Britain and many other countries. Chris Patten, the last governor of Hong Kong, gave a robust rebuttal to these statements. His response emphasised the universality of human values and human rights that protect all of humanity regardless of race, colour or creed, especially the most vulnerable – women, children, minorities, indigenous peoples, workers, refugees, displaced persons … People are people, all are part of the human race, was his message.

The concept and purpose of law in China is unlike that in the West.

Traditionally, it had more to do with administrative control and the maintenance of a moral and social (Confucian) order than with protection of the individual. Its underlying purpose was to maintain the power of the rulers. The Legalist structure of law codified by the First Emperor in the third century BC consisted of a vast number of hard and fast rules with which to keep the people in order. In one form or another this continued throughout Chinese history. In 1604 Chu-hung, a Buddhist monk in China, issued *The Record of Self-Knowledge* which listed 202 Good Deeds and 279 Bad Deeds with the number of points each would earn. During the Qing dynasty (1644–1912) the penal code listed 436 main statutes and some 1,900 sub-statutes which provided specific penalties for specific crimes. It listed 813 capital offences. Political offences merited the most savage punishments.

Mao Zedong abolished the law as a means of governance. Some 60,000 lawyers and judges were dismissed, and many imprisoned. All the laws enacted by the Nationalist government of Chiang Kai-shek were cancelled. For twenty-five years, law did not exist. It was seen by the new Marxist government as a tool of the ruling class in support of bourgeois capitalism. But there were many regulations, including (from 1951) the suppression of counter-revolutionaries, under which the vast *laogai* system of prison camps was founded. The Communist Party decided everything, and Party policies carried the weight of law. From 1957 Party organs could imprison anyone without legal process being applied. In 1959 the Ministry of Justice was abolished.

Mao died in 1976. In 1982 Deng Xiaoping introduced a radically new constitution largely to serve the needs of his policy of 'opening' China to modernisation and the influx of foreign capital and know-how. China then tried to construct a legal system from scratch. But in 1980 there were only about 3,000 people in the whole of China who had any acquaintance with the law, and these were mostly old men who had been persecuted under Mao. Early plans to train large numbers of lawyers were never carried out. Almost no books on law could be found. By Western standards, the new legal system was seriously deficient, for it was still essentially designed to serve the needs of the state. Thus, prior to the Law on Lawyers in 1997, the firm duty of a defence lawyer was to help the state elicit a confession from an accused person and to ensure that the correct punishment was exacted. The status of lawyers was then changed from being 'state law workers' to that of practitioners providing legal services for society, who are obliged to safeguard the legitimate interests of their clients. But it was still the case that defence witnesses could be arrested and tortured to change their evidence, that suspects had no legal right to remain silent and that the Communist Party would ignore legal proceedings when arresting and sentencing political dissidents. In 2000, the number of lawyers in China was stuck at about 100,000 – nowhere near the training of 2 million lawyers, 1 million judges and 1 million defence lawyers being talked about in 1985.

Thanks to early pressure from the UN and from many governments and NGOs, the Chinese authorities are now beginning to understand about human rights law and practice. There are 'Human Rights Dialogues' with the UN, the European Union and governments in Britain, Australia, Norway and the US, along with seminars, workshops, university degree and other specialist and general courses on human rights law and its administration for government officials, judges, prosecutors, lawyers, police, prison officials, Chinese students of law and teachers of human rights. A huge effort is involved. The task is enormous but, as UN High Commissioner for Human Rights Mary Robinson remarked, 'how else do you embed a culture of human rights in the largest population in the world?' In February 2002 *Xinhua* announced the first edition of a new bimonthly magazine, *Human Rights*, published in Chinese and English by the 'China Society for Human Rights Studies'. In July 2002 Zhang Yishan, China's deputy permanent representative to the UN, called for exchanges and cooperation in the field of human rights. Governments, universities, law societies and human rights organisations are already all engaged. Also, during 1992–5 there was a major project on 'China and Constitutionalism' organised at New York's Columbia University, including Chinese lawyers, in which the problems of the Chinese constitution were thoroughly examined, including its references to human rights. It was found that 'the current Constitution fails to impose any real restrictions on the ruling [Communist] party either in letter or spirit'. Chinese participants used the project to draft constitutional provisions intended to be put into effect in a future China. In December 2002 Xu Wenli, a prominent Chinese dissident just freed from imprisonment, said: 'There is a strong awakening of consciousness within Chinese society towards democracy, freedom and human rights.'

Human rights education is a necessary start, but it cannot be wholly effective until there is a fundamental change in people's hearts towards other human beings, whoever they may be. A Chinese friend of mine living in London, whom I have known for twelve years, said to me in March 2001: 'You know, John, you have spoken to me about human rights many times in our conversations but until last week, when I read in a newspaper about the grief felt by a husband and his wife in China at the required abortion of their second child and saw their pictures of great sadness, I never really felt it. Now I know what you mean.'

On 27 March 2001 the Chinese government lit a fuse which may detonate a legal bomb and blow China's centralist system of government apart. In the process, it may give Tibet a chance for autonomy or independence. On that day the Chinese government ratified the International Covenant on Economic, Social and Cultural Rights (ICESCR). In Article 1 this declares that:

(1) All peoples have the right of self-determination. By virtue of that right they freely determine their political status and freely pursue their economic, social and cultural development.

(2) All peoples may, for their own ends, freely dispose of their natural wealth and resources without prejudice to any obligations arising out of international economic cooperation, based upon the principle of mutual benefit, and international law. In no case may a people be deprived of its own means of subsistence.

(3) [in part] The State Parties to the present Covenant … shall promote the realisation of the right of self-determination, and shall respect that right, in conformity with the provisions of the Charter of the United Nations.

Within two years, by March 2003, the Chinese government was obliged to submit a report on the present situation in China with respect to the thirty-one articles in the covenant. Then started a series of five-year Periodic Reports on progress with compliance, which could take place through changes to the Chinese constitution, the introduction of specific legislation and/or changes in administrative practice. The Committee on Economic, Social and Cultural Rights is the UN treaty body responsible for the implementation of this covenant. Each year the committee makes a report to the Human Rights Commission which is debated, with resolutions resulting.

Article 1 of the International Covenant of Civil and Political Rights (ICCPR) is identical to Article 1 of the ICESCR, above. China signed the ICCPR on 5 October 1998, but the government has not yet ratified it. To become binding on a state, international covenants and other legal instruments have first to be signed by an authorised person in the state and then ratified by its government. Signing is a declaration of intent that ratification will follow in the future. Ratification is a solemn commitment by a government. The processes of compliance then come under the scrutiny and rules of the appropriate treaty body in the UN, with regular reports required from the state. Together these two international covenants comprise a powerful obligation to honour the 'right of self-determination' to all peoples in China, although one is sufficient.

If a people, such as a distinct ethnic group, have no freedom to determine their political status and thus cannot freely pursue their economic, social and cultural development as they wish, then they may not be able to protect themselves as individuals from the harsh and oppressive actions of the controlling power. Tibet is just one example. Witness also the people of Chechnya, Kosovo and East Timor, to mention three other recent tragedies; they all felt that they could not develop in their own ways because the states that had power over their territories wanted them to conform to their will, beliefs and ways of life. East Timor, after a long and bloody struggle, eventually won the right of independence from Indonesia, with the help of the UN, only in May 2002.

Thus one of the most important and fundamental human rights is the 'right of self-determination'. Where there is a serious dispute on, say, whether such a people wish to remain part of a much larger state or to become separate, wholly or in part, to ascertain what kind of political system a people want there may be a referendum, in practice likely to be held under the supervision of the UN.

The key word is 'people'. In 1990 a UNESCO 'Meeting of Experts on Further Study of the Rights of People' concluded that in the context of the rights of people under international law, including the right of self-determination, 'people' are to be defined as a group of individuals who have some or all of seven specified characteristics: a common historical tradition; racial or ethnic identity; cultural homogeneity; linguistic unity; religious or ideological affinity; territorial connection; and common economic life. Also, they must be of a certain number, which need not be large; they must have the will to be identified as a people, or the consciousness of being a people; and, possibly, the group must have institutions or other means of expressing its common characteristics and its will to identity. While this is not conclusive – other criteria have been considered from time to time – the UNESCO formulation has found favour with many international lawyers.

'Peoples' may also be minorities, indigenous populations or nationalities. All such titles involve essentially the same idea. The Chinese call Tibet one of their many 'national minorities' but that does not make it possible for them to deny Tibetans the right of self-determination if they are deemed to be a 'people' in international law and satisfy the criteria. The right of self-determination is a genuinely 'collective right' vested in a group of people, not in a government or a state – indeed, it is a right against the state which presently administers or controls that people.

The options for 'political status' can include acceptance by the people of full incorporation within the larger state in which those people live, varying by degrees and kinds of autonomy or self-government within a state, or complete independence, as in many former colonial territories. Slovakia achieved independence when it split from Czechoslovakia, Slovenia when it split from Yugoslavia, Eritrea when it split from Ethiopia, East Timor when it split from Portugal and then Indonesia. It should be up to the people freely to decide these fundamental matters. This implies, first, the existence of some kind of democratic process (for example, a referendum) through which the will of the people can be freely expressed and, second, the willingness of the highest authorities in the land to accept the expressed will of the people.

The Human Rights Committee of the UN has made clear that realisation of the right of self-determination is an essential condition for the effective guarantee and observance of individual human rights and for the promotion and strengthening of those rights. If a group of people are being oppressed and have no say over how they are governed, then they are in no position to have any of their individual rights fully protected. It is also true that denial of human rights to a people may justify the exercise of their right of self-determination. Thus there is a double relationship between human rights generally and the right to self-determination.

Self-determination is more than just a moral principle. It is a 'right' in international law. Lawyers are, however, cautious in expressing its exact status. Opinions differ but 'it probably forms part of customary international law' (which would render it obligatory for all states whether they like the idea or not), perhaps even *jus cogens* – the most decisive and final norm of general international law from which no lessening or diminution of the law ('derogation') is permitted. The trend of expert opinion is towards acceptance of the higher status, *jus cogens*.

In 1945 its already high status was expressed as a principle in Articles 1 and 55 of the charter that established the UN itself (Article 1 states that 'the purposes of the United Nations are ... to develop friendly relations among nations based on respect for the principle of equal rights and self-determination of peoples'). Later it was established as a specific goal in three major international instruments of the UN:

1. The Declaration on the Granting of Independence to Colonial Countries and Peoples (1960);

2. The International Covenant of Civil and Political Rights (1966), in Article 1;

3. The International Covenant of Economic, Social and Cultural Rights (1966), in Article 1.

It is significant that the 'right of peoples to self-determination' comes as Article 1 in both international covenants, not as some obscure footnote. The question, therefore, is whether the Tibetan people have this right.

On 20 December 1961 a resolution was passed by the UN General Assembly which called for the 'cessation of practices which deprive the Tibetan people of their fundamental human rights and freedoms, including their right to self-determination' and it expressed the hope that 'Member States will make all possible efforts, as appropriate, towards achieving the purposes of the present resolution'. This was re-affirmed in a further resolution in 1965. But General Assembly resolutions, although indicative of a worldview, are not binding on states.

There have been two important unofficial investigations into the question of self-determination for the Tibetan people held almost simultaneously. The first, in November 1992, consisted of hearings by the Permanent Tribunal of Peoples (PTP) meeting in Strasbourg. The PTP was established in Bologna, Italy, in June 1976, because there is no UN or other official court in which those who claim the right of self-determination within a state can plead their case. It was an attempt to remedy this deficiency through the conduct of hearings by the parties in public with an impartial verdict by distinguished persons, and to provoke the UN itself into establishing such a court with international authority.

The PTP first appoints the tribunal that will consider a case. For the Tibet hearings the PTP appointed Professor François Rigaux, a Belgian professor of international law from Louvain, as President, and eleven other members, professors of international law, a judge, a barrister and four journalists and writers. Both the prosecution and the defence called witnesses to present their evidence before the tribunal for cross-examination, and there was much published written material available, some provided by the Chinese government. After the tribunal had considered the evidence presented, in twenty-four pages they presented their verdict. The conclusion was that the Tibetan people did have the right of self-determination.

The second investigation was through the Conference of International Lawyers on Issues Relating to Self-Determination and Independence for Tibet (CIL). I devised and organised it along with Lord David Ennals, Chairman of the Organising Committee; it comprised twenty-nine distinguished international lawyers, together with the secretary-general of International Alert, an NGO specialising in international conflict resolution. They met in

London in January 1993. The chairman was The Hon. Justice Michael Kirby, at the time President of the Court of Appeal of New South Wales, Australia, and Chairperson of the International Commission of Jurists. The lawyers included five judges, five barristers and attorneys and seventeen professors and lecturers in international law. The Chinese declined to attend, and the Chinese ambassador in London 'strongly insisted that arrangements for this conference be cancelled'. He argued that:

> As is known to all, Tibet has been an inalienable part of China's sacred territory since the thirteenth century. The Tibetan people are a member of the big family of the Chinese nation. This is a fact recognised by governments the world over. The so-called 'Tibetan question' has been fabricated by a very small number of separatists in an attempt to split Tibet from China. Some people, in disregard of the history and reality that Tibet has been a part of China, raise the issue of 'self-determination for the Tibetan people' and preach 'the independence of Tibet' with the ulterior motives of interfering in China's internal affairs. This can by no means be tolerated by the Chinese government and the whole Chinese people – including the people of Tibet. China will not be represented at the Conference of International Lawyers on Issues Relating to Self-Determination and Independence for the Tibetan People [sic] as the theme of the conference violates the universally acknowledged basic norms governing international relations, namely respect for the sovereignty and territorial integrity of other countries.

Most of the international legal experts present at the conference knew nothing about Tibet beforehand. Some were apologetic about this, but to the organisers it was an advantage; they came with an open mind. Justice Kirby, in his opening remarks, requested that 'the nature and approach of the conference should be one of integrity, with decisions not based on slogans or the heart alone, but on evidence and principle … Because of [China's stated position] the participants must, as lawyers of principle, test propositions and not simply accept them because they are stated.'

In addition to published evidence, there were eleven special reports on evidence written for the conference which summarised the Chinese position on the matters to be discussed, then the Tibetan position and finally other views. No conclusions were drawn. They were examined in two Committees on Evidence, each chaired by a practising judge who then reported his conclusions to the main conference. Frequent references were made during the subsequent discussion of legal matters to this large body of evidence.

The report from the conference, edited by the conference *rapporteurs* Robert McCorquodale and Nicholas Orosz (and published in 1994), was the result.

It became evident from the CIL that there is much more to the issue of self-determination than the narrow application of the law, which makes its adjudication quite complex. For example, Professor Richard Falk's view is that:

> The application of self-determination raises questions of morality and politics in a very pronounced way. Recent history seems to be illuminating both the emancipatory role of self-determination as well as its potentially destructive impacts as a vehicle for ultra-nationalism. To validate a claim for self-determination it is increasingly helpful to demonstrate that its realisation will not have destructive effects but, on the contrary, will help resolve outstanding conflicts and create favourable economic and political conditions for the people affected. The Tibetan struggle has renounced violence and is therefore very much dependent on waging a symbolic war on the terrain of legitimacy.

The Chinese have argued elsewhere that with fifty-five different 'national minorities' in China, to grant self-determination to the Tibetans would trigger the other fifty-four minority peoples to claim and to expect the same benefits. These national minorities in total amount to over 91 million persons and occupy about 30 percent of China's territory. It is a serious and important question whether it is realistic to expect that all the other fifty-four minorities – or even a majority of them – would claim the same benefits from granting autonomy or independence to Tibet and whether severe 'disruptive effects' in China might result. This matter was not addressed at the CIL.

In summary, both the PTP and the CIL concluded that Tibetans were a 'people' for the purposes of international law; that, consequently, they had the right of self-determination; that the Tibetan people wished to exercise their right of self-determination; and that the Chinese authorities had denied them that right.

There were, of course, many other important conclusions from both investigations, some of which will be mentioned later. The CIL benefited from oral evidence from the leading author of the history of Tibet, Dr Alastair Lamb, who has written five substantial books on the subject, and from the presence of two leading experts on Chinese law: Professor Alice Tay, Professor of Jurisprudence at the University of Sydney, Australia, and Perry Keller, then Lecturer in Law at the University of Manchester, UK, who presented one of the papers.

The Chinese ambassador did not appear correct in many of his assertions, in particular his claim that the theme of the CIL conference violated 'the universally acknowledged basic norms governing international relations, namely respect for sovereignty and territorial integrity of other countries'. The UN has declared in the 'Principles of International Law' that:

> Nothing in the principle of equal rights and self-determination shall be construed as authorising or encouraging any action which would dismember or impair, totally or in part, the territorial integrity or political unity of sovereign and independent states [and, most importantly, it goes on to say] conducting themselves in compliance with the principle of equal rights and self-determination of peoples and thus possessed of a government representing the whole people belonging to a territory without distinction as to race, creed, or colour.

The first part of this quotation from the 'Principles of International Law' is the Chinese position, often repeated. But the second part imposes a requirement of legitimacy on a government which wishes to rely on the principle of territorial integrity. This qualification is important because China's government does not conduct itself in compliance with the above principles. Furthermore, the UN 'does not permit this right of non-interference [in the internal affairs of another state] to impede discussion and decision when the principle of self-determination is at stake'. The same legal principle on which China relies includes also the duty of every state to promote and observe human rights and fundamental freedoms, which patently China does not, in Tibet. One cannot select the bits that support one's argument and ignore the bits which impose conditions on its application – these 'Principles of International Law' have to be taken together.

Furthermore, as already shown, the right of self-determination has a very high status in international law. The International Court of Justice said, in the East Timor case, that it is binding on all states. What is or is not customary international law and thus binding on all states stems from Article 38 of the Statute of the International Court of Justice, which refers to it 'as evidence of a general practice accepted as law'. Leading international lawyers are seeking a general recognition among states of a certain practice as 'obligatory'. The Chinese ambassador was, therefore, not stating the whole truth in his letter to Justice Kirby and was incorrect in his assertion on the basis of the lack of 'legitimacy' of the Chinese government. Now, since 27 March 2001, the Chinese government has accepted a legal duty in respect of the rights of peoples to self-determination.

Given the strength of the democracy movement in China, as expressed especially in June 1989 in Tiananmen Square and more recently by Chinese dissidents, the question whether the Han Chinese themselves have the right of self-determination is extremely important for the future of China. One may say that *prima facie* the Han Chinese are a 'people' for the purposes of international law because they distinguish themselves so clearly from their own national minorities and from all foreigners (whom they used to consider 'barbarians'). Many of these minorities also see themselves as being ethnically, culturally and linguistically different from the Han Chinese. The Han appear to meet all of the criteria agreed by the group of experts considering the Rights of Peoples at the UNESCO meeting in February 1990 for being a 'people'.

On 18 December 1998 President Jiang Zemin declared to the nation that 'China would never tread the path of democracy ... and [that] China would crush any challenge to the Communist Party monopoly on power'. That is a clear enough indication of the denial of the right of the Chinese people for self-determination. The tragic events of Tiananmen Square and the large number of demonstrators all over China showed that the authorities have denied a proportion of the Chinese people their evident desire for a system through which the people's wishes can be fully addressed. Within China, no plans can be openly discussed or seriously considered for the introduction of, say, a federal or confederal system of government, as has occurred amongst Chinese dissidents abroad. However, as mentioned earlier, Hu Jintao wants the Communist Party to 'undertake a sweeping systemic project' to increase public participation in government and to enforce the rule of law. He wants a political process to emphasise 'official accountability and responsiveness to meet the needs of the Chinese people'. The future looks bright.

What about other human rights in China? The government of China has ratified six other international instruments of great importance and relevance both to its own Han people and to Tibetans. The complete list follows (the dates refer to their ratification by China):

1. The Convention on the Elimination of all Forms of Discrimination against Women (4 November 1980)

2. The Convention on the Elimination of all Forms of Racial Discrimination (29 December 1981)*

3. The Convention on the Prevention and Punishment of the Crime of Genocide (18 April 1983)*

4. The International Convention on the Suppression and Punishment of the Crime of Apartheid (18 April 1983)

5. The Convention Against Torture and other Cruel, Inhuman or Degrading Treatment or Punishment (4 October 1988)

6. The Convention on the Rights of the Child (2 March 1992)

7. The International Covenant of Economic, Social and Cultural Rights (27 March 2001)

(The conventions marked * above have acquired the status of 'absolute norms' in international law and are therefore obligatory on all states.)

Hu Yaobang was Party General Secretary when the first four of these conventions were ratified; Zhao Ziyang was General Secretary for No. 5, and Jiang Zemin for Nos 6 and 7.

To illustrate how the system works, here are some details from China's implementation of The Convention Against Torture. The Chinese government ratified this on 4 October 1988. It came into force in China on 3 November 1988. The Chinese government's Initial Report to the Committee Against Torture (CAT), the UN treaty body for this convention, was dated 1 December 1989, one year later as required. Jiang had just become the new Party General-Secretary and Li Peng was Premier. It included the statement:

> Torture, an act which endangers society, has yet to be eliminated in China. Due to a weak sense of the legal system [and] the serious influence of privileges, the phenomenon of torture still exists in some localities.

The Second Periodic Report was due four years later, on 2 November 1993, but it was submitted more than two years late, on 2 December 1995. The Third Periodic Report was due on 2 November 1997 but was again two years late (November 1999). These are simply delaying tactics. The deadlines are known, and to be on time is simply a matter of forward planning.

The CAT considered this third report in three meetings held in May 2000. While it reported some 'positive aspects' in implementing its previous recommendations, including China's assurances that the convention is binding on China's law-enforcement and judicial organs, there were seven 'Subjects of Concern', including 'the continuing allegations of serious incidents of torture, especially involving Tibetans and other national minorities', and eight

'Recommendations'. One of them is 'To incorporate a definition of torture into its domestic law that fully complies with the definition contained in the Convention'. It may seem remarkable that, twelve years after ratifying the convention, China still did not have the correct definition of 'torture' incorporated into its domestic legislation, as required by law.

Other recommendations related to the question of monitoring the treatment of prisoners and the conducting of 'prompt, thorough and effective impartial investigation of all allegations of torture'. Prison officers will not tell on their colleagues, and great trouble is taken by prison officers to prevent details about torture, beatings or other illegal activities in prisons from being revealed to the outside world by those who have been released. Informers of the true position in Chinese prisons from personal experience can be re-arrested and punished for 'revealing state secrets'. Tibetans who subsequently escape to India are safe, and that is where most of the published information comes from. But the Chinese authorities say that such reports are 'all lies'.

The main problem is that the CAT system is too weak in allowing China (and not China alone) to escape from its obligations. Inviting the Chinese government 'to consider' doing something or to 'make recommendations' is a completely inadequate response from the CAT, but under the present regulations it cannot go further. At least it has highlighted that China itself recognises that it violates some of these human rights provisions, and the CAT publicly declares China in breach of its legal obligations.

There is no established mechanism for obtaining reliable information about the treatment of prisoners. This exposes the fundamental contradiction inherent in the convention. While it is left to the governments of the contracting states to implement the convention, torture is usually practised with their tacit approval and by those at the apex of political power for their self-preservation and for the survival of the centralist system over which they preside. There is, however, light on the horizon. The arrest of the former dictator of Chile, Augusto Pinochet, based on the UN Convention Against Torture, has shown that present and former heads of state can no longer automatically expect immunity when they are outside their domestic jurisdiction, for example while travelling abroad.

Moreover, there now exists a permanent International Criminal Court (ICC). It has jurisdiction over the worst crimes both within and between states: genocide, crimes against humanity, war crimes and crimes of aggression. Whilst encouraging individual states to investigate and prosecute the perpetrators of such crimes under their own domestic or international law – whether such persons are heads of state, military commanders or others – if they do not do so the ICC will exercise its jurisdiction. The ICC Statute is a vast document comprising 13 parts, 128 articles and hundreds of paragraphs. The downside is that China, the US, Israel and four other states voted against its introduction. The US is trying to obtain a specific exemption regarding the surrender of its nationals to the Court. Moreover, the ICC will be dependent upon states' compliance to investigate and to enforce sanctions. There is, at present, no provision for sanctions against non-compliant states.

At the time of writing, the 1997 report of the International Commission of Jurists, 'Tibet: Human Rights and the Rule of Law', is the latest authoritative legal report on the situation in Tibet. It is very thorough both in reviewing the period since China's invasion of Tibet in 1950 and in describing the situation then. The ICJ found that since the beginning of 1996 there has been a further escalation of repression in Tibet marked by an intensive re-education drive in the monasteries and the requirement for monks and nuns to sign loyalty pledges to Chinese socialism or face expulsion. Photographs of the Dalai Lama in public places were forbidden. This escalation of repression followed the 1994 Chinese 'Third National Forum on Work in Tibet', which identified the Dalai Lama as the root cause of Tibet's instability, and mapped out a new strategy for the region. The report concluded that:

> Tibetans are a 'people under alien subjugation', entitled under international law to the right of self-determination, by which they freely determine their political status. The Tibetan people have not yet exercised this right, which requires a free and genuine expression of their will [which the Chinese have not yet permitted].

The ICJ therefore called for a referendum in Tibet under UN supervision to ascertain the wishes of the Tibetan people. The question has arisen: what about the increasingly large Chinese population residing in the TAR? Will it have a vote? An international case shows the problem. In 1985 the Security Council established a UN mission for a referendum in Western Sahara (MINURSO) which would allow the Saharawi people 'to choose freely and democratically' between independence and integration with Morocco (Morocco had occupied the former Spanish colony after Spain's departure). This would be in the context of the declared right of the people of the Western Sahara to self-determination. The Referendum Commission stated that 'all Saharawis 18 years or more that are included in the 1974 Spanish Census [before the Moroccan occupation] will have the right to vote … all Saharan refugees counted in the Census will be able to return to the Territory to participate in the referendum'. At the same time a 'solid and demonstrable' link with the territory was required.

The referendum scheduled for January 1992 was delayed – and is still delayed – because of disagreement over the identities of those able to vote. Morocco was flooding the territory with its own citizens in anticipation that their votes would be included.

In his address to the European Parliament, the Dalai Lama emphasised that the Tibetan people must be the 'ultimate deciding authority' and that the outcome of any negotiations should contain a procedural plan to ascertain the wishes of the Tibetan people in a nationwide referendum. In 1995 China rejected the notion of a referendum in Tibet as 'a mean trick' aimed at splitting China.

If the Han Chinese were to be recognised as a 'people' with the right of self-determination, or the Tibetans, Uyghurs or Inner Mongolians, then perhaps all would make similar claims. So the greatest likelihood is that the Chinese government will resist them all. Comparably, Indonesia argued that if East Timor had the right of self-determination it would lead to the whole of Indonesia splitting apart. While this could have been true – it did not happen – it did not need to be debated, because East Timor was previously a colony of Portugal while the rest of Indonesia was part of the Netherlands and thus unique. Tibet, too, is unique because of its history.

The United Nations Declaration on the Granting of Independence to Colonial Countries and Peoples of 1960 set up a 'Committee of 24' for its implementation. It scrutinised cases on the basis of their right of self-determination. Although most colonies then gained independence, in 1990 the UN General Assembly announced the beginning of the 'International Decade for the Eradication of Colonialism' aimed at 'the elimination of the last vestiges of colonialism by the year 2000'. In 1995 the General Assembly expressed its concern about the 'negative impact which the non-participation of certain administrating powers has had on the work of the Committee of 24'.

If Tibet is *de facto* a colony of China then it may be possible to use this Declaration as a means of having its right of self-determination scrutinised and determined. In 1997 the Unrepresented Nations and Peoples Organisation (UNPO), an NGO based in The Hague, undertook a major study into the question: 'Is Tibet a colony of China?' An eighty-three-page report, 'China's Tibet: the World's Largest Remaining Colony', began with an independent legal expert identifying the characteristics and common features of a 'colony'. Armed with this common understanding, an independent mission of three eminent persons – a professor of international law in the Netherlands, a member of the Dutch parliament and a member of the senate of the Republic

of Ireland, all foreign affairs experts – visited Tibet unofficially, as well as Nepal
and India. They sought answers about the presence or absence of the defining
features in Tibet which would, in their judgment, decide whether Tibet was
or was not *de facto* a colony of China. The evidence led unmistakably to
their conclusion that, 'despite China's insistence that Tibet is an integral and
inalienable part of China, the study which we have undertaken shows that
at least *de facto* Tibet must indeed be regarded as a colony of China'. But
the very narrow interpretation by the Committee of 24 of the right of self-
determination closed this possibility for progress.

Gerry Simpson has remarked that, while the right of self-determination is
invoked in international law more often than any other right, and while
over the years it has grown in prestige, the number of opportunities for its
application has diminished. The constraining factor was the work of the
Decolonisation Committee. The criteria for acceptance as a 'colony' were
drawn very narrowly and many seemingly good cases were rejected. He
also argues that 'the association of self-determination with decolonisation
represents an historical aberration' and that a broadening of the definition is
now overdue. Self-determination has become more a privilege than a right.
There are, however, some successes. It was applied to Bosnia and Croatia in
the former Yugoslavia (but not to Kosovo), to Namibia and South Africa, and
to East Timor (but not to Chechnya).

 The underlying problem is that there is no international mechanism as part
of the UN for scrutinising, conciliating and if necessary arbitrating claims by
peoples within a state for their right of self-determination, except if they are
deemed to be a 'colony'. There is no international tribunal or court to hear such
claims. The International Court of Justice in The Hague was set up to hear
disputes between states – only states may be parties in cases before the Court.
Tibet has not been recognised as a state separate from China, even though
all the evidence points to Tibet's being independent prior to the invasion in
1950. It is, however, a manifest failure of the UN system and of its Secretary-
General, Kofi Annan, that no mechanism for the resolution of such disputes
within states has been developed. The UN is controlled by its member states.
The problem is that no state would vote for the introduction of a mechanism
which might lead to its own dismemberment or disintegration – China and
Russia are both permanent members of the Security Council. The British
government has not considered the future of Northern Ireland or Gibraltar as
issues of their right of self-determination. The formation of the International
Criminal Court is a precedent for such a specialist court.

 An effective international legal mechanism must be found for the impartial consideration of the right of self-determination. During the eleven years 1990–2000 there were fifty-six major armed conflicts worldwide, of which all but three were conflicts within states. Every situation is different. The complexities are many and frequently baffling. In resolving a situation one would not want to create a worse one, as Professor Richard Falk has argued. Historical precedents may be unclear. Strong feelings will be expressed by both parties, frequently anger and hatred. One side may be heavily armed and the other side weak – even, as in Tibet, adhering strictly to the principle of nonviolence. There have been many proposals, but none has won sufficient support from UN member states. This is a major tragedy. Now that the International Criminal Court has been established, it is high time that an International Commission and an International Court of Self-Determination, or their equivalent, were established (on which Ruth West and I have done a great deal of work), otherwise, as Gerry Simpson has argued, 'a failure to recuperate the law of self-determination will consign this legal principle to the margins of global disorders'.

In the broader picture, the whole of international human rights law and humanitarian law covering armed conflict has been undermined by the actions of the US since 11 September 2001 in waging its 'war on terror'. The likelihood of the UN's being able to successfully promote such a new International Court, or even extending the jurisdiction of the International Court in The Hague, especially with China having a veto, is just about nil.

TWELVE

Negotiating with China

'The easiest way to get what you want is
to help others get what they want.'
Deepak Chopra, *The Seven Spiritual Laws of Success*

In almost any scenario for the future, Tibetans will have to negotiate with China if they are to achieve autonomy. The Chinese do not, however, seem comfortable with the whole idea of negotiation. It is alien to their thinking. What the Chinese appear to prefer is to dissolve the problem, to eradicate it, thus avoiding the need for negotiation (a very Taoist approach). In Tibet they have been trying to dissolve the problem for more than fifty years, and have not succeeded. However, if the Chinese are put in a position where they have to negotiate, or if they expect to gain more than they would otherwise lose, they will do so.

The Chinese know that they are highly skilled and experienced negotiators. Sun Tzu is, so to speak, on their side, and his principles are in their bones. They treat negotiation as a psychological game, to be won with craftiness, subtlety and skill at minimum cost, if possible in the short term but, if not, most certainly in the long term. In diplomatic negotiations, not only do they nearly always seem to win, but they also leave their opponents in a state of near-nervous breakdown. They have immense confidence in their ability to come out best in a negotiation with Tibetans. They did it once before.

In June 1998, as mentioned in Chapter Six, US President Bill Clinton – on his visit to Beijing – urged President Jiang Zemin to negotiate with the

Dalai Lama. The Chinese president responded warmly by saying that 'the door to dialogue and negotiation is open' and acknowledged that the issue was political, not religious. But he added two conditions: first, that the Dalai Lama must publicly state and make a commitment that Tibet is an inalienable part of China; second, that he must recognise Taiwan as a province of China. These conditions have been repeated many times.

What are we to make of these two demands? Since the Dalai Lama cannot accept that Tibet is an inalienable part of China, there seems to be no way forward. But studies show that the Chinese will set what they know to be impossible conditions if progress is to made in a negotiation. As Lucien Pye remarks: 'The Chinese seem to have no hesitation in raising what they must understand are unacceptable demands ... clearly the Chinese do not expect their ultimatums to be treated at face value but rather they are trying to say, "unless you are willing to make a modest change the situation is impossible".'[1]

Most foreign governments acknowledge that Tibet is now a part of China. (The British government sits on the fence and regards Tibet as autonomous whilst recognising the special position of the Chinese authorities there. It does not recognise Chinese sovereignty over Tibet, nor does it recognise Tibet as being independent.) International law affecting China also covers Tibet and in that sense confirms Chinese sovereignty.

The Chinese are known to transpose a desired hypothetical future situation as if it existed today. Jiang fervently desired Taiwan to be part of China, so perhaps in his perception it was as good as being true. Indeed, in his July 2001 major speech (see Chapter Eight), he said, 'we are fully capable of checking any attempt to split China by seeking Taiwan's independence'. This sounds as though he believed that Taiwan was already part of China.[2]

What the Tibetan foreign minister in Dharamsala actually replied was that 'His Holiness stated during his March 1997 visit to Taiwan that this is a matter which must be discussed and decided between China and the people of Taiwan. Confrontation and use of military force will help neither China nor Taiwan'. The Chinese then accused the Dalai Lama of being 'insincere'. The Tibetan side – preferably the Dalai Lama himself – might have responded with counter-proposals, enticing the Chinese to move in step with conditions likely to be more acceptable.

When the curtain rises and the two sides warily face each other across a negotiating table, how will they size each other up? The Chinese will start with many advantages. They will be brimming with self-confidence. They occupy Tibet; they rule it, maintain law and order, have military forces and defensive positions; they have poured billions of *yuan* into the territory, and they have the means to stop Tibet politically 'splitting' from the motherland. Moreover, Tibet is of crucial importance to their programme of Western Development. To the Chinese, control is simply the other side of the coin of sovereignty. Control is inherent in its very concept. So, in their eyes, they have no necessity in principle or practice – except for international opinion – to withdraw their control, and every incentive to stay put.

Moreover, it is the Tibetans who want to negotiate, not the Chinese. If the talks break down, providing the Chinese can make it appear the fault of the Tibetans, they will not be upset. The world's governments will look the other way. China appears to hold all the cards. If Tibetans avoid China's strengths, attack China's weaknesses and play to their own strengths, their position is likely to improve.

Tibetans know that right is on their side, which will give them strength of purpose. Taking the long view, they know that ordinary human decency will, in the end, prevail. Democracy and human rights are world concerns. Sometimes there are steps backwards, but the thrust of world opinion and practice is forward. Tibetans are 'going with the flow'.

International law is firmly on the side of Tibetans. The Chinese government has solemnly undertaken to implement seven international covenants and conventions including the ICESCR. There is every reason to expect that an official tribunal would confirm that Tibetans are a 'people' within international law distinct from the Han Chinese, and have the right of self-determination. China is in contravention in Tibet of at least four other international conventions which they have ratified. They are vulnerable on all these matters.

The sustained practice of Buddhism gives its practitioners powerful minds, a depth of spiritual awareness and a profound understanding of human nature. Tibetans can use these in negotiation. Buddhist monks have long training in oral disputation of great subtlety, and thus could be formidable opponents.

The international campaign in support of Tibet is truly a 'people' campaign, nonviolent and not relying on governments or businesses. It has over 330 support groups worldwide. Many leading politicians, lawyers and other prominent people, including some leading Chinese dissidents, are Tibet supporters. In scale, scope and persistence, it is unique in world freedom movements. It is also a spiritually based campaign, bringing out people's finer instincts, supported by many hundreds of thousands of ordinary people – mostly non-Buddhists – who find the continuing Chinese occupation of Tibet intolerable. Tibetans know that they are not alone. Moreover, Tibet campaigners have shown themselves to be brave, innovative and clever in getting their messages across. China will not want such people to disrupt the showpiece 2008 Olympic Games.

Finally, China is extremely anxious that the Western Development strategy be a success, for the benefit of its own continuing development and to win the hearts of the Tibetans. Article 2 of the ICSECR reads: 'All peoples may, for their own ends, freely dispose of their natural wealth and resources.' If Tibetans are a 'people' they can endeavour to assert this right in their own territories and thus frustrate, or at least delay, the use of their 'natural wealth and resources' for purposes of which they disapprove. Strong opposition from Tibetans (and Uyghurs) to particular projects could create problems for China which they might wish to avoid.

In preparation for a negotiation, as Ernest Bevin, the British foreign minister during and immediately after the Second World War, said, 'The first thing to decide before you walk into any negotiation is what to do if the other chap says "no".' Habitually, the Chinese prepare for negotiations with extreme thoroughness. The Chinese government will know before the Tibetans when they will be willing to negotiate. Therefore they can choose the timing when they are ready, and the Tibetans risk seeming at a disadvantage or ill-prepared.

Tibetans will need first to prepare evidence, ready and updated, to be used when the occasion arises. This might include, for example, Chinese actions in Tibet which appear to have violated the international covenants China has ratified; the experience of different forms of autonomy and self-government in other countries; different forms of democracy; and the experiences of Hong Kong and Taiwan. Tibetans will also need several versions of a draft 'Basic Law in Tibet', since the Chinese will want to know: 'What will it mean for us? Are our interests protected?'

Planning for a sound strategy should be a major preoccupation. Western experience shows that good negotiators spend a significantly longer time planning for the long term and considering strategic issues than do average negotiators. The Chinese always think very long-term. Experience elsewhere also shows that, strategically, a good negotiator will prepare at least five options per negotiable issue (in case of a 'no'), whereas an average negotiator will have prepared three options or fewer. Detailed work will reveal the possibilities. Flexibility is essential in negotiations, as well as knowing one's own sticking points and listening intently what the other side appears to be saying about theirs.

Good negotiators plan on an issue basis rather than sequentially ('first we will negotiate A, that will lead to B', and so on). Planning a negotiation on an issue basis gives more flexibility. Also, separate work teams can develop the details on specific issues simultaneously, both strategically and tactically, the sequencing of issues being decided by agreement – on which the Chinese will have views as the negotiations proceed. They will want to sequence the issues to their own advantage, as will the Tibetans.

Training will be an early necessity. Probably at least twice as many negotiators should be trained as are likely to be needed at any one time. They could be used like reserves in a game of football, to be called into the negotiation as seen to be advantageous. It would be essential to include as many Tibetans as possible with recent experience in Tibet, otherwise the team's competence could be challenged. Some negotiating teams have both a chief negotiator and a leading speaker. Their roles are different, and their personalities and strengths should reflect this.

Looking back over his thirty years in China and the key negotiations in which he was involved, Sir Percy Cradock remarks that 'on the British side certainly, much of the trouble stemmed from a failure on our part to forecast Chinese reactions accurately and with sensitivity, to allow for the idiosyncracies of their approach, to give sufficient weight to Chinese pride and nationalist sentiment, even at times to admit that there was a distinct Chinese position deserving attention and a measure of respect … the essential gift is the ability to put oneself in the others' shoes.' He adds that 'all negotiators should have a feel for the workings of the Chinese mind … this was a negotiator's irreplaceable attribute'.[3] The Chinese find US and British actions just as puzzling. During the Hong Kong negotiations 'there were deep suspicions that we were seeking to give Hong Kong true independence rather than a high degree of autonomy as part of China'.[4] This is the case with Tibet today.

The protracted and often tortuous negotiations leading to the transfer of Hong Kong to the Chinese in 1997, while under fundamentally different circumstances, have many lessons for the Tibetans which are explored below. The governance of Hong Kong is an example of what Deng Xiaoping referred to, originally in the context of Taiwan, as 'one country, two systems', and so is to be carefully studied. Many people expected to see Hong Kong totally absorbed into the Chinese system, but that did not happen. Also, the Hong Kong experience is the latest example of the twists and turns of Chinese negotiating tactics. Fortunately it has been well written about, by Chris Patten himself, reporter and documentary-maker Jonathan Dimbleby and others.[5] Patten was a Member of Parliament in Britain, a cabinet minister and Chairman of the Conservative Party. He was widely recognised as a wise and experienced political heavyweight, passionately in support of ordinary people sharing in the democratic process, of the universality of human rights and of the rule of law. His appointment as Governor of Hong Kong in 1992 terminated at its handover to the Chinese at midnight on 30 June 1997.

The Hong Kong negotiations had a deadline determined by history. Tibet has no such imperative, so every possible opportunity has to be grasped. The three visits to China and Tibet by the Dalai Lama's envoys in 2002, 2003 and 2004 should be seen *as though* they were the first stage of a negotiation, and now Hu Jintao has given a lead.

If the new team on the Politburo Standing Committee signified a willingness to contemplate some form of 'genuine autonomy' for the Tibetans, the outline plan could be first a negotiated joint declaration as a statement of agreed intent and as a framework for more detailed negotiations. Such a declaration could lead to the formation of a 'Basic Law for Tibet' within that framework. This would normally progress through meetings between officials on both sides. However simply 'genuine autonomy' is conceived, if it is to mean anything worthwhile to the Tibetans, the Basic Law would be a complex document.

The general aim of the negotiation must surely be to give enduring satisfaction to both sides, for then the agreement will be long-lasting. But this will be achieved only if they both feel that they have won something significant from it. The easiest way to get what you want is to help others get what they want. The principles of reciprocal favours and of compromise are ingrained in Chinese behaviour. Ideally, therefore, both sides should plan their strategy on the basis of 'win-win' (we both win something significant) as the most desirable outcome. While this appears to be the normal Chinese starting assumption, in the practice of negotiation, to outsiders, it has appeared to be more like 'win-lose' (they win, you lose).

What might give the Chinese particular satisfaction at the end of the negotiations, to enable them to feel that they had won something worthwhile? It is not difficult to draw up a shopping list, and being aware of such possibilities can help the Tibetans form their strategy.[6] Even if there is a major change of heart at the top which embraces some political change – which now seems possible – the leadership will still want to ensure that its own interests are safeguarded, including, no doubt, defence, Western Development, internal security and the welfare of Chinese residents in Tibet. So there are bound to be detailed negotiations to recognise these.

Agreeing on an agenda for the framework of a joint declaration is crucial. Both sides will pay great attention to this. It will be difficult to achieve the right balance between flexibility and trying to tie down the Chinese into accepting a serious negotiation which will cover the issues on which the Tibetans want to reach agreement. The Chinese will want to omit discussion of matters where they are weak and include matters where the Tibetans are weak.

In the spirit of 'Entice the Tiger to Leave the Mountain',[7] a Chinese tactic, a location for the negotiations would be preferable that detached the Chinese from their familiar home station, Beijing, and caused them to move elsewhere. In Beijing they would feel psychologically safe and invincible. If the Tibetans have to go to Beijing to negotiate, as they did in 1951, they would be at a psychological and practical disadvantage. All their rooms for private meetings could be bugged, and the Chinese would control, or try to control, their communications system to the Dalai Lama and the government-in-exile. If a neutral location could not be agreed upon, then Hong Kong would be a good option.

The Chinese might demand secrecy in the negotiations. By this they might mean the very fact that talks were being held at all should be kept secret, perhaps to spare embarrassment and a loss of face for the Chinese leaders. They would not like to see their own people after all the calumny heaped upon the Dalai Lama, that they were now negotiating with him. But that kind of secrecy should be resisted. 'Public diplomacy works with the Chinese, private diplomacy does not.'[8] If a deal were to be struck secretly that then proved to be unacceptable to Tibetans, most probably it could not be renegotiated. It is safer to assume that the Tibetans would have only one chance, which would be final. So it must be open.

For example, in the negotiations for the handover of Hong Kong there was, in 1991, a secret negotiation and an agreement between the British and Chinese governments over the Court of Final Appeal. When eventually published, it was rejected by the Legislative Assembly of Hong Kong and by its legal profession. The problem was that it gave the Chinese National People's Congress in Beijing the right to overturn any judgment reached by the Hong Kong Court of Appeal. It was not until 1995 that the matter was settled after much acrimony, although after 1997 the Chinese had their way. There are risks in openness, but more risks in secrecy.

Also, Chris Patten resisted the Chinese demand for secrecy in his proposed negotiations to extend the franchise for choosing members of the legislature. His main reason was that he wanted to attract the support of both the non-Chinese leadership in the existing system of government and of the ordinary people in Hong Kong in what would be a remarkably difficult negotiation. Public support would, he thought, be crucial. Patten did more than reject secrecy. He went out to meet the people of Hong Kong, held large public meetings and had 'phone-ins'. He cultivated excellent relations with the press and made sure it understood his policies. Tibetans might want to attract support from Tibetans in Tibet, in exile and from others internationally. The European Parliament has consistently supported the Tibetan cause, and it would be helpful to have their active support when the time comes. The UN has been involved in many such situations.

The Chinese might be very fussy about exactly who can be on the Tibetan negotiating team. In the September 1988 offer of negotiations the Chinese stated their conditions on attendance, which the Tibetans ignored (see Chapter Six) and did not even attempt to negotiate. In the Hong Kong negotiations, the Chinese insisted that since the talks could take place between the two sovereign powers only, no servant of the Hong Kong government was entitled to a place at the table. Patten remarked that 'it was a rather elaborate theological point and you certainly couldn't explain it to a Martian. You couldn't actually explain it to any human being.'[9] A minister of state at the Foreign Office, Alastair Goodlad, then told the Chinese that the point was non-negotiable. The more-or-less secret 'talks about talks' went on for more than six weeks – and then the Chinese announced that talks would resume according to Patten's conditions, including no secrecy.

It is obvious and most important to be absolutely clear at the end of the negotiations what the words agreed to actually mean and whether they can be interpreted in a different way from what was intended. Patten, apropos the 1991 negotiation between the British prime minister John Major and the Chinese, over the construction of the new Hong Kong airport (prior to the handover of the whole territory in 1997), wrote:

> The Chinese regarded this mega-project, the biggest civil engineering project in the world, as a way of exercising political control over Hong Kong ... A memorandum of understanding was signed by the British and Chinese premiers which, it was claimed, would clear the way for the rapid planning and construction of the airport. Hardly had it been signed than Chinese officials were offering imaginative interpretations of what it really meant. The memorandum's exact meaning was still unfortunately the subject of debate four years later.[10]

The same was true of the joint declaration treaty between the two sides, agreed in 1984 and considered sacrosanct. But, as Patten later remarked, 'they're in the throes of defining words in the Joint Declaration in their own terms.'[11]

The style and tactics of a negotiation are crucial to their success. The Chinese tactical approach to negotiating is developed essentially from *The Art of War*, almost regardless of the subject matter of the negotiation. Other, more straightforward people find this baffling, maddening, impossible to get to grips with. 'Uniqueness' is a basic feature of Chinese diplomacy. So throughout a negotiation one has to be aware of traditional Chinese modes of thinking and behaviour, many of which Tibetans would appreciate. Chinese negotiations generally display a relational style, based on Confucian harmony in interpersonal relationships. Informal meetings over a meal are important to the Chinese in establishing friendship at the beginning and perhaps later in resolving particularly difficult issues. This style based on harmony and friendship would also suit the Tibetans well (but is the opposite of the Western transactional style, which is more businesslike and confrontational). The term 'friends' has a special meaning for the Chinese, wider in scope than in the West, to include, for example, 'people one calls on in time of need'.

While friendship and trust are key aspects of Chinese culture and can be positive in smoothing the path towards success for both sides, there is another side to these pleasing attributes. The purpose of establishing establish a basis of friendship and trust might be to make the other side feel that this positive relationship would be in serious jeopardy unless they agreed to the Chinese position. 'Friendship' can be seen, therefore, as a form of entrapment. One may have to risk losing friendship to retain one's position. 'It is the tension of the relationship game that gives dealings with the Chinese much of their distinctive quality'.[12]

The Chinese do not like direct confrontation. They see it as being unfriendly, rude and perhaps leading to a loss of face. They do not like saying 'no' to a specific request, which they feel might cause offence. The same point can be made with greater subtlety and thus save face. So they might say 'yes' or 'probably' when they really mean the opposite. Thus, nonverbal communication can be very important – a nod of the head may not mean 'yes' but simply, 'I hear what you are saying'. Instead of making the point directly, they may approach it indirectly so that not only does the point itself soon become obvious, but the reasons why the point is being made also become clear.

Chinese thinking tends to be circular rather than linear. Different or dissimilar things are complementary opposites and together form a unity (hence, no doubt, Mao Zedong's interest in dialectics – the metaphysical contradictions in Marxism and their resolution). A concept thus also embraces its opposite. Tibetans think holistically in a similar fashion; the concept of death, for example, also embraces the prospect of a new life.

The Chinese are also like Tibetans in finding a common cosmology in the interrelationships between man, nature and heaven – all are part of a higher universe, and in their harmony people find great satisfaction. In China, *feng shui* is much respected as a practical expression of good living of taking advantage of natural forces and avoiding creating problems for oneself.

The Chinese are also acutely aware of impermanence in everything, the central precept of the *I Ching* (Book of Changes). So are the Tibetans, as the concept is a central feature of Buddhism. Nothing is fixed for all time (not even Tibet as an inseparable part of China). Change is constant. Thus, flexibility in negotiation is fundamental, supported by mutual trust, not being tied down by too many details and providing for contingencies. Likewise, divination (foretelling the future) is well-known in both China and Tibet. Indeed, the *I Ching* has its close counterpart in Tibet.

So, in many fundamentals there is common ground between Chinese and Tibetans, which should be helpful in negotiation. This is hardly surprising since the two peoples have had interactions since antiquity and Buddhism was at one time a powerful common link. However, in practical negotiation there is another side to the Chinese which Tibetans do not share. It can make all the difference between winning and losing.

'Craftiness' is a characteristic of Chinese negotiating, applied through the medium of psychological games which are endless in their possibilities. GOH Bee Chen explains the subtleties of 'The Thirty-Six Strategies',[13] originating in and developed from *The Art of War* – some of which have become part of Chinese folk lore – like No. 18 ('Catching the Leader in Order to Win'), the aforementioned No. 15 ('Entice the Tiger to Leave the Mountain') and No. 35 ('Chain Links', mentioned below). They also include, for example, No. 27 ('Be Clever but Pretend to Be a Fool'), intended to lead the opposition to become overconfident; and No. 20 ('Catch the Fish in Muddy Waters'), intended to ensure that a disappearance is not noticed.

One of the most prominent Chinese practices is what the Japanese have called 'swaying tactics'.[14] These may not be directly related to the substance of the negotiations but would be intended to draw more concessions from the other side, to undermine its position and prestige or to influence and modify its outlook. Tibetan negotiators and the Dalai Lama might be accused by the Chinese of 'not being friends of China' or 'having no sincerity towards a dialogue'. The latter was the Chinese response to Madeleine Albright, the US Secretary of State at the time, when she called for a dialogue with the Tibetans during a visit to Beijing. The Chinese might use such accusations as attempts to force concessions.

The Chinese might also try to put Tibetans on the defensive by making use of any supposed 'faults' or 'errors' the Tibetans have or are accused of having committed in the past, or of having broken a previous agreement or understanding. To respond that any such faults, errors or accusations are extraneous to the negotiations today could bring a Chinese response in turn that this very attitude testifies to a lack of sincerity and genuine desire for friendly ties with China. Also, the Chinese will be extremely well-briefed on all violations alleged against them by Tibetans, even the smallest of incidents, and may make full use of them at awkward moments during the negotiation. The purpose would be, again, to put the Tibetans on the defensive. But two can play at that game. By way of example, from Chris Patten again:

> One after another, Chinese officials – over the table or from the depths of their white antimacassared chairs – would accuse me of having broken the Joint Declaration and Basic Law.
>
> 'How have I done so?' I would respond. 'Show me where.'
>
> 'You know that you have done so,' they would reply, 'you must have done so or else you wouldn't have said it.'
>
> 'But where?'
>
> 'It is not for us to say; you know you have erred.'
>
> 'Give me a single instance,' I would argue.
>
> 'Well,' they would usually claim, somewhat lamely, 'you have at least broken the spirit of the Joint Declaration and the Basic Law.'
>
> 'What do you mean by "the spirit"? Do you just mean that you disagree with me? Why not then discuss what I have done? Put forward your own proposals.'
>
> 'We cannot put forward our own proposals until you return to the spirit of the text.'
>
> The arguments twisted and turned, the greased pig wriggled about the room, defying capture.[15]

The issue behind this confrontation was Patten's determination to extend the democratic legitimacy of the legislature in Hong Kong. The Joint Declaration was the 1984 treaty that defined the terms under which the sovereignty of Hong Kong would be transferred from Britain to China in 1997. The Basic Law was China's codification of the joint declaration into the constitutional and legal framework for the governance of Hong Kong as a Special Administrative Region of China. Patten had found some elbow room in which to extend the franchise within the previously agreed framework. Given that Patten went to Hong Kong as Governor in 1992 in the aftermath of the Tiananmen Square tragedy in 1989, to try to introduce more democracy was a heroic venture.

It is common practice, when the words of a document do not say what the Chinese want them to say, to make reference to 'the spirit of the document'. In a negotiation with the Japanese in the mid-1970s 'the Chinese team looked offended and stated that [the Japanese] argument was contrary to the spirit of the Joint Communiqué signed in 1972 … and that China had to question seriously the "political philosophy" of the Japanese negotiator.'

Patten was also a victim of what George Shultz, a former US Secretary of State who was familiar with Chinese negotiating tactics, called the 'post-visit blast'. Patten wrote:

> No sooner had the aircraft doors closed on my exhausted departure from the harangues, the antimacassars and the carefully calibrated (or just unthinkingly ill-mannered) snubs than Lu Ping [head of the department in the Chinese government responsible for Hong Kong] held a press conference at which he said that there would be no negotiations until I dropped my 'triple negotiation package' – that is, proposals which allegedly breached the Joint Declaration, the Basic Law and the 'secret understanding'. [This was a 1990 secret exchange of correspondence between the foreign secretaries of Britain and China which the Chinese did not think Patten had seen, but he had. The Chinese did not know this and thought that they had scored a triumph. Patten wrote later that they were merely an exchange of possibilities, but Jonathan Dimbleby has revealed that they were more important than that.][16]

Patten also found that between the end of the negotiation and the production of the Chinese-printed version of what had been agreed upon, a few extra paragraphs had mysteriously appeared that had not been agreed to. He regarded this as 'just a try-on'. It would be worth forgoing the champagne and the bonhomie of the farewell to undertake a thorough cross-check of the final document before departure, he advised.

The Chinese could try to throw the Tibetans off-balance with personal accusations against members of the Tibetan negotiating team, to humiliate them and bully them into submission. Patten was called, day after day, 'a criminal who would be condemned for a thousand generations'; 'the whore of the East'; 'a strutting prostitute'; 'a sly lawyer'; 'a clown'; 'a serpent'; 'a dirty trickster'; 'an assassin'; 'the Triple Violator'; and, even more exotically, 'the tango dancer'. ('It takes two to tango,' he had said.)[17]

Such descriptions, applied in similar vein also to the Dalai Lama in recent years, are simply traditional Chinese expressions of disapproval towards someone who refuses to agree with them. Repetition indicates that being rude is not having the desired effect. Patten dismissed it as 'background noise' and, sometimes privately, when he was most exasperated, 'bullying ineptitude'. However, 'having decided that they were not going to able to bully us into backing down, the Chinese resorted to another stratagem: a longer-term sapping of our defences, the painstaking and relentless attempt to isolate me from my civil service, from London and from the [Hong Kong] community', wrote Patten.[18] This also happened to the Tibetans in negotiating the Seventeen-Point Agreement in 1951 (see Chapter Four).

Other offensive tactics may include unilaterally setting a framework for the negotiation, laying down the basic ground rules designed to draw the maximum number of concessions from the other side or which inhibit their effectiveness. The Chinese might produce their own basket of items for negotiation and refuse to change them. However, if it suits them, the Chinese will abandon ground rules and agenda items without notice. They might also insist on the use of certain 'principles' which may look reasonable initially, such as (in the case of the Japanese) the 'principle of equality and mutual benefit', which turned out to be crucially in favour of the Chinese at a later stage. Experience shows, however, that when a Chinese negotiator wants to reach an accord he will quietly drop any such principles which previously had seemed set in stone, as the Chinese did eventually in the Hong Kong negotiations, on which Patten remarked: 'Hey, presto. They moved. So we did make progress.'[19] But if the Tibetans counter by proposing their own principles then the Chinese may respond, as they did to the Japanese, that they 'do not want to waste time in empty argument'.

They might also say that 'it is improper to discuss questions on which the Chinese government alone has jurisdiction', questions which may be crucial to the Tibetan position. The Chinese might also make pre-emptive bids on key issues. They could attempt to present a judgment on their part as an established fact and thus to pre-empt any possible counter-argument. They might claim that their view represents 'the facts' and that any other view 'ignores the facts'. All these tactics were used earlier in the 1951 negotiations with the Tibetans. The Chinese could go to great lengths to make the other side speak first, and then refuse to give their own views – except later on another occasion – until the other side has revealed too much of its case to have any defensive position left.

The Chinese might accuse the other side of being vague, equivocating, abstract, imprecise or unclear. Thus they could try to force it to abandon any qualifications that it might have to a Chinese proposal and force an agreement with the Chinese interpretation. Use of the word 'insufficient' might also be designed to bring the other side nearer to their own position.

The Chinese could try to shift the reference point for the present discussion to a future situation when certain Chinese policies allegedly benefiting the Tibetans will have been achieved. This tactic, mentioned earlier, makes use of hypothetical historical trends. They might also point to all the benefits Tibetans have allegedly received from the Chinese occupation, as compared with the previous feudal system (however, this would be illegitimate; the true comparison should be between today's situation in Tibet and what the Tibetans would have achieved by today in the absence of the Chinese occupation. There is no doubt that the Dalai Lama would have improved the situation anyway – as demonstrated by his actions since 1959.) Some careful comparisons, for example, of the educational attainments of Tibetan children in Tibet today, by age and sex, with those in exile today in the same categories, could be very significant.

As recently as 1999, then Premier Zhu Rongji said, in a private meeting, 'we repeatedly enjoined lower levels of government not to provide false statistics ... I cannot say that the statistics are very accurate, but I think it is fair to say that our industrial and business figures are quite accurate'[20] (if only one could feel confidence in that). Jasper Becker, who has had long experience in China, writes that 'intense secrecy and the manipulation of information' still characterise Chinese statistics. Information from the huge quantity of statistics collected evidently still 'travels up through the bureaucracy, and every layer revises it to conform to the targets set by its superiors. As quoted earlier, 'anyone who spends time working in China eventually comes to doubt even basic facts.' All Chinese statistics should be treated with great caution in any negotiations with them.

There appear to be some differences between the style of cadres/diplomats and of politicians in negotiating with the Chinese. A Chinese negotiator was seen by Richard Solomon in 1995 to be 'sitting cold and taut as a steel spring, sternly unapproachable, suspicious, impenetrable, a rigidly disciplined agent reading his lines with mechanical precision. He is able, persistent, imperturbable – and frustratingly predictable in style. Negotiating with him is an ordeal, because he makes it so.' More succinctly, Chris Patten in 1993 described the chief Chinese negotiator as a 'bureaucratic speak-your-weight machine ... seventeen rounds of negotiation saw no real Chinese movement on anything'. (This was probably an example of the 'Chain Links' strategy referred to above: one tries to exhaust an opponent by employing a succession of crafty techniques, one after the other, for weeks on end, until the opponents become totally fed up and agree to something they shouldn't have.)

It takes an exceptional person to break through. Sir Percy Cradock described his own diplomatic approach to negotiations with the Chinese as generally a 'frontal approach to the topic in hand, logical and step-by-step, as in eighteenth-century pitched battles'.[21] But in 1982 Prime Minister Margaret Thatcher, in direct negotiations with the Chinese leadership, 'recognised no such rules' and conducted a species of guerrilla warfare, appearing suddenly behind the lines or firing from unconventional angles. She often operated from behind a smokescreen of her own making, a series of remarks which were commonplace, or even off the point, and which induced a false and fatal sense of security on the part of her listeners. Then, amidst the dross and the chaff, would come a missile, a question or comment of such relevance and penetration that it destroyed the opposition. It should be mentioned, however, that on the main British proposal with which they started the negotiations – that they should transfer sovereignty to the Chinese but retain control of the administration in Hong Kong to preserve its famously successful trading and financial operations – the Prime Minister was totally defeated.

Patten's conclusion was that 'the Chinese are bullies':

> ... I think there's a certain amount of awe in dealing with China, which surprises me. Why should one play the game entirely by their rules? Why should one accept their definition of what a "principled position" is or what "consultation" is? We wouldn't do it with others, so why should we do it with China?[22]

Patten quoted with approval the view of a former chief secretary of the Hong Kong government that 'the Chinese style is not to rig elections, but they do like to know the results before they are held'.[23] In negotiating a widening of the franchise for an elected Legislative Council in Hong Kong, in 1993 Patten felt that 'the Chinese were obsessed with the need to control the legislature after 1997' and 'they wanted the right to exclude any elected members of whom they did not approve'. They threatened that if they did not get their way after 30 June 1997, when British control ceased, they would simply close down the democratically elected Legislative Council and replace it with their own version. So in December 1995 the National People's Congress in Beijing appointed 130 candidates for the sixty seats of a Hong Kong 'provisional legislature' to be elected by a Chinese-appointed selection committee of 400 persons. This legislature had no powers because the Legislative Council still existed. It met outside Hong Kong on Saturday mornings to plan the legislation it would pass once the Chinese took over on 1 July 1997. This occurred on the due date, and most citizens of Hong Kong then lost their democratic rights. Worse still, the provisional legislature had been empowered by the National People's Congress to prepare for laws to inhibit human rights and civil liberties.

It would also be most important how the head of the executive would be chosen. His (or her) initiatives within his jurisdiction and the resources at his command, his interpretation of the laws he would be required to implement and his executive actions could make all the difference between a compassionate administration and one which leaned towards control and severity. In Hong Kong the selection committee which elected the new legislature also chose the person from four candidates who would be the new chief executive after the transfer of power. The person so elected, Tung Chee-hwa (C. H. Tung), already indicated by Jiang Zemin, was very unpopular and was sacked in March 2005 together with 300 top officials, many loyal to Jiang, thus increasing Hu Jintao's control.

A negotiation with the Chinese would endeavour to resolve all matters concerning Tibet and, most fundamentally, exactly what 'autonomy' would mean. The Dalai Lama's approach since 1988 has been 'top down' – 'genuine autonomy' except for defence and foreign relations. For all its simplicity, it has not yet led to a meaningful dialogue and negotiation with the Chinese authorities. Perhaps China could not see, within this framework, how its own essential interests would be met.

The 'one country, two systems' of Hong Kong is an obvious possibility for Tibet. Although Hong Kong has many freedoms absent in China which would be welcome in Tibet, there appears to be a slow convergent approach towards 'one system', China's way. This will be confirmed or denied in 2007 when, according to the Basic Law, the chief executive and the legislature will be freely elected by the Hong Kong people.[24] The Tibetan situation is, however, different.

In seeking an approach that may recognise the interests of Tibet and China more closely it may be possible to negotiate a portfolio of government authorities over which, through negotiation, Tibetans would be granted full control on some matters without even consulting the Chinese ('consultation' as giving them the right of veto, to secure their prior consent[25]). There could also be some activities jointly controlled with the Chinese, and the residual activities could come under full Chinese control – three categories in all. We might call this a 'bottom-up' approach to the problem. Here are some suggestions:

Category One: Government Policies for Tibetan Determination Alone

Tibetans would no doubt want religious freedom, obviously for Tibetan Buddhists but also for the possibility that the Chinese population might want to establish centres of Chinese Ch'an Buddhism and Tibetan Muslims might want their own mosques in Tibet. A Religious Affairs Department could bring the Tibetan Buddhist monasteries, nunneries and institutes under full Tibetan control in all Tibetan occupied areas, without restriction or interference by the Chinese. This bold step would transform the attitude of Tibetans and bring them joy and hope. The future of Buddhism in Tibet would be secure. If there were to be a wider agreement on some form of autonomy acceptable to the Tibetan people, there would be no need for monks and nuns to demonstrate against China.

Good health and education are the foundations of a successful society in all that it wants to achieve. The comparatively poor health of Tibetans, especially in rural areas, is shocking. Health education in rural areas is almost non-existent. The present system is failing most Tibetan people. Tibetan control over hospitals and clinics, using Tibetan medicine with other holistic and allopathic systems as appropriate, is essential. Clinics and small hospitals in rural areas with properly trained staff are much needed. The issue of funding would require separate investigation, but much help can come from abroad.

Tibetan education is also a crucial issue and could be more of a problem, but it would be right, in the TAR especially, where (according to Chinese statistics) the resident population are about 92 percent Tibetan, that the school system should be run by Tibetans. Chinese residents in Tibet could still have their own schools within the framework of a Tibetan Department of Education, with, say, Tibetan compulsory as a second language. Included would also be training programmes for school leavers and others, to provide for the development of small rural industries and other occupations. Tibetans should also control their own universities.

Most Tibetans live by agriculture and animal husbandry, so Tibetans should be responsible for national agriculture and nutritional policies and applications. The Chinese interests in agriculture are different, relying more on wheat and less on barley, for example.

A rural enterprise agency could also be run by Tibetans to help small businesses flourish in small townships and rural areas. This would help to keep young people in the countryside engaged in a diverse range of activities. Not everyone wants to earn their living on the land.

The control and development of the 'infrastructure for living in Tibet', in towns and villages in rural areas, could also be accorded to Tibetans in the TAR – roads, electricity, gas, water, local planning, public housing, building regulations and forests, rivers, wildlife and plants. Secondary roads in rural areas would be a priority. Chinese people could have the right to express their views where their populations are significant.

Category Two: Joint Determination

Then there may be a number of jointly controlled activities, with Tibetans and Chinese working together. Here unanimous voting, or codetermination, should be the guiding principle for all major strategic decisions (majority voting for less essential matters). Both Tibetans and Chinese would have to agree what should be done in the legislature or in joint committees of the government – and would have to go on meeting until they did agree, without coercion on either side. If, ultimately, there is no agreement, then the proposal would have to be reformulated or even dropped. This would prevent domination by either side. It would take some experience to work well, as Chinese and Tibetans get to know and trust each other to find mutually acceptable solutions.

China would never surrender Tibet's share of Western Development to a Tibetan administration. It is too important for the future of China. Over 100 key infrastructure projects were launched in the TAR in 2003, amounting to US$ 1.45 billion. But mineral and other natural-resource developments are crucial both to China's interests and to Tibet as part of its spiritual homeland. Some places – mountains, lakes and rivers – are environmentally and spiritually sensitive, and Tibetans must be able to protect them. Priorities for the Tibetan people will not be the same as those for China.

Article 9 of the Chinese constitution reads in part: 'All mineral resources, waters, forests, mountains, grasslands, unreclaimed land ... are owned by ... all the people, including Tibetans; moreover, Article 2 of the ICSECR would appear to give Tibetans as a 'people' the right to 'freely dispose of their natural wealth and resources'. So Tibet's case for codetermination with the Chinese for the development of all natural resources and for taxing them where appropriate is very strong.

Codetermination is likely to be the best that could be achieved for the position of Han Chinese residing in the TAR and for the movement of Han Chinese into Tibet. Both sides would have strong views. Some form of control would have to be agreed. It would not be easy. Control of the police, security, the judiciary and the running of prisons could be by Tibetans and Chinese. Adherence to the international human rights conventions that China has ratified would be the guiding principle, even if the Chinese government has not introduced the appropriate legislation or administrative decisions.

The infrastructure development of major towns and cities in Tibet, where the Chinese may be in the majority, is also right for codetermination as both Chinese and Tibetans will have strong interests.

There could be US, British, Indian, Nepalese and other consulates or legations in Tibet. Tibet's foreign relations (except boundaries) could be jointly determined to safeguard China's interests. The land used for defence should also be codetermined. Likewise, air traffic rights to fly into and over Tibet should be jointly determined (the five 'Freedoms of the Air'). These are important matters for negotiation.

Finally, the question of funding would have to be addressed. There could be local taxes decided by a Tibetan assembly, with or without some national taxes imposed by the centre.

Category Three: Chinese Determination

Other activities could be solely for the Chinese to control, including territorial boundaries, foreign alliances, air traffic control systems, and customs and excise.

In this way, sovereignty could be divided between power over people and power over territory. China would retain sovereignty over the extent of the territory of all Tibet. Citizenship would be derived from the state, the People's Republic of China, and nationality would be derived from the Tibetan nation; passports could show both.

All the above would require negotiation in detail.[26] It would be much more complex than a 'top-down' agreement with the Chinese government. Hence it would give more opportunities to display craftiness in negotiation. But it might be more persuasive in bringing the Chinese government to the negotiating table because they could see that some of their interests of great concern, such as economic development and internal security, would be properly recognised. Any form of autonomy carved out of a totalitarian state would require strong institutions and laws for it to survive – otherwise it would be eroded, small steps at a time. With experience, over time, Tibetans alone could assume more responsibility. The new Politburo Standing Committee under Hu Jintao's leadership could authorise investigation of such a fundamental change with the aim that Tibetan and Chinese people should live in peace and harmony.

Perhaps the way into a negotiation would be to start, as the Tibetan envoys have done, by clarifying the true situation in Tibetan areas and the hopes and fears of the people, and to recognise Chinese hopes and fears as well. It would also do to explain and clear up any possible misunderstandings about what is meant by 'autonomy' – for example, that sovereignty is not 'all or nothing', but can apply differently to different policies; the next step would be to begin negotiating just one aspect of autonomy, such as religion, as the envoys evidently have done, to build confidence and mutual trust. Given positive experience with this on the ground, the scope for autonomy can then be widened.

What Now?

'Without bold thinking, Chinese and Tibetans
are unlikely to find the common ground
necessary to make China a multi-ethnic state
that is comfortable with itself.'
Extract from an open letter to the
Standing Committee of the Chinese Politburo
(Orville Schell, San Francisco Chronicle,
June 24, 2001)

The Standing Committee of the Politburo has now had time to settle in to the job of running China under President Hu Jintao. There are already hopeful signs of a new political realism – except concerning Tibet. The 23 May 2004 White Paper will disappoint all those who felt that some progress was being made with the three visits to China by the Dalai Lama's envoys in 2002, 2003 and in September 2004 (a planned official visit to Tibet by Gyalo Thondup was cancelled by the Chinese authorities). The White Paper will infuriate the younger Tibetan activists who seek independence, and we may expect some reaction. However, issuing it at this time may indicate that now the Chinese are indeed prepared to negotiate.

In any event, as the Dalai Lama teaches, 'NEVER GIVE UP. Develop the heart, be compassionate not just to your friends but to everyone. Work for peace in your heart and in this world.' So this apparent rebuff is an opportunity to be especially compassionate, to think again, to open minds and to pursue new ideas – which this book has tried to do. It recognises that 'autonomy' except for defence and foreign affairs is now insufficient because it fails, for example, to take account of China's urgent priority and the huge scale of Western Development, and that the Chinese resident population in the TAR (presently around 6–7 percent) will grow fast when the Golmud–Lhasa railway is operational.

As the scale and scope of Tibetan autonomy increases with satisfactory experience, the need will arise for both a president and a prime minister. Andorra, a small independent state perched high in the Pyrénées between France and Spain, has two presidents, one drawn from each country – evidently a popular arrangement. Similarly, in the TAR there could be two presidents, one from China and one from Dharamsala. Their functions would not be like presidents in the US or France, but more like Switzerland or Germany with strictly limited powers but with important roles in times of political crisis.

As shown in Chapter Twelve, negotiating with the Chinese is always difficult. However, for both sides to be successful in negotiating a settlement which will have long-lasting effects there has to be a change of heart amongst the Chinese leadership and their cadres in Tibet, otherwise it would be a rerun of 1951 and after.

Is it perhaps too soon to expect this? It may take more than a generation for a people who have been so sorely assaulted by the Cultural Revolution and Strike Hard campaigns to recover fully. Perhaps we are not there yet; or perhaps the Chinese leadership simply has too many more pressing problems to resolve, and Tibet can wait a bit. Nevertheless, 'never give up' means just that: carrying on despite adversity. So let us take matters a bit further.

We must be aware of history, but not be ruled by it. History means so much to the Chinese, understandably so. But, actually, what happened in the thirteenth or eighteenth centuries is completely irrelevant to today's situation, as are the Opium Wars and Hong Kong's past dating back to 1841. Recent history in Tibet, China and Hong Kong *is* more relevant, but not all of it. China uses history to set the agenda. The May 2004 White Paper is a classic example. There is, however, a higher-level agenda which the White Paper did not mention. International law is the civilised way to conduct affairs in matters of war and peace, in settling disputes and in instilling the culture of human rights and respect for all people. The 'rights of people to self-determination' is a powerful principle to which the government of the People's Republic is committed. It cannot wriggle out of it by saying, 'It was Jiang Zemin who ratified it, not Hu Jintao' and 'anyway, Tibet is an internal matter'.

If Tibetans are a distinct people separate from the Han Chinese, as two major investigations have found is the case, and if they want to claim that right, then the law is on their side. So Tibetan people must have their say (as should the Chinese people themselves). There should be a well-conducted survey amongst Tibetans in Tibet and in the Tibetan diaspora asking what it is they want for their political future, including of course the possibility of the *status quo*. The Tibetan government-in-exile should consult as widely as possible to find out whether there is a general will amongst Tibetans who are able to respond, perhaps using the media to communicate with those in Tibet to request the UN to hold such a survey, which must be, and be seen to be, independent and completely confidential as to the views expressed. It would not be a 'mean trick aimed at splitting China', as the Chinese claimed when the proposal for a referendum was made in 1995, but an attempt to 'find the truth from the facts' and a civilised way to proceed. The dispute has gone on for more than fifty years, and it is high time it was resolved.

If the Tibetan people said they wanted a higher degree of autonomy, which cannot be assumed without enquiry, the implications would be even wider than indicated so far. President Hu's first public statement about Tibet in January 2004 referred to Tibet as *an inseparable part of Chinese territory*. Whether 'inseparable' is really much different from 'inalienable' is arguable, the important point being that nothing is fixed for all time – change is constant. Sovereignty is not an 'all or nothing' principle. Tibet could be autonomous within Chinese territory. With new people at the helm, anything is possible; with Hu as President and General Secretary of the Communist Party, and with Wen Jiabao as Premier with the wide range of executive responsibilities, real progress could be made. This time the hardliners must not hold them back.

If Tibet followed Scotland and acquired a substantial degree of autonomy with a wide portfolio of activities in the territory of the TAR, 'meaningful autonomy', as the Dalai Lama now prefers to call it, for the development of laws and for good administration, there should be a Tibetan constitution, a legislature and a government. Given the scale of China's continuing involvement in Tibet, in matters for which they would have sole responsibility and in those to be decided jointly, the legislature would have to be in some way joint, with equal status for the two peoples. Thus it might be sensible to make provisions in the Basic Law that a proportion of the permanent population should determine the proportion of seats in the legislature, subject to not less than one half of the seats being held by Tibetans. The speaker of this parliament should be Tibetan, with a Chinese alternate. As explained in Chapter Six, the Dalai Lama in exile has ensured that the Assembly of People's Deputies in Dharamsala and the Kalon Tripa (the prime minister or chief executive) should be democratically elected without having competing political parties. Primaries are first held to select candidates and the main elections are held between those in the lead. However, if the Chinese insist that only 'patriots' (of China) are fit to rule, as apparently in Hong Kong, that the Chinese should have a majority in the legislature or could reject those elected Tibetans they did not like, and if codetermination meant that the Chinese always got their way, then autonomy in Tibet would fail.

The Basic Law should also specify the extent of the proposed jurisdiction. The territory of the TAR would be at its heart and where self-rule should start. There is good reason why jurisdiction should in some way extend to the Tibetan Autonomous Prefectures, counties and other areas which have a significant Tibetan population to the east in what were Kham and Amdo, because most Tibetans live there. This will be difficult and controversial. In Qinghai, for example, 22.5 percent of its population is ethnic Tibetan, one-third scattered in rural areas. The Communist Party secretary and the governor of Qinghai would not like to see their jurisdiction over such a large section of their population taken away from them, and most likely Hu would not agree to it. Sichuan has nearly 1.3 million Tibetans who account for only 1.5 percent of its population, more than one half scattered in rural areas.[1] While groupings of Tibetan communities could form regional assemblies with organic links to the TAR, 'autonomy' in these areas might have to be different from that in the TAR. Detailed investigations would reveal what is possible. Much would depend on how Hu develops his desire to increase public participation in government. The whole Tibetan area, when defined, could become a territory of China with self-rule.[2]

In 845 AD the Chinese emperor Wu Tsung destroyed 4,600 Buddhist monasteries in China and dismissed their monks and nuns because of their potential political threat to his power and authority. Mao Zedong did the same in Tibet over 1,100 years later because they represented the 'four olds' which had to be destroyed to make room for socialism. Jiang Zemin, like Emperor Wu, saw Buddhism as a potential political threat and contained it whilst threatening the Dalai Lama as being the leading 'splittist'.

Yet Tibet has remained basically nonviolent despite fifty years of provocation, and the Dalai Lama has constantly sought an accommodation with China which would satisfy the Tibetan people through 'genuine autonomy'. He is a Buddhist monk and an honourable man, with great wisdom and infinite patience, a person who can be trusted. He has no political ambitions for himself, only to serve the Tibetan people. Buddhism and the Dalai Lama pose no political threat to the Chinese state. He has no hidden agenda. When that message is finally understood in Beijing it may be opportune for a technical and spiritual dialogue to take place between Tibetan and Chinese Buddhists. The Dalai Lama has said that 'in future we need to encourage and foster an exchange of knowledge and experience amongst our different traditions and improve communications amongst us.'[3] Tibetan Buddhism has remnants of the earlier Bon religion, and Chinese Buddhism has been influenced strongly by Taoism (likewise, Buddhism in Japan has been strongly influenced by Shinto; such influences between religions are called 'syncretic'). The regeneration of Buddhism in China today suggests that, when the time is right, a dialogue between Tibetan and Chinese Buddhists could be a useful measure of confidence-building between the two peoples on the path towards mutual trust. The first such dialogue took place in 1954 when the Dalai Lama went to Beijing as a guest of Mao Zedong, and gave teachings to Chinese Buddhists.

It is most likely that a few more dialogues between the Dalai Lama's envoys and Chinese officials will have to be held primarily to explore each other's minds, to be clear that the words and concepts used and the underlying assumptions are clearly understood by both sides – clearing the decks, so to speak, and building mutual confidence and trust – the White Paper notwithstanding. The meaning of 'autonomy' and its related concept of 'splittism' have been particular obstacles to dialogue. They are so rooted in the Chinese psyche that even in June 2004 the Chinese ambassador, in persuading the Russian leadership not to permit the Dalai Lama to visit Buddhists in a predominately Buddhist Russian republic (Kalmykia), claimed that the Dalai Lama 'wanted Tibet to secede from China', which is, of course, nonsense.

When such matters have been clarified, President Hu and the Standing Committee may then feel able to hold more formal talks, leading to a UN enquiry into what the Tibetan people themselves want. As Buddhists say, 'the root cause of hatred is fundamental and all-encompassing ignorance that blinds individuals and societies.' Otherwise, how can one explain that the Chinese ambassador to a powerful neighbour, and the Standing Committee of the Politburo, have not understood that for more than thirty years the Dalai Lama has been arguing for more autonomy within China, not independence? The ignorance is indeed fundamental. And when a young Tibetan intellectual trained in China writes the truth – a woman named Oser, who wrote *Notes on Tibet* – what happens? Almost as soon as the book was published, in May 2004, it is banned throughout China. Basic statistics are distorted by the hierarchy of cadres, and the scale and growth of the GDP in the TAR are misinterpreted. How can anyone at the top make wise and sensible policies if the information they receive through the usual channels is so distorted?

Indeed, it is apparent that many of Tibet's problems stem from China's own internal problems, going back centuries but especially in the last fifty years or so. Several authors foresee an internal collapse of China (e.g. Chang), its problems seemingly insurmountable. If that happened, Tibet could perhaps grab its chance. However, the Chinese people and leaders are well capable of resolving them all, in due time, although not necessarily all at the same time. Their men and women have remarkable talents, and great energy and determination. In some fields they have achieved the highest international standards. Other authors foresee the possibility of war, particularly with the US (Bernstein, Chomsky), but this is much less likely than internal collapse. While Tibet is favoured by the US, Tibet would probably suffer more from the conflict than it would gain, even if the US won.

The evidence that China would be prepared at present to negotiate political autonomy for Tibet on any large scale is too slender upon which to build hope, and independence is impossible. But under President Hu, fundamental changes are in the air and a cautious small change in China's attitude towards Tibet could emerge.

It is common practice in China to experiment first with the application of radical new policies in one or a few locations and situations. So it is just possible that Tibet could be a testing ground for a new system of governance which would have a wider relevance in China – certainly in the Autonomous Region of Xinjiang and perhaps elsewhere.

There is also a higher-level issue. China today is, however, firmly in the 'materialist' or 'modern' phase of human evolution: it prioritises Western Development, economic growth, science, oppression, powerful weapons, concern for the preservation of its boundaries. Yet there are signs of moving towards what Deepak Chopra has called the 'intermediate zone', intermediate between materialism and the spiritual realm.[4] The regeneration of Buddhism, the spread of Christian faiths, and the local beliefs in gods in rural areas are signs of a widespread spiritual–religious resurgence and a search for meaning. Richard Falk, in his *Explorations at the Edge of Time*, writes in parallel but broader terms about the postmodernist attempt to 're-invent reality in a more holistic, less hierarchical imagery. Part of our challenge has to do with the rescue of the spirit … and a related feminisation of political life [that] finds power in *relations* rather than in *capabilities* for dominance and destruction.' The Green movement; the organic food and products movement; the preservation of increasingly rare species; care for the environment; more compassionate care for animals; complementary medicine; doing good deeds for their own sake and not for personal reward or gain: all these and more are part of the postmodern world. 'One of the most illuminating ways of imaging the future is studying the lives of exemplary citizen-pilgrims who are at work amongst us,' Falk writes. He is also against the artificialities and constraints of the state – 'the most menacing of these are artificial boundaries' – and the trouble they have caused in the world. Again, China is moving in this direction with, for example, its newfound emphasis on sustainable use of the environment and the prevention of environmental degradation. This is looking forward with hope into the twenty-first century, with China and Tibet in a leadership role. To redefine the boundaries of Tibet in the near future as a *territory of China with self-rule* would be a huge step forward.

When a settlement is reached and both the Chinese and the Tibetans are satisfied with the outcome, then – following the example of many other countries – a truth and reconciliation commission could prove immensely valuable. If exposure of the truth about Tibet's experiences could be authenticated in this more formal way, by holding hearings and presenting evidence, the search for reconciliation would be complete and effective. The millions of people who have suffered could feel that their suffering and pain were publicly acknowledged. The past could be exposed and put to rest. Archbishop Desmond Tutu was the heroic and compassionate chairman of South Africa's Truth and Reconciliation Commission. In launching the commission in February 1996, President Nelson Mandela described its simple purpose as 'healing our nation'. Should that occur in Tibet, the elderly Tibetan woman quoted earlier who, for the last fifty years has had a smile on her face but tears in her heart, would be filled with joy.

Appendix

The following is the full text of the speech made by then Vice-President Hu Jintao in Lhasa, at a rally celebrating the fiftieth anniversary of the 'Peaceful Liberation of Tibet' (19 July 2001):

Comrades and Friends,

Today, the ancient city of Lhasa is covered in gala decorations with red flags flying in Potala Square, and the Yarlung Zangbo River is gurgling delightfully. We members of the delegation from the Central Government, together with cadres and people of all ethnic groups in Tibet, are holding this grand celebration to mark the fiftieth anniversary of the peaceful liberation of Tibet with joy and elation. First of all, I wish to extend, on behalf of the CPC Central Committee, the NPC Standing Committee, the State Council, the CPPCC National Committee and the Central Military Commission, our warm congratulations and cordial greetings to workers, farmers and herdsmen, intellectuals, cadres and people from all walks of life of all ethnic groups in Tibet and to officers and men of the PLA Garrison and of units of the People's Armed Police Force (PAPF) and public security officers in Tibet. Our high tribute goes to all the comrades and friends who have contributed to the peaceful liberation, prosperity and development of Tibet, and our heartfelt thanks to the foreign friends who have cared for and supported the development and progress of Tibet.

Fifty years ago, the CPC Central Committee and Comrade Mao Zedong, having correctly assessed the situation, made a far-sighted, resolute and significant policy decision to liberate Tibet peacefully. The Central People's Government and the former local government of Tibet signed the Agreement on Measures for the Peaceful Liberation of Tibet, thus bringing about the peaceful liberation of Tibet. The peaceful liberation of Tibet was a major event in modern Chinese history and an epoch-making turning point in the course of development in Tibet. It symbolised that Tibet once and for all cast off the yoke of imperialist aggression and that the great unity of the Chinese nation and its great reunification cause have entered a new period of development. It ushered in a new era in which Tibet would turn from darkness to light, from backwardness to progress, from poverty to affluence and from seclusion to openness.

Over the past fifty years, which is just a blink of the eye in the long history of human progress, the ancient and fascinating land of Tibet has undergone unrivalled changes and worked unprecedented miracles on earth. Over the past fifty years, Tibet has achieved a leap forward in the historical development of social systems and embarked on a socialist road. With the abolition of feudal serfdom, under which the Tibetan people had long been suppressed and exploited, millions of erstwhile serfs who did not even have the minimum of human rights have now stood up and become masters of their own fate. Today people of all ethnic groups are fully enjoying political, economic, cultural and other rights and having complete control of their destiny.

Over the past fifty years, Tibet has made substantial headway in its economic development, and the living standards of its people have improved markedly. Through democratic reform, socialist transformation and reform and opening-up, the social productive forces of Tibet have been emancipated and developed in an unprecedented manner. Last year, the GDP of Tibet was more than fifty times that of 1959 when democratic reform started. The Autonomous Region has built up its infrastructure from scratch. The income of urban and rural residents has increased steadily, with the overwhelming majority of people out of poverty and some people leading comfortable lives. This stands in stark contrast to the plight of the destitute people in the old Tibet.

Over the past fifty years, the socialist spiritual civilisation in Tibet has been steadily enhanced and society has moved forward in an all-round way. Educational, scientific and technological, cultural, public health and other social undertakings have been developing vigorously. People of all ethnic groups in Tibet have generally had enhanced political awareness, higher ethical standards and scientific and educational levels. The fine traditional culture in Tibet has not only been protected, inherited and carried forward, but also substantiated to reflect people's new lives and meet the new requirements of social development called for by the times.

Over the past fifty years, solidarity amongst all ethnic groups in Tibet has been constantly strengthened and social stability there has been maintained on the whole. With the execution of the Party's policies on ethnic and religious affairs and the all-round implementation of the system of regional autonomy of ethnic minorities, the socialist ethnic relationship, which features equality, solidarity and mutual assistance, has been growing in strength. People's freedom of religious belief has been fully respected and protected. People of all ethnic groups have worked in unity and succeeded in foiling the separatist and disruptive activities of the Dalai clique and anti-China forces in the world time and again, and thus safeguarded stability in Tibet and national unity and state security.

With the passage of fifty extraordinary years, Tibet of today presents a scene of vitality and prosperity with economic growth, social progress and stability, ethnic solidarity and solid border defence. The people here are living and working in peace and contentment.

The credit for the remarkable achievements of Tibet in the past fifty years goes to the wise decision-making and correct leadership of the three generations of central collective leadership of the Party with comrades Mao Zedong, Deng Xiaoping and Jiang Zemin at the core respectively during different historical periods in Tibet 's development. The achievements are also attributable to the all-out support of the state to Tibet and the continual aid of the people across the country. The achievements are also the result of the concerted efforts by the people of all ethnic groups in Tibet, who have displayed the extraordinary spirit of fortitude, hard work, endurance, solidarity and utter devotion.

Reflecting on the past in light of the present, one should bear in mind where his/her happiness comes from. At this moment, we deeply cherish the memory of proletarian revolutionaries of the older generation such as Mao Zedong and Deng Xiaoping who initiated and laid the foundation for the development and progress of Tibet. We also deeply cherish the memory of the martyrs and heroes who dedicated their youth, wisdom, strength and even invaluable lives to the revolution, construction and reform in Tibet and to the defence of the frontier of the motherland. Their heroic names and meritorious deeds will be eulogised through the ages and go down in history!

The course of fifty years of storms and vicissitudes has brought to light a great truth: it is only under the leadership of the Communist Party of China, only in the embrace of the big family of the motherland and only by firmly taking the socialist road with Chinese characteristics that Tibet can enjoy today's prosperity and progress and an even better tomorrow. This is the most important conclusion that we have drawn from the fifty years of Tibet's development and also the fundamental principle that must be followed in building and developing Tibet in the days to come.

Comrades and Friends, Tibet is in the south-western frontier of the motherland, with a vast stretch of land and a most important strategic position.

The development, stability and security of Tibet have a direct bearing on the fundamental interests of people of all ethnic groups in Tibet as well as ethnic solidarity, national unity and state security. It is the common aspiration and mission of people of all ethnic groups in China, the Tibetan people included, to build on the prosperity and progress and maintain stability and solidarity in Tibet.

At present, China has entered a new stage of development in which it will build a well-to-do society in an all-round manner and accelerate the socialist modernisation drive. Tibet has also entered an important period of faster development and maintenance of stability. Recently, Comrade Jiang Zemin made an important speech at a rally in celebration of the eightieth anniversary of the founding of the Communist Party of China. He systematically summarised the achievements and basic experience of the eighty-year-long struggle of our Party, profoundly expounded the scientific connotation of the important concept of the 'Three Represents', correctly answered major questions that need to be studied and resolved for Party-building in the new historical period and further identified the objectives and tasks of the Party in the new century. This important speech is a Marxist programmatic document which will guide our efforts to advance the great cause of building socialism with Chinese characteristics and the new and great project of Party-building. It also provides a strong ideological weapon for accelerated development of Tibet in the new century. Not long ago, the CPC Central Committee and the State Council held the fourth working conference on Tibet, at which a magnificent blueprint for Tibet's development for the first few years of the new century was mapped out and the guiding principles of vital importance for the work of Tibet were formulated. According to the plan of the conference, the Central Government and all localities throughout the country will intensify their support for Tibet and help create even more favourable conditions for its development. As one of the priority regions in the development of China's west, Tibet is faced with unprecedented opportunities for development.

The Central Government ardently hopes that the vast number of cadres and people of Tibet will earnestly study and implement the essential points of President Jiang Zemin's important speech on 1 July and the spirit of the fourth working conference on Tibet, seize the opportunities and make good use of them, and forge ahead in a pioneering spirit in an earnest effort to move the Tibetan economy from step-by-step development to leapfrog development and Tibetan society from relative stability to lasting peace and stability.

Rapid economic development is the fundamental condition for realising the interests of all ethnic groups in Tibet and also the basic guarantee for greater ethnic unity and continued stability there. Cadres and people of all ethnic groups in Tibet should further emancipate their minds, update their concepts and press ahead with the reform and opening-up so as to create a sound social and institutional environment for economic development. It is essential to work hard, practise economy, make careful plans and calculations and cherish and make good use of Government investment and financial assistance by other regions of the country to ensure full economic and social returns for aid projects. It is essential to rely on your own efforts, work assiduously, truly depend on your own enthusiasm, initiative and creativity, and bring them into full play. It is essential to vigorously develop an economy with distinctive local characteristics by making full use of abundant local resources and speed up strategic readjustment to your economic structure in a bid to turn your rich natural resources into actual economic strength. It is essential to implement the strategy of revitalising Tibet through science and education in a comprehensive manner, advocate a social environment of respect for knowledge and talented people, and work hard to advance science, technology and education so that you may truly depend on scientific and technical progress and improved quality of the work force for economic growth. It is essential to pay great attention to the environment, step up the protection and improvement of the ecosystem so as to achieve a sustainable economic and social development in Tibet.

Greater ethnic unity and lasting social stability are where the fundamental interests of people of all ethnic groups in Tibet lie. Without ethnic unity and social stability, its economy cannot develop smoothly and its people cannot enjoy their work and lives. Cadres and people of all ethnic groups in Tibet should always hold high the banners of patriotism and ethnic unity, bear in mind that 'the Han people and ethnic minorities are inseparable from each other, so are ethnic minorities themselves' and that people of all ethnic groups should truly share weal and woe. It is essential to stick to and improve the system of regional ethnic autonomy and further consolidate and develop the socialist ethnic relationship of equality, solidarity and mutual assistance. It is essential to correctly and comprehensively implement the Party's policy of freedom of religious belief so that people of all ethnic groups will unite and cooperate with each other politically, respect each other's beliefs and throw all their weight behind faster development and continued stability in Tibet. It is essential to fight unequivocally against the separatist activities by the Dalai clique and anti-China forces in the world, vigorously develop a good situation of stability and unity in Tibet and firmly safeguard national unity and state security.

The PLA Garrison, PAPF units and the law enforcement departments in Tibet are the strong pillars and loyal guards in defending the frontier of the motherland and maintaining stability in Tibet. They are an important force in the building of both material and spiritual civilisations. They should carry forward the fine traditions and work style, improve and stiffen themselves, strengthen unity between the government and the army, between civilians and the armed forces, and between the police and the people, and make new contributions to the stability and development of Tibet.

Comrades and Friends, Tibet is a beautiful and richly endowed region of our great motherland. The industrious and talented people of all ethnic groups in Tibet have, in a long historical development, made outstanding contributions to the creation of a glorious culture of the Chinese nation and creation of a unified multi-ethnic country. In the last half a century in particular, the Tibetan people have written brilliant chapters in the development and progress of Tibet and added new glory to the big family of our socialist motherland. We feel profoundly proud of the past and immensely confident about the future. Let us rally around the leadership of the CPC Central Committee with Comrade Jiang Zemin at the core, hold high the great banner of Deng Xiaoping Theory, take the important thinking of the 'Three Represents' as the guide, work together unremittingly with one heart for a new socialist Tibet of unity, prosperity and civilisation, and for the great rejuvenation of the Chinese nation!

Source: Xinhua *in English, 19 July 2001, Lhasa.*

Notes

Introduction
1. I should have warned against involvement with the International Monetary Fund (IMF), however; see Joseph E. Stiglitz's *Globalization and its Discontents*, Penguin Books, 2002. On p. xiii Stiglitz writes that 'decisions at the [IMF] were made on the basis of a curious blend of ideology and bad economics ... [they] prescribed outmoded, inappropriate, if "standard", solutions without considering the effects they would have on the people in the countries told to follow these policies.'

Prologue
1. References in this book to 'Tibet' by itself refer to ethnic Tibet, where most Tibetans live, sometimes called 'historical Tibet'. The principal Tibetan areas are called U-Tsang (made up of U and Tsang), Kham and Amdo; collectively, Cholka-Sum. The territory U-Tsang in central Tibet, which in 1965 became the Tibet Autonomous Region (TAR) under the Chinese, has its capital at Lhasa (the seat of the Dalai Lama) and was the centre of government for almost all that area. A small part of this territory around Shigatse was the domain of the Panchen Lama, conferred on him by the Manchu emperor Yung Ch'eng in 1728. His monastery was at Tashilhunpo near Shigatse, about 190 miles west of Lhasa; it was also the centre of his authority, and today is the TAR's second-largest city.
2. Tibetans in Kham and Amdo (sometimes called 'Eastern Tibet' or 'Inner Tibet' – 'inner' being from the Chinese point of view) acknowledged the Dalai Lama as their spiritual authority, but they preferred to govern themselves until the Manchu emperors invaded their lands and, by the end of the eighteenth century, exercised much direct control. The Tibetan areas in Kham and Amdo became, at various dates, Tibetan Autonomous Prefectures and Counties in Chinese provinces. In Qinghai province there are seven such prefectures; Sichuan has three, Gansu province, two and Yunnan province, three. Each province has several counties, the lowest level in the administrative hierarchy, as shown below in the table derived from the Tibet Information Network (TIN)'s *Yearbook* for 2002, pp. 131–6. It was originally from the November 2000 Chinese

Census of Population. The composition of all Tibetans, except for a few in the 'other' category, is shown below.

	TAR	Sichuan	Qinghai	Gansu	Yunnan
Total population (million)	2.6	82.3	4.8	25.1	42.4
of which Tibetan (million)	2.4	1.3	1.1	0.4	0.1
Tibetan percentage	92.8%	1.5%	22.5%	1.8%	0.3%
Tibetan counties (number)	81	32	40	9	3

The Chinese population of the TAR as indicated is probably an underestimate because of the presence of military personnel and unregistered Chinese migrant workers, and because the census was taken in November when many Chinese workers might have returned to China to avoid the winter. Lhasa may be at least 70 percent Chinese; in other administrative centres this percentage is probably much lower, and still lower in rural areas.

3. Official concern about Serthar is thought to have been initiated much earlier by Yin Fatang, a military cadre from the Eighteenth Route Army of the PLA and Party Secretary in Tibet, 1980–5. He thought that right from its beginning, the institute would turn out to be dangerously 'splittist'. In 1990, Khenpo Jigme Phuntsok visited the Dalai Lama in India, and it may be that this alerted Chinese attention. Yin so advised President Jiang Zemin, who ordered an investigation by the United Front Department of the Chinese Communist Party. It reported that there was little or no evidence of 'splittism' at the Serthar Institute, but nevertheless some senior members of the leadership thought it should be cut back. Thus in June 2001 the decision was taken. Source: Tibet Information Network 'News Updates', 19 August and 18 November 2001; *Leaders in Tibet: A Directory* (TIN, Victoria Connor and Robert Barnett), 1997, p. 9 and *TIN News Review: Reports from Tibet*, 2001, pp. 50–7.

4. The Karze Tibetan Autonomous Prefecture in Sichuan, where Serthar is, is an area noted for its support for the Dalai Lama.

5. The actual number varied according to the number of visiting pilgrims at the time.

6. The institute kept strictly to the teaching of Buddhism and avoided politics. Successful students received a degree equivalent to a doctorate in Western universities, the highest formal academic qualification. It taught the four schools of Tibetan Buddhism (Nyingma, Kagyu, Sakya and Gelugpa) and thus was all-embracing. Many of its alumni became teachers at the Buddhist institutions from which they came; some stayed as teachers in the rapidly growing institute or for further study. Khenpo Jigme did, however, openly support the Dalai Lama, which was probably his downfall.

7. See the Tibetan Centre for Human Rights and Democracy (TCHRD)'s *Annual Reports* for 2001 and 2002, 'Freedom of Religious Belief and Practice'. These annual reports are also the source of much of the detailed information given in this prologue, and my debt to both the TCHRD and TIN is considerable.

8. See the December 2003 'Report on Education in China' by Katarina Tomasevski, Special Rapporteur on the Right to Education of the UN Human Rights Commission (Croatia).

9. See Andrew Fischer, *Poverty by Design: The Economics of Discrimination in Tibet* (Canada Tibet Committee), August 2002, p. 7. This important ninety-two-page economic study was presented at the August 2002 World Conference on Sustainable Development in Johannesburg. It is a devastating indictment of China's economic policies in Tibet.

10. Quoted in *Cutting Off the Serpent's Head: Tightening Control in Tibet, 1994–1995,* TIN and Human Rights Watch Asia, p. 68. The notion of 'patriotism' as a prime requirement for any leader in Tibet was Deng Xiaoping's idea. 'Patriotism' was a requirement for Hong Kong's chief executive, thus undermining the plan, at the time of the handover to the Chinese in 1997, that democratic elections for Tung Chee-hwa's replacement would be introduced in 2007. The Chinese-appointed first chief executive turned out to be most inadequate, and is regularly lambasted in Hong Kong's satirical magazine *Spike*, which is based on the popular British equivalent *Private Eye*. Tung Chee-hwa is patriotic, and this seems more important than that he be efficient.

11. This major speech was published in a special edition of *News from China*, July 11 2001.

12. Cf. Note no. 9 in this chapter.

13. Speech to the Fifth TAR Conference on Education, 26 October 1994. See *Racial Discrimination in Tibet*, TCHRD, September 2000, p. 72.

14. Catriona Bass, *Education in Tibet: Policy and Practice since 1950*, Zed Books in association with TIN, 1998, p. 154.

15. See *Tibet 2002 Yearbook*, TIN, 2003, pp. 107–9.

16. Bass, pp. 151–2.

17. See *The Status of Tibetan Women 1995–2000* (prepared by the Tibetan Women's Association for the Beijing +5, the twenty-third special session of the United Nations General Assembly, 'Women 2000: Gender Equality, Development and Peace for the Twenty-first Century'), June 2000, p. 30.

18. Zhu Kaixuan, 'Report to the National People's Congress Standing Committee on Educational Work', quoted in *Racial Discrimination in Tibet* (TCHRD), September 2000, p. 65.

19. See *Tibetan Review*, December 2003.

20. Quoted in *Racial Discrimination in Tibet* (TCHRD), September 2001, p. 35.

21. Source: New Progress in Human Rights in the Tibet Autonomous Region (Information Office of the State Council of the People's Republic of China), February 1998.

22. See *Delivery and Deficiency: Health and Health Care in Tibet* (Tibet Information Network), November 2002, p. 9.

23. See TIN *Tibet 2002 Yearbook*, p. 18.

24. See *The Status of Tibetan Women 1995–2000*. For a historical survey of birth control policies in Tibet, see *Children of Despair: An Analysis of Coercive Birth Control Policies in Chinese-occupied Tibet* (Free Tibet Campaign), August 1992.

25. See TCHRD *Annual Report 2001*, 'The Right to Housing'.

26. Jasper Becker, 'Empire Building', in *The Independent Review*, 24 March 2003.

27. On discrimination in work generally, see *Racial Discrimination in Tibet* (TCHRD) September 2000, especially pp. 8–33.

28. During a three-week consultancy in Mongolia I visited many nomadic people in their *yurts* in high territory, far from any settlements. I saw that a nomadic way of life was a good use of land where climatic and geographical conditions are harsh, which the Mongolian authorities confirmed. Also, in 1987 during the seven-week scientific expedition to the high Himalaya in Nepal (see Introduction), at an altitude of about

16,000 feet, I saw the simply built wooden huts where villagers would stay during the summer months, tending their animals on the thin grassland while their herds from down the valley roamed. In early October, the snow-line just reached that area.

29. Some reports say that in 1988–9 Tibetans generally were paid the same as Chinese. See Bass, p. 81.

30. TCHRD *Annual Report 2003*.

31. For more details see *China's Great Leap West*, Tibet Information Network, November 2000.

32. Ronald D. Schwartz, *Circle of Protest: Political Ritual in the Tibetan Uprising*, Hurst and Company, London, 1994, pp. 135–6.

33. *Fire Under the Snow: Testimony of a Tibetan Prisoner*, Harvill Press, London, 1997.

34. The Ven. Bhagdro, *A Hell on Earth: A Brief Biography of a Tibetan Political Prisoner*, published by Bhagdro, 1998. See also Chris Michell, Ven. Bhagdro and the nuns of Drapchi Prison, *Tibetan Freedom Chants*, Oreade Music (ORW 60982), The Netherlands, 2001, a CD recorded live at Namgyal Monastery with Ven. Bhagdro chanting and with flute improvisations. It includes Bhagdro's spoken account of his torture under the Chinese, and some archival recordings by the nuns of Drapchi Prison. All the nuns in the recording have now been released.

35. *Torture: Quarterly Journal on Rehabilitation of Torture Victims and Prevention of Torture* (IRCT), Copenhagen.

36. Torture is used to extract information, enforce confessions and as straightforward punishment. An arrest might begin with self-tightening handcuffs, which may become so tight that, in the words of one former torture victim, 'blood ran from my finger-tips'; other frequent inflictions include punching, kicking, beatings all over the body with wooden clubs or sticks (some nail-studded), iron bars, rods or rifle butts; being held by the hair and having the head smashed against a wall; being attacked by specially trained dogs which savagely bite their victims; being burned with cigarette ends.

Interrogation can last several weeks and will generally involve, in addition to the above, the use of electric cattle prods to sensitive parts of the body including genitals, mouth and just below the ears, and on the soles of wet feet, 'causing my body to spasm and blood to come from my nose and mouth', according to one former victim. Another describes being 'hung upside down one foot above the ground by my hands chained together behind my back until sunrise the next day'; other torture methods in a similar vein can involve being hung upside down over a heated stove; being tied round a burning hot stovepipe for hours on end ('until I had burns all over and my boots were filled with water from sweating', reports one former victim); prolonged exposure to extreme cold; having water thrown over one's naked body in sub-zero temperatures; being made to stand barefoot outside on ice, so all the skin comes off the feet upon movement; being made to stand outside all day in the blazing sun without water.

There is deprivation of food and water. 'I took scraps of vegetables from the ditch when food was being prepared,' says one former victim, while another reports, 'there was ditch nearby with dirty laundry water running through it and while handcuffed behind my back I held a bowl with my teeth to get water when I thought the guards were not looking.'

Confessions may be made in an attempt to gain release, as in the case of one former prisoner: 'After one month of daily interrogation I could not cope with the situation any longer so I confessed to hitting a policeman with an iron bar. The officials wrote out this confession.' Punishment can involve all the above plus solitary confinement, gruelling exercises in the sun and extremely heavy labour outside, whatever the weather. Even the ill are forced to try and keep up; those who fail risk beatings, and many die this way.

37. Source: *The Status of Tibetan Women 1995–2000*, June 2000, p. 10.

38. *Tibetan Review*, December 2003.

39. Most of the above information comes from two reputable and reliable sources: the Tibetan Centre for Human Rights and Democracy (www.tchrd.org) based in Dharamsala, and the Tibet Information Network (www.tibetinfo.net) based in London, together with *Tibet News*, (www.tibetnews.com), a Canada-based international news service. TCHRD and TIN carefully interview the many thousands of Tibetans who have escaped over the mountains and cross-check their stories wherever possible. My own discussions with many Tibetans confirm the general picture, conveyed in the Prologue.

Chapter One

1. The *Tao Te Ching* is a Taoist treatise compiled in eighty-one chapters by Lao-tzu ('the Old Master') around 500 BC, said to have been an older contemporary of Confucius. While the chapters are short, they are pregnant with meaning. The quotation is a translation from the original Taoist text by Thomas Cleary, *The Essential Tao*, Castle Books, 1992, p. 9. It teaches that nothing is fixed or permanent, everything changes. As Cleary says (p.1), 'Tao is one of the most basic and comprehensive symbols in the Chinese language … a path, a way, a principle, a method, a doctrine, a system of order'.

2. See his *The Chinese*, John Murray, 2000, p. 2. This is thought to be partly due to under-reporting of the size of the population on account of China's 'one child' policy, any subsequent children being unreported.

3. TCHRD *Annual Report 2002*, p. 38.

4. Jonathan Spence gives a good example in *The Search for Modern China* (W. W. Norton and Company, second edn, 1999, p. 359). The phrases

> Everything prospers, Heaven is protective.
> The people are heroes. The place is famous.

read in a Cantonese accent and then reinterpreted according to the sound, become:

> Everything disintegrates, Heaven explodes.
> The people are extinct. The place is bare.

5. In the *pinyin* system, this is the First Emperor Qin. In Wade-Giles it would be 'Ch'in Shi-huang-ti'. *Shi* means 'first', *huang* 'emperor' and the suffix *ti* or *di* is an honorific meaning 'august'. There are several other versions, too ('Qin Shihuang', 'Qinshi Huangdi' and 'Shi Huangdi', for example). Most details of the First Emperor in this book are taken from *The Cambridge History of Ancient China*, Michael Loewe and Edward L. Shawghnessy, eds, Cambridge University Press, 1999, and Chapter One by Derk Bodde in *The Cambridge History of China, Volume One*, Denis Twitchett and Michael Loewe, eds, Cambridge University Press, 1986.

6. The so-called 'Warring States' were Yan, Qi, Wei, Zhao, Hann, Qin and Chu (Lu) and their main period of conflict was 481–222 BC, brought to an end by Qin Shihuangdi.

7. In 1975 a coffin was unearthed at Shuihudi in Hubei province containing the remains of a man, thought to be a local official, buried in 217 BC or shortly thereafter. In it were

also detailed records (on 1,155 strips of bamboo), field by field, of the crops planted and their present state, the local rainfall, the cattle owned by local farmers and other minute details of the agriculture of the area. See W. J. F. Jenner, *Tyranny of History: The Roots of China's Crisis*, Penguin Books, 1994, p. 22.

8. John King Fairbank and Merle Goldman, in *China: A New History* (The Belknap Press of Harvard University Press, 1998, p. 57), say very firmly that he did not build the Great Wall of China; but in *The Cambridge History of China, Volume One*, it is equally clear that the Great Wall was started in 221 BC by the First Emperor's most important general, Meng T'ien, and took ten years to build with some 300,000 men. Jonathan D. Spence probably comes nearest to the truth in *The Chan's Great Continent: China in Western Minds* (W. W. Norton and Company, 1998, p. 215), saying that Meng T'ien connected parts of already existing structures.

9. What survived were the remains of his vast mausoleum, built by some 700,000 labourers, and the many thousands of life-sized, truly remarkable ceramic soldiers buried in his tomb in Xi'an, discovered in 1974, to protect him in the afterlife from his many enemies. Buried with him were his many concubines, along with the workmen who knew where his treasures were hidden. His administrative system, however, survived.

10. Different authorities give different dates. Here I follow Mark Edward Lewis in 'The Warring States Political History', a chapter in *The Cambridge History of Ancient China*, p. 631.

11. Its original title was *Sun Tzu Ping Fa* ('The Military Method of Venerable Master Sun'). It is thought that Sun Tzu was probably Sun Wu (late sixth century BC), whose book led him to have an audience with King Ho-lu of Wu. Mark Edward Lewis calls him 'Sun Wu'. Mao Zedong, in his *Selected Works* (p. 187), called him 'Sun Wu Tzu'. *The Art of War* drew heavily on the earlier Taoist masterpiece *Tao Te Ching*, as well as the advisory precepts in the *I Ching*. Commentators have interpreted and added to the original work throughout the ages. I have found the most interesting to be Thomas Cleary's *The Art of War: Sun Tzu*, Shambhala Dragon Editions, 1988, and *Mastering The Art of War: Zhuge Liang's and Liu Ji's Commentaries on the Classic by Sun Tzu*, translated and edited by Thomas Cleary, Shambhala Dragon Editions, 1989.

12. Taken from the *Tao Te Ching*, Chapter Thirty-one, p. 72.

13. *The Art of War*, Chapter Three.

14. Cleary, *The Art of War*, p. 4.

15. Samuel B. Griffith, *Sun Tzu: The Art of War*, Oxford University Press, 1963, especially Chapter VI ('Sun Tzu and Mao Tse-Tung'). Griffith was a Brigadier General in the US Marine Corps with a detailed knowledge of early Chinese, an unlikely but fruitful combination. This enabled him to produce his own translation of the original (he also translated Mao's *On Guerrilla Warfare*). His military knowledge gives a special edge to his observations. Clearly he regards Mao Zedong as the best exponent of Sun Tzu's principles in modern times. That Mao often read *The Art of War* is also confirmed in Zhisui Li's *The Private Life of Chairman Mao*, Arrow, 1996, p. 83. Mao may have first learned about it from the ancient classics *San Kuo* ('Narrative of the Three Kingdoms') and *Shui Hu Chuan* ('All Men are Brothers'). See Edgar Snow, *Red Star Over China*, Victor Gollancz, London, 1937, pp. 130–1, being a reported series of discussions with Mao Zedong. See also Griffith, p. 45.

16. Capturing one of the enemy's leaders refers to the Tibetan Ngabo Ngawang Jigme, the former Governor-General of Kham based in Chamdo, the first town the Chinese captured during their invasion of Tibet in 1950. While in Chinese hands, he reported

to the Dalai Lama on his experiences and predicament, and suggested that he lead the Tibetan delegation at the forthcoming negotiation with the Chinese. The Dalai Lama accepted this suggestion. See also Chapter Four.

17. Chris Patten, *East and West*, Macmillan, 1998, p. 17. See also Chapter Twelve below for examples.

18. Simon Leys, *The Analects of Confucius*, W. W. Norton and Company, 1997, pp. xxi.

19. Elias Canetti, *The Conscience of Words*, Seabury Press, 1979, quoted in Simon Leys, *Analects*, p. xxi.

20. He lived in Lu, a small state at the base of the Shandong Peninsula neighbouring the much larger state of Qin, long before the First Emperor captured it. The great masters of China generally wrote down their ideas at times of intense turmoil, presumably in case they were killed and thus to preserve their teachings. This applied to Lao-tzu, Sun Tzu and Confucius.

21. Jonathan Spence, *The Search for Modern China*, p. 239.

Chapter Two

1. Much of the early part of this chapter is based on Philip Short's *Mao: A Life*, Hodder and Stoughton, 1999, along with Jonathan Spence's *The Search for Modern China* (W. W. Norton and Co.), second edn, 1990, and John King Fairbank and Merle Goldman's *China: A New History*, The Belknap Press of Harvard University Press, 1998, and other texts. I was mindful of Spence's warning that things historians believed they knew about China can be revised in quite a short space of time on account of new research and discoveries. Short includes much new material in his book about Mao that had not been previously published.

2. For details see Spence, p. 280, and Fairbank and Goldman, pp. 251–2.

3. China had supplied over 100,000 labourers to work with the Allies in Western Europe. See Spence, p. 267.

4. The whole episode is described with great clarity by Margaret Macmillan in *Peacemakers: Six Months that Changed the World*, John Murray, 2003 edn, pp. 331–53.

5. Short, p. 107.

6. Short, p. 109.

7. Short, pp. 111–2.

8. Russell had travelled extensively in China during 1920–1, and had visited Changsha in Hunan province. It is most likely that Mao had heard him speak, as the British philosopher attracted large audiences. See Spence, p. 305.

9. Short, p. 124.

10. Snow, *Red Star Over China*, p.47. Chiang Kai-shek's relationships with the Green Gang are also described in Spence, p. 350.

11. Short, p. 154.

12. Ibid., p. 171.

13. Ibid., p. 173.

14. Ibid., p. 212.

15. Spence, pp. 394–6.

16. See Thubron's *Behind the Wall*, 1987, p. 277.

17. Griffith, pp. 50–4.

18. Spence puts the casualties at much lower figures (see Spence, p. 423). Whatever the figures, the slaughter was horrific.

19. See Edwin Wickert, ed., *The Good German of Nanking: The Diaries of John Rabe*, Abacus, 1998, pp. 190, 204. It was the opinion of Chancellor Scharffenberg of the

German embassy at the time that the terrible treatment of the Chinese was revenge for the 'gruesome murder' of Japanese women and children at Tungchou. (See Wickert, p. 247.)

20. This was an ancient Chinese proverb; see Adeline Yen Mah, *A Thousand Pieces of Gold*, HarperCollins, 2002, p. xix. See also Pang-Mei Natasha Chang, *Bound Feet and Western Dress*, Bantam Books, 1997, p. 202.

21. The United Front agreement is described by Fairbank and Goldman, p. 316, the earlier one on p. 311.

22. Simon Sebag Montefiore, *Stalin: The Court of the Red Tsar*, Weidenfeld and Nicolson, 2003, p. 523.

23. Ibid., p. 536.

24. Short (p. 413) puts the figure of US support at US$ 300 billion, but Spence (p. 444) gives the sum of US$ 1 billion in lend-lease supplies (which need not have been paid for if they were used in the common cause against the enemy [Japan]) in addition to cash credits of US$ 500 million – a total of around US$ 1.5 billion. This is perhaps the more likely figure.

25. Short, p. 409.

26. Chancellor of Oxford University Chris Patten, as Governor of Hong Kong (1992–7) studied the book and its commentaries and, to his fury and frustration, experienced several examples of Sun Tzu-based Chinese negotiating tactics (see Chapter Twelve). Hu Yao-Su and Pierre Berthon, in an article on Sun Tzu in the *International Encyclopedia of Business and Management*, give a good account of comparisons between Sun Tzu and Clausewitz, which are reflected in different schools of thought on both the conduct of war and the nature of strategic management.

27. David Stafford, *Roosevelt and Churchill: Men of Secrets*, Abacus, 2000, p. 257.

28. She died in New York at the age of 106 on 23 October 2003. See her obituary and accompanying article in *The Independent*, 25 October 2003.

Chapter Three

1. On this early history see Michael C. van Walt van Praag, *The Status of Tibet: History, Rights, and Prospects in International Law*, Westview Press, 1987, pp. 1–2, and useful footnotes; Hugh E. Richardson, *Tibet and its History*, Shambhala, 1984, Chapter Two; Tsepon W. D. Shakabpa, *Tibet: A Political History*, Potala Publications, 1984; Professor Dawa Norbu, *China's Tibet Policy*, Curzon Press, 2001 and *Tibet and Her Neighbours: A History*, Alex McKay, ed., Hansjorg Mayer, London, 2003.

2. Evidently it stood 2 metres high. The Jokhang, the cathedral in the centre of Lhasa and the holiest temple in Tibetan Buddhism, was built in 652 AD to commemorate the princess's arrival in Tibet and to house the Akshobhya Buddha, which she brought.

3. On the pretext of the marriage of the Han princess to a foreign king, the Han court would send gifts to Tibet which, by ancient precedent, would have to be reciprocated. The return gifts from the Tibetans were perceived and recorded by the Han chroniclers as 'tribute' from a subordinate people. See Norbu, p. 24.

4. Traditionally, tea and silk in China had the status of currency.

5. This was the equivalent of what many Westerners might call 'cousins' to denote close friendship.

6. See China's *White Paper on Tibet*, 'Tibet – its Ownership and Human Rights Situation', Information Office of the State Council, Beijing, 22 September 1992, p. 1. See the complete text in Appendix 1 in van Walt van Praag, pp. 287–8.

7. Bonpos resemble, in their religious practices, the Tibetan Red Caps (there are also White Cap and Black Cap Bons); see Alexandra David-Neel, *My Journey to Lhasa*, p. 250. Some Bon practices were carried over into Buddhism. Burning juniper leaves and sandalwood for incense and offering barley grains and *tsampa* were also common in Bon as in Buddhism. Weddings had no religious or legal aspects, except in divorce, but animistic rites of the Bon era would be practised on the rooftops for good luck even into the twentieth century. Bon continues today, now in small groups in India and elsewhere (including the UK), having decamped from eastern Tibet when the Chinese invaded in 1950.

8. Chun-fang Yu, *The Renewal of Buddhism in China*, Columbia University Press, 1981, p. 3. There were several schools of Buddhism in China at this time, although after their persecution in 845 AD only the Ch'an and 'Pure Land' sects survived and flourished.

9. A vast hoard of over 400 beautiful Buddhist stone carvings, many of them in their original colours and dating mainly from the sixth century AD, were discovered in 1996 at the site of the Longxing Temple near Qingzhou in Shangdong province. Many others had been found at nearby sites. They illustrate the reverence in which Buddhism was held at that time in China. Thirty-three of them were exhibited at the Royal Academy, London, in June–July 2002. See *The Return of the Buddha*, Royal Academy of Arts, London, 2002, published for the exhibition. The Leshan Buddha, standing 233 feet high and carved into a cliff in Western Sichuan, dates from about the year 720 AD. It was restored in July 2002.

10. The Sakya sect is one of four principal sects: Nyingmapa is the oldest, Sakyapa is the second oldest and Kargyudpa and Gelugpa, from which the Dalai Lamas originated, follow. Sakya is a village with 100 or so monasteries grouped partly on and around a high mountain called Taktsenma, from which the Sakya River flows.

11. In truth the Sakya Pandita did not have authority over all Tibetans any more than Godan Khan ruled all of the Mongol empire, but it established an important relationship between the priests of Tibet and the Mongol rulers.

12. In January 1987 the Chinese government published a work of considerable scholarship and beauty on the twenty-five remaining early fifteenth-century *thangkas* (traditional cloth scroll paintings) about Phags'pa and the events of the time (originally there were thirty, but the other five have been lost). It is clear that Phags'pa was also a wise and subtle diplomat, and that his advice to the Emperor went far beyond spiritual matters. The propaganda value of this fine book, sponsored by 'The Research Institute of Literature and Art of China's Minority Nationalities Under the Central Academy of Minority Nationalities', lies in that the reader is led to accept that, because of this close relationship between the Tibetan *lama* and the Mongolian Emperor Kublai Khan, Tibet became (or was already) a minority nationality of China. In fact, after the fall of the (Mongolian) Yuan dynasty, the relationship between the Tibetan *lamas* and the *khans* in Mongolia continued, although outside China. The book referred to is titled *Thangka, Buddhist Painting of Tibet: Biographical Paintings of 'Phags-pa*, New World Press, Beijing, People's Publishing House of Tibet, January 1987.

13. Richardson, p. 41. Mary Craig, in *Kundun: A Biography of the Family of the Dalai Lama*, HarperCollins, 1997, gives the date as 1517. This is hardly likely, as Sonam Gyatso was born in 1534.

14. *Dalai* is a Mongolian word meaning 'ocean' and *lama* is a Tibetan term corresponding to the Hindi *guru*. The Dalai Lama himself says that to translate his title as 'Ocean of Wisdom' is a misunderstanding. Originally *Dalai* was a partial translation of the

name of Sonam Gyatso, the Third Dalai Lama and the person upon whom the title was conferred. A further misunderstanding is due to the Chinese rendering of the word *lama* which has the connotation of 'living Buddha'. The Dalai Lama has said this interpretation is mistaken. Tibetans and other Buddhists believe that only certain beings, of whom the Dalai Lama is considered one, can choose the manner of their rebirth. Such people are called *tulkus* ('incarnations'). See Tenzin Gyatso, *Freedom in Exile: The Autobiography of the Dalai Lama of Tibet*, Hodder and Stoughton, 1990, pp. 1–2.

15. Dudjom Rinpoche, quoted in Sogyal Rinpoche, *The Tibetan Book of Living and Dying*, Rider, first edn, 1992, p. 349.

16. Buddhists believe that the 'soul' is ephemeral, an illusion, and therefore has no real existence. Carl Jung uses the word poetically as meaning the 'psyche' and the 'collective unconscious'. See Dr C. G. Jung ,'Psychological Commentary', in *The Tibetan Book of the Dead*, Oxford University Press, 1960, p. xxxv. Jung also writes about the difficulty of translating Tibetan concepts into those which would be understood by the West. He relates *The Tibetan Book of the Dead* to *The Egyptian Book of the Dead*, with which there are many parallels.

17. Diki Tsering, the Dalai Lama's mother, describes many such personal experiences, especially of what we would call poltergeists. See Diki Tsering, *Dalai Lama, My Son: A Mother's Story*, edited and introduced by Khadroob Thondup (her grandson), Viking/Arkana, 2000.

18. Quoted in Sogyal Rinpoche, p. 305.

19. Ibid., p. 22.

20. This section is based on research from the Dalai Lama's autobiography and from Diki Tsering's book, as well as from Gilles van Grasdorf's *Hostage of Beijing: The Abduction of the Panchen Lama*, Element, 1999, pp. 49–54.

21. Rider, first edn 1992, second edn revised and updated, 2002.

22. This section is based on the writings of several Tibetan authors who have described everyday life in old Tibet – lamas, ordinary monks, aristocrats, lay people – and my own discussions with many Tibetans over the past fourteen years. Tibetan authors include His Holiness the Dalai Lama in some of his fifty-six published books, speeches and interviews; Palden Gyatso (*Fire Under the Snow*); Namgyal Lhamo Taklha (*Born in Lhasa*); Jetsun Pema (*Tibet: My Story*); Diki Tsering (*Dalai Lama, My Son: A Mother's Story*); Dawa Norbu (*Tibet: The Way Ahead*). There are also many other sources written by non-Tibetans, especially Hugh Richardson (*Tibet and its History*); Heinrich Harrer (*Seven Years in Tibet*); Robert Ford (*Captured in Tibet*); Alexandra David-Neel (*My Journey to Lhasa, Magic and Mystery in Tibet, Initiations and Initiates in Tibet*); Catriona Bass (*Inside the Treasure House* and *Education in Tibet*); and Mary Craig (*Tears of Blood: A Cry for Tibet*).

23. Tsering, p. 29.

24. For example, by the seventeenth century, the time of the Fifth Dalai Lama, Drepung Monastery west of Lhasa had 10,000 monks, 185 manorial estates with about 25,000 serfs and 16,000 herdsmen for its 300 pastures. It could levy its own taxes.

25. The matters described in this section became much more comprehensible to me after reading Dr Deepak Chopra's *Quantum Healing: Exploring the Frontiers of Mind/Body Medicine*, Bantam Books, 1989. Chopra is a much-respected endocrinologist and spiritual philosopher, and is the executive director of the Sharp HealthCare Institute for Human Potential and Mind/Body Medicine in San Diego, California. In this book

he writes that every cell in the body is a 'little sentient being' (p. 146) and that every molecule in the body has its own intelligence, that the mind and the body are as one – what he calls 'bodymind'.

26. Prof. Paul Ekman of the University of California, San Francisco, has studied the effects of meditation on the mind, and so has Prof. Richard Davidson at the University of Wisconsin, Madison. During meditation the latter showed a dramatic increase in activity of the left prefrontal cortex, a region of the brain associated with a sense of well-being and happiness. EEG (electro-encephalogram) readings confirm the changes due to meditation. Experiments are continuing. See *The Financial Times*, 13 February 2004.

27. Gyatso, p. 233.

28. Tsering, pp. 123–5, describes what happens during this event. I am also indebted to Karma Lundrup, a Tibetan shaman, for the following description of Tibetan oracular ritual.

    The Oracle, a medium, enters a trance and calls forth the Seventh Bumi, a higher being who then begins to speak. The Oracle has said that if one trusts him only halfway, one will receive only half the truth of the result under enquiry; obtaining the result also very much depends on the sincerity and integrity of the person asking the question. Obtaining the best answers will also depend upon current astrological disposition. While the Dalai Lama can order the State Oracle to answer his questions, ordinary people must ask the Oracle if he will advise them. On all really important matters the Dalai Lama may make a final decision in front of a gold-plated, very simple sandalwood standing Buddha, the most holy statue outside of Tibet.

29. Using the *I Ching* requires one to throw three coins six times or to select six times from forty-nine specially prepared yarrow sticks in a quite complex procedure (the exact procedures are given in the 1951 English translation of the *I Ching* by Richard Wilhelm and Cary F. Baynes, Routledge and Kegan Paul, third edn, pp. 721–4). One does this in a quiet place while meditating on the question asked, and throws the coins or selects the yarrow sticks when it is instinctively felt that the time is right to do so. A hexagram is constructed from the six results obtained, which correspond to six of the sixty-four situational interpretations in the *I Ching* itself. Jung, who studied the *I Ching* for over thirty years, coined the word 'synchronicity' to describe the element of guided chance according to which the words in the book form a response to the question asked. Mao Zedong used the *I Ching* in drawing up his plan of operation for the encirclement of the Nationalist forces in Tianjin and perhaps Peking, in September 1945, according to a private source in China.

30. See 'Tibetan Medicine: An Holistic Approach', *Men-Tsee-Khang Newsletter*, Autumn 2001, and Tom Dummer, *Tibetan Medicine and Other Holistic Health Care Systems*, Routledge, 1988. The literature on the subject is vast.

31. Glenn H. Mullin, 'A Long Look Homeward: An Interview with the Dalai Lama', available from the Tibetan Cultural Centre, Snow Lion Publications and Potala Publications, 1987, p. 27.

32. The decrees related to the duties and powers of officials and the rights of individuals (for example, to follow the beliefs of their own religious sects); the conduct of investigations of those accused of criminal offences (they were directed at discovering the truth); making arrests; listing the seriousness or otherwise of crimes; the fines to be imposed, usually in the form of religious penances (such as three days of prostrations before holy images, or providing 1,000 butter lamps); the powers of tax collectors and the

methods to prevent exploitation; indemnities for murder dependent upon the status of the person killed; compensation to be paid to an injured person by those who caused the injury; ways of settling unresolved cases (e.g. playing dice, picking out black and white pebbles from a bottle of water or boiled oil; oaths were permitted if the person had integrity); the fines imposed on thieves and robbers; divorce; adultery (sexual intercourse on one or two occasions might be condoned; for more than sixty occasions a fine of 60 *khels* could be imposed on the adulterer); and the final clause deals with ordinary human relations (the borrower of an animal was held to be responsible if the animal was lost or killed).

33. van Grasdorf, p. 128. This is the egalitarianism favoured so strongly by Mao Zedong.

Chapter Four

1. In May 1950 a small Communist force of about fifty soldiers entered Amdo and were preparing to enter eastern Kham. They were said to be seeking out Nationalists rather than invading Tibet, although they might have been testing the strength and readiness of Tibetan defences. In any event, they were repulsed. At the same time as the main invasion from the east in October 1950, a small Chinese force from Khotan in Xinjiang entered north-west Tibet. It was not significant in the events that followed. A detailed description of events around Chamdo during the attack and the capture of Ngabo in October can be found in Robert Ford's *Captured in Tibet*, George G. Harrap and Co. Ltd, 1957.

2. Tsering Shakya says that, in all, there were 2,500 men in the Tibetan army in eastern Tibet (see *The Dragon in the Land of Snows*, Pimlico, 1999, p. 14), but the force around Chamdo contained about 700 men according to Ford.

3. Ibid., pp.18–9.

4. Tibetans say he was sixteen.

5. Dawa Norbu, *Tibet: The Road Ahead*, Rider, 1997, p. 63.

6. Ibid., pp. xiii–xiv.

7. Quoted in Snow, p. 444.

8. Quoted in Shakya, p. 3.

9. Ibid., p. 24.

10. Ibid., p. 36. See also *Leaders in Tibet*, TIN, 1997, p. 159.

11. Taiwan and Korea were much more important than Tibet. In Philip Short's 782-page biography *Mao: A Life*, Tibet receives only four brief passing references and no mention of Mao's thoughts on the subject in an otherwise very thorough book.

12. Quoted in Shakya, p. 67.

13. Ibid., p. 90.

14. Ngabo Ngawang Jigme, *A Great Turn in Tibetan History*, New Star Publications, Beijing, 1991; *On Tibetan Issues*, New Star Publications, Beijing, 1991.

15. Richardson, p. 187. See also Shakya Tsering's historical introduction to TIN's *Leaders in Tibet*, pp. 7–8.

16. van Grasdorf, p. 126.

17. China's *White Paper on Tibet*, special supplement, Information Office of the State Council, 24 September 1992, p. C1/10.

18. Gyatso, pp. 123–31.

19. Quoted in *China's Current Policy on Tibet*, Department of Information and International Relations, Dharamsala, 29 September 2000, p. 38.

20. See *A Poisoned Arrow: The Secret Report of the 10th Panchen Lama*, TIN, 1997. Subsequent quotations are from this report.

21. Ibid.
22. Ibid. For cadres to report the truth – that their policies had failed – would get them into trouble. Mao may have been told that Tibet was enjoying unparalleled prosperity and happiness as a result of his policies, and to have even glanced at the Panchen Lama's report could have convinced him that the Panchen Lama was lying.

Chapter Five

1. Thomas Cleary's translation in *The Essential Tao*, Castle Books, 1992, is: 'Heaven and earth are not humane; they regard all beings as straw dogs. Sages are not humane; they see all people as straw dogs.' In his *Lao-Tzu: 'My Words Are Easy to Understand': Lectures on the Tao Teh Ching*, North Atlantic Books ,1981, p. 34, Cheng Man-jan explains that in ancient times straw dogs were used as ritual sacrifices in place of real animals: 'Once they had fulfilled their function they were cast aside, thus giving rise to the observation in the text that no feelings of humanism are involved ... the sage treats people just as heaven and earth treat the myriad things: as if they were straw dogs.'
2. The Manchus did not like railways. The first track in China was laid in 1875 by Jardine, Matheson and was ceremonially torn up by outraged officials, who supervised its demolition from the comfort of their sedan chairs. Later, local governors-general raised foreign money and developed their own railways in different parts of China. Their attempted nationalisation by the Manchus contributed to that dynasty's downfall.
3. Gu Yang, *Foreign Direct Investment and Technology Transfer in China 1979–94*, PhD thesis, University of Manchester, 1997, p. 181.
4. Roy Jenkins, *Churchill*, Macmillan, 2001, p. 835. The US was also keen to use atomic weapons at the end of the Korean War if the North Koreans or the Chinese did not adhere strictly to the ceasefire line. Dwight D. Eisenhower was President, and he was meeting Winston Churchill (back as Prime Minister) and then-Foreign Secretary Anthony Eden at a summit in Bermuda. The British pair were horrified at Eisenhower's statement to this effect (p. 873).
5. Mao thus violated a basic principle of Sun Tzu's, that an absentee civilian leadership that interferes ignorantly with field command 'takes away victory by deranging the military'. Cleary, *The Art of War*, p. 20.
6. Jung Chang, *Wild Swans*, Flamingo, 1993, pp. 242–3.
7. Short, pp. 436–7.
8. For the reasons see Elena Veduta, *Revitalizing Socialist Enterprise*, ed. John Heath, Routledge, 1993, Chapter Two.
9. Fairbank and Goldman, p. 353.
10. Short, p. 447.
11. Ibid., p. 449.
12. Remarkably, it was to be revived again in President Jiang Zemin's speech of 1st July 2001 (see Chapter Eight).
13. Li Zhisui, *The Private Life of Chairman Mao*, Arrow, 1996, p. 201.
14. Short, p. 479.
15. Li., p. 4–5.
16. Li, pp. 234–5.
17. The full 'cost' of such steel included an enormous number of accidents. As a result, China became a leader in the successful treatment of severe burns and complex limb reconstruction. See Frances Wood Hand, *Grenade Practice in Peking: My Part in the Cultural Revolution*, John Murray, 2000, p. 13.
18. Andrew J. Nathan in Li, p. xi.

19. Simon Leys, *The Chairman's New Clothes: Mao and the Cultural Revolution*, Allison and Busby, 1977, p. 18.

20. Gu, p. 182.

21. Becker, p. 352.

22. Short, p. 533.

23. Leys, p. 30.

24. Fairbank and Goldman, p. 391.

25. The name was invented by an unknown student at the Qinghua University Middle School, Beijing, where the Cultural Revolution began.

26. One of the most moving, eloquent, intelligent and perceptive testimonies is by Nien Cheng, *Life and Death in Shanghai*, Flamingo, 1995 (first published by Grafton in 1986). Zhang Chunqiao, in charge of Shanghai at the time of Cheng's ordeal, later became a member of the Politburo and one of the so-called 'Gang of Four'. See also the remarkable testament of Ting-xing Ye, *A Leaf in the Bitter Wind*, Bantam Books, 2000. She also writes with eloquence, passion and direct experience about Shanghai during the Cultural Revolution, but from the perspective of a fourteen-year-old girl; finally, Jung Chang in *Wild Swans* writes about the tragedies of her strongly pro-Communist but bitterly disillusioned parents (pp. 374–408).

27. Nicholas D. Kristof and Sheryl Wudunn, *China Wakes*, Nicholas Brealey Publishing, 1995, pp. 73–5. These reports are based on secret, detailed official records kept by local authorities at the time, obtained by Kristof in the 1980s.

28. Li, p. 8.

29. Ibid., p. 114.

30. Short, p. 551.

31. Ibid., p. 594.

32. Henry Kissinger, *The White House Years*, Boston, 1979, pp. 1058–9.

33. He was, of course, hardly the only great leader to have such a predilection for young women and to use his lofty position to secure his gratification; one can think of many names.

34. Li, pp. 4–5.

35. This according to Simon Leys (which, of course, was an alias Pierre Ryckmans, the distinguished specialist on Chinese art and literature), p. 243. Jiang allegedly committed suicide in prison in 1991 (Joe Studwell, *The China Dream: The Elusive Quest for the Greatest Untapped Market on Earth*, Profile Books, 2002, p. xvi).

36. She had an aversion to noise, light, cold and heat, and she was a compulsive quarreller (Andrew J. Nathan in Li, p. xii). She had a great many imaginary illnesses and insisted upon taking 'cures'. However, once she had a real job helping Mao plan the Cultural Revolution, all these symptoms disappeared.

Chapter Six

1. See *His Holiness the 14th Dalai Lama of Tibet*, Committee for the Sixtieth Enthronement Anniversary Celebration and the Fiftieth Anniversary of His Holiness the Fourteenth Dalai Lama Assuming State Responsibility, December 2000. The 1963 constitution can be found in the *Constitution of Tibet*, Bureau of His Holiness the Dalai Lama, New Delhi, 10 March 1963.

2. See Mullin, p. 25.

3. For these and the following details see *Tibetan Refugee Community: Integrated Development Plan – II, 1995–2000*, Planning Council, Central Tibetan Administration of His Holiness the Dalai Lama, May 1994.

4. See *PADME Project Summary*, *PADME Loan Guidelines for Unemployed Youths* and *PADME Training Programme Status*, May 1999 (internal documents).

5. Jetsun Pema, *Tibet: My Story*, Element, 1987, pp. 141–63.

6. My daughter Claire Heath, an experienced homoeopath, helped me considerably in identifying the effects of trauma and in supplying me with five different possible homoeopathic remedies, depending on the symptoms. See also Peter Chappell, *Emotional Healing with Homoeopathy*, Element, 1994, especially Chapters One and Two.

7. An example from my case notes: one man had difficulty sleeping, with frequent nightmares, acute headaches and flashbacks to his experiences of torture; his hands frequently trembled, so that he could not write or draw; he experienced frequent hot flushes, especially in his head; his stomach pains were sometimes crippling; he had loss of appetite, sudden and unexplained outbursts of anger, was generally lacking in energy and felt subdued.

8. The Tibet Relief Fund in London, of which at the time I was a trustee, kindly provided the framework for this project, and funding came from the Miriam Dean Fund.

9. As a result of the report on the first year of operation, the Miriam Dean Fund felt that the 'goal post had been moved' to include all Tibetans who arrived in exile requiring treatment as a result of their experiences in Tibet. The Fund wanted to maintain the centre for survivors of torture only. Dr Beate was not prepared to turn away those Tibetans who asked for her help but who had not been physically tortured. In spite of strong support for her continuation from Tibetan *lamas*, especially those whom she had successfully treated, the Department of Health of the government-in-exile became less supportive than they had been earlier.

10. See *The Question of Tibet and the Rule of Law*, International Commission of Jurists, p. 71. The ICJ is a non-governmental organisation founded in 1952 and based in Geneva, whose task is to 'defend the Rule of Law throughout the world and to work towards the full observance of the provisions in the Universal Declaration of Human Rights'.

11. Pema, pp. 141–63.

12. Hu Yaobang's six main recommendations were:

    Tibet must be given full rights to exercise regional autonomy;

    There would be a period of recuperation during the first three years in which people in Tibet would be exempt from paying taxes and meeting state purchase quotas;

    A flexible economic policy suited to Tibet's special conditions should be adopted;

    A greater part of the state subsidy should be used for the development of agriculture and animal husbandry;

    Tibetan culture, language and education should be developed following socialist orientation;

    The Party's policy on minority cadres should be implemented and should promote unity between Chinese and Tibetan cadres.

13. Shakya, p. 411.

14. There is some further explanation in the Dalai Lama's 1990 autobiography; see Gyatso, pp. 274–9.

15. News compilation, TIN, 22 October 1992.

16. Shakya, p. 375.

17. From the Chinese embassy press release, New Delhi, 28 September 1988, quoted in Shakya, p. 426.

18. Gyatso, pp. 247–8.

19. Ibid., p. 285.

20. This is a global campaign based in the US, established in March 2000 for direct economic action to achieve independence for Tibet. Its three goals are:

The restoration of Tibetan independence;

The return of the Dalai Lama to Tibet as 'the sovereign head of state of a free and democratic nation';

The establishment of a 'genuinely liberal and democratic Tibetan nation, based on the rule of law and humanist principles common to Buddhism and the enlightened philosophies of the world, first proclaimed by the Dalai Lama in his draft constitution of 1963'.

Source: Jamyang Norbu Jamyang Norbu, *Rangzen Charter: The Case for Tibetan Independence*, published privately, third revised edn, September 2000.

21. Ibid.

22. Mao Zedong, in an interview with Edgar Snow at Pao An, July 1936 (see Snow, p. 387).

23. Quoted in *Cutting Off the Serpent's Head*, p. vii.

24. Quoted in *China's Current Policy on Tibet*, Department of Information and International Relations, Dharamsala, 29 September 2000, p. 9.

25. TIN news review: *Reports from Tibet*, 2001, pp. 14–6.

26. The Black Hat itself was presented to the Fifth Karmapa by Emperor Yung-lo of China in the fifteenth century, and still exists today. The First Karmapa, Dusum Khyena, lived from 1110 to 1193 AD. The Kagyu lineage has a purely oral transmission of teaching and learning, unbroken for 890 years. (See Nik Douglas and Meryl White, *Karmapa, the Black Hat Lama of Tibet*, Luzac, London, 1976.)

There were two high *lamas* who had been taught personally by the Sixteenth Karmapa, and three others whom the Seventeenth Karmapa also regarded as his teachers – including the present Dalai Lama. They all escaped to India; the Seventeenth Karmapa applied for seven years to leave Tibet to receive his teachings, and had asked that, alternatively, the two high *lamas* should be permitted to visit him in Tibet. But the Chinese refused these requests. They had been attempting to indoctrinate him with socialist policies, and saw him as a possible leader, authenticated by the Dalai Lama, whom Tibetans could respect. He was enthroned by the Chinese government in September 1992, and became their official representative amongst the Tibetan people. The Chinese were not going to let him slip from their grasp, and clearly did not want him to have the correct and traditional Buddhist teachings. So, to receive the necessary transmissions indirectly from the Sixteenth Karmapa and from the other *lamas* (thus maintaining the centuries-old tradition), he took matters into his own hands and escaped.

However, in December 2003 a member of the Karma Kagyu school of Buddhism, Lama S. N. Singh, claimed in a legal suit before the High Court in New Delhi that only the Kagyu sect had the right to appoint the Karmapas, not the Dalai Lama (who is from the Gelugpa sect), as in the case of the Seventeenth Karmapa. Clearly, there are high politics involved here as well as religious affairs.

27. 'Kasur' means he was a former minister.

Chapter Seven

1. Merle Goldman, *Sowing the Seeds of Democracy*, Harvard University Press, 1994, p. 48.

2. Studwell, p. 30. Joe Studwell is the editor of *China Economic Quarterly*. He lived and worked as a freelance journalist in Hong Kong and Beijing from 1991 to 2000.

3. The backwardness of Chinese technology and the problem of overmanning were soon exposed. The Japanese-built plant at Baoshan used 0.8 tons of coal per ton of steel; a Chinese plant of similar scale at that time used 15 tons. The Japanese sintering plant employed fifty people; a similar-capacity Chinese sintering plant employed 5,000. During Phase One (1978–85), most of the plant was made in Japan, and the Japanese managed the production and delivery of Chinese-built equipment. All of it was delivered on time and to the required quality. In Phase Two (1985–92), the Chinese produced and delivered a high proportion of the component equipment themselves – but 90 percent of suppliers delivered late, and many products were of sub-standard quality.

   By 1992 the Baoshan plant employed 31,000 people, whereas a Chinese plant of similar capacity employed 400,000. Japanese management systems were unknown to the Chinese and included time management of maintenance and delivery, lean production, total quality control, teamwork and zone leader accountability (the next 'zone leader' in the production process is the *client*). Baoshan also set up its own research and development (R&D) department, whereas in China, as in the Soviet Union, R&D was conducted in separate institutes and was not closely related to industrial needs. All this was vastly expensive to the Chinese, especially as the Japanese kept loading surcharges on to the agreed costs, and many of the materials transferred by the Japanese could have been bought at a fraction of the cost in the open market. This was China's first major experience of negotiating such a contract, and the learning process was costly, but the whole project was of enormous benefit to China. The above information comes from Gu Yang's PhD thesis, *Foreign Direct Investment and Technology Transfer in China 1979–94*, University of Manchester, 10 February 1997 (cited earlier). The special study of the Baoshan steel project is to be found on pp. 503–41 in vol. 2, and was based on many interviews with the management. (I was the external examiner for this thesis, and am very grateful to Dr Gu for being able to draw upon her research.)

4. It still is the policy in the Democratic People's Republic of Korea (aka North Korea), where it is known as *juche*.

5. In 1980 Joseph E. Stiglitz, who became the chairman of the Council of Economic Advisors under US President Bill Clinton, and who was then the chief economist and senior vice-president of the World Bank, visited China to speak with the leadership. He strongly advised a gradualist policy in the transition from their planned economy towards a more market economy, which Deng Xiaoping adopted, as opposed to a 'big bang' approach being advocated by many other development economists at the time. See Stiglitz, pp. xx–xi.

6. Fox Butterfield, *China: Alive in the Bitter Sea*, Coronet Books, Hodder and Stoughton, 1982, p. 412.

7. In 1984 there followed thirteen Economic and Technical Zones in 'Open Coastal Cities' – all former Treaty Ports; the following year the three 'Delta Regions' (Yangtse River Delta, Pearl River Delta and Amoy Delta) were established on a similar basis to the SEZs. Links were set up between these special areas and related developments inland.

8. Nevertheless, even deducting 2–3 percent, these statistics are of doubtful quality. For example, instead of China's economy growing at around 7–8 percent as the figures show for 1998–9, Thomas Rawski, an American specialist in these matters, reckons

that China's economy may have shrunk: -2.2 percent in 1998 and -2.5 percent in 1999. There are no definitive figures.

9. Quoted in Gu, p. 183.

10. Quoted in Colin Mackerras et al, *The Beijing Tragedy: Implications for China and Australia*, Griffith University, Centre for the Study of Australia–Asia Relations, 1989, p. 3.

11. Ye, p. 285.

12. Butterfield, p. 402.

13. See Goldman for the full story on Hu Yaobang.

14. Much of what happened during the period leading up to 4 June 1989 and its aftermath is a matter of public record. This section, however, draws heavily on *The Tiananmen Papers*, compiled by Zhang Liang (no doubt a pseudonym), Andrew J. Nathan and Perry Link, eds, Little, Brown and Company, 2001. The book reveals in remarkable detail how the Chinese leadership saw matters, what they decided to do and how. The question of veracity is discussed at length by Orville Schell on pp. 459–74. The key questions – who really was behind the release of these documents and for what purpose – have not been answered.

15. Zhang, p. 74.

16. Ibid., p. 11.

17. Ibid., p. 107.

18. Becker, p. 354.

19. Zhang, p. 199.

20. Ibid., p. 217.

21. Ibid., pp. 268–72.

22. Ibid., p. 358.

23. Kristof and Wudunn, pp. 87–9. See also Kate Adie, *The Kindness of Strangers*, Headline, 2002, especially Chapter Fourteen.

24. Zhang, p. 425.

25. Nathan, in Zhang, p. xxiii.

26. Patten, p. 17. Nicholas Kristof remarks that 'there is something about Li [Peng], a combination of arrogance and hard-line political principles, which grates on many Chinese'. He believes that 'he got where he is only because of support from his foster parents, Zhou Enlai and Deng Yingchao ['Sister Deng']'. See Kristof and Wudunn, p. 129.

Chapter Eight

1. For more details of his life see Bruce Gilley, *Tiger on the Brink: Jiang Zemin and China's New Elite*, University of California, 1998.

2. The plant also produced Audi cars in a joint venture with Volkswagen. When I saw the engine plant on site built by General Motors (GM), it was idle and covered in dust. For more details on GM's problems and disasters in China see Studwell, pp. 142–4.

3. Gilley, p. 178.

4. Quoted in Becker, p. 255.

5. This administrative structure is, however, still far from realising Mahatma Gandhi's vision of India as a patchwork of largely self-governing rural communities.

6. Oceana Publications, Dobbs Ferry, New York, 1975.

7. See, for example, Elazar's *Federal Systems of the World: A Handbook of Federal, Confederal and Autonomy Arrangements*, Longman, 1994, and *Governing Peoples and Territories,*

Institute for the Study of Human Issues, Philadelphia and the Jerusalem Institute for Federal Studies, Jerusalem, 1982, and Hannum's *Autonomy, Sovereignty and Self-Determination: The Accommodation of Conflicting Rights*, University of Pennsylvania Press, revised edn, 1996.

8. See article by Charles A. Radin in *The Boston Globe*, 10 June 2000, (www.tibetnews.com). At the earlier meeting in London in September 1992, which I attended, a slightly different version was put forward which aroused some controversy. See Yan Jiaqi, 'A Future Federal System for China' in *In Quest of a Better China*, The Forum Team of the Alliance for a Better China, Global Publishing Co. Inc., 1993, pp. 79–85.

9. In China the internet is closely controlled by the state, allegedly employing some 100,000 cyber-police. See the 'Executive Summary', in TCHRD's 2002 *Annual Report*, p. 2; Nina Hachigian, 'China's Cyber Strategy', *Foreign Affairs*, March/April 2001; and 'Harvard student finds China blocks hundreds of websites', AFP/New York, 6 September 2002, www.tibetnews.com.

10. Liu Hong, *Startling Moon*, Headline Review, 2001, pp. 3–4.

11. See Tyrene White, 'Village Elections: Democracy from the Bottom Up?', in *China: Adapting the Past, Confronting the Future*, Bruce Dickson, political ed., Center for Chinese Studies, University of Michigan, 2002, pp. 181–9.

12. See Noam Chomsky, *Hegemony or Survival: America's Quest for Global Dominance*, Hamish Hamilton, 2003, p. 138.

13. Becker, p. 362.

14. 'China, "Striking Harder" than ever before', Amnesty International report, 6 July 2001.

15. See Harry Wu and Carolyn Wakeman, *Bitter Winds: A Memoir of my Years in China's Gulag*, John Wiley and Sons, 1994.

16. See, for instance, *The Independent*, 1 December 2000.

17. *The Times*, 2 February 2002.

18. The head of News Corporation's Asian operations is Rupert Murdoch's son, James. He has been outspoken in attacking opponents of the Chinese government, allegedly saying that the democracy movement in Hong Kong should learn to get used to the absolutist rule of Beijing and should not try to destabilise the government. See *The Independent*, 1 April 2001.

19. Studwell, p. 253.

20. See Foreign Affairs Committee of the House of Commons, Session 1993–4, 'Relations between the United Kingdom and China in the period up to and beyond 1997', 23 March 1994, vol. II, paragraph 475.

21. The National People's Congress (NPC) is the legislature and supreme organ of state power in China. It has a Standing Committee of 200 members which drafts laws and treaties. From March 1988 it was chaired by Li Peng, and in March 2003 Wu Bangguo took over. Wu is an electronic engineer and spent most of his life running State-Owned Enterprises (SOEs). He has also been a strong supporter of Jiang Zemin. The NPC has nearly 3,000 members, indirectly elected by lower-level People's Congresses. Essentially, it rubber-stamps decisions made by the Communist Party, but recently its members have become bolder in their questioning. It meets for two to three weeks once a year. The State Council is the highest organ of state administration. Its chairman was Premier Zhu Rongji, and is now Premier Wen Jiabao. It has an Executive Board of some fifteen members. Below the State Council are the ministries and commissions, which together form the government of China, along with some SOEs. Its composition is decided by the NPC acting on Communist Party recommendations. At the highest

level of the Communist Party is the Standing Committee of the Politburo, with nine members including the General Secretary, Hu Jintao. It is the principal maker of policy in China. Wu Bangguo and Wen Jiabao are also members. See Chapter Nine.

22. See UNDP Project Documents CPR/91/512/A/12/99 and CPR/91/513/B/01/99.
23. Mine was on reforming the SOEs. It followed a 260-page report on the same subject based on international experience, which earlier I had been commissioned to write by the Chinese government.
24. Becker, p. 311.
25. Ibid.
26. Ibid., p. 32.
27. See *The New York Times*, 20 April 2001 and *The New York Sun*, 21 April 2001.
28. See TCHRD's *Annual Report*, 2000, Chapter Five.
29. Fairbank and Goldman, p. 452.
30. The name means 'The Practice of the Wheel of the Dharma'. The principles and spiritual beliefs of Falun Gong are called the *Falun Dafa*.
31. Xinhua, the official Chinese news agency, 1 February 2001. For ten years Luo Gan had been in charge of security in China. On his role, see Andrew J. Nathan and Bruce Gilley, eds, *China's New Rulers: The Secret Files*, Granta Books, 2003, p. 110.
32. Jonathan Fenby, *Dealing with the Dragon: A Year in the New Hong Kong*, Little, Brown and Company, 2000, p. 264.
33. See Kate Westgarth, *China Review*, Issue 27, Winter 2003, pp. 22–4.
34. These were exposed most recently by Studwell; by Gordon G. Chang in *The Coming Collapse of China*, Random House, 2001; and by others (including the writers of a special survey of China in *The Economist*, 15 June 2002, the distribution of which was banned in China).
35. Gordon Chang, p. 311.
36. Some books, such as the best-seller (in the West) *Shanghai Baby* by Wei Hui (Robinson, London, 2001), are banned in China because of the 'immorality' and Western free-living lifestyles they portray. A high proportion of such books published in English are by Chinese women now living abroad.
37. Gordon Chang, p. 165; Becker, p. 157.
38. The picture of Chinese managers in general painted by Ji Li, Ping Ping Fu, Irene Chow and T. K. Peng is not flattering. See their 'Societal Development and the Change of Leadership Style in Oriental Chinese Societies', *Journal of Developing Studies*, vol. 18, issue 1, April 2002: 'Chinese leaders, in order to protect their organisational status, would withhold information and power from their subordinates … Chinese supervisors regularly play down or deny the contributions of subordinates so that their own position can be secured.'

Bad management and gross exploitation can be found in many places. In the mid-1990s, for example, 'the textile and garment industries still employed children and young adults to work 14 hours a day, 7 days a week, who sleep by their looms. If you lose an arm in the loom you're fired' (Kristof and Wudunn, p. 347). Such cases are reminiscent of China in 1923 (see Chapter Two of this book) – except that the 'eighteen hours a day, seven days a week' has been reduced to fourteen hours, seven days.

39. Studwell, p. 197.
40. See Note no. 208.
41. These include Stu Fulton (Pricewaterhouse Coopers); Nicholas R. Lardyé (an American specialist on China's financial system – see his *China's Unfinished Economic Revolution*,

Brookings Institution, 1998, and in particular his 'Fiscal Sustainability: Between a Rock and a Hard Place', *China Economic Quarterly* , Q2, 2000); Zhong Jiyan (Chinese Academy of Social Sciences); Edward Steinfeld (professor at MIT); and Studwell, in whose book (ibid.) the above are mentioned, especially in Chapter Nine.

42. See the full text in the special edition of *News From China*, 11 July 2001.

43. Basing education on Confucius meant there was little or no development of mathematics or the sciences. Mathematics was hindered by two factors. Zero was not in regular use in the Chinese system of counting until the twentieth century; it was a blank space on the abacus. Complex calculations were possible but cumbersome. The concept of infinity, likewise a problem, also came into use in the twentieth century. That neither was commonplace significantly retarded scientific development (see Charles Seife, *Zero: The Biography of a Dangerous Idea*, Souvenir Press, 2000). Perhaps this is why Jiang put science foremost in his 'Three Represents' speech.

44. This would include both State-Owned Enterprises and communally owned local enterprises.

45. This was Mao's Leninist development of the Marxist 'dictatorship of the proletariat' – the industrial workers. Adding 'peasants' was in line with Mao's respect for the innate capabilities of the peasants, their great superiority in numbers compared to industrial workers in China and the basis of his support. Intellectuals are, however, now included as amongst the working class.

46. Kristof and Wudunn, pp. 224–39.

47. This figure was according to Peng Peiyun, the minister in charge of the Chinese Family Planning Commission, in 1992. See *In Quest of a Better China*, p. 126.

48. Chang has lived and worked in China for almost twenty years, most recently in Shanghai as counsel to an American law firm.

49. However, in 1991 it was estimated that about 70 percent of these losses were 'policy-induced losses', not the fault of management. In principle, there could be a rapid turnround. See Gu, p. 91.

50. The figure of 200 million is from Studwell, p. 189, and includes some indirectly managed state enterprises and a proportion of collective workers in smaller publicly owned enterprises. The percentage figure is from Gordon Chang, p. 207.

Chapter Nine

1. This is according to Oliver August, writing in *The Times* on 15 November 2002. August reported a long conversation, which seemed genuine, with Liu Bingxia in her home. But Nathan and Gilley (p. 66) write that after Hu Jintao's mother died, he and his two sisters were brought up by their grandparents. Nathan and Gilley's book was a translated and edited version of secret Chinese documents called *Disidai* ('The Fourth Generation'), with later additions from interviews with the person (going under the pseudonym Zong Hairen) who made them available. Hu has the reputation of being a very private person.

2. See Mure Dickie and Richard McGregor, 'Stars in his Eyes: Hu Jintao One Year On', *China Review*, Winter 2003, Great Britain–China Centre, and Geoffrey Howe, 'China's Role in a Shrinking World', in the same issue.

3. This is the central theme of Gidon Gottlieb's *Nation Against State: A New Approach to Ethnic Conflicts and the Decline of Sovereignty*, Council of Foreign Relations Press, New York, 1993 (especially pp. 2–3; 21). When Premier Wen Jiabao was in Washington on his first official visit to the US on 4 December 2003, he made reference to Tibet's being 'an inalienable part of Chinese territory'.

4. On 21 March 2004 at 8 PM, the Lhasa-based Tibet TV3 inadvertently (?) broadcast a background image of the Tibetan flag for less than five seconds. It was spotted, and as a result the director of TV3 was demoted and the entire staff underwent 're-education' and wrote self-criticisms of their error. See www.tibetnews.com, 25 March 2004.

5. This consists of nine persons: Hu himself (Party General Secretary, President of the PRC, Vice-Chairman of the Central Military Commission), born December 1942; Wen Jiabao (Premier), born September 1942; Zeng Qinghong (Vice President); born July 1939; Wu Bangguo (Chairman of the National People's Congress), born July 1941; Jia Qinglin (Chairman of the Chinese People's Political Consultative Conference), born March 1940; Huang Ju (Vice-Premier), born September 1938; Wu Guanzheng (Secretary of the Central Commission for Discipline Inspection), born August 1938; Li Changchun (member, Politburo Standing Committee), born February 1944; Luo Gan (member, Politburo Standing Committee), born July 1935.

6. See Nathan and Gilley, especially pp. 91–100, and TIN's *Tibet 2002*, p. 41.

7. Wenran Jiang, 'Prosperity Based on Poverty and Disparity', *China Review*, Great Britain-China Centre, Spring 2004, Issue no. 28.

8. Nathan and Gilley, pp. 83–90. Geoffrey Howe (see Note no. 284) believes Zeng is 'probably the most powerful member of the Politburo'.

9. Nathan and Gilley, p. 219.

10. See Richard Bernstein and Ross M. Munro, *The Coming Conflict with China*, Alfred A. Knopf Inc., 1997, pp. 22–3.

11. Ibid., p. 23.

12. Chomsky, p. 152.

13. Bernstein and Munro, p. 33.

14. Some of the political complexities of US involvement with the Taliban in Afghanistan concern the proposed pipeline, which the US has much desired.

15. *Stockholm International Peace Research Institute (SIPRI), Yearbook 2001*, Oxford University Press, 2001, pp. 326; 353.

16. Ibid., p. 257.

17. Patten, p. 296.

18. For more on the region, see the excellent book by Christian Tyler, *Wild West China: The Taming of Xinjiang*, John Murray, 2003; see also Michael Dillon, 'Ethnic, Religious and Political Conflict on China's Northwestern Borders: The Background to the Violence in Xinjiang', *IBRU Boundary and Security Bulletin*, Spring 1997, pp. 80–6, and the same author's 'Muslims in Post-Mao China', *Journal of Muslim Minority Affairs*, vol. 16, no. 1, 1996.

19. See Jonathan Spence, *Treason by the Book*, Allen Lane, Penguin Press, 2001, a remarkable historical 'whodunnit' which gives clear insight into the beliefs and practices of Emperor Yongzheng and into Chinese society at that time.

20. Non-Han people in the Xinjiang Uyghur Autonomous Regions, as well as those who have emigrated abroad, still do not refer to the area as 'Xinjiang', which they see as having Chinese imperialist and colonial connotations, but as 'East Turkestan'.

21. The Xinjiang Production and Construction Corporation was originally called the 'Xinjiang Production and Construction Corps'; the name was changed in the late 1990s to reflect its strong economic role. Its tentacles are vast. According to Tyler (p. 194), it produces 40 percent of Xinjiang's cotton, a major crop, and farms one third of its arable land.

22. Chris Patten, lecture at the Royal Institute of International Affairs, 6 September 2002.

The text of this speech is available at http://europa.eu.int/comm/external_relations/ news/patten/sp02_368.htm.

Chapter Ten

1. *Tibet Bulletin*, July–August 2001.
2. They should have been selling at full cost, including depreciation based on replacement cost of the vehicles and equipment, plus the full costs of replanting and maintenance, plus perhaps a fixed and low profit margin. Wrong pricing from a state enterprise gives the wrong market signals.
3. For more details, see *China's Great Leap West*, Tibet Information Network, November 2000, especially Chapter Four.
4. Dam construction is seen as the answer, combined with hydro-electricity to help combat the great power shortage. But there are major conflicts with the environment. At the time of writing, the latest problem is the proposed construction of thirteen dams on the Nu River in Yunnan province in the far south. The Nu becomes the Salween, which flows into Myanmar and forms the border with Thailand. The gorge through which the river flows in China has been called the 'Grand Canyon of Asia'. Another hydro-electric dam in the National Park at Mugetso Lake in Sichuan has also run into environmental opposition, with high-level political implications. The Huaneng Company of Beijing, which will share the costs and the revenues with the local authority, is owned by the son of Li Peng, the former Chinese premier (Li senior is also a strong supporter of the proposal). Source: Radio Free Asia report, 12 July 2003; see also www.tibetnews.com, 13 July 2003.
5. See the *New York Times* article by Jim Yardley, 10 March 2004, or www.tibetnews.com, 16 March 2004.
6. *China's Great Leap West*, p. 22.
7. Brunel (1806–59) was one of Britain's three great pioneering engineers in the middle of the nineteenth century (along with Joseph Locke and Robert Stephenson). In 1833 he became the engineer of the Great Western Railway, responsible for building the main line to the west of England. It is still regarded as the best piece of railway engineering in the whole British railway system.
8. Much of the information in this section is based on the following: Gabriel Lafitte, 'Fast-tracking Tibet', *Harvard Asia Pacific Review*, Summer 2001, reprinted in *Tibetan Bulletin*, July–August 2001; related reports in *Tibetan Bulletin*, September–October 2001; Zhao Qinghua, 'New Projects to Balance China's Resources', *The Independent*, 1 October 2001; Shishir Gupta, 'Diverging Tracks', *India Today*, 17 September 2001 via World Tibet Network News; and John Ackerly, 'Slow Train Coming', *Tibet News*, no. 19, Autumn 1995.
9. See Ma Jian, *Red Dust*, Chatto and Windus, 2001, pp. 104–12, for a contemporary description.
10. *Tibetan Bulletin*, September–October 2001.
11. The first runs along a shorter route than Golmud–Lhasa, but at more than three times the cost (US$ 7.7 billion). It will be from Lanzhou (in Qinghai province) to Lhasa via Nagchu (Chinese: Nagqu), north of Lhasa, linking with the Golmud–Lhasa line. The second is from Chengdu (the capital of Sichuan province), also via Nagchu to Lhasa, at an expected cost of US$ 9.3 billion. The third is the more southerly route from Dali (near Xiaguan, in Yunnan province) via Nyingtri (Chinese: Nyingchi) due west into Lhasa, expected to cost US$ 8 billion. The forward plan is to complete these by 2038. They can be seen as three more routes by which migrants can enter Tibet and trade

can be conducted. Tibet, even as it is known today, will become unrecognisable. The authorities are planning for a Lhasa five times its present size in the next fifteen years.

12. 'No. 1: Highways', *Foreign Investment in Tibet*, Australia Tibet Council, Aid Group, August 1998.

13. It is part of the Tsonub (Chinese: Haixi), Mongol, Tibetan and Kazakh Autonomous Prefecture.

14. Liu, p. 37.

15. 'No. 2: Fertilizers', *Foreign Investment in Tibet*, Australia Tibet Council, Research Office, September 1998.

16. Paul Hawken, in *The Ecology of Commerce*, HarperBusiness, 1993, p. 142, points out that the Menominee American Indians have, for the past 135 years, managed a sustained yield on their 234,000 acres of forest and have produced 2 billion board-feet of sawn timber while preserving the forest stock.

17. Helena Norberg-Hodge, *Ancient Futures: Learning from Ladakh*, Rider, 1991.

18. Hawken, p. 103.

19. See Gu, p. 318, and also W. A. Byrd and Lin Qingsong, *China's Rural Industry: Structure, Development and Reform*, Oxford University Press, 1990.

20. These include the Tibet Relief Fund (part of the Tibet Society of the United Kingdom); Appropriate Technology Asia (formerly Appropriate Technology for Tibetans), which now includes assistance to very poor Chinese families; the Tibet Foundation; the Samye Ling Monastery in Scotland; and The Peak Enterprise Program, founded by Elsie Walker in 1997 (in association with the TAR Federation of Industry and Commerce, Lhasa, and The Mountain Institute; this organisation manages worldwide projects to help people living in high mountain areas to develop new businesses, and has been working in Tibet since 1986).

21. See Carole Samdup, 'The Right to Development on the Tibetan Plateau', *Human Rights Tribune*, Spring 2002, vol. 9, no. 1, and www.tibetnews.com, 11 August 2002.

22. See www.tibet.com/aidTibet.html.

23. *The China Daily*, December 2003, reported that 'more than 120,000 people died in work-related accidents from January to December 2003 ... an average of 300 Chinese lose their lives every day in industrial accidents'. Also, many workers, especially in the toy-making industries (China supplies some 70 percent of the world's toys) and in the garment trade, suffer appalling conditions. See Jasper Becker, 'Sweatshop hell for China's toy makers "worse than ever"', *The Independent*, 24 December 2002. The conditions described mirror those reported above in Chapter Two relating to working conditions in 1923.

24. For example, any plant that draws large quantities of water upstream from a river and disposes of its toxic effluent downstream from the plant should be required to reverse the procedure. If it was made to dispose of its effluent upstream from the plant and to draw its intake from downstream, the owners would soon clean up its production system to remove harmful waste.

25. Hawken, p. 173.

Chapter Twelve

1. Lucien Pye, *Chinese Commercial Negotiating Style*, Rand Corporation, 1982, pp. 72–3.

2. *The Chinese Statistical Yearbook 2000* does not list Taiwan as a region or province of China, but gives the main social and economic indicators of 'Taiwan Province' separately in Appendix 1.

The independent and authoritative *Times Atlas of the World* (2000 edn) does not list Taiwan as a province of China. On the other hand, in the *UNDP Human Development Report 2001*, Taiwan is always referred to as 'Taiwan (Province of China)'. The UNDP has many projects in China, and undoubtedly this was considered rather diplomatic.

3. Sir Percy Cradock, *Experiences of China*, John Murray, 1994, p. 266.
4. Ibid., p. 211.
5. In addition to Patten and Cradock, see Jonathan Dimbleby, *The Last Governor*, Warner Books, 1998.
6. For example, perhaps, as issues for negotiation not be to given away lightly:

   Being assured of the welfare of any Han Chinese remaining in Tibet and the maintenance of some privileges.

   Keeping control of things that matter most to them (e.g. sovereignty, central administration for some important matters, control over Tibet's natural resources, control over the media, police and internal security, passports and visas) while also:

   Giving way to Tibetans only on matters which are of very little consequence to the Chinese.

   Agreeing to relax the grip on Tibet in many specific ways that would look good internationally, especially in religious matters, but perhaps only to the extent that they have been increased in recent years (which may have been part of their long-term strategy anyway) while giving way on nothing else.

   Gaining the things that China really wants, which are thought to be within the Tibetans' control (e.g. closing down the international campaign).

   Negotiating an agreement apparently favourable to Tibet, thereby gaining international approval, while being confident that in the longer term they can interpret it imaginatively to undermine its effectiveness.

7. GOH Bee Chen, *Negotiating with the Chinese*, Dartmouth Publishing, 1996, pp. 137–57.
8. See Dr David Shambaugh, School of Oriental Studies, London University, Foreign Affairs Committee of the House of Commons, Session 1993–94: 'Relations between the United Kingdom and China in the period up to and beyond 1997', 23 March 1994, para. 163.
9. Quoted in Dimbleby, pp. 216–8.
10. Patten, pp. 40–1. For an analysis of this situation see Michael S. Bennett, 'Financing the Chek Lap Kok New Airport: A Case Study in Amending the Sino–British Joint Declaration on the Question of Hong Kong', *Journal of Chinese Law*, vol. 9, no. 1, Spring 1995.
11. Dimbleby, p. 418. In fact the two documents, the Memorandum of Understanding and the November Fourth Accord, represented 'significant victories for the Chinese, weakening the principles set forth in the Joint Declaration'. See Bennett, ibid.
12. Richard H. Solomon, *Chinese Negotiating Behaviour*, RAND Corporation, 1995, p. 168.
13. Chen, pp. 134–57.
14. Ogura Kazuo, 'How the "Inscrutables" Negotiate with the "Inscrutables": Chinese Negotiating Tactics vis-à-vis the Japanese', *China Quarterly*, no. 79, September 1979, p. 24.
15. Patten, p. 69.
16. Ibid., p. 66; Dimbleby, pp. 169–75.
17. Dimbleby, p. 187; Patten, p. 69.

18. Patten, p. 72.
19. Dimbleby, p. 234.
20. Quoted in *China's Great Leap West*, pp. 15–6.
21. Cradock, p. 176.
22. Dimbleby, p. 191.
23. Sir David Ackers-Jones, Foreign Affairs Committee of the House of Commons, Session 1993–94: 'Relations between the United Kingdom and China in the period up to and beyond 1997', 23 March 1994, vol. 2, para. 445.
24. In 1996 Tung Chee-hwa was elected by a committee of 400 persons, approved by Beijing.
25. Chris Patten, ibid., para. 446.
26. Dimbleby, p. 525, points out that Sir Percy Cradock's strong objection to Chris Patten's approach to negotiating was that the latter was very confrontational, while the former espoused cooperation. But, Patten believed, cooperation would lead ultimately to the Chinese winning the argument – there had to be the right balance.

Epilogue
1. Thus the difficulties are evident. Qinghai province, with a population of 4.8 million, has forty separate Tibetan counties, while Sichuan province, with a population of over 82 million, has thirty-two. Some geographical grouping may be necessary to allow all Tibetan groups above a certain number of people to participate. (See the table in Note no. 3.)
2. Hong Kong is a 'Special Administrative Region of China'. 'Administration' is generally taken to mean 'government' or the 'executive', and not to include the legislature. 'Self-rule' includes the legislature and any other activities of governance.
3. See 'Relevance of Buddhism in the New Century', *Tibet Foundation Newsletter*, Winter 2004, p. 3.
4. Deepak Chopra, *How to Know God; The Soul's Journey into the Mystery of Mysteries*, Rider, 2000, p. 4.

Select Bibliography

Principal Books and Reports Cited or Read

On China

Ackers-Jones, Sir David, 'Relations between the United Kingdom and China in the period up to and beyond 1997' at the Foreign Affairs Committee of the House of Commons, Session 1993–4, 23 March 1994, vol. II.

Amnesty International, many reports, including 'China, "Striking Harder" than ever before', 6 July 2001.

Becker, Jasper, *The Chinese*, John Murray, 2000.

Becker, Jasper, 'Empire Building', *The Independent Review*, 24 March 2003.

Bernstein, Sir Richard and Munro, Ross M., *The Coming Conflict with China*, Alfred A. Knopf Inc., 1997.

Bodde, Derek, Chapter One in Twitchett, Denis and Loewe, Michael, eds, *Cambridge History of China*, vol. 1, Cambridge University Press, 1986.

Butterfield, Fox, *Alive in the Bitter Sea*, Coronet Books, Hodder and Stoughton, 1982.

Byrd, W. A. and Lin, Qingsong, *China's Rural Industry, Structure, Development and Reform*, Oxford University Press, 1990.

Chang, Gordon, *The Coming Collapse of China*, Random House Business Books, 2001.

Chang, Iris, *The Rape of Nanking; The Forgotten Holocaust of World War II*, Basic Books, 1997.

Chang, Jung, *Wild Swans*, Flamingo, 1991.

Chang, Pang-Mei Natasha, *Bound Feet and Western Dress*, Bantam Books, 1997.

Chen, GOH Bee, *Negotiating with the Chinese*, Dartmouth Publishing, 1996.

Cheng, Man-jan, *Lao-Tzu: 'My Words Are Easy to Understand': Lectures on the Tao Teh Ching*, North Atlantic Books, 1981.

Cheng, Nien, *Life and Death in Shanghai*, Flamingo, 1995.

Chun-fang, Yii, *The Renewal of Buddhism in China*, Columbia University Press, 1981.

Cleary, Thomas, *The Art of War, Sun Tzu*, Shambhala Dragon Editions, 1988.

Cleary, Thomas, *Mastering The Art of War: Zhuge Liang's and Liu Ji's Commentaries on the Classic by Sun Tzu*, Shambala Dragon Editions, 1989.

Cleary, Thomas, *The Essential Tao*, Castle Books, 1992.

Colmer, Michael, *The Executive I Ching, The Business Oracle*, Blandford Press, 1987.

Cradock, Sir Percy, *Experiences of China*, John Murray, 1994.

Da Chen, *Colours of the Mountain*, Arrow, 2000.

Dimbleby, Jonathan, *The Last Governor*, Warner Books, 1998.

Fairbank, John King and Goldman, Merle, *China: A New History*, The Belknap Press of Harvard University Press, Enlarged Edition, 1999.

Falun Gong, www.falungong.org.uk.

Fenby, Jonathan, *Dealing with the Dragon: A Year in the New Hong Kong*, Little, Brown and Company, 2000.

Feng, Gia-Fu and English, Jane, *Lao Tsu: Tao Te Ching*, Wildwood House, 1973.

Gao, Anhua, *To the Edge of the Sky*, Penguin Books, 2001.

Gilley, Bruce, *Tiger on the Brink: Jiang Zemin and China's New Elite*, University of California Press, 1998.

Gittings, John, *China Changes Face: The Road from Revolution 1949–1989*, Oxford University Press, 1989.

Goldman, Merle, *Sowing the Seeds of Democracy in China*, Harvard University Press, 1994.

Griffith, Samuel B., *Sun Tzu: The Art of War*, Oxford University Press, 1963.

Gu, Yang, *Foreign Direct Investment and Technology Transfer in China 1979–94*, unpublished PhD thesis, University of Manchester, 1997.

Human Rights in China, New York, www.hrichina.org.

Hutchings, Graham, *Modern China: A Companion to a Rising Power*, Penguin Books, 2000.

Information Office of the State Council, Beijing, China, *White Paper on Tibet: Tibet: Its Ownership and Human Rights Situation*, 22 September 1992.

Information Office of the State Council, Beijing, China, *White Paper: Regional Ethnic Autonomy in Tibet*, 23 May 2004.

Jenner, W. J. F., *Tyranny of History, The Roots of China's Crisis*, Penguin, 1994.

Kristof, Nicholas D. and Wudunn, Sheryl, *China Wakes The Struggle for the Soul of a Rising Power*, Nicholas Brealey Publishing, 1995.

Lewis, Mark Edward, 'Warring States, Political History', in Loewe, Michael and Shawghnessy, Edward L., eds, *The Cambridge History of Ancient China*, Cambridge University Press, 1999.

Leys, Simon (alias Ryckmans, Pierre), *The Chairman's New Clothes: Mao and the Cultural Revolution*, Allison and Busby, 1977.

Leys, Simon (alias Ryckmans, Pierre), *The Analects of Confucius*, W. W. Norton and Company, 1997.

Li, Zhisui, *The Private Life of Chairman Mao*, Arrow, 1996.

Mah, Adeline Yen, *Falling Leaves: The True Story of an Unwanted Chinese Daughter*, Penguin Books, 1997.

Mah, Adeline Yen, *Watching the Tree to Catch a Hare*, HarperCollins, 2000.

Mah, Adeline Yen, *A Thousand Pieces of Gold*, HarperCollins, 2002.

Ma, Jian, *Red Dust*, Chatto and Windus, 2001.

McKay, Alex, ed., *Tibet and Her Neighbours: A History*, Edition Hansjorg Mayer, 2003. (Papers presented at a 'History of Tibet' conference held at St Andrews, Scotland, September 2001.)

Miles, James A. R., *The Legacy of Tiananmen: China in Disarray*, University of Michigan Press, 1997.

Nathan, Andrew J. and Link, Perry, eds, compiled by Zhang, Liang, *The Tiananmen Papers*, Little, Brown and Company, 2001.

Nathan, Andrew J. and Gilley, Bruce, *China's New Rulers: The Secret Files*, Granta Books, 2003.

Patten, Chris, *East and West*, Macmillan, 1998.

Patten, Chris, speaking at the Foreign Affairs Committee of the House of Commons, 23 March 1994.

Patten, Chris, lecture at the Royal Institute of International Affairs, 6 September 2002.

Pye, Lucien, *Chinese Commercial Negotiating Style*, Rand Corporation, 1982.

Royal Academy of Arts, London, *The Return of the Buddha*, exhibition catalogue, 2002.

Shambaugh, Dr David, in 'Relations between the United Kingdom and China in the period up to and beyond 1997', Foreign Affairs Committee of the House of Commons, Session 1993–94, 23 March 1994.

Sharf, Robert H., *Coming to Terms with Chinese Buddhism: A Reading of the Treasure Store Treatise*, Kuroda Institute, 2002.

Short, Philip, *Mao: A Life*, Hodder and Stoughton, 1999.

Snow, Edgar, *Red Star Over China*, Victor Gollancz, 1937, also Random House, 1938.

Solomon, Richard H., *Chinese Negotiating Behaviour*, RAND Corporation, 1995.

Spence, Jonathan, *The Chan's Great Continent, China in Western Minds*, W. W. Norton and Company 1998.

Spence, Jonathan, *The Search for Modern China*, W. W. Norton and Company, second edn, 1999.

Spence, Jonathan, *Treason by the Book*, Allen Lane, The Penguin Press, 2001.

Studwell, Joe, *The China Dream: The Elusive Quest for the Greatest Untapped Market on Earth*, Profile Books, 2002.

Terrill, Ross, *The New Chinese Empire and What it Means for the United States*, A Cornelia and Michael Bessie Book, Basic Books, 2003.

Theroux, Paul, *Riding the Iron Rooster: By Train Through China*, Penguin Books with Hamish Hamilton, 1989.

Thubron, Colin, *Behind the Wall*, Penguin Books, 1987.

Tomasevski, Katarina, Special Rapporteur on the Right to Education of the UN Human Rights Commission, *Report on Education in China*, December 2003.

United Nations, 'Declaration on Principles of International Law Concerning Friendly

Relations and Co-Operation among States in Accordance with the Charter of the United Nations', United Nations, 24 October 1970.

Wei, Hui, *Shanghai Baby*, Robinson, 2001.

Wei, Jingsheng, *The Courage to Stand Alone: Letters from Prison and Other Writings*, Viking, 1997.

White, Tyrene, *Village Elections: Democracy from the Bottom Up?*, chapter in Dickson, Bruce; *China: Adapting the Past, Confronting the Future* (Centre for Chinese Studies), University of Michigan, 2002.

Wickert, Edwin, ed., *The Good German of Nanking: The Diaries of John Rabe*, Abacus, 1998.

Wilhelm, Richard and Baynes, Cary F., *I Ching*, Routledge and Kegan Paul, third edn, 1951.

Wood, Frances, *Hand Grenade Practice in Peking: My Part in the Cultural Revolution*, John Murray, 2000.

Wright, Elizabeth, *The Chinese People Stand Up*, BBC Books, 1989.

Wu, Harry and Wakeman, Caroline, *Bitter Winds: A Memoir of My Years in China's Gulag*, John Wiley and Sons, 1994.

Yan, Jiaqi, 'A Future Federal System for China', in *In Quest of a Better China*, ed. The Forum Team of the Alliance for a Better China, Global Publishing, 1993.

Ye, Ting-xing, *A Leaf in the Bitter Wind*, Bantam Books, 2000.

Zhu, Ling, 'Free Compulsory Education: A Study by the Chinese Academy of Social Sciences', *China Daily*, 17 May 2004.

On Tibet

Australia Tibet Council, Aid Group, 'No. 1: Highways', *Foreign Investment in Tibet*, August 1998.

Australia Tibet Council, Research Office, 'No. 2: Fertilizers', *Foreign Investment in Tibet*, September 1998.

Barnett, Robert, in McKay, Alex, ed., *Tibet and Her Neighbours: A History*, Hansjorg Mayer, 2003.

Barnett, Robert and Akiner, Shirin, *Resistance and Reform in Tibet*, Hurst and Company, 1994.

Bass, Catriona, *Inside the Treasure House: A Time in Tibet*, Victor Gollancz, 1990.

Bass, Catriona, *Education in Tibet: Policy and Practice Since 1950*, Zed Books in association with Tibet Information Network, 1998.

Bhagdro, the Venerable, *A Hell on Earth*, privately published by The Ven. Bhagdro, 1998.

Brown, Mick, *The Dance of Seventeen Lives: The Incredible True Story of Tibet's 17th Karmapa*, Bloomsbury, 2004.

Bureau of His Holiness the Dalai Lama, New Delhi, *Constitution of Tibet*, 10 March 1963.

Campaign Free Tibet, *Children of Despair: An Analysis of Coercive Birth Control Policies in Chinese Occupied Tibet*, August 1992.

Craig, Mary, *Tears of Blood: A Cry for Tibet*, HarperCollins Religions, 1992.

Craig, Mary, *Kundun: A Biography of the Family of the Dalai Lama*, HarperCollins, 1997.

David-Neel, Alexandra, *My Journey to Lhasa*, Virago Press, 1983 (first published in 1927).

David-Neel, Alexandra, *Magic and Mystery in Tibet*, Thorsons, HarperCollins, 1997 (first published as *With Mystics and Magicians in Tibet*, Penguin Books, 1931).

David-Neel, Alexandra, *Initiations and Initiates in Tibet*, Rider, 1970 (first published in 1931).

Department of Information and International Relations, Dharamsala, *The Legal Status of Tibet: Three Studies by Leading Jurists*, 1989.

Department of Information and International Relations, Dharamsala, *International Resolutions and Recognitions on Tibet 1959 to 1997*, March 1997.

Department of Information and International Relations, Dharamsala, *China's Current Policy on Tibet*, September 2000.

Department of Information and International Relations, Dharamsala, *His Holiness the Fourteenth Dalai Lama of Tibet on the Occasion of the Sixtieth Anniversary of his Enthronement and the Fiftieth Anniversary of His Assuming Political Power of Tibet*, December 2000. (This is a useful summary of all the Dalai Lama's activities, political progress, fifty-six books and 478 foreign visits to fifty-six countries, as well as of the constitution of the Tibetan government-in-exile, etc.)

Department of Information and International Relations, Dharamsala, *China's Railway Project: Where Will it Take Tibet?*, August 2001.

Department of Information and International Relations, Dharamsala, *Height of Darkness: Chinese Colonisation on the World's Roof – Tibetan Response to Beijing's White Paper of 8 November 2001*, 10 December 2001.

Douglas, Nik and White, Meryl, *Karmapa, the Black Hat Lama of Tibet*, Luzac, 1976.

Drummer, Tom, *Tibetan Medicine and other Holistic Health-Care Systems*, Routledge, 1988.

Ennals, Lord and Hyde-Chambers, Frederick R., 'Tibet in China', *International Alert*, August 1988.

Evans-Wentz, W. Y., ed., *Tibet's Great Yogi Milarepa: A Biography*, Oxford University Press, 1969 (first published in 1928).

Fischer, Andrew, *Poverty by Design: The Economics of Discrimination in Tibet*, Canada Tibet Committee, August 2002.

Fleming, Peter, *Bayonets to Lhasa*, Oxford University Press, 1961.

Ford, Robert, *Captured in Tibet*, George G. Harrap, 1957.

French, Patrick, *Tibet, Tibet: A Personal History of a Lost Land*, HarperCollins, 2003.

van Grasdorff, Gilles, *Hostage of Beijing: The Abduction of the Panchen Lama*, Element, 1999.

Gyatso, Palden with Shakya, Tsering, *Fire Under the Snow: Testimony of a Tibetan Prisoner*, Harvill Press, 1997.

Gyatso, Tenzin (His Holiness the Dalai Lama), *A Policy of Kindness: An Anthology of*

Writings by and about the Dalai Lama, Snow Lion Publications, 1960.

Gyatso, Tenzin (His Holiness the Dalai Lama), *My Land and My People: Memoirs of the Dalai Lama of Tibet*, Potala Corporation, 1962.

Gyatso, Tenzin (His Holiness the Dalai Lama), *Constitution of Tibet*, 10 March 1963.

Gyatso, Tenzin (His Holiness the Dalai Lama), *Collected Statements, Interviews and Articles*, Information Office, Central Tibetan Secretariat, revised edn, 1986.

Gyatso, Tenzin (His Holiness the Dalai Lama), *Freedom in Exile*, Hodder and Stoughton, 1990.

Gyatso, Tenzin (His Holiness the Dalai Lama), *Ocean of Wisdom: Guidelines for Living*, Harper and Row, San Francisco, 1990.

Gyatso, Tenzin (His Holiness the Dalai Lama), *Ethics for a New Millennium*, Little, Brown and Company, 1999.

Gyatso, Tenzin (His Holiness the Dalai Lama), 'World Peace', *Caduceus*, no. 51, Spring 2001.

Gyatso, Tenzin (His Holiness the Dalai Lama) & Cutler, Howard C. MD, *The Art of Happiness; A Handbook for Living*, Coronet Books, Hodder & Stoughton 1998.

Harrer, Heinrich, *Seven Years in Tibet*, Rupert Hart-Davis and the Book Society, 1953.

Harrer, Heinrich, *Return to Tibet*, Weidenfeld and Nicolson, 1984.

Foreign Affairs Committee of the House of Commons, Session 1993–94, 23 March 1994, 'Relations between the United Kingdom and China in the period up to and beyond 1997', vol. II.

Information Office of the State Council, Beijing, *Tibet's March Towards Modernisation*, 8 November 2001.

Information Office of the State Council, Beijing, special supplement, *China's White Paper on Tibet*, 24 September 1992.

Information Office of the State Council, Beijing, *New Progress in Human Rights in the Tibet Autonomous Region*, February 1998.

International Commission of Jurists, *The Question of Tibet and the Rule of Law*, Geneva, 1959.

International Commission of Jurists, *Tibet and the Chinese People's Republic: A Report to the International Commission of Jurists by its Legal Inquiry Committee on Tibet*, Geneva, 1960.

International Commission of Jurists, *Tibet: Human Rights and the Rule of Law*, Geneva, 1997.

Jigme, Ngabo Ngawang, *A Great Turn in Tibetan History* ,New Star Publications, Beijing, 1991.

Jigme, Ngabo Ngawang, *On Tibetan Issues*, New Star Publications, Beijing, 1991.

Johnson, Sandy, *The Book of Tibetan Elders*, Constable, 1997.

Lamb, Alastair, *Tibet, China and India 1914–1950*, Roxford Books, 1989.

Mackerras, Colin, *China's Minorities: Integration and Modernisation in the Twentieth Century*, Oxford University Press, 1994.

Mackerras, Colin et al, *The Beijing Tragedy: Implications for China and Australia*,

Griffith University, Centre for the Study of Australia–Asia Relations, 1989.

McCorquodale, Robert and Orosz, Nicholas, eds, *Tibet: The Position in International Law – Report of the Conference of International Lawyers on Issues Relating to Self-determination and Independence for Tibet, London 6–10 January 1993*, Hansjorg Mayer, Stuttgart, 1994.

Michell, Chris, *Tibetan Freedom Chants: The Ven Bhagdro and the Nuns of Drapchi Prison*, CD, Oreade Music ORW 60982, 2001.

Mullin, Glenn H., *A Long Look Homeward: An Interview with the Dalai Lama*, The Tibetan Cultural Center, Snow Lion Publications, 1987.

Nolan, Peter, *China's Rise, Russia's Fall: Politics, Economics and Planning in the Transition from Stalinism*, Macmillan, 1995.

Norberg-Hodge, Helena, *Ancient Futures: Learning from Ladakh*, Rider, 1991.

Norbu, Dawa, *Tibet: The Road Ahead*, Rider, 1997.

Norbu, Dawa, *China's Tibet Policy*, Curzon Press, 2001.

Norbu, Jamyang, *Rangzen Charter: The Case for Tibetan Independence*, published privately, third revised edn, September 2000.

Planning Council, Central Tibetan Administration of His Holiness the Dalai Lama, *Tibetan Refugee Community: Integrated Development Plan II, 1995–2000*, May 1994.

Planning Council, Central Tibetan Administration of His Holiness the Dalai Lama, *PADME Promotional Agency for Development of Micro-Enterprises: Project Summary*, unpublished, 1999.

Planning Council, Central Tibetan Administration of His Holiness the Dalai Lama, *Loan Guidelines for Unemployed Youths*, unpublished, 1999.

Planning Council, Central Tibetan Administration of His Holiness the Dalai Lama, *Training Programme Status*, unpublished, 1999.

Pema, Jetsun, *Tibet: My Story – An Autobiography*, Element, 1997.

Pommaret, Françoise, *Tibet: Turning the Wheel of Life*, Thames & Hudson, New Horizons, 2003.

Research Institute of Literature and Art of China's Minority Nationalities Under the Central Academy of Minority Nationalities, *Thangka: Buddhist Painting of Tibet – Biographical Paintings of Phags'pa*, New World Press, Beijing, The People's Publishing House of Tibet, January 1987.

Richardson, Hugh E., *Tibet and Its History*, Shambhala, second edn, revised and updated, 1984.

Schwartz, Ronald D., *Circle of Protest: Political Ritual in the Tibetan Uprising*, Hurst and Company, 1994.

Shakabpa, Tsepon W. D., *A Political History*, Potala Publications, 1984.

Shakya, Tsering, *The Dragon in the Land of Snows: A History of Modern Tibet Since 1947*, Pimlico, 1999.

Sogyal Rinpoche, *The Tibetan Book of Living and Dying*, Rider, first edn, 1992.

Sogyal Rinpoche, *The Future of Buddhism and Other Essays*, Rider, 2002.

Takla, Namgyal Lhamo, *Born in Lhasa*, Snow Lion Publications, 2001.

Tibetan Women's Association, *The Status of Tibetan Women 1995–2000*, June 2000.

Tibet Centre for Human Rights and Democracy (TCHRD) report, *The Next Generation: The State of Education in Tibet Today*, 1997.

Tibet Centre for Human Rights and Democracy (TCHRD) report, *Racial Discrimination in Tibet*, September 2000. (Contains Kaixuan, Zhu, *Report to the National People's Congress Standing Committee on Educational Work*.)

Tibet Centre for Human Rights and Democracy (TCHRD) report, *Drapchi Prison*, June 2001.

Tibet Government-in-Exile, *Guidelines for International Development* and other reports: www.tibet.com/aidtibet.html.

Tibet Information Network and Human Rights Watch/Asia (privately funded and independent NGOs), *Cutting Off the Serpent's Head*, 1996.

Tibet Information Network (www.tibetinfo.net), *A Poisoned Arrow: The Secret Report of the 10th Panchen Lama*, 1997.

Tibet Information Network (www.tibetinfo.net), Connor, Victoria and Barnett, Robert, *Leaders in Tibet: A Directory*, 1997.

Tibet Information Network (www.tibetinfo.net), *China's Great Leap West*, November 2000.

Tibet Information Network (www.tibetinfo.net), *Delivery and Deficiency: Health and Health Care in Tibet*, November 2002.

Tibet Information Network (www.tibetinfo.net), *Mining Tibet: Mineral Exploitation in Tibetan Areas of the PRC*, November 2002.

Tsering, Diki, Thondup Khedroob, ed., *Dalai Lama, My Son: A Mother's Story*, Viking/Arkana, 2000. (In the book her name is also spelt 'Dekyi'.)

van Walt van Praag, Michael, *The Status of Tibet: History, Rights, and Prospects in International Law*, Westview Press, 1987.

Other Relevant Texts

Adie, Kate, *The Kindness of Strangers*, Headline, 2002.

Anderson, Benedict, *Imagined Communities*, Verso, revised edn, 1991.

Blaustein, Eric, *Constitutions of Dependencies and Territories*, Oceana Publications, 1975 and onwards.

Brownlie, Ian, *Principles of Public International Law*, Clarendon Press, fourth edn, 1990.

Canetti, Elias, *The Conscience of Words*, Seabury Press, 1979.

Chappell, Peter, *Emotional Healing with Homoeopathy*, Element, 1994.

Chomsky, Noam, *Hegemony or Survival: America's Quest for Global Dominance*, Hamish Hamilton, Penguin Books, 2003.

Chopra, Dr Deepak, *Exploring the Frontiers of Mind/Body Medicine*, Bantam Books, 1989.

Chopra, Dr Deepak, *How to Know God: The Soul's Journey into the Mystery of Mysteries*, Rider, 2001 edn.

Crawford, James, ed., *The Rights of Peoples*, Oxford University Press, Clarendon Paperbacks, 1988.

Dillon, Dr Michael, 'Ethnic, Religious and Political Conflict on China's Northwestern Borders: The Background to the Violence in Xinjiang', *IBRU Boundary and Security Bulletin*, Spring 1997.

Dillon, Dr Michael, 'Xinjiang: Ethnicity, Separatism and Control in Chinese Central Asia', *Durham East Asian Papers 1*, Department of East Asian Studies, University of Durham, 1995.

Dillon, Dr Michael, 'Muslims in Post-Mao China', *Journal of Muslim Minority Affairs*, vol. 16, no. 1, 1996.Elazar, Daniel J., *Governing Peoples and Territories*, Institute for the Study of Human Issues, Philadelphia and the Jerusalem Institute for Federal Studies, Jerusalem, 1982.

Elazar, Daniel J., *Federal Systems of the World: A Handbook of Federal, Confederal and Autonomy Arrangements*, Longman, 1994.

Falk, Richard, *Explorations at the Edge of Time*, Temple University Press, 1992.

Falk, Richard with Johansen, Robert C. and Kim, Samuel S., eds, *The Constitutional Foundations of World Peace*, State University of New York Press, 1993.

Gottlieb, Gidon, *Nation Against State: A New Approach to Ethnic Conflicts and the Decline of Sovereignty*, Council of Foreign Relations Press, New York, 1993.

Hannum, Hurst, *Autonomy, Sovereignty and Self-Determination: The Accommodation of Conflicting Rights*, University of Pennsylvania Press, revised edn, 1996.

Havel, Vaclav, *Disturbing the Peace: A Conversation with Karel Hvizdala*, Faber and Faber, 1990.

Hawken, Paul, *The Ecology of Commerce*, HarperBusiness, 1993.

Hayer, Priscilla B., 'Fifteen Truth Commissions, 1974 to 1994: A Comparative Study', *Human Rights Quarterly*, no. 16, 1994.

Heath, John, ed., *Revitalizing Socialist Enterprise: A Race Against Time*, Routledge, 1993.

Hu, Yao-Su and Berthon, Pierre, 'Sun Tzu', in Warner, Malcolm, *International Encyclopedia of Business and Management*, Thompson Learning, first edn, 1999.

Jenkins, Roy, *Churchill*, Macmillan, 2001.

Jung, Dr Carl G., *On the Nature of the Psyche*, Routledge and Kegan Paul, 1982.

Jung, Dr Carl G., *Psychology and the East*, Routledge and Kegan Paul, 1978.

Kissinger, Henry, *The White House Years*, Little, Brown and Company, 1979.

Macmillan, Margaret, *Peacemakers: Six Months that Changed the World*, John Murray, 2003.

Man, John, *Genghis Khan: Life, Death and Resurrection*, Bantam Press, 2004.

Marx, Karl, *Capital [Das Kapital]*, J. M. Dent and Sons, 1930.

Miles, Martin, *Homoeopathy and Human Evolution*, Winter Press, 1992.

Montefiore, Simon Sebag, *Stalin: The Court of the Red Tsar*, Weidenfeld and Nicolson, 2003.

Olson, Mancur, *The Rise and Decline of Nations*, Yale University Press, 1982.

Seife, Charles, *Zero, The Biography of a Dangerous Idea*, Souvenir Press, 2000.

Stiglitz, Joseph E., *Globalization and its Discontents*, Penguin Books, 2002.

Stafford, David, *Roosevelt and Churchill: Men of Secrets,* Abacus, 1999.

Tyler, Christian, *Wild West China: The Taming of Xinjiang*, John Murray, 2003.

United Nations Development Programme, *United Nations Development Report,* 2001.

Principal Journals and Journal Articles Cited or Read

Bennett, Michael S., 'Financing the Chek Lap Kok New Airport: A Case Study in Amending the Sino–British Joint Declaration on the Question of Hong Kong', *Journal of Chinese Law*, vol. 9, Spring 1995, no. 1.

Foreign Affairs, March/April 2001.

Griffiths, Stephen Iwan, *Nationalism and Ethnic Conflict: Threats to European Security*, Stockholm International Peace Research Institute (SIPRI) research report no. 5, 1991.

Howe, Lord Geoffrey, 'China's Role in a Shrinking World', *China Review*, Great Britain–China Centre (www.gbcc.org.uk), Winter 2003.

Journal of Developing Studies, Vol. 18, Issue 1, April 2002.

Kazuo, Ogura, 'How the "Inscrutables" Negotiate with the "Inscrutables": Chinese Negotiating Tactics vis-à-vis the Japanese', *China Quarterly*, no. 79, September 1979.

Mure, Dickie and McGregor, Richard, 'Stars in His Eyes: Hu Jintao One Year On', *China Review*, Great Britain–China Centre (www.gbcc.org.uk), Winter 2003.

Men-Tsee-Khang, Institute of Tibetan Medicine and Astrology, newsletters, esp. *Tibetan Medicine: An Holistic Approach*, Autumn 2001.

Samdup, Carole, 'The Right to Development on the Tibetan Plateau', *Human Rights Tribune*, Spring 2002.

Simpson, Jerry, chapter in McCorquodale, Robert, ed., *Self-Determination in International Law*, Ashgate/Dartmouth, 2000, originally published in the *Stanford Journal of International Law*, 1996.

Stockholm International Peace Research Institute (SIPRI), *Yearbook* for 2001, 2002, 2003, Oxford University Press.

'Symposium on Constitutionalism: Introduction', *Journal of Chinese Law*, vol. 9, no. 1, Spring 1995, Columbia University Center for the Study of Human Rights, the Chinese Legal Studies Center of the Columbia Law School and the East Asian Institute.

Tibetan Bulletin, The Official Bi-Monthly Journal of the Tibetan Administration of the Dalai Lama: www.tibet.net.

Tibet Alive, The Journal of the Tibet Society and Tibet Relief Fund of the UK: www.tibetsociety.com.

Tibet Information Network (TIN), current news, annual reports, images.

Tibet News reports: www.tibetnews.com.

Tibetan Centre of Human Rights and Democracy, *Annual Report* for 2000, 2001, 2002 and 2003.

Tibetan Centre of Human Rights and Democracy, news items: www.tchrd.org.

Tibetan Envoy, magazine of the Gu-Chu-Sum Movement of Tibet (ex-political prisoners' association, founded September 1991).

Tibetan Review, issues since 2001.

Torture, The Quarterly Journal on Rehabilitation of Torture Victims and Prevention of Torture, published in Denmark. See especially special supplement *Torture in Tibet 1949–1999*, 1999.

Wenran Jiang, 'Prosperity Based on Poverty and Disparity', *China Review*, Great Britain–China Centre (www.gbcc.org.uk), Spring 2004.

Other Sources

China Central Television 9 (CCTV9), Sky TV. State broadcasting channel, news and current affairs in China; includes Tibet, www.cctv9.tv or www.cctv9.com/english.

International Alert (UK)

International Campaign for Tibet (US)

Tibet Support Groep, Nederland, The Netherlands

Xinhua, the official Chinese news agency (www.xinhuanet.com/english/china.htm)

Index